Praise

The Lost
of Siberia

A *SUNDAY TIMES* BOOK OF 2020:
'Extraordinary.'

'The ultimate quest for the oddest objects – pianos – in the
most unlikely place – Siberia. But Roberts makes it much more
than that, an elegant and nuanced journey through literature,
through history, through music, murder and incarceration
and revolution, through snow and ice and remoteness, to
discover the human face of Siberia. I loved this book.'
PAUL THEROUX

'An impressive exploration of Siberia's terrifying past.'
GUARDIAN

'A quixotic literary adventure.'
FINANCIAL TIMES

'A sparkling debut by an outstanding and gifted author.
A brilliant guide to Russia of the past and the present, set
around an extraordinary search for the heart, soul
and lost keyboards of centuries gone by.'
PETER FRANKOPAN

'An extraordinary encounter with a wildly fascinating and
astonishingly ill-known region . . . This is a wonderful book.'
SUNDAY TIMES

'These pages sing like a symphony . . . Roberts controls the
narrative drive as if with a pianist's foot pedals and modulates
the tone between the flats of long motor journeys
and the sharps of emotional intensity.'
WALL STREET JOURNAL

'A noble quest to understand the dazzling respect
for music embedded in Russian culture.'
COUNTRY LIFE

'The poetic idea of finding exquisite old pianos in
an otherwise elemental wilderness is only
one of many fascinating strands.'
SYDNEY MORNING HERALD

'Marvellous . . . a masterful example of modern
historical travel writing.'
INDEPENDENT

'A richly observed cultural history . . . thrilling.'
NEW STATESMAN

'Fascinating account of Siberia's horrific legacy told with
great verve . . . Roberts is a wonderfully lyrical writer.'
OBSERVER

'A masterpiece of modern travel literature with
words that sing from its pages. A definitive
exploration of Russia's wild east.'
LEVISON WOOD

'An amazing tour-de-force . . . it touches your soul.'
RADIO NEW ZEALAND

'Beautifully written . . . A unique short history
of Russia from Catherine the Great to Putin . . .
A sense of the extraordinary marks every page.'
HISTORY TODAY

'Captures Siberia's wildness, but favours its enchantments.'
TIMES LITERARY SUPPLEMENT

'Courage, patience, erudition and a sympathetic
imagination . . . A travel book of rare quality.'
DERVLA MURPHY

'Utterly absorbing . . . Roberts displays an empathy
and understanding worthy of this deeply
haunted, strangely fascinating land.'
BENEDICT ALLEN

'Stories endure in this compelling debut.'
WANDERLUST

'Beautifully nuanced prose . . . It is an existential journey
through the literature, history and music of one of the wildest
and fiercest places on earth.'
THE IRISH TIMES

'*Lost Pianos*' great truth is that out of pain, darkness,
and calamity, music emerges as solace, and
pianos, a source for celebration.'
SAN FRANCISCO CLASSICAL VOICE

'One of those magical books that captures the
imagination and draws you into the beauty and majesty
of Siberia . . . A book to savour and remember.'
HELEN RAPPAPORT

'A modern-day Freya Stark.'
TATLER

'Roberts jolts the sleepy Siberia of our imaginations
into 2020, and the result is a cannot-put-it-down
tale of music and humanity.'
GOOP

'Beautiful writing off the beaten track.'
PIANIST

'Utterly fascinating and revealing to anyone who only knows
Siberia through its Great Myth as a forgotten, frozen Nowhere.'
CHRISTOPHER SOMERVILLE

'An intoxicating journey into the wilds of Siberia.'
STELLA MAGAZINE

'To say that Sophy Roberts' *The Lost Pianos of Siberia*
is among the unexpected works of history
in recent memory is an understatement.'
CHRISTIAN SCIENCE MONITOR

'I loved this book – such a wonderful idea,
and so beautifully written.'
STEVEN ISSERLIS

THE LOST PIANOS OF SIBERIA

Sophy Roberts

BLACK SWAN

TRANSWORLD PUBLISHERS
Penguin Random House, One Embassy Gardens,
8 Viaduct Gardens, London SW11 7BW
www.penguin.co.uk

Transworld is part of the Penguin Random House group of companies
whose addresses can be found at global.penguinrandomhouse.com

Penguin
Random House
UK

First published in Great Britain in 2020 by Doubleday
an imprint of Transworld Publishers
Black Swan edition published 2021

A CIP catalogue record for this book
is available from the British Library.

ISBN
9781784162849

Typeset in 10.29/14.33pt Sabon Next LT Pro by Jouve (UK), Milton Keynes.
Printed and bound in Great Britain by Clays Ltd, Elcograf S.p.A.

The authorized representative in the EEA is Penguin Random House Ireland,
Morrison Chambers, 32 Nassau Street, Dublin D02 YH68

Penguin Random House is committed to a sustainable
future for our business, our readers and our planet. This book
is made from Forest Stewardship Council® certified paper.

FSC
www.fsc.org

MIX
Paper from
responsible sources
FSC® C018179

For John, Danny and Jack

'Once a certain idea of landscape, a myth, a vision, establishes itself in an actual place, it has a peculiar way of muddling categories, of making metaphors more real than their referents, of becoming, in fact, part of the scenery.'

SIMON SCHAMA
Landscape and Memory

'Objects have always been carried, sold, bartered, stolen, retrieved and lost. People have always given gifts. It is how you tell their stories that matters.'

EDMUND DE WAAL
The Hare with Amber Eyes

'My piano is to me what his vessel is to the sailor, his horse to the Arab, nay even more, till now it has been myself, my speech, my life . . . I confided to it all my desires, my dreams, my joys, and my sorrows. Its strings vibrated to my emotions, and its keys obeyed my every caprice.'

FRANZ LISZT
Franz Liszt, *Gesammelte Schriften*, Volume II

Contents

PART THREE

Goodness Knows Where · 1992–Present Day

Author's Note

TRAVEL EAST BY TRAIN from Moscow and the clip of iron on track beats out the rhythm of your approach towards the Ural Mountains. This band of hills separates Western Russia from Siberia, rising in Kazakhstan and following an almost direct line up through Russia to the Arctic Ocean. The train passes lazy trails of chimney smoke, gilded churches, and layers of snow stacked like bolts of silk, with the rhythm of the journey – the sluggish gait, the grinding stops into gaunt platforms and huddled towns – much as early travellers described Russian trains in the fashionable Siberian railway sketches of the time. These days, however, fellow passengers are few; most Russians now fly to and from Siberia rather than use the railways.

During the time of the last Tsar, travellers on the country's most iconic train of all – the *train de luxe Sibérien*, running for some five-and-a-half thousand miles from Moscow to Vladivostok on Russia's Pacific coast – described an ebullient opulence, with passengers dripping in 'diamonds that made one's eyes ache', and music from a Bechstein piano. Siberia's railway was dizzy with ambition: 'From the shores of the Pacific and the heights of the Himalayas, Russia will not only dominate the affairs of Asia but Europe as well,' declared Sergei Witte, the statesman and engineer responsible for building the track at the end of the nineteenth century. In the fancy tourist carriages, there was a busy restaurant panelled in mahogany, and a Chinese-style smoking lounge, the train presided over by a heavily perfumed fat conductor with a pink silk handkerchief. French-speaking waiters came and went with Crimean clarets and beluga caviar, pushing through carriages decorated with mirrored walls and frescoes, a library, a darkroom for passengers to process camera film, and according to adverts promoting Siberia to tourists, a hairdressing salon, and a gym equipped with a rudimentary exercise bike. Sing-songs tumbled out of the dining car as if it were a music hall, with the piano used like a kitchen sideboard to stack the dirty dishes on.

At no point on this great Eurasian railway journey, then or now, was there a sign saying 'Welcome to Siberia'. There was only the dark smudge bestowed by cartographers denoting the Ural Mountains – a line that conjures up something vaguely monumental. In reality, the Urals feel closer to a kind of topographical *humph*, as if the land is somehow bored, the mountains showing as bumps and knuckles and straggling knolls. There is no dramatic curtain-raiser to the edge of

Siberia, no meaningful brink to a specific place, just thick weather hanging over an abstract idea.

Siberia is difficult to pin down, its loose boundaries allowing each visitor to make of it whatever shape they want. In a drive for simplicity to organize these indistinct frontiers, I have therefore provided a few notes to explain my parameters.

The breadth of Russia has been squashed and squeezed into chapter maps in a struggle to fit this vast territory on to a single page. What makes it even more challenging is that aside from China, this country has more international borders than any other nation. In this Author's Note I also give explanations about the time periods and terminology, which can get complicated in Russia. If my definitions are in any way reductive, it is because I am not a historian. If they are Eurocentric, it is because I am English; any journey to Siberia is one I take from the West to the East – physically, culturally, musically. This book – written for the general reader, about a hunt that is sometimes more about the looking than the finding in the so-called 'land of endless talk' – is a personal, literary adventure. More nuanced scholarly research and further reading is indicated in the Source Notes and Selected Bibliography.

My Siberia covers all the territory east of the Ural Mountains as far as the Pacific, which is the 'Siberia' defined on imperial Russian maps up until the Soviet period. It is an extremely broad interpretation, which includes the Far North and the Russian Far East, taking in dominions lost and gained during the eighteenth and nineteenth centuries. I therefore apologize in advance with the full knowledge that I have not subscribed to modern administrative boundaries or prevailing political correctness about who or what is Siberian. I have instead gone by Anton Chekhov's description: 'The plain of Siberia begins, I think, from Ekaterinburg, and ends goodness knows where.'

There were three significant revolutions in early twentieth-century Russia. The first was in January 1905, after government soldiers opened fire on peaceful protesters in St Petersburg in what became known as 'Bloody Sunday'. Vladimir Ilyich Ulyanov, known by his alias, Lenin, and Leon Trotsky became the main architects of the two socialist revolutions in 1917 – the February Revolution, and the October, or Bolshevik, Revolution. I tend to refer to the events of 1917 collectively as the Russian Revolution, unless otherwise stated.

As archival evidence has emerged during the last few decades, historians have been able to piece together more authoritative figures relating to Siberian exile under the Tsars, and prisoner numbers in the Soviet Gulag.[*] Some of the most reliable current statistics[†] for a basic understanding of the scale are as follows: from 1801 to 1917, more than a million subjects were banished to Siberia under the Tsarist penal exile system. From 1929 to 1953, 2,749,163 forced labourers died in the Soviet Gulag.[‡] There are many more numbers, and unknowable quantities of suffering, but I make little further mention of death tolls and prisoner counts. This is because official

---

[*] GULAG is an acronym for the Main Administration of Camps – in Russian, *Glavnoe upravlenie lagerei* – which is now more commonly used as a proper noun to describe the whole horrifying system of Soviet penal labour.

[†] At the time of this book's first publication: 2020.

[‡] Numbers relating to Tsarist exile are taken from Daniel Beer's *The House of the Dead* (London: Allen Lane, 2016). Anne Applebaum's Pulitzer Prize-winning *Gulag: A History* (London: Penguin, 2004) hesitantly cites the Gulag death toll. Both books are critically important to an understanding of the statistics, while both also acknowledge the unreliability of any final number.

figures are untrustworthy and other counts remain reluctant estimates.

I use 'Russia' to describe the country prior to the end of the Russian Civil War, which ran from 1918 to 1922, when the 'Reds' (Bolsheviks, later known as communists) fought the 'Whites' (anti-communists, with some factions retaining Tsarist sympathies). The USSR refers to the Union of Soviet Socialist Republics, or Soviet Union, formed in 1922, which expanded to comprise Russia and fourteen surrounding republics. After the breakdown of the Soviet regime following a tumultuous period of economic restructuring known as perestroika, Russia changed its name. On 31 December 1991, it became known as the Russian Federation, which I shorten to Russia for the sake of simplicity. To track these political changes, as well as key moments in the history of Siberia, please refer to the brief Chronology at the end of the book.

Until 31 January 1918, Russian dates conformed to the Julian, or Old Style, calendar, which ran between eleven and thirteen days behind the Gregorian, or New Style, system. I use the Old Style for events that took place inside Russia before the Revolution. I use the New Style thereafter.

Sometimes I am the one out of synch. Although this book is written as a continuous journey for narrative coherence, my various research trips were not all taken in the order they are documented. Sometimes I had to return to a location to deepen my research. I also had to work with opportunistic leads, inclement weather and unpredictable scrutiny from Russia's FSB, the state security and surveillance apparatus and a direct descendant of the KGB. I mostly travelled Siberia in winter, not summer. The main reason for this was a dangerous allergic response to the region's mosquitoes – as vicious as the Siberian legend suggests, that they were born from the ashes of a cannibal.

The Great Patriotic War is a term widely used by Russians to refer to the Soviet experience of the Second World War. I have used the most familiar, Western version of people's names. I have tended to avoid patronymics, as well as the feminine forms of a surname customarily used for Russian women. Nicholas II is the common name by which most readers will know the last Tsar. The other Nikolais I met, along with the Alekseis, Marias and Lidiyas, I don't anglicize. I like the sound of their Russianness, though these decisions are idiosyncratic. The transliteration of Russian to English follows the Library of Congress system in the Source Notes and the Selected Bibliography only.

All interviews have relied on interpreters, who have stuck as close as possible to the spirit of intention, as per the advice of the Hungarian composer Franz Liszt about transcribing orchestral works to the piano: 'In matters of translation there are some exactitudes which are the equivalent of infidelities.' Many of my interviews were digitally recorded. Original direct quotes were re-checked with sources, and sometimes subsequently amended to refine meaning.

I relied on one interpreter more than any other: Elena Voytenko, whose fortitude helped me through many a black hole in Siberia. On a number of my trips to Russia, I was also joined by the American photographer Michael Turek. I picked up all manner of local guides, from music teachers to mountain-rescue specialists. I travelled 'on the hoof' wherever a lead might take me, by plane, train, helicopter, snowmobile, reindeer, amphibious truck, ship, hovercraft and taxi. I also hitched lifts with oil and gas workers. False leads induced a certain amount of backtracking, which was another reason for return visits.

Author's Note

Siberia's Altai Region (capital, Barnaul) is contiguous with the Altai Republic (capital, Gorno-Altaysk); the latter is the more remote and mountainous. For simplicity, I use the term Altai to cover both. I have gone by the modern designation of Russian place names (since 1991, cities have generally gone back to their pre-Revolution names). St Petersburg I refer to by its current name as well as Petrograd (from 1914 to 1924) and Leningrad (the name from Lenin's death until the end of the Soviet Union in 1991). Again, my decision is idiosyncratic. The events that took place in this city during the Leningrad Siege from 1941 to 1944 were so monumental, the name is hard to cleave from specific historical incidents. This is not so true of Novonikolaevsk, now known as Novosibirsk. Before starting this book, I hadn't heard of either.

PART ONE

Pianomania
1762–1917

'Liszt. It is only noon. Where are those brilliant carriages travelling from every direction going with such speed at this unusual hour? Probably to some celebration? Not at all. But what is the reason for such haste? A very small notice, brief and simple. Here's what it says. A virtuoso announces that on a certain day, at two o'clock, in the Hall of the Assembly of the Nobles, he will play on his piano, without the accompaniment of the orchestra, without the usual prestige of a concert . . . five or six pieces. Upon hearing this news, the entire city rushed. Look! An immense crowd gathers, people squeeze together, elbow each other and enter.'

– Journal de St-Pétersbourg, August 1842

1

Music in a Sleeping Land:
Sibir

E ARLY ON IN MY travels in Siberia, I was sent a photograph
from a musician living in Kamchatka, a remote peninsula
which juts out of the eastern edge of Russia into the fog of the
North Pacific. In the photograph, volcanoes rise out of the flat-
ness, the scoops and hollows dominated by an A-shaped cone.
Ice loiters in pockets of the landscape. In the foreground stands
an upright piano. The focus belongs to the music, which has
attracted an audience of ten.

A young man wearing an American ice-hockey shirt

crouches at the pianist's feet. With his face turned from the camera, it is difficult to tell what he is thinking, if it is the pianist's music he finds engaging or the strangeness of the location where the instrument has appeared. The young man listens as if he might belong to an intimate gathering around a drawing-room piano, a scene that pops up like a motif in Russia's nineteenth-century literature, rather than a common upright marooned in a lava field in one of the world's most savage landscapes. There is no supporting dialogue to the photograph, no thickening romance, as happens around the instruments in Leo Tolstoy's epic novels. Nor is there any explanation about how or why the piano ended up here in the first place. The image has arrived with no mention of what is being played, which is music the picture can't capture anyway. Yet all sorts of intonations fill the word 'Siberia' written in the subject line of the email.

Siberia. The word makes everything it touches vibrate at a different pitch. Early Arab traders called Siberia Ibis-Shibir, Sibir-i-Abir and Abir-i-Sabir. Modern etymology suggests its roots lie in the Tatar word *sibir*, meaning 'the sleeping land'. Others contend that 'Siberia' is derived from the mythical mountain Sumbyr found in Siberian-Turkic folklore. Sumbyr, like 'slumber'. Or Wissibur, like 'whisper', which was the name the Bavarian traveller Johann Schiltberger bestowed upon this enigmatic hole in fifteenth-century cartography. Whatever the word's ancestry, the sound is right. 'Siberia' rolls off the tongue with a sibilant chill. It is a word full of poetry and alliterative suggestion. But by inferring sleep, the etymology also undersells Siberia's scope, both real and imagined.

Siberia is far more significant than a place on the map: it

is a feeling which sticks like a burr, a temperature, the sound of sleepy flakes falling on snowy pillows and the crunch of uneven footsteps coming from behind. Siberia is a wardrobe problem – too cold in winter, and too hot in summer – with wooden cabins and chimney stacks belching corpse-grey smoke into wide white skies. It is a melancholy, a cinematic romance dipped in limpid moonshine, unhurried train journeys, pipes wrapped in sackcloth, and a broken swing hanging from a squeaky chain. You can hear Siberia in the big, soft chords in Russian music that evoke the hush of silver birch trees and the billowing winter snows.

Covering an eleventh of the world's landmass, Siberia is bordered by the Arctic Ocean in the north and the Mongolian steppe in the south. The Urals mark Siberia's western edge, and the Pacific its eastern rim. It is the ultimate land beyond 'The Rock', as the Urals used to be described, an unwritten register of the missing and the uprooted, an almost-country perceived to be so far from Moscow that when some kind of falling star destroyed a patch of forest twice the size of the Russian capital in the famed 'Tunguska Event' of 1908, no one bothered to investigate for twenty years. Before air travel reduced distances, Siberia was too remote for anyone to go and look.

In the seventeenth century, wilderness was therefore ideal for banishing criminals and dissidents when the Tsars first transformed Siberia into the most feared penal colony on Earth. Some exiles had their nostrils split to mark them as outcasts. Others had their tongues removed. One half of their head was shaved to reveal smooth, blue-tinged skin. Among them were ordinary, innocent people labelled 'convicts' on the European side of the Urals, and 'unfortunates' in Siberia. Hence the habit among fellow exiles of leaving free bread on windowsills to help bedraggled newcomers. Empathy, it seems, has been seared into the Siberian psyche from the start, with these small acts of kindness the difference between life and death in an unimaginably vast realm. Siberia's size also stands as testimony to our human capacity for indifference. We find it difficult to identify with places that are too far removed. That's what happens with boundless scale. The effects are dizzying until it is hard to tell truth from fact, whether Siberia is a nightmare or a myth full of impenetrable forests and limitless plains, its murderous proportions strung with groaning oil derricks and sagging wires. Siberia is all these things, and more as well.

It is a modern economic miracle, with natural oil and gas reserves driving powerful shifts in the geopolitics of North Asia and the Arctic Ocean. It is the taste of wild strawberries sweet as sugar cubes, and tiny pine cones stewed in jam. It is home-made pike-and-mushroom pie, clean air and pure nature, the stinging slap of waves on Lake Baikal, and winter light spangled with powdered ice. It is land layered with a rich history of indigenous culture where a kind of magical belief-system still prevails. Despite widespread ecological destruction, including 'black snow' from coal mining, toxic lakes, and forest fires contributing to smoke clouds bigger than the EU, Siberia's abundant nature still persuades you to believe in all sorts of mysteries carved into its petroglyphs and caves. But Siberia's deep history also makes you realize how short our human story is, given the landscape's raw tectonic scale.

In Siberia's centre, a geographical fault, the Baikal Rift Zone, runs vertically through Russia to the Arctic Ocean. Every year the shores around Lake Baikal – the deepest lake on Earth, holding a fifth of the world's fresh water – move another two centimetres apart, the lake holding the kinetic energy of an immense living landscape about to split. It is a crouched violence, a gathering strain, a power that sits just beneath the visible. The black iris of Russia's 'Sacred Sea' is opening up, the rift so significant that when this eye of water blinks sometime in the far future, Baikal could mark the line where the Eurasian landmass splits in two: Europe on one side, Asia on the other, in one final cataclysmic divorce. Above all, Baikal's magnificence reasserts the vulnerability of man. Beneath the lake's quilt of snow in winter lies a mosaic of icy sheets, each fractured vein serving as a reminder that the lake's surface might give way at any moment. Fissures in the ice look like the surface of a shattered mirror. Other cracks penetrate more deeply, like diamond necklaces suspended in the watery blues. The ice tricks you with its fixity when in fact Baikal can be deadly. Just look at how it devours the drowned. In Baikal there is a little omnivorous crustacean smaller than a grain of rice, with a staggering appetite. These greedy creatures are the reason why Baikal's water is so clear: they filter the top fifty metres of the lake up to three times a year – another strange endemic aberration like Baikal's bug-eyed nerpa seals, shaped like rugby balls, whose predecessors got trapped in the lake some two million years ago when the continental plates made their last big shift. Either that or the nerpa are an evolution of ringed seal that swam down from the Arctic into Siberia's river systems and got stuck – like so much else in Siberia, unable to return to their homeland, re-learning how to survive.

Because Siberia isn't sleeping. Its resources are under immense pressure from a ravenous economy. Climate change is also hitting Siberia hard. In the Far North, the permafrost is melting. More than half of Russia balances on this unstable layer of frozen ground, Siberia's mutability revealed in cracks that slice through forlorn buildings, and giant plugs of tundra collapsing without a grunt of warning. Bubbles formed of methane explode then fall in like soufflés. But no one much notices – including Russians who have never visited, whose quality of life owes a debt to Siberia's wealth – because even with modern air travel there are Siberians living in towns who still refer to European Russia as 'the mainland'. They might as well be marooned on islands. Take Kolyma in Russia's remote north-east, flanking an icy cul de sac of water called the Sea of Okhotsk. This chilling territory, where some of the worst of the twentieth-century forced-labour camps, or Gulags, were located, used to be almost impossible to access except by air or boat. Even today, the twelve hundred miles of highway linking Kolyma to Yakutsk, which is among the coldest cities on Earth, are often impassable. In his unflinching record of what occurred in the camps, Aleksandr Solzhenitsyn's choice of words – *The Gulag Archipelago* – is therefore rooted in fact, even if the phrase carries an immense metaphorical weight.

The Soviet Gulag – scattered throughout Russia, not just Siberia – was different from the Tsarist penal exile system which came before the 1917 Revolution, although the two are often confused. The Tsars could banish people to permanent settlement in Siberia, as well as condemn them to hard labour. Under the Soviets, the emphasis was on hard-labour camps only, wound together with curious methods of 'cultural education'. Once your sentence was up (assuming you survived it), you could usually return home, though there were exceptions. Both systems had a great deal of brutality in common, with the Tsarist exile system turning Siberia into a prodigious breeding ground for revolutionary thought. Trotsky, Lenin, Stalin – they all spent time in Siberia as political exiles before the Revolution. So did some of Russia's greatest writers, including Fyodor Dostoevsky, who in the mid-nineteenth century described convicts chained to the prison wall, unable to move more than a couple of metres for up to ten years. 'Here was our own peculiar world, unlike anything else at all,' he wrote – 'a house of the living dead.'

Yet under winter's spell, stories about the state's history of repression slip away. Siberia's summer bogs are turned into frosted doilies and pine needles into ruffs of Flemish lace. The snow dusts and coats the ground, swirling into mist whenever the surface is caught by wind, concealing the bones of not only Russians but also Italians, French, Spaniards, Poles, Swedes and many more besides who perished in this place of exile, their graves unmarked. In Siberia, everything feels ambiguous, even darkly ironic, given the words used to describe its extremes. Among nineteenth-century prisoners, shackles were called 'music', presumably from the jingle of the exiles' chains. In Solzhenitsyn's *The Gulag Archipelago*, to 'play the piano' meant having your fingerprints taken when you first arrived in camp.

But there is also another story to Siberia. Dotted throughout this land are pianos, like the humble, Soviet-made upright in the photograph of a Kamchatka lava field, and a few modern imported instruments. There is an abundance of beautiful grand pianos in a bitterly cold town called Mirny – a fifties Soviet settlement enriched by the largest open-cast diamond mine in the world – and more than fifty Steinway pianos in a school for gifted children in Khanty-Mansiysk at the heart of Western Siberia's oil fields. Such extravagances, however, are few and far between. What is more remarkable are the pianos dating from the boom years of the Empire's nineteenth-century pianomania. Lost symbols of Western culture in an Asiatic realm, these instruments arrived in Siberia carrying the melodies of Europe's musical salons a long way from the cultural context of their birth. How such instruments travelled into this wilderness in the first place are tales of fortitude by governors, exiles and adventurers. The fact they survive stands as testimony to the human spirit's need for solace. 'Truly, there would be reason to go mad if it were not for music,' said the Russian pianist and composer Pyotr Tchaikovsky.

Russia's relationship with the piano began under Catherine the Great – the eighteenth-century Empress with a collector's habit for new technologies, from musical instruments to her robotic timepiece made up of three life-size birds: an owl which twists its head, a peacock which fans its tail (you can almost see the breast rising for a breath), and a rooster which crows on every hour.* Catherine was also the inheritor of Peter the Great's Westernizing legacy when his founding of St Petersburg in 1703 first 'hack[ed] a window through to Europe'. Sixteen years after Peter's death came the Empress Elizabeth, another modernizer, who introduced a musical Golden Age with her affection for European opera. Elizabeth's extravagant spending habits on Italian tenors and French troupes affected the musical tastes of the Russian elite – a trend which continued after 1762 when Catherine became Empress and augmented Elizabeth's mid-century influence and generous patronage of the arts. European culture thrived

* The clock can still be found encased in a protective glass box in the State Hermitage Museum in St Petersburg. The birds lie still for most of the week, but every so often their two-hundred-year-old mechanisms are carefully wound to give visitors a glimpse of the performance that captivated the Empress.

in St Petersburg, even if the deeper questions surfacing in Western Europe – in books by, for example, Jean-Jacques Rousseau, the philosopher whose theories about the pursuit of individual liberty and the natural equality of men inspired a generation of Romantics – had no place in the Russian court.

While revolution brewed in France, Catherine remained entirely deaf to criticism around Russia's oppressive system of serfdom, which was such a significant source of imperial wealth. Russian men, women and their children born into feudal bondage were not only vassals employed to work the fields but were also trained as singers and dancers to lighten the manorial gloom. As instrumental music developed, serf orchestras became a distinctly Russian phenomenon, with one well-known musical fanatic of Catherine's time insisting his entire staff address him only in song. Others were sent abroad to study music – a fashion which continued into the nineteenth century. In 1809 when two of these serf musicians were unhappily recalled to Russia from their training in Leipzig, they took their revenge, and murdered their master by cutting him up into pieces in his bedroom. In Leipzig, not only had they heard beautiful music; they had also tasted liberty.

Punishment was Siberia, where unlucky serfs were routinely exiled without trial for far more trivial transgressions, from impudence to taking snuff. When the dissident Aleksandr Radishchev chronicled the horrors of the Russian system of feudal slavery in his 1790 book, *A Journey from St Petersburg to Moscow*, Catherine cranked up her response.*

---

* 'It is thought that by the end of her reign well over half the population of the Russian Empire had become a slave class, every bit as subjugated as the Negro slaves of America.' A. N. Wilson, *Tolstoy* (London: Hamish Hamilton, 1988).

She exiled her most high-profile naysayer to the penal colony of Siberia, which was rapidly expanding its barbaric shape. When Austria, Prussia and Russia began to carve up Poland and what became known as the Western Provinces – a region that roughly included Lithuania, Ukraine and Belarus – Siberia received the first trickle of educated Polish rebels.* Presiding over their fate as exiles were Catherine's governors, one or two of whom took keyboard instruments with them to their postings in the back of beyond.

This was a time when the instrument was still developing, when even the names of keyboard instruments betrayed an identity problem. The German word *Klavier* sometimes referred to a harpsichord, spinet, virginal or clavichord. The word 'clavichord', if correctly used, referred to an instrument which, like the piano, used a percussive hammer action on the strings rather than the pluck of a harpsichord's plectrum. Sometimes called 'the poor man's keyboard', it was an instrument which could respond to a player's fingers, their trembling, sympathetic pauses and emotive intent: 'In short, the clavichord was the first keyed instrument with a soul.' Confusingly, however, 'clavichord' sometimes also referred to the 'fortepiano' – the instrument, which translates as 'loud-soft', devised by the Italian maker Bartolomeo Cristofori for the Medici family at the turn of the eighteenth century. What made Cristofori's invention groundbreaking wasn't just the piano's relative portability (unlike an organ): its improved dynamics and

---

* 'Polish' is a simplification of the cultural nuances of the time, but is generally used to discuss the various ethnicities – Polish, Lithuanian, Belarusian, among others – sharing a region on Russia's western edge with constantly shifting borders during the eighteenth and nineteenth centuries.

musical expression created the illusion there was an entire orchestra in the room.

'Until about 1770 pianos were ambiguous instruments, transitional in construction and uncertain in status,' observes one of the twentieth century's foremost historians on the subject. Catherine's treasured square piano, or *piano anglais*, is the perfect example of this evolutionary flux. In 1774, at the dawn of the piano's vogue, the Empress ordered this new-fangled keyboard instrument from England, made by London's first manufacturer, a German immigrant called Johann Zumpe. It was the instrument *du jour*, owned by everyone from Catherine's great friend the French philosopher and lexicographer Denis Diderot, whose *Encyclopédie* declared keyboard playing a crucial accomplishment in the education of modern women, to English royalty. Within ten years of its invention, versions of this instrument were being made in England, France, Germany and America. According to one contemporary British composer, Zumpe couldn't make his pianos fast enough to gratify demand.

Catherine's 1774 *piano anglais*, its decorative cabinetry as pretty as a Fabergé egg, now stands behind red rope in Pavlovsk, an eighteenth-century Tsarist pleasure palace outside St Petersburg which functioned as one of Russia's most important centres of musical life. The piano is displayed alongside a Sèvres toilet set gifted to the imperial family by Marie Antoinette. The Zumpe, which would have been a novelty at the time, has a certain sweetness when playing a slow *adagio*, but there is also an older, courtlier twang and a tinny thud of keys. Only when the technology's powerful hammer action improved, thicker strings were stretched to higher tensions, and the pedals were finessed to allow for even better control of the 'loud-soft' expression, would the piano's potential expand into the instrument we know today. This next dramatic phase in piano technology, thriving in the first three decades of the nineteenth century, pushed the instrument into concert halls all over Europe as its more robust mechanisms became better able to tolerate the passions of the virtuoso. In 1821, the French factory Erard patented the 'double escapement' action, which allowed for much more rapid repetition of a note without releasing the key. This was when the piano also began to migrate more widely – a trend witnessed by James Holman, a blind Englishman who travelled to Siberia in 1823 for no other reason, it would seem, than to furnish himself with a stack of drawing-room anecdotes. He wrote in his account: 'One lady of my acquaintance had carried with her to the latter place, a favourite piano-forte from St Petersburg at the bottom of her sledge, and this without inflicting the least injury upon it.'

Violent. Cold. Startlingly beautiful. That stately instruments might still exist in such a profoundly enigmatic place as Siberia feels somehow remarkable. It becomes nothing less than a miracle when one learns that not only did Catherine's 1774 Zumpe survive a twentieth-century wartime sojourn in Russia's terra incognita, but that other historic pianos are still making music in sleepy Siberian villages. Where wooden houses seem to cosy up together for warmth, there are pianos washed up and abandoned from the high-tide mark of nineteenth-century European romanticism. This was one of the most important periods in the popularization of the piano, when a new breed of virtuoso performer became its most convincing endorsement.

Soon after arriving in Russia in 1802, the Irish pianist John Field – the inventor of the nocturne, a short, dream-like love poem for the piano – could name his price as both a performer and a teacher in the salons of Moscow and St Petersburg. Field sounded the first chord, as it were, in the Russian cult of the piano, but it was the celebrity of the Hungarian Franz Liszt which turned the Russian love of the instrument into a fever in the 1840s.

Women grabbed at strands of Liszt's iconic bobbed hair to wear close to their chest in lockets. Fans fought over his silk hankies, coffee dregs (which they carried about in phials) and cigarette butts. German girls fashioned bracelets from the piano strings he snapped and turned the cherry stones he spat out into amulets. In Vienna – one of the great capitals of

An 1842 drawing of Liszt playing to a frenzied Berlin crowd, the scene not unlike a modern rock concert.

European music – local confectioners sold piano-shaped biscuits iced with his name. When Liszt left Berlin for Russia in the spring of 1842, his coach was drawn by six white horses and followed by a procession of thirty carriages. When he played in St Petersburg in April, the infamous 'smasher of pianos' – a reputation derived from the broken instruments Liszt left in his wake – drew the largest audience St Petersburg had ever seen for such an event.

Liszt leapt on to the stage rather than walked up the steps. Throwing his white kid gloves on to the floor, he bowed low to an audience who lurched from complete silence to thunderous applause, the hall rocking with adulation as he played on one piano, then another facing the opposite direction. At a performance for the Tsarina in Prussia two years earlier, Liszt had broken string after string in his tortured piano. In St Petersburg, his recital was somewhat more successful – a spectacular display of the instrument's range, jamming rippling notes into music packed with an intense and violent beauty. When John Field heard Liszt perform, he apparently leaned over to his companion, and asked, 'Does he bite?' Liszt was considered 'the past, the present, the future of the piano', wrote one contemporary; his solo recital to a throng of three thousand Russians 'something unheard of, utterly novel, even somewhat brazen . . . this idea of having a small stage erected in the very centre of the hall like an islet in the middle of an ocean, a throne high above the heads of the crowd', wrote another witness to this groundbreaking event. Liszt's talent was capable of instigating a kind of musical madness, according to Vladimir Stasov, the Russian critic present at Liszt's St Petersburg debut. Stasov went with his friend Aleksandr Serov to hear him play:

We exchanged only a few words and then rushed home to write each other as quickly as possible of our impressions, our dreams, our ecstasy ... Then and there, we took a vow that thenceforth and forever, that day, 8th April, 1842, would be sacred to us, and we would never forget a single second of it till our dying day ... We had never in our lives heard anything like this; we had never been in the presence of such a brilliant, passionate, demonic temperament, at one moment lurching like a whirlwind, at another pouring forth cascades of tender beauty and grace.

Liszt's Russian tour had a significant effect on the country's shifting musical culture – not least the validation Liszt gave to Russia's nascent piano industry when he played on a St Petersburg-made Lichtenthal in an important musical year. In 1842, Mikhail Glinka's *Ruslan and Lyudmila* – considered the first true 'Russian' opera for its native character and melody – premiered in St Petersburg. Liszt, who developed a keen affection for Russian folk music, thought the opera marvellous.

While Glinka's opera was influential, it was still the piano and the splendid character of the virtuoso which enthralled the aristocracy, with instruments being snapped up in Russia now they were no longer a technical rarity. 'You will find a piano, or some kind of box with a keyboard, everywhere,' observed one mid-century Russian journal writer: 'If there are one hundred apartments in a St Petersburg building, then you can count on ninety-three instruments and a piano-tuner.' It was the same story all over Europe. That same year, the London piano maker Broadwood & Sons was one of the city's twelve largest employers of labour. Grand Tourists – upper-class men on a coming-of-age culture trip through Europe – couldn't live away from home without a piano. According to a well-thumbed guidebook, *How to Enjoy Paris in 1842*, most English families who came to the city for any length of time would want to hire or buy a piano. In Britain alone, the five-year period from 1842 saw sixteen patents issued for new piano technology.

With every development in the instrument's functionality, the piano's increasingly expressive capacity was greeted with a flurry of composition. With an emerging merchant class hungry for new luxuries, state subsidies were encouraging a home-grown industry. Russian piano-making was thriving, an early Russian-made salon grand piano costing not much more than a couple of rows of seats at Liszt's 1842 performance in St Petersburg.

A Russian family pictured with their piano in the 1840s, when the piano became an important symbol of prestige.

As the century progressed, piano technology kept improving, with iron (as opposed to wooden) frames, new ways of stringing, and the development of the upright piano – described by one historian as 'a remarkable bundle of inventions', its size and portability well suited to the homes of the swelling middle classes. In 1859, Henry Steinway, a German piano maker who emigrated to New York, patented the first over-strung grand piano, which gave concert instruments greater volume. A richly textured musical establishment evolved not just with piano-playing in Russia but across all sorts of musical genres and institutions – in opera, ballet, symphony orchestras,

St Petersburg-made Becker pianos on show at the Paris World Fair of 1878, with the Shah of Persia listening in to the demonstration. In 1900, the Fair's Russian pavilion caused another sensation, with an advert for the new Trans-Siberian Railway. A painted panorama, scrolled past the windows of the display carriage, compressed the five-and-a-half-thousand-mile-long trans-Siberian journey into a famously pretty sales pitch. The reality, remarked some travellers, did not always prove quite so picturesque.

conservatories and amateur musical societies. Around the turn of the twentieth century, Russia's contribution to classical composition was riding high. Tchaikovsky and Nikolai Rimsky-Korsakov had joined Europe's first rank. Luminaries among Russian piano-players included Anton and Nikolai Rubinstein, and Sergei Rachmaninoff. A Russian national style had fully developed, which was influencing (and even eclipsing) the rest of the Western world. Russia was winning accolades for its instrument-makers at the World Fairs.

Then the chaos of the 1917 Revolution ruptured the country's cultural patrimony. A number of high-profile musicians fled for Germany, France and America. As the Tsarist regime fell apart, Gobelin tapestries, even Van Dyck paintings, were scooped up by departing gentry and opportunistic foreigners in a hurry to leave town with whatever treasures they could salvage. Precious violins were sneaked out under greatcoats, and pianos were tied on top of trains fleeing Russia through Siberia into Manchuria and beyond.

In 1919, one of St Petersburg's music critics sold his grand piano for a few loaves of bread. 'Loot shops' opened up in St Petersburg and Moscow to deal in *objets d'art* stolen from the rich. During the Russian Civil War, which lasted until 1922, manor houses were raided or burnt. In the aftermath, half-surviving instruments were reconstructed. Pianos were built with jumbled parts, such as a Bechstein keyboard on Pleyel legs.

Two decades later, during the Great Patriotic War, the country's most significant national treasures were sent to Siberia for safekeeping, including state-owned instruments from Leningrad and Moscow, the country's best ballerinas and Lenin's embalmed corpse. Not long after, pianos taken from the USSR's Western Front,* from the likes of Saxony and Prussia, ended up travelling eastwards with the country's Red Army soldiers to adorn many a Siberian hearth. As the Nazis advanced, Russians fled their own cities on the European side of the Urals, the trauma of war driving civilians deeper into Siberia, sometimes with an instrument. Other pianos were lost to the German advance or chopped up into firewood. One piano, today in the hands of a well-known musician, was pushed up on its side to black out windows during the Siege of Leningrad when the Nazis starved the city in one of the darkest civilian catastrophes of a horrifyingly bloody century.

Meanwhile, the old expertise in Russian piano-making was changing with the politics. 'Art belongs to the people,' Lenin said in 1920: 'It must have its deepest roots in the broad mass of workers. It must be understood and loved by them. It must be rooted in and grow with their feelings, thoughts and desires.' The Soviet government encouraged the production of thousands of instruments, which were distributed through the USSR's newly formed network of music schools. Piano factories opened in Siberia. Piano rental schemes were introduced for private citizens, with a buoyant market for uprights able to fit into snug Soviet apartments.

This dynamic musical culture, its provincial and social reach far exceeding the equivalent education systems in the West, fell away after 1991 when Boris Yeltsin became the first freely elected leader of Russia in a thousand years. Yeltsin

* Confusingly, most non-Russian readers will know this as 'the Eastern Front', where the Allies fought Germany for control of Eastern Europe. For the Soviet Union, however, this was most definitely a *Western* Front. The Soviets' Eastern Front centred around the invasion of Japanese-held Manchuria in 1945.

immediately set about dissolving the Soviet Union by granting autonomy to various member states. He also overhauled government subsidies in the move to a free-market economy, inducing a chain reaction of dramatic hyperinflation, industrial collapse, corruption, gangsterism and widespread unemployment. As the masses crashed into poverty, the privatization of Russian industries benefitted a few friends of friends in government, who bought oil and gas companies at knock-off prices. Russia's famous oligarchy was born at the same time as generations of communist 'togetherness' were overthrown.

Whether or not Yeltsin's time was a good or a bad thing for Russians remains a moot point. For pianos, it was a catastrophe. The musical education system suffered. As a new rich evolved, tuners learned how to make a mint by doing up old instruments and selling them off as a kind of bourgeois status symbol. They painted broken Bechsteins white to suit an oligarch's mansion, decorated them with gold leaf, and occasionally told tall stories about some kind of noble history to increase the piano's value in a new and naive market. This was a time when Russia was giddy with opportunity and new ways of doing things. It was also a country demoralized by communism's failure: many people wanted to believe in a rosier version of the past.

Numerous instruments were left to rot in Siberia, either too big to move from apartments, or ignored in the basements of music schools long after the funding had run out. Often all that is left of a piano's backstory can be gleaned only from the serial number hidden inside the instrument – stories reaching back through more than two hundred years of Russian history. Yet there are also pianos that have managed to withstand the furtive cold forever trying to creep into their strings. These instruments not only tell the story of Siberia's colonization by the Russians, but also illustrate how people can endure the most astonishing calamities. That belief in music's comfort survives in muffled notes from broken hammers, in beautiful harmonies describing unspeakable things that words can't touch. It survives in pianos that everyday people have done everything to protect.

In the summer of 2015, I encountered Russia's piano history for the first time. It was something new for me: the mysterious, illogical power of an obsession when I started looking for an instrument in Siberia on behalf of a brilliant Mongolian musician. Part of me had always been intrigued by Siberia – a curiosity which had existed since my childhood, when the white space on my globe stretched further than my imagination was capable of. Like Timbuktu, or Ouagadougou, Siberia resonated in a way I couldn't quite explain, with my bookcase telling the story of a bibliophile's relationship with a place I assumed I would never visit. When I finally did, something else took hold – a kind of selfish madness to finish what I had started, while at the same time knowing that in a place as vast as Russia the finish might also never come. I began to make digressions into territory I didn't expect pianos to ever lead me, travelling further and further from my home in England in pursuit of an instrument I don't even play. It didn't matter if causality started to fracture – from A, I had to go to C because of what B had told me – because I had begun to fall for Siberia's unpredictability, for the serendipitous connections and untold experiences that belong to people who make up one of the greatest storytelling nations in the world. I soon realized that what is missing can sometimes tell you more about a country's history than what remains. I also learned that Siberia is bigger, more alluring and far more complicated than the archetypes might suggest – much bigger, in fact, than all the assumptions I had made when my plans began to germinate, then proliferate, and I found myself caught up in the momentum of travelling a ravishingly surprising place.

All this because of a friendship which formed back in the summer of 2015 with a young Mongolian woman called Odgerel Sampilnorov. Odgerel and I were both staying with a German friend, Franz-Christoph Giercke, in Mongolia's Orkhon Valley, close to Karakorum, the site of the historic capital of Genghis Khan's empire, not far from the border with Siberia. The Giercke family spent their summers in a ridgeline of *gers* – the nomads' round-shaped wood-and-canvas tents, which were pitched a long way from where the road runs out in the fenceless steppe. Odgerel had formerly worked as a piano teacher to Giercke's daughter and her Mongolian cousins, using an old instrument he had trucked in from the modern capital, Ulaanbaatar.

'When we first met, Odgerel was only nineteen years old, but within a few hours of hearing her play, I had an epiphany,' recalled Giercke. 'Not only did she have a great feeling for Johann Sebastian Bach and the Germany of the seventeenth century, for Bach's religious devotion and suffering, but she could evoke emotions and memories going back to my East German childhood in Magdeburg and Leipzig. She could play all the key piano pieces of the eighteenth, nineteenth and twentieth centuries. She could play them by heart, never needing a written score. Mozart, Beethoven, Handel, Mendelssohn, Chopin, Liszt, Schumann, Rachmaninoff, Tchaikovsky, Scriabin. I'd never heard talent like it.'

With Giercke's help and others', Odgerel studied for nine years at a conservatory in Perugia in Italy. By the time I met her, her playing was sublime. The old instrument was gone, and she gave recitals on Giercke's Yamaha baby grand, followed by dinners of roasted goat, each animal cooked from the inside out with a bellyful of hot rocks. Outside the *ger*'s wooden door was a wide plateau cupped by mountains, the steppe's velvet folds studded with tombs and ancient standing stones left by successive waves of nomadic people. Yaks and horses, more numerous than people in Mongolia, grazed on the riverbank below. Inside the tent, the gathering included a Sherpa cook, a local shaman nicknamed The Bonesetter, and Tsogt, a Paris-trained opera singer from Inner Mongolia who was also a consummate archer. The baritone's neck was always crooked from trying to fit into the *ger*'s low opening to listen to the piano concerts, the music's deep, poignant conflicts floating up through an opening in the roof fashioned from a spoked wheel of painted wood.

One night, Giercke shook his head with irritation. The piano was a modern Yamaha, and out of sorts. It played with an even temper, but in his opinion, the sound wasn't up to what it was before. Perhaps the steppe's dry climate had finally caused it damage. Perhaps Odgerel's tuner needed to return sooner than planned. Giercke leaned over and whispered in my ear his frustration, 'We must find her one of the lost pianos of Siberia!'

That evening, he handed me a novel by an American author, Daniel Mason, about a British piano tuner who travelled up the Salween River into a lawless nineteenth-century Burma. The tuner was tasked to fix a rare 1840 grand piano belonging to an enigmatic army surgeon employed by the British War Office. The Erard functioned as a symbol of European nineteenth-century colonization in Asia, with many of

33

the book's themes recalling Joseph Conrad's story of Kurtz, the painter, musician and ivory hunter who 'goes native' in *Heart of Darkness*. In Mason's book, whenever the Erard was played, the music brought peace to the warring tribes. Giercke, who had a little bit of Kurtz to him, liked the idea of living 'upriver' with a spectacular piano; he saw no reason for a good piano hunt to be cast as fiction, nor to doubt there being pianos in Siberia in the first place: 'If you, Sophy, would find a piano and bring it here, our story would be real.' Giercke was a filmmaker and well travelled in Central Asia. He knew enough about the region's history to believe that there would be instruments out there. He liked the idea of a piano bringing joy to his adopted country, and Odgerel having an instrument of her own – playing it in the Orkhon Valley in summer, and at her home in Ulaanbaatar in winter.

Through that dusty Mongolian summer, Odgerel and I became friends. We talked about her childhood, how her father was a basketball coach and her mother a gymnast. Odgerel's family were Buryats, an indigenous group with strong Buddhist and shamanistic roots from close to Lake Baikal. In the thirties, members of her family were persecuted under Stalin, when nomadic pastoralism was replaced with collective herds, their Buddhist religion was suppressed, monasteries closed, their intelligentsia killed, and their homeland – defended in a 1929 rebellion that saw some thirty-five thousand Buryats killed – cut up into smaller territories. Some of Odgerel's relatives fled to Mongolia.

While Odgerel's story stayed with me, it was her music which moved me. The more I listened to her play, the more I wondered how an historic piano would sound different in the steppe – an instrument which still resonated with the gentler

Odgerel Sampilnorov's family. Her Buryat ancestors, originally from near Lake Baikal in Siberia, are pictured in the first image.

timbre of the nineteenth century: the moody nocturnes of John Field, the sparkling elegance of Chopin's Ballades, the earthy texture of Tchaikovsky's 'Russian Rustic Scene'.* You don't need a thundering concert piano in a space as intimate as a Mongolian *ger*. An interesting European instrument with a mellow voice would duet well with the plaintive *morin khuur*, the Mongolian horsehead fiddle. The combination was something Odgerel was also beginning to champion as a unique Eurasian style.

We talked a little about the difficulties that might lie ahead, and our mixed motivations. If I were to go and look in Siberia, I would need to understand the story of pianos in Russian culture and how and why these instruments had travelled east in the first place. I love nothing more than listening to people talk, whether in the pages of books, or across a table sharing a meal. Odgerel loves music; she wanted a piano with good sound. Giercke loves all of these things too, but above all, the spirit of adventure. Offering to help pay for the endeavour, he said that only in trying to take on something difficult would something interesting ever happen.

'We made our plans in this way: If we could do it, it would be good, and a good story. And if we couldn't do it, we would have a story, too, the story of not being able to do it.' This is how John Steinbeck described his trip to the USSR in the aftermath of the Second World War with the photographer Robert Capa. Steinbeck's approach appealed to me. So did Anton Chekhov's, who declared his intention to travel across Siberia in a letter to his publisher in 1890: 'Even assuming my excursion is an utter triviality, a piece of obstinacy and caprice,

---

* *Dumka*, op. 59.

yet just you consider and then tell me what I'm losing by going. Time? Money? Will I undergo hardships? My time costs nothing. I never have any money anyway.' In a fug of piano music, Mongolian vodka and late nights talking under a starry sky, a trip to Siberia sounded almost implausibly exciting. Then summer turned to autumn, and back home in England my mood darkened with the leaves and the seasonal malaise. I moved on from the idea of undertaking any Siberian piano hunt until eight months later, when I flew to the Russian Far East. Only when I started travelling deep into the Russian forest did I realize I could no more unsnag the idea of Siberia's lost pianos than set out coatless into cold so extreme it makes your tears freeze into the lines around your eyes.

2

Traces in the Snow:
Khabarovsk

I F YOU MEASURE SIBERIA's width from the Urals in the west to the last spit of land that makes up the Chukotka Peninsula on Russia's Arctic seaboard, then Siberia is wider than Australia, its Pacific edge just fifty miles shy of North America to the east. In Siberia, there are lakes that are called seas, with some parts so thinly populated that travellers past and present have frequently compared Siberia to the moon.* This analogy

---

* The contemporary American author Ian Frazier recounts a story about Westerners flattering the seventeenth-century Tsars with the idea that their territory 'exceeded

would work if it weren't for the animal life that thrives in Siberia's icy vaults. Once upon a time, when Eurasia wasn't such a mighty, contiguous landmass, the Urals formed the shore of an epicontinental sea dividing Europe from Asia. Flora and fauna migrated across the land when sea levels fell, except for one species that managed to more or less respect the borders of this long-forgotten biogeographical divide: a plucky little Siberian newt you seldom find west of the Urals. A fierce swimmer and evolutionary hero, the pencil-long *Salamandrella keyserlingii* can live for many years inside the permafrost, in temperatures hitting fifty degrees below. In *The Gulag Archipelago*, Solzhenitsyn describes how in Stalin's labour camps, higher thoughts of ichthyology would be cast aside for a mouthful of the prehistoric flesh. If famished convicts were ever to chance upon such a thing, he pictured the scene: the salamander would be frantically thawed on the bonfire and devoured *'with relish'* by hungry convicts elbowing each other out of the way.

On a cold winter morning in March 2016, I landed in the city of Khabarovsk in the Russian Far East, an eight-hour flight from Moscow and about a day's drive from the Pacific, where the coast is so choked with ice you can walk out on to a frozen ocean. It felt about as far from home as I could get while remaining on this planet. With the idea of Siberia's lost pianos nagging at my conscience, I had made a couple of cursory attempts to see if my quest had legs, but the real purpose of my

---

the size of the surface of the full moon'. It didn't matter that it was potentially untrue: 'To say that Russia was larger than the full moon sounded impressive, and had an echo of poetry, and poetry creates empires.' This is one of my favourite lines ever written about Siberia – a remark which speaks to the power of the great Siberian myth. *Travels in Siberia* (New York: Farrar, Straus and Giroux, 2010).

trip wasn't to find an instrument for the Mongolian pianist I had befriended. I had come to track something far rarer – to write about the Siberian, or Amur, tiger. If there were a decent story to tell, I would sell it to a British newspaper. In winter, when the forest is covered in snow, it is easier to see a tiger's footprints.

Panthera tigris altaica, an icon of the Russian wilderness under heavy federal protection, is on a fragile edge. There are only an estimated five hundred of these creatures surviving in the wild, their rarity almost on a par with the few snow leopards left in Siberia's Altai Mountains close to Mongolia, and the Amur leopard, which is down to eighty or so animals where Russia borders China and North Korea. For centuries, the Chinese came foraging for ginseng roots in these eastern forests, and to poach tigers for traditional medicine. Then in the late nineteenth century, big-game hunters shot them for trophy pelts until tiger hunting was banned in Russia in 1947. These days, professional conservationists are lucky to encounter a wild tiger more than once or twice in a lifetime. Before the Korean tiger researcher and filmmaker Sooyong Park started his work in 1995, less than an hour's footage had ever been recorded of Siberian tigers in the wild.

I arrived in Khabarovsk expecting everything to be dead and infirm, unbearably cruel and devoid of enchantment. Siberia had functioned for more than three centuries as a prison. It had been shredded by revolution, civil war, Stalin's reign of terror and the impact of the Great Patriotic War. I turned eighteen in 1991, the year the USSR collapsed. Twenty-five years later and numerous post-Soviet images were seared into my mind: a factory here, an abandoned tank there, and a sickly forest eaten away by industrial pollution.

Not that I was unique in my preconceptions. In 1770, Catherine the Great complained to the French Enlightenment philosopher Voltaire: 'When this nation becomes better known in Europe, people will recover from the many errors and prejudices that they have about Russia.' When Tchaikovsky met Liszt in 1877, he remarked on his nauseatingly deferential smile, which was heavily loaded with condescension.

'Pay no heed to the boasting of Russians; they confuse splendour with elegance, luxury with refinement, policing and fear with the foundations of society,' wrote the French traveller the Marquis de Custine, of the Russia he found around the time Liszt was in St Petersburg. 'Up to now, as far as civilization is concerned, they have been satisfied with appearances, but if they were ever to avenge their real inferiority, they would make us pay cruelly for our advantages over them.' De Custine – described by one historian as a camp, gossipy travel writer – was a powerful influence in the West's early (and enduring) perception of backwards Russia: 'The Russians have gone rotten without ever ripening!' he wrote in 1839, citing a well-known aphorism of the time. If the West still looks down on Russia, it has an even more pronounced attitude towards Siberia – and it was ever thus. 'There are few places on the earth's surface about which the majority mankind have such definite ideas with so little personal knowledge as Siberia,' observed a British economist travelling through the country in 1919.

On first encounter, Khabarovsk was wrapped in this fog of stereotypes. It was a leaden sprawl in monochrome with neither the brutal beauty of Moscow nor the peppermint-coloured grace of St Petersburg. There was a museum about a bridge, another about fish, a third about the history of gas extraction. The snow was dirty, like the midnight stipple on an old television channel. Trails from smokestacks streaked the sky with worry lines. Signs of urban prosperity were thin: a European-style boulevard with blushes of pink paint, and a promenade with white railings used as a set for wedding photographs beside the frozen Amur River. At least I hadn't come in summer, when the surrounding forest turns to swamp blackened with mosquitoes, their wings pricking the surface like drizzle, their swollen corpses falling into every spoonful of soup.

Aleksandr Batalov, the local tiger researcher I had come to meet, didn't speak much at first. In his middle sixties, he was broad and short, with grey eyes and wide shoulders honed by the pull-ups he practised on a bar that hung across the doorway of his cabin in the forest. He wore a pair of felt boots gifted to him by a colonel in the Russian army, and mismatched camouflage fatigues. Following us in another van out to the forest was a driver carrying food supplies and extra blankets. The driver's face was sallow, scored by a lifetime of pulling hard on cigarettes, his lack of charisma matching a description that the early-twentieth-century explorer Vladimir Arseniev gave to the local men who joined him on his expeditions through this territory. 'The Siberians were selected not for their social qualifications,' he wrote, 'but because they were resourceful men accustomed to roughing it.'

Arseniev was right. Our driver was efficient when the engine coughed and cut, but not once did he attempt conversation. The Uzbek cook at Aleksandr's research base wasn't much of a talker either, leaving me to wonder how the Silk Road town of Samarkand and the golden roads that once led to it must have hit a catastrophic slump in fortune for a man to venture here, to abandon the fat peaches of his native

Fergana Valley in Uzbekistan for Siberia's bony fish. For the Uzbek, it was unclear if Siberia marked the end of the road, or a new beginning.

We rumbled out of Khabarovsk, passing workers gathered at the bus stops, their breath suspended in the air. We passed a shopping mall on the city's outskirts, where a few months prior, a brown bear had wandered in. The bear was shot and bundled into the back of a white van, head hanging like a teddy without its stuffing. Aleksandr then described a boar that had recently rammed the doors of a Khabarovsk hotel. Each of Aleksandr's stories implied that Siberia was teeming with wildlife, when a century ago, Dersu Uzala, the indigenous trapper who led Arseniev's expeditions, warned of the environment's demise: he gave it ten years before all the sable and squirrel would be gone.

Dersu Uzala belonged to the Nanai tribe, also called 'the fishskin Tatars' after their habit of using dried fishskins for clothes. In the late sixteenth century, Siberia's population comprised almost a quarter of a million indigenous people living as nomads, fishermen, hunters and reindeer herders. The Nanai were one among around five hundred unique Siberian tribes. Belief systems were shamanist and animist.

This mix began to change in the seventeenth century. Religious dissidents who refused to sign up to reforms in the Russian Orthodox Church fled east of the Urals to escape repression in European Russia. They formed 'Old Believer' communities, which still exist today. The process of Russian cultural assimilation among minorities picked up under Catherine the Great, with a rapid expansion in Siberian trade. Disease, brought in by the influx of outsiders, also spread into indigenous communities. By the middle of the seventeenth

Dersu Uzala, photographed c. *1906, acted as a guide for Vladimir Arseniev's expedition, and twice saved his life. In 1975, the story was turned into an Oscar-winning film,* Dersu Uzala, *by the Japanese director Akira Kurosawa.*

century, Russian settlers – as opposed to just convicts, who were only ever a small proportion of Siberia's new population – were outnumbered by indigenous Siberians at a ratio of around three to one. By the end of the nineteenth century, that ratio had changed, with five citizens of Russian descent to one indigenous Siberian. With these demographic shifts – not unique to Russia, given what the Europeans were up to with their overseas colonies – Orthodox Christianity soon prevailed. Forced collectivization in the Soviet period, as well as a stringent 'Russifying' political ideology, then brought the last of Siberia's indigenous outliers into line. Shamanism, banned by Lenin in the twenties, is no longer close to what it was before. With the old blood mixed up with the new, Slavic features are found in faces that look a little Korean, Mongolian, even Native American. Siberia's original hundred-odd languages are disappearing. The Kerek tongue, spoken in the Far North, is close to extinction. There are more tigers left in Siberia than there are Itelmen-speaking people.

There had been fresh snowfall overnight in Khabarovsk. The further we drove, the thicker the drifts. By the time we turned off the road at the village of Durmin, the track was smothered. Marsh grasses arced under the weight, and seedheads nodded like silver pom-poms. In the solitude, it was hard to imagine the Russian taiga – the so-called 'tipsy forest', named after the skinny, deracinated trees – rustling with sable. This relative of the marten once thrived in the wooded belt between Russia's grassy southern steppe and the northern tundra inside the Arctic Circle. From the mid-sixteenth century, sable was Russia's 'soft gold', accounting for up to ten per cent of the state income, its silken fur, each dark chocolate hair tipped in silver as if sprinkled in morning frost, drawing bands of ruffian Cossack mercenaries. Answering to the Tsars, the Cossacks colonized Siberia so rapidly, they reached the Pacific within sixty-odd years of making their first incursion over the Urals.

Aleksandr spotted a field mouse on the road, which we just avoided running over. 'Don't look after the shrew, and we have big problems,' he said, explaining how the natural chains are breached with every felling of an oak tree. When predator and prey lose their place in the world, tigers are forced to migrate into territory where they don't belong. He told me

An eighteenth-century engraving of an indigenous Siberian fur trapper. The indigenous people were heavily exploited, earning a copper kettle in return for the equivalent skins they could squash inside the vessel.

to listen out for ravens, which cluster around a kill. He wanted to show me a nuthatch, which was his favourite bird. Between sharing facts about the forest, Aleksandr talked a little about politics – how the socialist idea was a good one, though other nations wouldn't have stood it for so long. Russians have an ability to endure, he said, to test an idea from the beginning to its end. He described the vacuum that was created, and his disappointment, when the USSR disintegrated. He talked about the riverside cabin of his Siberian childhood, how it was surrounded by rolling wheat fields and mountains where he used to collect berries which his grandmother folded into yoghurt. A large basket took two hours to fill. It was on expeditions like this that he learned to observe the behaviour of animals, including hares, birds, roe deer, foxes and wolves. At the age of five, he spied on a family of cranes, hiding himself in the pond so that only his eyes and nose were above the water. But the cranes got angry and attacked him.

Bit by bit, Aleksandr began to reveal his motivations for protecting a species he feared could no longer protect itself. It didn't matter that he rarely found a tiger. Like the researcher Sooyong Park, who has written so eloquently about his years sleeping in hides waiting for Siberian tigers, Aleksandr was content looking for its tracks and trying to reason with the loggers damaging the habitat on which not just the tiger but also its prey depend. Aleksandr was fascinated by the tiger's status in Russian culture. He described all sorts of superstitions around tigers – like the one about a priest who in Tsarist times wore a tiger skin under his cassock to avoid being bitten by the town's stray dogs – and gruesome true stories. A few years ago, a good friend – a game warden – woke up to fresh tracks, recorded the sighting in his diary and then set out for another winter cabin. Along the way the tiger ambushed him.

Then Aleksandr grabbed my hand, squeezed it and stopped the van. On the ground ahead of us was a perfect line of pugmarks – each wide pad fringed with four round toes. As I cautiously stepped out of the truck and put my hand against the pugmark in the snow, the scale became real. The front paw pad measured nine centimetres at its widest point. A six-year-old tiger, said Aleksandr, and probably a male.

For another mile, the tracks followed a straight line then looped off the road, where the tiger had wandered off to add its scratch marks to a tree. Aleksandr said we mustn't follow. If a tiger has prepared itself for an attack, there is no way a man can act quickly enough. Tigers are clever, with a capacity for premeditated revenge. They like walking in our footsteps, said Aleksandr, preferring the feel and efficiency of compressed snow.

We drove on at a crawl, until we came to the impression where the tiger had been sleeping and left its barrel-shaped belly pushed into the pack. Golden strands of hair were still embedded in the white. A few steps beyond, there were scarlet specks of blood, the stain so fresh that the colour was still bright with life. This would have been enough – to touch the blood from a Siberian tiger's kill – until we turned another bend in the track. The tiger was sleeping, perhaps eighty metres distant, in the middle of the road. When he raised his head, I could see the dazzling stripes, the crystal snow falling off his back, the poise of his long tail, which had nothing to do with fear.

That night, I had difficulty sleeping. When a log hissed then snapped in the fire, I thought of the single bite it takes a tiger to break the neck of a deer. But it wasn't fear that was keeping me awake; it was intoxication. Part of me wanted to leave Durmin and the discomforts of Siberian life – the anxious nights, the frozen meat hung up in the porch waiting for a clumsy hacking from the Uzbek cook – but a far larger part of me wanted to stay.

There was something bewitching about the taiga now I was inside the forest, something which ran deeper than those glinting incisions of curling waterways you see from the air, the forest scrawled with tightly folded S-bends as if the land is whispering somehow. There is a covert charm to Siberia, like the maps by Semion Remezov, who drew up the first significant cartographic record of the region at the end of the seventeenth century, when Peter the Great posted him to the Western Siberian town of Tobolsk.*

---

* Two of Remezov's maps are published on the endpapers of this book.

Remezov had a cartographer's eye for the dimensions of the land, and an illustrator's flourish. His maps are decorated with elaborately inked fortresses, sickle lakes and wooded copses. Many of Remezov's manuscripts are dotted with Siberian creatures – flying horses, a pack of wolves, horned antelopes – and effortlessly fluid line-drawings of grand cathedrals, weaponry and soldiers. His work is still the most perfect distillation of Siberia's lures, rendered in beautiful, calligraphic loops. Painted in watery blues, the tributaries reach across the pages like the veins of the Empire itself, each spur as finely drawn as a fishbone. Remezov drew Siberia with a delicacy that belies its ferocious reputation, from the fraying rivers spilling into lakes the shape of love-hearts, to forests hollowed out by lazy streams making their northern journey to the Arctic.

In my mind's eye, Siberia began to burn with possibility, in the faults and folds of a landscape full of risk and opportunity. Names began to roll out of the emptiness: Chita, Krasnoyarsk, the River Yenisei, which is one of Siberia's four great rivers, along with the Amur, Lena and Ob. I was captivated by how marvellous it would be to find one of Siberia's lost pianos in a country such as this. What if I could track down a Bechstein in a cabin far out in the wilds? There was enough evidence in Siberia's musical story to know instruments had penetrated this far, but what had survived?

On my last evening in the forest, I mentioned the idea to Aleksandr over another thin broth of dill and fish-heads with boiled white eyes – the notion of returning to Siberia to look for an instrument.

At first, Aleksandr didn't address my idea. He talked about his personal history, and his father's songs. In the Siberian village where Aleksandr was raised, his father had been a music teacher and accordion player; his melodies were well remembered. Aleksandr told me about a musician who ten years before had wanted help moving an old piano into his home in Khabarovsk. He described dragging it to the apartment block then up numerous flights of stairs. Then Aleksandr went back to scanning his camera-trap footage of tigers, leaving me to picture a piano being hauled across pavements of ice. Nothing more was mentioned about music until the last morning as we readied to leave the forest. Aleksandr reminded me of the tiger we had encountered on the path, and the snow pricked with blood. The sighting would be my talisman, he said.

'You must give it a go,' he urged. 'The tiger will bring you luck.'

In my last hours with Aleksandr, a powerful attachment formed in my mind, that I might find as much enchantment in the historical traces of instruments through Siberia as Aleksandr did in the footprints of a rare animal. Instead of tigers, I would track pianos. By knocking on doors looking for instruments, I would be drawn deeper into Russia and perhaps find a counterpoint in music not only to Siberia's brutal history but to the modern images of this country reported by the anti-Putin media in the West. Driving back out of the forest, I passed the spot where I had seen the tiger. If the silver birches were spirit trees, as the Nanai people believed, I wondered if I should have made a passing act of totemism to persuade Siberia to keep me safe.

When I returned to England, I started looking for good leads. I contacted Pyotr Aidu, a Russian concert pianist who had amassed a Moscow orphanage for abandoned instruments. In his collection, there was an 1820 English Broadwood, and a Russian-made Stürzwage wearing the scars of a firework

detonated under its lid – a good brand, much overlooked, and
one I should look out for, he advised. He said there were voices
worth seeking out in old instruments. In his opinion, restored
pianos have better sound than their modern counterparts.

Others disagreed. Numerous piano experts told me that
all the reconstruction in the world wouldn't necessarily make
a dead piano sing again. I was told Siberia was a terrible place
for pianos, especially because of the low humidity in winter. I
was warned that there were strict laws to protect against arte-
facts of more than a hundred years old leaving the country;
more than fifty years, and a piano would need, at the very
least, special permission. I decided to home in on Siberia's old
trade routes, including the Trans-Siberian Railway towns that
thrived in the nineteenth century, at the same time as Russian
pianos spread east. I would use television adverts, social media
and local radio channels to track down private instruments
with stories. I would need Siberia's piano tuners on my side.
They would know best where history was still to be found in
Russian homes. That was by far the most important part to
me: gathering the stories, then seeing where they led.

As I marked up my map, I started to understand more
clearly how the Tsars' expansion into Siberia, and their establishment of the exile system, coincided with the state's desire
to bring European piano-making to Russia – and how instruments had trickled into this wasteland over the course of three
centuries, contributing to the waves of Russification across old
Siberia and lost indigenous cultures. Part of me hoped that the
piano, which was such a magnificent symbol of European culture, hadn't yet made it into a nomad's tent. Every piano I
found would be a victory, but I also wanted to seek out the
corners of Siberia which had been left untouched – the parts

not even Catherine the Great had managed to pull into line during a reign that helped turn Russia into a European musical nation, and Siberia into a synonym for fear. I not only needed to travel into the musical history of the nineteenth and twentieth centuries, but also to look at the piano's domination, its shifting dominions, and its social role. Only then would I understand the value of something precious in the physical peripheries of Russia at a time when piano music was experienced 'live', before radio and recorded music shrank the world. By following the pathway of an object, I would get closer to understanding the place. I would learn that an object is never just an object – that each piano sings differently because of the people who used to play it and polish its wooden case.

3
Siberia is 'Civilized':
St Petersburg to the Pacific

W HEN I VISITED TOBOLSK for the first time, it was blowing a snowstorm. The weather softened everything – my mood, my expectations. This small town in Western Siberia with its white citadel, circular, frilled towers and windowless walls was built on top of a pleated escarpment. It seemed to belong to the pages of a fairy tale, Tobolsk's profile glittering with the bulbous gold and turquoise domes of the Russian Orthodox religion. Beside the church stood a seminary – the oldest in Siberia, from which nineteenth-century missionaries were despatched all over the Empire, even to Russian America, when the Tsars' colonial possessions extended to Alaska and parts of what is now California.* Standing at the heart of this old Siberian capital, I was close to the site where an important battle took place in 1580 when the Cossack adventurer Ermak Timofeevich ventured east across the Urals with an army of less than a thousand men to defeat the last Sibir khan – an achievement the Tsar rewarded with new chainmail. Unfortunately for Ermak, the weight of his fashionable new armour led to his drowning when he toppled into a river nearby.

Ermak's story, both mighty and bathetic, marked the beginning of Siberia's colonization, which saw the Russian Empire expand its territory by more than a hundred times. But if Tobolsk was a symbol of imperial Russia's glory, the town was also testimony to the punitive tyranny of the Tsarist regime. Before the rise of the Eastern Siberian city of Irkutsk under Catherine the Great, Tobolsk was the main sorting house for Siberia's incoming exiles. Among them were prisoners of war, including a large Swedish contingent picked up at the 1709 Battle of Poltava – a victory over the Swedish Empire that forever changed the power balance in north-east Europe, to Russia's advantage. The Swedes not only provided the necessary labour for redirecting the river systems which wind beneath Tobolsk; they also imparted a significant civilizing influence. In 1720, the Scottish traveller John Bell observed the Swedes' effect on Tobolsk's culture. He expressed surprise to find such a variety of musical instruments, with the Swedes responsible for introducing several useful arts 'almost unknown'

---

* Russian America existed from 1733 to 1867, when the territory was sold to the United States for a paltry US$7.2 million.

before their arrival. Bell attended various concerts with these officer convicts, who also worked as teachers for the Russians.

The Swedes joined the system of penal labour devised by Peter the Great under a late-seventeenth-century initiative called *katorga*, which banished men and women to Siberia with forced-labour terms. Sometimes amnesty was granted for high-profile political prisoners, usually with a changeover of Tsar, but otherwise marked exiles – the worst offenders with their nostrils split, branded and scarred by a kind of barbed whip called the knout – were deemed 'officially dead' in the eyes of the law. For exiles, there was also no return, which was a highly effective way not only to punish people, and push 'undesirables' out of sight and out of mind, but to colonize Russia's acquisitions. With this ambitious penal system to manage, Tobolsk attracted its fair share of officialdom – governors, educators and their wives, and, inevitably, pianos. I had traced and found a few interesting instruments – a beautiful nineteenth-century French Erard, serial number 75796, which had been irretrievably damaged by a burst pipe as recently as 1988. There were a score of pre-Revolution, Russian-made grand pianos, but in poor condition. The civil war had been hard on Tobolsk, said Aleksei, a chatty, energetic one-time priest who had trained at the seminary. He offered to help with my search – a chance encounter that rolled into a whole day of looking when he changed his plans to accommodate a stranger.

Aleksei was tall, handsomely dressed in a black suit, his charismatic presence, whispered my interpreter, reminding her of all the images she had in her head of Peter the Great. He had bright blue eyes, and an even brighter voice that seemed to make the air move differently when he spoke. I suppose both of us were a little bit in love with him. This was partly because Aleksei was everything I didn't expect of Russian Orthodoxy – a wit, without the long, grave beard I associated with his religion, his cheerfulness so abundant that I soon stopped thinking about the tragedy of the drowned Erard and Tobolsk's other half-sounding instruments. When Aleksei was studying at the seminary, his favourite game was doing roly-polies off the hill beneath the church in his long black cassock. He would tumble off the edge of the escarpment towards a thicket of wooden houses that flowed beneath the hill like spring's muddy snowmelt.

In the lee of this ledge, Aleksei took me to the Lower Town, where the great and good once lived, including Catherine's governor, Aleksandr Aliabiev, a keen patron of the musical arts, and a significant symbol of Catherine's expanding cultural influence. The governor's son, also called Aleksandr Aliabiev, became a well-regarded pianist and composer who trained in St Petersburg. After serving his country in the Napoleonic Wars, Aliabiev junior was exiled back to Tobolsk for his alleged involvement in a murky gambling murder, with his most popular song, 'The Nightingale', composed during his stint in Tobolsk jail on a piano a Sister of Mercy arranged to be brought to his cell. At least, that's how the legend goes – one among many that congregate in this old part of town. Aliabiev's music, however, is eclipsed by the far larger story lurking among Tobolsk's nineteenth-century boulevards. In the old Governor's House, the last Tsar and his family were kept under house arrest by the Bolsheviks in 1917 before being moved to Ekaterinburg, where they were eventually murdered. The family's German music teacher had travelled with them to Tobolsk from St Petersburg. With no piano among their luggage, the Romanovs' captors therefore had to acquire an instrument, along with other pieces of furniture, from merchants who lived nearby. It was a piano often played by the Empress when she was left by herself, waiting for news of their fate while the civil war intensified.

Aleksei said Tobolsk's archivists were looking for the Empress's instrument, but so far without success. He took me up the rickety stairs of the mansion, which workmen were busy renovating in order to turn it into a museum. They showed me handwritten notes from the late nineteenth and early twentieth centuries which they had found between the floorboards. That such scraps of history might still lie in cracks like these felt somehow reassuring. Then, when we were finishing up for the day, Aleksei suggested I meet some of his friends who were studying at the seminary. He led me into the priests' canteen, a bare white room where nine men were already gathered: three of them bearded, four in cassocks, the rest in high-collared, brass-buttoned black suits.

The priests' demeanour was deadly serious. They had twenty minutes, they said, before their absence would be noticed. One of them fiddled with a heavy crucifix around his neck like an awkward teenager. Another straightened his back as if he were being pulled tall by a puppet string. With no ceremony, concert hall or church, they started to sing, led by a wide-chested choir regent. For the next ten, fifteen minutes, they barely paused in their plaintive chants, their naked voices making the hairs stand up on the backs of my arms. Something felt innately right about these people – in their precise commitment to their art, and their passionate belief in a divinity greater than themselves. I felt reassured that in a part of the world associated with fear I was now among Siberians for whom music mattered as much as air.

*

I am no musician, but music moves me. Catherine the Great, on the other hand, claimed her musical ear was deaf as a post. '[I]t's just noise to me,' she wrote wryly to a friend, with one account claiming she was assigned court musicians to tell her when to clap. She possessed enough of an ability, however, to remark on her husband's even more inferior talents when she complained how Peter, grandson of Peter the Great and heir to the Romanov dynasty, used to scratch on a violin in the imperial boudoir in between playing with toy soldiers. Throughout the five-hour-long orchestral concerts at court each week, her husband would play lead violin, to Catherine's disgust. There was no creature unhappier than herself, Catherine claimed, with her caustic epistolary wit, except for Peter's spaniels, which he continually thrashed.

Catherine's remarks also have to be taken with a pinch of salt. This brilliant, German-born princess might have professed to lack any natural ability for music, but its advancement under her rule was significant, given the country was lagging behind Western Europe's state of development when she first arrived in Russia in 1744. In the countryside, the peasantry were drumming their feet to the plucking of the balalaika, a traditional three-stringed guitar. Beyond the Romanov court, folk song dominated. A French traveller who ventured to Tobolsk in the year of Catherine's coronation described a lamentable state of affairs: music in the most sophisticated Siberian towns rang with the sound of bad violins, which were nothing more than pieces of hollowed wood. The Russian Orthodox Church relied on liturgical chants, with instrumental music banned. In 1762, when Catherine's inept husband expired in shady circumstances – perhaps by throttling, possibly by poisoning, though the official version of events had his death put down to haemorrhoidal colic – Catherine began to change the Empire for ever by consolidating the country's territorial reach, as well as Russia's status as a formidable cultural power.

Catherine was an avid reader. She bought Diderot's entire library, followed by Voltaire's, and she sanctioned Russia's first private printing presses. Her instinct for art collecting was second to none, and she adored English gardens and Scottish architects. Like the vast art collection she acquired, music was a means to establish power and prestige – above all, to bring Russia closer to Europe. She acquired an affection for opera, and opened a theatre where it could be performed in the Hermitage. This gave birth to a national tradition which later influenced the operatic styles and aesthetics in other European countries, including Italy. Her reign – the longest in Russia's imperial history – also established the infrastructure for Russia's piano tradition to root as Catherine tipped the balance in the country's appropriation of European habits.

Until Napoleon invaded Russia in 1812, and France fell from grace, the Russian aristocracy spoke French over their native tongue. Russian men cut their beards so that they might look more like Europeans. Following the latest French fashions, Russian women donned red-heeled shoes, laced themselves into whalebone corsets, and added the odd beauty spot à la Marie Antoinette. Even diseases were fashionably French, with *la grippe*, observed Tolstoy in *War and Peace*, 'being then a new word in St Petersburg, used only by the elite'. Throughout Catherine's reign, Russia's aristocracy travelled abroad. They brought back with them a taste for opera, chamber music and the new orchestral arrangements coming out of Paris, Leipzig and Vienna, as well as growing curiosity for the new instrument affectionately referred to as 'the one with little hammers'.

Clavichords began to appear in Catherine's court as her ambassadors engaged foreign teachers and commissioned new musical compositions. The Moscow house belonging to Catherine's friend Ekaterina Dashkova, a talented harpsichordist, was cluttered with these new keyboard instruments, which was a direct reflection of the Empress's Enlightenment ideas and approbation of European accomplishments. The German harpsichordist Hermann Raupach not only encouraged private concerts; he also taught keyboard at St Petersburg's Imperial Academy of Fine Arts.

Year by year, Russia's musical culture developed. In 1776, Catherine was persuaded to hire the Italian composer Giovanni Païsiello as court conductor – the first musician, she wrote, who could turn her inclement ear. What is less clear is whether it was the conductor's appearance she found attractive, or his musical talents. Another of her lovers – Grigory Orlov, a dashing, music-loving officer – made a note of it when he watched Catherine wrap a fur coat round the shoulders of this enchantingly handsome, dark-haired Italian while he sat playing the harpsichord.

Whatever it was in Païsiello that Catherine found so engaging, it was enough to ensure that he stayed in Russia for the next seven years, composing numerous keyboard pieces for women of nobility – preludes, capriccios, rondos, a sonata or two. Catherine hired him to teach fortepiano to her son, the future Tsar Paul I, and his wife, the inquisitive, musically talented Maria Feodorovna. After Païsiello came Giuseppe Sarti, an Italian composer-conductor and favourite of Catherine's most influential paramour, Prince Grigory Potemkin – a political genius whose passion for music was as intense as his love-making was renowned. Potemkin was Catherine's true

Catherine the Great listening to a performance by Giovanni Païsiello. During his seven-year tenure in Russia, Païsiello composed extensively, and gave piano lessons. This drawing was made by Edoardo Matania in 1881.

companion in a revolving door of bed-fellows, whose musical obsession ran so deep he would send his courier to Milan to fetch a piece of sheet music. Potemkin's most significant English biographer writes how he required his choir to be with him at all times – to perform at breakfast, lunch and supper. They also had to join him in the field of war.

With Potemkin by her side, Catherine began to turn into a powerful benefactor of the musical arts. Other noble ladies took lessons at the educational institutions in St Petersburg that Catherine patronized. Foreign teachers serviced an eager market. In September 1791, the music-obsessed Russian envoy to Vienna urged Potemkin to employ a willing Mozart. Unfortunately for Russia, by the end of the year both Potemkin and Mozart were dead.

Mozart had gone to his grave in Vienna struggling to pay his medical bills, unable even to afford firewood. Russia, meanwhile, had been paying its lead musicians so well that Potemkin's favourite composer was given a village in Ukraine. At the same time, in St Petersburg's glamorous musical circles, profound changes were underway with the rising influence of Catherine's daughter-in-law, Maria Feodorovna, whose support of performers and musical education made her a spectacular catalyst for the country's nascent piano-making industry. Ten years before Potemkin was mulling over the Mozart hiring, Maria Feodorovna had made a trip to Vienna – the city of Haydn and Beethoven, or 'clavierland' as Mozart called it – where she had attended the piano duel of the century: Muzio Clementi versus Wolfgang Amadeus Mozart. The event, attended by the great and the good, pitted the two musicians against each other in a kind of eighteenth-century boxing ring.

For Mozart, the encounter was worth no more than a passing comment. '[Clementi's] greatest strength is his passage in thirds, but he has not an atom of feeling or taste – in short, he is a mere machine,' Mozart remarked in a letter to his father. For Clementi, the event presented a new opportunity; he was quick to hobnob with the Russian ambassador in order to exert his influence in Russian society.

Clementi began exporting his English brand of pianos to Russia – advising his colleagues to 'make hay while the sun shines', now the piano was in a much more robust state of development, along with music publishing. In this same period, concert promoters started to hire out privately owned halls in St Petersburg for public performances. Clementi, however, couldn't resist showing disdain for his new Russian customers. He complained of them being 'slippery' in payments, 'cursedly stingy', possessing 'good ears for sound tho' they have none for sense and style'. As for the Emperor himself, 'nothing less than a trumpet could make its way through his obtuse tympanum'. The instruments constantly suffered from the climate – 'keep them some time in a very warm room, in order to discover whether the wood dont warp, or any other mischief don't ensue,' Clementi advised his London office. In spite of these hurdles, the orders came rolling in, from bankers, generals and the imperial family. Also nudging into the Russian market, observed the avaricious Clementi, was the French piano maker Sébastien Erard, and the English maker John Broadwood. To counter the foreign invasion, a home-grown piano-making industry began to take off in Moscow and St Petersburg, with state-sponsored tax-breaks luring artisans from Western Europe (especially the German-speaking lands) to set up shop inside Russia's borders. These émigrés could be sure of lucrative sales, as well as subsidies to help transport pianos into Siberia.

Clementi had a head start on the competition. Through his pupil and sales representative in Russia, the Irish composer and performer John Field, Clementi was able to show off his pianos' capabilities to Russian customers. Worked to the bone, Field – whom Clementi called 'a lazy dog' – functioned like Clementi's musical puppet. In March 1804, Field became the first virtuoso to truly reveal the emotional depth of the piano to the Russians when he made his public debut in St Petersburg. His performance brought the audience to their feet. Newspapers and journals poured praise upon the Irishman. 'Not to have heard Field,' wrote an actor friend of the musician, 'was regarded as a sin against art and good taste.' As for St Petersburg, the people's obsession for the instrument caused one musical commentator to dub the city 'pianopolis'.

Field's teaching – his students included Aleksandr Aliabiev, who wrote 'The Nightingale' in Tobolsk jail, as well as Mikhail Glinka, who described the pianist's fingers falling on the keys like 'drops of rain that spread themselves like iridescent pearls' – made Field so much money, he once used a hundred-rouble note to light his cigar. On another occasion, Field's dogs chewed his concert earnings. It was a symbol of the sometimes luxurious, often turbulent life Field was to pursue in Russia for the next thirty years, his eccentric genius revealed in the way he wore his stockings inside out, his white tie skewed, and his waistcoat buttoned all wrong. Intemperate and adored, Field was in such a strong position by 1815 that he could reject an invitation to become Russia's court pianist. By 1823, that job was taken by another brilliant virtuoso who had taken St Petersburg by storm: Polish-born Maria Szymanowska.

When Russia opened its doors to Europe's growing troupe of performers, they functioned as dazzling endorsements of an instrument that had by now gripped Russia's heart. In 1838, the German pianist Adolf Henselt – the man with 'the velvet paws', as Liszt described his touch – moved to St Petersburg. In 1839, the Swiss virtuoso Sigismond Thalberg thundered into Russia, along with Marie Pleyel – the pretty French prodigy known as 'the female Liszt'. Passing through St Petersburg at the same time, Pleyel battled (and defeated) Thalberg in a pianistic duel. '[E]verything is full of fire, of energy; the piano speaks under her brilliant fingers. It has a soul,' wrote a reviewer for *Journal de St-Pétersbourg*. When Clara Schumann played for the Tsar in the Winter Palace in 1844, she described the scene as a fairy tale in *One Thousand and One Nights*. The truth was probably more mundane. 'The Russian rouble had a very good clink to German ears,' wrote Stasov, Russia's foremost music critic at the time.

I found a book by an American music historian,* which dug deep into the archives of Russian piano-making. Her description of the industry's proliferation and the distribution of the instruments further east was one of the reasons I took confidence early on that my 'fieldwork' looking for pianos in Siberia might glean results. By 1810, six Western entrepreneurs had set up piano workshops in Russia, including a St Petersburg factory founded by the Bavarian-born maker Jacob Becker. This single workshop built more than eleven thousand pianos before the century was out. Orders for instruments came thick and fast, including from Siberia, where pianos had already penetrated in the first half of the century. East of the Urals, music teachers were paid two to three times the amount they earned in Western Russia. In these new towns of the expanding Empire, the piano played an even more important social role than it did in a Moscow drawing room. A piano was a 'highly respectableising piece of furniture', observed a British musicologist of the nineteenth century, to affirm one's European education.

In the 1870s, the Imperial Russian Musical Society opened branches in the Western Siberian cities of Omsk, Tomsk and

---

* A book I kept close at hand for three years: Anne Swartz, *Piano Makers in Russia in the Nineteenth Century* (Bethlehem: Lehigh University Press, 2014).

Tobolsk, with the intention of educating both audiences and musicians. Bookstores selling popular sheet music began to pop up. Piano shops also opened, to ease the distribution of instruments further east. As the century progressed, only a few foreign-made Broadwoods and the odd German Blüthner made it through Russia's protective trade barriers. This gave the likes of Becker with his home-grown pianos a clear run to dominate the ever-growing domestic market.

And then the wheel of fate turned. After the 1917 Russian Revolution, the Becker factory became state property, and was renamed Red October. For a while, the USSR's system of musical education, which spread deep into the provinces, kept up demand for inexpensive Soviet-made instruments. Tens of thousands of uprights were distributed into small towns, with piano factories even opening in Siberia, in Tyumen and Vladivostok. But after perestroika, the old art of piano-making fell away. By the turn of the millennium, the industry had almost died completely. The Red October factory closed in 2004. A piano maker in Kazan turned to coffin-making before going bust. In the same month I saw the Amur tiger, it was reported that the last of Russia's piano factories had closed.

So great was the tragedy, there were now men of influence trying to reverse the trend. When I first latched on to this story, the Irkutsk-born classical pianist Denis Matsuev – among the great virtuosos of the twenty-first century – was campaigning to bring back the lost art of Russian piano-making. When we later met in Moscow, he talked about the high level of musical education among Russians, and how he still owned his family's first Soviet piano: a Tyumen upright, made in one of the main towns along the Trans-Siberian Railway. The network of music schools had birthed extraordinary careers throughout the history of the Soviet Union, in addition to engendering a unique culture of appreciation. The Russian audience is completely different from the Carnegie Hall audience in New York, Matsuev explained. But Siberians trump them both: 'They understand everything. They are my number one audience,' he said, describing the perfectly attentive 'suspicious silences' he experienced east of the Urals. I would understand soon enough, he said, when I had spent more time in Siberia.

But would I? Part of me was anxious that I can only respond to music in the way I did to the singing priests – the feeling of not knowing what is happening, or why it even matters, except that it does in the moment it is experienced. Unlike so many Russians who benefitted from the Soviet education system, I have no formal musical knowledge. By putting instinct over intellect, and trust before prejudice, there was of course a risk some scoundrel would undo me, and that I would end up with an expensive box of strings no better than the thudding upright Giercke had first bought. But on the other hand, Tobolsk's singing priests had given me confidence. They had persuaded me to pause for a moment, to believe in people who make all the time in the world to help a stranger who turns up unannounced. They had also held a mirror to my own shortcomings. Time has a life of its own in Siberia. It has a depth and dimension which makes you feel that days shouldn't be hurried – the opposite of how our time is construed in the West. So when the priest I had befriended suggested I should stay a while longer before I caught the last train out, I wanted to more than anything. But such is the trouble with Siberia. The map is always goading you with how much more territory there is still left to cover.

4

The Paris of Siberia:
Irkutsk

IN THE RUSSIAN STATE NAVAL ARCHIVES in St Petersburg, there is a revealing set of customs papers documenting the travails of a little clavichord – the earliest known record of such an instrument making it across Siberia. It belonged to a socially ambitious naval wife called Anna Bering who, in the 1730s, took this precious instrument from St Petersburg to the Sea of Okhotsk, and then travelled another six thousand miles home again on a magnificent transcontinental journey of exploration using only sleighs, boats and horses. Anna was married to Vitus

Bering, a Danish-born sea captain in the service of Peter the Great. Known as the 'Russian Columbus', Bering's job was to establish a postal route across Siberia, build ships on Russia's Pacific coast, and then penetrate the American Northwest. Anna, along with her clavichord, accompanied him.

If the scale of Siberia is dumbfounding, it is even more so when the map is traced with instruments like Anna's, which wove their way across the Empire before reasonable means of travel existed. They journeyed along Siberia's expanding trade routes, usually setting off in the dead of winter when the ground was good for sledges, rather than in summer, when Siberia turned into a mire of mud covered with mosquitoes. Siberia's rivers were another hindrance for travellers: instead of winding across the Empire from west to east, or vice versa, all the big waterways flowed south to north before emptying into a frozen Arctic Ocean.

Overland travel became easier when the Great Siberian Trakt opened during the reign of Catherine the Great. This was the main post road that ran from the brink of Siberia in the Ural Mountains to the city of Irkutsk, located close to Lake Baikal. The journey was infamous – a bumpy highway covered with slack beams of wood. The discomfort of traversing the road's length by sledge recalled the sensation of a finger being dragged across all the keys of a piano, even the black notes, remarked a nineteenth-century Russian prince, who served as an officer in Siberia. 'It is heavy going, very heavy,' observed Anton Chekhov in 1890, 'but it grows still heavier when you consider that this hideous, pock-marked strip of land, this foul smallpox of a road, is almost the sole artery linking Europe and Siberia! And we are told that along an artery like this civilisation is flowing into Siberia!'

Various methods available for travelling on ice in Siberia, according to the Jesuit explorer Father Philippe Avril in his 1692 work, Voyage en divers états d'Europe et d'Asie.

Chekhov had considered himself well prepared for his journey from Moscow through Siberia to reach the Tsarist penal colony of Sakhalin Island in the Russian Pacific, where he wrote an important piece of journalism about the brutality of the exile system. His mistake was the choice of season. Chekhov undertook his Siberian travels in spring – during *rasputitsa*, an evocative Russian word, as sticky as clods of earth, used to describe the muddy conditions that come with the thaw. He used a *tarantass*, a horse-drawn carriage with a half-hood, no springs, and wheels that could be interchanged for runners for the ice. Chekhov packed big boots, a sheepskin jacket, and an army officer's waterproof leather coat, as well as a large knife – for hunting tigers, he joked. 'I'm armed from head to foot,' he wrote to his publisher. He passed chain gangs of convicts. The company he kept was poor. The coachmen were wolves. The women, who couldn't sing, were colourless, cold and 'coarse to the touch'. Inevitably, he got stuck in the seasonal mud, his *tarantass* caught like a fly in gooey jam.

Travellers put up with the unpleasantness because until the Trans-Siberian Railway arrived at the end of the nineteenth century, the Great Siberian Trakt was the only significant road nourishing Siberia with new blood from

The tarantass – *depicted here crossing a tributary of Lake Baikal – was described by an English traveller in Russia in 1804 as a 'wooden Machine precisely like a Cradle where People place their Beds and Sleep thro' the entire of a Winter Journey'.* The Russian Journals of Martha and Catherine Wilmot *(London: Macmillan and Co., 1935).*

European Russia – or at least what had survived the journey over Western Siberia's malarial Baraba Steppe. As for the lures of Irkutsk, they might not have been quite on a par with St Petersburg – everything in Siberia ran a hundred years behind the rest of Russia, noted an early visitor – but its relative cosmopolitanism provided some relief for travellers. When Chekhov visited, he remarked that Siberia was a place you rarely heard an accordion, blaming the lack of art and music on a pitiless struggle with nature, as if survival and culture were mutually exclusive. But Irkutsk, known as the Paris of Siberia, was an exception. Chekhov thought it 'a splendid town' lively with music and theatre, as well as 'hellishly expensive', with a very good patisserie.

Irkutsk was sophisticated for the provinces, an upwardly mobile town where it was important to the educated classes to grasp any threads of connection with European culture, which Catherine's reign had encouraged. In 1782, the Imperial Academy of Sciences in St Petersburg despatched thirteen hundred books to Irkutsk. A public library went up, designed according to the fashionable European Russian style prevalent in the capital. An orchestra was founded, and a school teaching no less than five foreign languages. By the time of Catherine's death in 1796, Irkutsk had turned into a critical junction of the two main trans-Siberian routes.

The southern route out of Irkutsk wound east over Lake Baikal, the water traversed either by sledge in winter or by ferry in summer. The road then spurred down towards the dusty Russia–China border town of Kiakhta, a famous staging post on the Eurasian tea route. The north-easterly passage from Irkutsk to Siberia's Pacific rim was more forbidding: a thirty-day winter journey by dog-sled, reindeer-sled and horse-drawn cart east along the Yakutsk–Okhotsk Trakt to reach the shipbuilding yard of Okhotsk. One fifth of all the silk reaching Western Europe passed through Irkutsk, along with rhubarb – a precious commodity thought to be a miracle cure for a myriad of maladies – and a large share of China's tea. For anyone of influence travelling across the Russian Empire, Irkutsk was an economic and geopolitical crucible in the heart of Eurasia – a significance symbolized by the elegant belfry at the top of the Church of the Raising of the Cross still dominating a small hill at the city centre where Arthur Psariov, a veteran of the Soviet–Afghan War,* has been ringing the church bells for the last three decades.

We had met the first winter of my search when Arthur led me through the nave, passing a tall priest with the poise of a chess piece, his neck held stiff in a rigid golden cassock. Incense drifted across the altar from a swinging ball and chain, the ball's to-and-fro setting the measured pace of the priest's holy incantations. Inside the bell tower, Arthur knew where the stairs' rungs were weak, the wood spongy, the old nails unreliable with rust. When he skipped a step, I did the same, placing my feet into the crinkled prints he left in the thin membrane of frost that coated the tower's throat, each staging post in the plexus of narrow steps more treacherous than the next.

At the top of the bell tower, its sides open to the weather, the snow absorbed the babble of the divine service going on downstairs: the priest chanting, *babushki* arriving with their trolley bags of shopping, the clunk and burst of heavy doors. The octagonal platform was topped with a stone cupola, its

---

* Fought from 1979 to 1989 in support of the Afghan communist government.

underbelly webbed with struts, many of them in poor repair. Circling the belfry was a balcony, its rim beaded in ice. Arthur warned me not to stand too close to the edge. Three of the wooden balusters were missing. Others were barely holding their place, hanging like loose teeth.

Beneath me lay the city's wide boulevards. On a shallow incline stood historic wooden houses, and a few other bell towers puncturing the sky, their cupolas skinned in green, gold and peacock blue. With snow unable to stick to their pitch, the domes caught the sun, their satisfying shapes exactly as the author Jules Verne described them, like pot-bellied Chinese jars.

I looked for the train track to orientate me, and the river which runs through Irkutsk, winter's grip holding it in frigid stasis. In the stillness, two figures in black moved through the whiteness below. One man shovelled snow from the cemetery path. Another swept up behind him, clearing the graves. I looked at them and wondered how they came to be there. Was the one with the dragging leg descended from a murderer, a tea trader, a political exile or a free settler? Or were they Old Siberians, born of the earliest Russian peasants, who intermarried with the indigenes? The pull of private histories is always present in Siberia. Every face informs the enigmatic texture of a place where the legacy of exile lingers, like the smell of incense, or the feeble gleam of traffic lights, with the complexity of Russia's identity, and the mix of Europe and Asia, evident not just in the jumbled architecture of the Siberian baroque church I stood on top of in a snow-breeze in winter, but in the routes reaching out from every side.

Arthur guided me by the elbow to the edge of the belfry. He wanted to show me the nineteenth-century bell, which had been made in Berlin. The other bells came from the foundry towns ribboning the River Volga – a thousand-year-old tradition of Russian bell-making which had been significantly disrupted by the twentieth century's atheist Soviet regime. In Irkutsk, the Soviets had turned the oldest church, into a cobbler's shop, and another into a film studio. Bogoyavlensky Cathedral was used as a bakery, and the bell tower to store salt. These were fates to be preferred over that suffered by Moscow's Cathedral of Christ the Saviour. Though now rebuilt, it was torn down under Stalin's orders and turned into Russia's largest open-air swimming pool.

Arthur started to play – softly at first, the resonance making the snow tremble on the belfry's flimsy balustrade as the bell's tongue licked its copper skirt. Then the patterns started to build until all eight bells were singing. Arthur pushed and pulled the ropes with his hands, while his feet worked pedals to strike the largest bells, the pace an exhilarating distillation of music's power, of chords at once melodically familiar and outlandishly foreign.

For five or six minutes Arthur held the city in thrall, sweat riding down the sides of his temples, his body moving with the ease of a dancer, not a giant of a man in clumsy shoes. The sequences quickened until the deepest bell tolled three bass notes. With the sound eddying over Irkutsk, I imagined the townspeople looking up. Would they ever know the identity of this person who found such intense pleasure in such an improbable place? When the last note began to fade, Arthur turned around to face me, wiping his brow.

'I can play most things, except rock 'n' roll,' he said, a broad smile reaching across his face.

*

In 1591, a bell was among the first exiles to Siberia – the weight of a horse, cut down from the belfry in Uglich, a town on a bend in the River Volga in European Russia. The bell had committed the crime of being tolled as a rallying call to urge the citizens to join a small, bold and foolhardy uprising against the state. In response, and to establish his legitimacy, the Tsar Regent executed two hundred of the Uglich townspeople. In a final sadistic twist, those exiled to Siberia were forced to carry the Uglich bell, itself subject to a public lashing, some thirteen hundred miles across the Ural Mountains to Tobolsk. Like the men who bore the instrument on its journey, who had their tongues cut out, the bell was also rendered mute by having its clapper removed. It was a terrifying symbolic act: by silencing music in the belfry, the regime was exerting the alarming reach of its power over every facet of Russian life.

Nor did the horror abate after the Revolution, when the Tsarist exile system was effectively relaunched as the Soviet Gulag. Victims travelled in cattle wagons on the railways to Siberia's mines and ports. Kolyma-bound prisoners would then sail by Stalin's convict ships into some of the darkest corners of Soviet Russia, populating the regime's network of forced-labour camps with political opponents and *urkas* (prison slang for legitimate thieves, murderers and criminals).

For some, the experience was made bearable with the smallest of survival strategies. Fyodor Dostoevsky – who endured four years as a convict in Siberia, living with dripping ceilings, rotten floors, filth an inch thick, and convicts packed like herrings in a barrel – was given a copy of the New Testament by an exile's wife, and taught a fellow prisoner to read. The tiger conservationist Aleksandr Batalov spoke about a friend who spent decades in a Stalinist labour camp; he said his friend's study of the migrating birds around the camp was the thing that stopped him going crazy. Varlam Shalamov, a poet who spent a total of seventeen years in the Soviet Gulag, found no such comfort. He wrote about the terror of indifference, how the cold that froze a man's spit could also freeze the soul.

I came to Irkutsk in pursuit of a piano which represented the opposite of Shalamov's tears: the instrument belonging to Maria Volkonsky, the wife of one of the nineteenth century's most high-profile political exiles. It functioned like a fulcrum in Siberia's piano history, marking the moment when classical music in this penal wasteland was invested with a keen sense of European identity and pride, the piano's Siberian story beginning with a poorly conceived rebellion in St Petersburg on 14 December 1825. It was the day of the

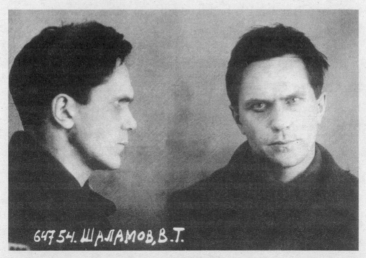

An official NKVD (secret police) photograph of Varlam Shalamov following his January 1937 arrest for 'counter-revolutionary' activities.

winter solstice – an event traditionally bound to all sorts of ideas about birth, death and change.

Before dawn was up, a group of men gathered in the city's Senate Square with the intention of deposing the Tsarist regime. The Decembrists, as the rebels came to be known, comprised noblemen, gentlemen and soldiers – including Maria Volkonsky's husband, Sergei. Having fought alongside the peasantry during the Napoleonic Wars, Russia's elite had come to admire the stoicism of their fellow countrymen. Liberal idealists all, the Decembrists not only wanted emancipation for Russia's beleaguered serfs; they also sought to replace the country's political structure with a constitutional monarchy, or even a republican form of government – a response to the despotism of the Romanovs, which had defined the dynasty's long lineage since 1613.

Dissent had stepped up after Catherine the Great's death. Her son, Tsar Paul I, had enjoyed a brief, tyrannical tenure before assassins strangled him with a sash in 1801. Paul's murder was probably a good thing for music. Suspicious of Western thought to the point of paranoia, Paul formalized a ruthless backlash to Catherine's flirtations with the Enlightenment. He banned any kind of foreign-printed book or pamphlet from entering Russia, including sheet music.

The next in line, Tsar Alexander I, had a reformer's spirit. He relaxed state censorship but failed to progress emancipation in any meaningful way. After the trauma of Napoleon's invasion of Russia in 1812, when Moscow was all but burnt to the ground, Alexander governed with almost schizophrenic swings. He tried to improve the exile system, introducing new rights for convicts; he also fell under the influence of a demonic Russian general, Aleksei Arakcheyev, who was obsessed with turning the Empire into a military state. Alexander took increasingly draconian measures against liberal foreign influence. In 1823, he banned Russian students from entering certain German universities, lest they be exposed to seditious ideas.

When Alexander died childless in 1825, leaving the country in a state of bankruptcy, Alexander's brothers hesitated to fill the throne. The Russian crown, gossiped contemporary chroniclers, was being passed around the family like a cup of tea nobody wanted to drink. Constantine, the elder of Alexander's siblings, had already run off to Poland, where he had fallen in love with a Catholic pianist (after Constantine first heard the ten-year-old prodigy play, his wife often invited Chopin to their Polish residence, convinced his music calmed Constantine's difficult nerves). Alexander's youngest brother, Nicholas, was also slow to act and take up the vacant throne; he needed to be cautious lest any advances he made be considered a coup. For the Decembrist revolutionaries, this messy two-week interregnum therefore presented the perfect opportunity to advance their plans for revolt.

But while the Decembrists' motives were impassioned, their regiments were not. When the men began to assemble in Senate Square, there was a smaller force of rebel soldiers than the Decembrists had hoped. In addition, one of the main leaders deserted. Despite these setbacks, the Decembrists refused to disperse, so Nicholas ordered a cavalry squad to break up the rabble. Only with the whine of cannon fire did the men eventually retreat to a frozen River Neva, where Nicholas's soldiers blitzed the ice with artillery. By nightfall, the revolt was quashed. The perpetrators were rounded up. On the same day as the Decembrist Revolt, also referred to as the First Russian Revolution, Nicholas I declared himself Tsar.

Close to six hundred suspects were put on trial. Five men were hanged, including the poet and publisher Kondraty Ryleev, who was executed holding a book by Byron in his hand. When the rope snapped on the first attempt, one of the prisoners reportedly quipped: 'What a wretched country! They don't even know how to hang properly.' Another of the condemned men remarked on the privilege of dying not once but twice for his country. Whether any of these remarks are true is beside the point: the myth of the Decembrists' martyrdom took root when Tsar Nicholas I ordered the execution to continue, and the gallows were strung with new rope.

With the hangings complete, a core of more than a hundred men were identified as coup leaders and sent to Siberia for hard labour, some for life.* They were stripped of their wealth and privileges. As they were members of some of the grandest, most decorated families in Russia, this was the high-society scandal of the time. It was talked about all over Europe, with the vengeance in Nicholas's response also changing Russians' perception of banishment forever. Prior to 1825, very little compassion had existed for the men, women and children sent to Siberia. After 1825, political exiles were regarded with far greater sympathy. As for the eleven women who elected to follow their Decembrist husbands and lovers into exile, they were revered as living saints. Under the rules of banishment, the women had to leave their children behind in European Russia. Any offspring conceived in exile would be forbidden from inheriting their family's titles or estates.

---

* Among the exceptions was Nikolai Turgenev (uncle to the novelist Ivan Turgenev), who was out of the country on the day of revolt, and never returned to face the Tsar's ire.

The five Decembrists hanging from the gallows, sketched in Pushkin's notepad. Pushkin was closely linked to the revolt, having gone to school with some leading Decembrists. His 1817 poem 'Ode to Liberty' was also cited by some conspirators as an influence. As a result, Pushkin was brought before the Tsar and restrictions placed on his freedom of movement and expression.

One of the most high-profile Decembrists banished for life was Prince Sergei Volkonsky – a childhood playmate of the Tsar's, whose mother was a principal lady-in-waiting to the Dowager Empress. Sergei's wife, Maria, came from an equally elite family. Her father, General Raevsky, was one of the heroes of Napoleon's defeat in 1812. With her knowledge of literature, music and foreign languages, Maria was a descendant of Catherine's 'Enlightened' Russia. She was also a well-known beauty, her abundant black curls and olive skin earning her the nickname *la fille du Ganges*.*

Maria decided to abandon her enchanted circle – as well as her infant son, who would die aged two – and follow her husband into exile. It became one of the most talked about tragedies of a feverishly romantic century. 'All her life was this one unconscious weaving of invisible roses in the lives of those with whom she came in contact' is how Tolstoy described the heroine, modelled on Maria, in his unfinished mid-nineteenth-century novel *The Decembrists*. Maria's actions inspired paintings, music and Pushkin's poetry, as well as a love of the piano on the other side of the Urals, when she took a clavichord some four thousand miles from Moscow to join her husband deep in the Siberian taiga.

The instrument, kept close at hand throughout Maria's exile, was a gift from her sister-in-law Zinaida Volkonsky – a keen patron of the virtuosos, who hosted one of the most well-regarded cultural salons of the period. When Zinaida threw a leaving party in Moscow on the eve of Maria's Siberian journey, Maria sat close to Zinaida's piano, and Pushkin

* The phrase was Pushkin's. He reportedly fell in love with Maria when she was barely out of her childhood during a holiday he took with her family in Crimea.

close to Maria. She wanted her friends to sing so that she wouldn't forget their voices in exile. Shortly afterwards, she set off for Siberia with the clavichord Zinaida had strapped to her sledge. It was a remarkable journey, the instrument travelling all the way from Moscow to the eastern side of Lake Baikal. What the local Buryats would have made of this Russian princess as they watched her passage across the lake is hard to picture. The Buryats thought the Milky Way was 'a stitched seam', and the stars the holes in the sky. When meteors flashed, Siberia's indigenous tribes described it as the gods peeling back 'the sky-cover to see what is happening on Earth'. The sight of Maria bundled up in her ermine furs must have appeared out of this world to them, like a visitation from another planet.

Maria spent her first few months in exile in the town of Nerchinsk, near the Mongolian border, living in a small Cossack hut. She was allowed to visit Sergei's cell twice a week. At first the men were forbidden to receive packages from relatives in European Russia, so the women began to sneak money into Siberia through secret channels in order to buy the prisoners extra privileges. When a French-born couturier arrived in Nerchinsk in pursuit of her Decembrist lover, she turned up with hundreds of roubles stitched into her clothes. She also smuggled in Italian sheet music for Maria. The women were pushy, persistent and resourceful. As for the Decembrists' prison commander, he soon got the measure of their capabilities, remarking 'he would rather deal with a hundred political exiles than a dozen of their wives'.

The men were moved a year later to a prison at Chita, also east of Lake Baikal. Later, the Decembrists were transferred to a new jail at Petrovsky Zavod, in a nearby valley, where the wives were allowed to share their husband's room. Maria's clavichord moved into the windowless prison, which was far gloomier than the one at Chita. As the years went by, children were conceived. Maria learned to speak Russian, as opposed to the French of her aristocratic childhood. She gave birth to a little girl, who died after only two days. Her next two children, a son and a daughter, survived.*

While family provided comfort to a few of the Decembrists, it was through culture – for many, music in particular – that they were able to maintain some kind of connection to the lives they had left behind, helped along by relatives sending books, paints and large sums of money from home. 'What remarkable fighters they were, what personalities, what *people*!' wrote the nineteenth-century Russian journalist Alexander Herzen of the gentlemen revolutionaries. The Decembrists represented everything brave and humane that was missing from Tsar Nicholas I's lightless reign. 'I have been told, – I don't know whether it is true, – that wherever they worked in the mines in Siberia, or whatever it is called, the convicts who were with them, improved in their presence,' wrote Tolstoy.

The Decembrists teamed up to create a small academy in exile. They set up carpentry, blacksmith and bookbinding workshops, and ran lectures on subjects from seamanship to anatomy, physics to fiscal theory. They established a library, which they filled with thousands of books sent by their relatives (according to one account, a collection that numbered nearly half a million). Another building was turned into a

---

* The Volkonsky love story wasn't perfect. Various historians suggest Maria's two children were the progeny of her long affair with Sergei's friend and fellow Decembrist the charismatic Alessandro Poggio, who ran the prisoners' vegetable garden with Maria's husband.

An 1832 drawing by fellow Decembrist Nikolai Bestuzhev of the Volkonskys in their cell at Petrovsky Zavod.

music room for piano, flute and strings. Locals came to study, and to attend the Decembrists' concerts and musical soirées. The prisoners dreamed up imaginary lands, inventing sea stories about the distant oceans, and found comfort in the smallest delights of nature. The Borisov brothers, for instance, went on to build a huge Siberian insect collection. Meanwhile, the school the Decembrists created during their prison years benefitted hundreds of Siberian peasant children.

When Sergei Volkonsky's decade-long hard-labour sentence was up, the Volkonskys had greater freedom to influence Siberian culture, specifically in and around Irkutsk, where they were required to settle in exile. The Volkonskys were allocated a plot in swampy taiga. This was when Maria's two

The Volkonskys' manor house in Irkutsk.

surviving children learned the native Siberian dialect. Then, in 1844, the Volkonskys bought a house in town.

Year by year, Maria gained confidence under a sympathetic new governor, who became a visitor to her musical salons. She expanded Irkutsk's hospital for orphans, fought for musical education to be introduced in schools, and raised money to build the town's first purpose-built concert hall – civic duties that earned her the sobriquet 'the Princess of Siberia'. When a classical pianist from Tobolsk came to play in Irkutsk, Maria broke protocol for an exile's wife: she went to the concert, and was given a standing ovation. Sergei led a humbler life; he grew a long beard and frequented the market with a goose under his arm. Nicknamed 'the peasant prince', he was simple and unostentatious, deeply respected by Siberians who sought his help. He made numerous friends among the locals, with whom he shared his knowledge of agriculture and strand of liberal political philosophy. Meanwhile, elsewhere in Europe, Sergei's lifelong quest for fairer government looked like it might be coming of age. During the 1848 Spring of Nations, absolutist regimes were toppling and a reformist press was on the rise. Prussian liberals got their constitution, and elective assemblies. In Hungary, serfdom was finally outlawed.

When I visited the Volkonskys' two-storey house in Irkutsk, now a museum, frost laced the panes and dulled the glow of lamps inside. Upstairs there was a pyramid piano – an instrument of peculiar shape and height, like a concert piano turned up against the wall. The museum staff said it probably belonged to the family's Florentine music teacher, who had lived in one of the outbuildings. Downstairs, there was a beautiful Russian-made Lichtenthal, which Maria's brother delivered from St Petersburg. The Lichtenthal, made by a piano maker who had moved to Russia following the Belgian revolution of 1830, was the grandest instrument Maria owned. It was also the most potent surviving symbol of her affection for music, given that Maria's original clavichord, which had travelled on her sledge from Moscow to Siberia, had disappeared – when or where, no one was quite sure.

As for the Lichtenthal, the instrument behaved awkwardly when a museum worker tried to make the prop stick hold up the lid. The keys were sticky, like an old typewriter gluey with ink. He struck the keys until the softened notes – muted by a layer of dust, perhaps, or felt that had swollen in the damp – started to appear. At first the sound was reed-thin, no louder than the flick of a fingernail on a bell. Inside the piano, the amber wood still gleamed, the strings' fragile tensions held in place by tiny twists around the heads of golden, round-headed tuning pins. The Lichtenthal, said the museum worker, was full of moods that made it challenging to tune. In Siberia, violent swings in humidity and heat can shrink the wood. The soundboard, a large, thin piece of wood which transforms vibrations into musical tones, can easily crack. Different makers devised different solutions to this problem. Mozart's favourite maker would deliberately split a piano's soundboard by exposing it to rain and sun, and would then wedge and glue it back together so that it might never break again.

I traced the Lichtenthal's restorer who had picked the yellowed ivory tops off the keys to clean them, re-spun the bass strings, and repaired the veneer.* I also wanted to talk to the piano's current keepers, to see whether they might know of other noble instruments of its type. One thing led to another and via various other city institutions, I was connected with an Irkutsk piano tuner who seemed to hold the keys to my quest. Cutting an elegant figure with a tuning hammer in his leather satchel, he said he had a private collection of forty historic instruments. His most prized piano was a rare 1813 grand which he had bought for a few kopeks from an army general in the early nineties. It was an Andreas Marschall, serial number 5, traced back to a very old Danish maker. He said it was in such bad condition that it was just a box and strings, but one day he wanted to do it up.

I made an appointment to visit the tuner's Siberian workshop a few months later, but when I arrived back in Irkutsk, he didn't show up as we had agreed. When I found the numbers of other tuners working in Irkutsk, they seemed

* Given its grand provenance, the Lichtenthal was sent from Irkutsk to St Petersburg for a major restoration in the nineties. The then museum director organized delivery of the instrument by military plane to a restorer called Yuri Borisov – a man I went to meet, dubbed 'The Last of the Mohicans', trained by one of the original pre-Revolution masters from the Becker factory.

reluctant to talk. Feeling the cold of being an outsider in Siberia, I eventually persuaded one of them to act as my paid guide. We drove out to a small apartment, where he was restoring a Bechstein grand. He said it originally belonged to a local cultural activist who had brought the piano to Irkutsk from Moscow in the thirties. The piano was broken up into all its parts with the soundboard laid out like an old drunk waiting to die. It was positioned in front of an electric fire to help dry it out, the keys and strings a jumble on the floor. One day he would finish the restoration, he said; there was a market for these grand pianos in Russia. He showed me another private instrument in his home: an upright Smidt & Wegener piano which he had reason to believe belonged to, or was played by, the wife of Mikhail Frunze, a Red Army commander in the Russian Civil War. The tuner opened the piano up to show me where he had found three gold coins, dated 1898, minted with the face of Tsar Nicholas II. The tuner had sold the coins during perestroika to help make ends meet.

I would find many more secrets like this, said a local musicologist: Siberia's pianos were full of hidden treasures, like the grand piano her teacher used to own. Inside its workings, the woman had concealed all her jewellery. The piano was her teacher's family safe. But she warned me I would also need to keep my wits about me, because there were all sorts of complications with proving provenance in Russia. I knew there would also be stories people *wouldn't* want told. There was a risk that my research might reveal the original, rightful owner of an instrument, which could open up a cat's cradle of restitution claims. There would be others who wouldn't want to talk of the past – any part of it. 'Some things I cannot speak of,' said a piano expert I met in Western Siberia: 'We envy countries which provide easy access to what happened to their families, but here it is different. Access to archives isn't easy. It's not open source. It's expensive. My generation belongs to the war children. We lost one or two of our parents, and ever since have been seeking the truth.' We all do what we can to keep on going, warned another tuner; stories shift to fit our needs. He said there are pianos with the serial number painted on to the soundboard, and then those with a number moulded into the cast-iron frame. You can repaint a soundboard, he said, but you can't change a number cast in metal.

This was always going to be my biggest challenge – looking for reliable truth. I wasn't after a fancy piece of furniture to show off in the equivalent of a Mongolian parlour. I couldn't have cared less, in fact, how a piano looked. I wasn't here to fiddle with serial numbers, or pursue old pianos painted up in glossy colours. Such an instrument would be ill matched to a musician like Odgerel, who needed pure sound reinforced by a retrievable inner story. Odgerel's musical perception was so authentic, she could render J. S. Bach's 'Chaconne'* with an exceptional depth of feeling. She could communicate the composer's unquestioning faith in the divine. More than anything, Odgerel understood how struggle can invest the act of musical creation with the conviction of felt experience.

'Bach tells us about tragedy and pain in a musical language. Whenever I read about the triumph of the Resurrection I cannot feel very much, but when I play "Chaconne",' Odgerel told me, 'the story comes alive. Bach taught me how to breathe.'

---

* J. S. Bach's 'Chaconne' was the final movement of his Partita No. 2 in D Minor, and was written for violin. Italian composer Ferruccio Busoni transcribed Bach's music for the piano between 1891 and 1892.

Was it the same for Maria Volkonsky? What did a piano mean to her in exile? Did Siberia allow her to live more intensely than she could have ever done in high society back home? Was it empowering in nineteenth-century Russia to be disconnected from the period's suffocating rules and expectations around her gender and class? Because despite the privations of their exile, the Decembrists didn't view Siberia as a place only of *katorga*. 'The further we moved into Siberia, the more it improved in my sight,' observed the Decembrist Nikolai Basargin: 'To me, the common folk seemed freer, brighter, even better educated than our Russian peasantry – especially more so than our estate serfs. They better understood the dignity of man, and valued their rights more highly.' Siberia, you see, never had a history of serfdom. There were the exiles who came as prisoners of the state, but there were also many, many more migrants who ventured into Siberia for the taste of freedom – to live far from the reach of the Tsar and the moral reprimands of the Russian Orthodox Church.

5

Pianos in a Sandy Venice:
Kiakhta

I N 1856, WHEN MARIA VOLKONSKY made her last visit to Lake
Baikal, she described watching the forest animals coming
in to drink as if Siberia were a Garden of Eden rather than her
prison for the last thirty years. She was leaving Siberia. The
new Tsar, Alexander II, had granted amnesty to the twenty-
odd surviving Decembrist rebels. Some of the men had already
committed suicide before the amnesty came through. Others
had lost their wits. One or two were trying to make their living through teaching, farming watermelons, making opticals,

or even drawing butterflies for German museums. Among those who stayed on voluntarily after the amnesty was Mikhail Küchelbecker, who was shackled to Siberia by an unfulfilled love affair with a local girl. His headstone stands on the eastern shoreline of Lake Baikal.

I spent almost three weeks poking around the lake, making three different visits. But however hard I wished it, Baikal's seductive lures – the winter ice, the summer sward crackling with crickets, the red-barked cedar trees arcing out from cliffs – didn't deliver on the piano discoveries I needed. The settlements were too thin. There was more for me in Kiakhta, the old tea traders' town on the Mongolia–Russia border depicted by Karl Marx and Friedrich Engels as if it were one of the most important centres of nineteenth-century world trade. In Kiakhta, I had been told about a rare Bechstein grand piano.

My tipster was the Mongolian opera singer, Tsogt, who used to stand at the door of the tent in the Orkhon Valley trying to fit into the narrow opening to listen to Odgerel play. He was a Buddhist and a Buryat whose ancestors, like Odgerel's, had fled the Lake Baikal region in the thirties. His family ended up in Inner Mongolia, which is a part of China. He had trained in music in Beijing. He had also lived for a while in Ulan-Ude, the capital of Buryatia, one of the Russian Federation's autonomous republics, and a half-day's drive from Baikal's eastern shore. A bear of a man, Tsogt wore leather boots designed with upturned toes so as to tread softly on the snow, and a traditional Mongolian felted *del* robe, belted below the waist, which made his belly look like a beer casket. We had travelled together across western Mongolia in 2001. Over the years, I had grown fond of Tsogt. I liked watching his tough front fall away in the presence of Bach. So I hired him early on to help look for pianos.

For a while, I heard nothing. Then I received a short and intriguing email: 'I'm back from Siberia. I find only one grand piano. C. Bechstein – Serial number 7050. Year is 1874. From very little place. No other people has old piano.'

Given the Bechstein's date, which was before a railway looped south beneath the lake, the piano may have taken a number of different routes. It could have travelled the rutted road running along the craggy south coast. It could also have crossed the lake by boat in summer, or by sledge in winter, or travelled on the *Baikal*, a British-built icebreaker. The ship, made of parts transported to Russia in pieces, sometimes took up to a week to make the winter crossing – from port to port, less than fifty miles – carrying twenty-five Trans-Siberian Railway cars on her specially designed deck. The carriages would be uncoupled at the water's edge and shunted on to the ship's on-board rails. In the depths of winter in 1904, when the ice was too thick for even the ship to break, a seasonal track was laid over Lake Baikal's frozen surface instead. The first engine across plunged straight through the ice – a blank white canvas which these days is carved by the lonely movements of the few fishermen who still live along Baikal's shores, the lake's frozen surface scored with lines from snowmobile tracks and black dots where the fishermen have cut holes. The sweeps and curves look like the drawings of Wassily Kandinsky – an avant-garde, turn-of-the-century Russian artist obsessed by Russian ethnography, the 'double faith' combining paganism and Christianity, as well as the relationship between music and painting, between sound, points, lines and planes.

Kandinsky's great-grandmother claimed Buryat–Mongol

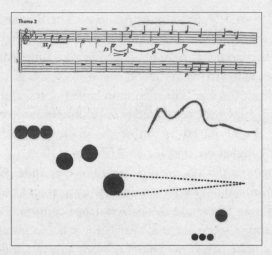

Wassily Kandinsky's theory of music's relationship to art, from his 1926 work, Point and Line to Plane.

blood. His father was a tea merchant from Kiakhta. One side of the Kandinsky family, who became fabulously rich over the course of the nineteenth century, were descended from church robbers and highwaymen, or so the story goes. Before Kandinsky's time, when his relations were living in a taiga village east of Lake Baikal, the family were visited by Decembrists, including Sergei Volkonsky, who were entertained by the music from several pianos that the Kandinskys owned.

If the Kandinsky history gave Kiakhta a sprinkling of glamour, the snobbery of nineteenth-century travellers gave the town a rather different reputation. 'There was not a lady without a large hat decorated with what looked like an entire flower-bed,' remarked Elisabeth von Wrangell, wife of the governor of Russian America, who ridiculed the local merchants' wives when she stopped by Kiakhta on her twelve-thousand-mile journey from St Petersburg to America. 'The Russians, after all that they have borrowed from their western neighbours, remain barbarians at bottom,' observed Alexander Michie, a Scotsman who tarried in Kiakhta on an 1863 passage through Siberia from Peking: 'Their living in large houses, and drinking expensive wines, serve merely to exhibit, in more striking colours, the native barbarism of the stock on which these twigs of a higher order of life have been engrafted.'

I encountered a scene of complete decrepitude. Wooden homes tumbled out over a sandier landscape than I had so far got used to in Siberia. In this barren steppe country, the snow didn't seem to settle like it did further north, but hung in the air like smoke. Kiakhta's churches were largely windowless, sometimes steeple-less, and its roads so pitted it was sometimes easier to walk the streets than find a car. The once-grand façades of wooden houses were smeared with graffiti, and one of the cemeteries smelled of urine. There was a menacing stasis to both Kiakhta, where the merchants had their homes and trading houses in the nineteenth century, and Troitskosavsk, the adjacent settlement, which was once populated by the shops, schools and administrators. It felt as though the town was only just surviving, its edge of existence marked by a thin line of trucks lingering for a couple of lazy hours as they waited to cross the border between Russia and Mongolia.

Yet once Kiakhta had been so lively. During its pre-Revolution heyday, the town's club put on balls and musical events. Concerts by European pianists visiting Kiakhta were advertised in Irkutsk, Tomsk and Chita. At one time in history, there were enough good pianos in town to justify a tuner travelling here all the way from Kiev.

A nineteenth-century account called the town Asia's

'Sandy Venice'. Tea caravans, loaded up on to camels, would arrive from Mongolia, looking like the merchants and their ships that once sailed into Italy's great maritime capital. Up to a hundred horses filled the yard of a Kiakhta merchant's home. Mansions shimmered with winter gardens. The merchants' wives ordered their dresses from the Paris couturier The House of Worth, and filled their cellars with rare wines. The merchants also had summer cottages, or dachas, with bathing pools and a boating lake. The children were given donkeys with miniature carriages, and piano lessons from Polish political exiles. At Christmas-time, tables were loaded with champagne. Dressed in masks and festive costumes, the first families of Kiakhta would parade through town with a small orchestra and a local composer. The party would continue through the night to other merchants' homes, where they danced quadrilles and waltzes.

The reason for this wealth was unique in Russia: for every consignment of tea that passed through this border, Kiakhta's merchants creamed off a tidy local tax, part of which was invested in local philanthropy. It worked brilliantly until the money started to show signs of drying up after 1869, when the access provided by the Suez Canal took business from Eurasia's camel trains. When the Trans-Siberian Railway was built many miles to the town's north, Kiakhta's relevance began to wane even further. By the first decade of the twentieth century, Siberia's richest marketplace no longer teemed with Chinese, or crates of tea stacked in pyramids taller than the merchants' homes. But Kiakhta was still very, very wealthy. Right up until the Revolution, it remained a place where pianos – like Kiakhta's Bechstein grand, which Tsogt had found on my behalf – tinkled with mazurkas and other Polish dances. The

Bechstein was thought to be connected to the Lushnikov merchant family, said the guide who showed me around the town's splendid museum the first time I came.

I went to find the Lushnikov residence where the piano would have stood, close to Kiakhta's Resurrection Cathedral, which once had columns made of crystal. On top of a small hill looking down on Mongolia, I found the house where the Lushnikovs hosted scientists and explorers, many of whom were stopping on their travels to Central Asia, whether looking for new species, or seeking out the holy secrets of Tibet. Kiakhta was also where Grigory Potanin buried his wife, the brilliant Russian explorer Aleksandra Potanina, who was among the first women to win a gold medal from the Imperial Russian Geographical Society. During her funeral, the

A late-nineteenth-century photograph of Aleksei Lushnikov, pictured with his wife, Klavdia, and their family at their country residence situated about twenty miles outside Kiakhta.

Lushnikov house was overflowing with mourners. Her husband was among the nineteenth century's most outspoken advocates for an independent Siberia and an end to the exile system. When the American journalist George Kennan stopped in Kiakhta in the 1880s on his epic journey across Siberia to report on the Tsarist exile system, he too visited the Lushnikovs' home. 'We were very often surprised in these far-away parts of the globe to find ourselves linked by so many persons and associations to the civilized world,' remarked Kennan.

The Lushnikovs were in fact a powerful example of the Decembrists' reach and influence, the family's lives testament to an extraordinary moment in Siberian culture. The matriarch, Klavdia Lushnikov – a Kandinsky cousin – was educated in Irkutsk at the Institute of Noblewomen. Standing at the centre of the Kiakhta intelligentsia, she was a gifted pianist, nicknamed 'Lushnikova the Liberal', who became well known for her musical salons. Twice a week, she would gather the women for

The American journalist George Kennan pictured next to his Siberian tarantass, c. *1885.*

lectures on literature, politics and economics. She had married the millionaire tea trader Aleksei Lushnikov – a sophisticated man born into a modest family in the nearby Selenga Valley. Aleksei had been educated from the age of eight by Mikhail and Nikolai Bestuzhev, two Decembrists who had made an impressive job of exile by farming and teaching in the region after their hard-labour sentences were up. As for Aleksei Lushnikov's children, one daughter studied sculpture with Rodin in Paris. Another daughter went on to sing at the Tbilisi Opera House.

Both Bestuzhevs were well qualified to act as teachers – Nikolai in particular, whose story is so full of charm and conviction. A musician, scientist and painter, Nikolai was responsible for most of the surviving portraits of his fellow Decembrists in Siberia. During exile, he relied on colour pigments sent by Maria Volkonsky's sister-in-law Zinaida, who also posted seeds for the Decembrists' vegetable garden. The gentle countenance in Nikolai's self-portrait is hard to square with the image of a violent revolutionary who briefed the Tsar's would-be assassin on the morning of the Decembrist Revolt. He made his journey to Siberia with a volume of the *Rambler* tucked into his luggage – an English periodical full of elevated prose and humanist ideas encouraging greater social mobility between classes.

While Nikolai tended to paint the Decembrists' lives in rosier hues than their grubby reality, he still communicated the sorrow of exile with a moving depth. He drew his compatriots reading, talking, painting, often in lonely thought. He depicted their prison as if it were an English landscape, and the Decembrists' children playing with kites. He also painted that famous image of Maria Volkonsky sitting with her narrow back to the artist in the Volkonskys' cell, her right hand on the piano. The picture is a reminder of how fragile Beethoven

Aleksei Lushnikov's daughters in the 1870s; the family pictured at a Russian-made Becker piano.

must have sounded in this part of the world, rendered into quivering melodies on Maria's clavichord – ghost sounds from the salons of Europe played on this weak and imperfect instrument, its parts fixed up by the convict with the so-called 'golden fingers'. Nikolai was also an able engineer. He made hats, jewellery from the Decembrists' old fetters (coveted by fashionable women in Kiakhta and Irkutsk as rings), cradles and coffins. He was an expert watchmaker. Many years after his release, Nikolai had finessed his chronometer designs developed in prison. He made a clock, which kept time at his house near Kiakhta: 'In spite of a frost of twenty-five degrees, it went perfectly,' said his fellow Decembrist Baron Rozen.

With the Bestuzhevs as his teachers, Aleksei Lushnikov therefore received one of the most unusual educations in nineteenth-century Siberia for a child of such modest roots. By the time he had entered the service of a Kiakhta merchant, Lushnikov could recite pages of Pushkin by heart. Once he had made his fortune, Lushnikov opened Kiakhta's first printing house, and founded its first newspaper, the *Kiakhta Page* – one of many that flourished in the late nineteenth century when Siberia was developing lively journalism, its own universities and home-grown intelligentsia. Lushnikov subscribed to all sorts of politically progressive magazines and newspapers, including *The Bell*, printed in London by the émigré Alexander Herzen, who became Russia's first independent political publisher. Although prohibited by the Tsarist government, *The Bell* was distributed to Siberia by the Kiakhta trading caravans, with Kiakhta's merchants providing a safe house and funds to others in Herzen's circle.

The democratic values which flowed out of Lushnikov's home – like many of the Kiakhta merchants, Lushnikov

contributed generously to the city's library, museum, orphanage and schools – were sustained by the lifelong friendship the
family kept up with both Bestuzhevs. Nikolai visited the Lushnikovs frequently to paint dozens of portraits of the Kiakhta
elite. Before he died, he entrusted many of his paintings to
Lushnikov, a collection lost in the post in the 1870s, according
to one account. There was also a trunk Lushnikov asked
nobody to open until twenty-five years after his death. He kept
the key on a chain with a crucifix around his neck. Both the
key and the trunk vanished, presumably in the chaos of the
Russian Civil War.

That was why the Bechstein felt so remarkable, even if it
was sad and weary, the piano's bald hammers and loose strings
barely able to produce a sound. Located in one of the museum's cold corners, its bones were chilled from a draught that
slunk in through the windows. I pressed for more information, with calls and a second visit to Kiakhta two years later.
Locals helping me around town also spoke of the Lushnikov
connection; that was how the story ran. One of the archivists,
a woman who was new to me when I returned to Kiakhta, said
she would make some further investigations. 'I suspect it is a
legend,' she said after a while. 'People say it is the Lushnikovs',
but these things are hard to prove.'

Before I left Kiakhta for the last time, I went back to the Lushnikov mansion. I walked around the back to try and peek
through the windows. A man answered the door. He let me
into the only room of the house still occupied.

On the ground floor, there was just enough room for a
cooker and a bed, which the man shared with his four-year-
old son. He couldn't remember how long he had lived there,

but it was from around the time that he got work helping Kiakhta's Father Oleg clean up the church in the nineties. Back then, there had been another family living on the second floor of the house, but otherwise there hadn't been anyone else he could recall for twenty-five years. The decaying wood was too dangerous; the roof had fallen in. As we talked, the dogs were circling again outside. In the stableyard, a man who had offered to help me fell to the ground in an epileptic fit.

On my last night in Kiakhta, I slipped into the back of the Trinity Cathedral – the town's largest abandoned church, opposite the old trading houses – through a gap in some metal railings. The nave, missing its dome, looked like a skull that had been trepanned for a post-mortem. The masonry was loose, the ground tangled with undergrowth and broken glass.

I didn't know what I had expected to find, especially in the dark, but as soon as I was beyond the cordon, it felt as if something bad had happened here, that I was walking unquiet earth. I had read about Kiakhta in the Russian Civil War, how the massacres were so brutal, the museum's records of events were deliberately destroyed. When the enemy was approaching, the White Army killed some sixteen hundred Reds in Kiakhta in a cold-blooded orgy of bayonets and poison.

The tea millionaires scattered. Some of them were murdered, others fled to the Pacific ports via the Trans-Siberian trains. Kiakhta was in chaos, derived not only from the fallout of the Russian Civil War but from the Mongolian Revolution of 1921 just across the border. Leading the army of Mongol revolutionaries was a madman with an identity crisis: an Austrian-born German warlord – Baron von Ungern-Sternberg, known as the Bloody White Baron – who had originally attached himself to imperial Russia as a Tsarist officer, then 'went rogue'. Believing he was an incarnation of Genghis Khan, von Ungern wanted to reinstate Mongolia's old Buddhist theocracy. To achieve his goal, he enacted a reign of terror against the Bolsheviks, which eventually brought him back to the Russia–Mongolia border territory. In the Mongolian town abutting Kiakhta, a suspected 'Red' met his death in a baker's oven. In Kiakhta, the Baron's enemies were locked into a room, and cold water sprayed on to their naked bodies. They were frozen to death rather than shot, so as not to waste bullets, the Baron's

Baron von Ungern-Sternberg, photographed in Mongolia in the early 1920s.

capacity for murder said to be so bottomless that he was constantly inventing new ways of killing. One of his methods of execution was to tie his victim to two trees bent to the ground, which, when released, split the body in two.

The currents of history swirled among the cathedral ruins – the story about the Bestuzhev drawings which went missing in the post, the trunk full of Decembrist secrets, the merchants' pianos the tuner from Kiev came to fix. If none of this had happened – no 1917 Revolution, no White Baron, no

The Kiakhta Bechstein, photographed in the town's museum in 2016.

Russian Civil War – what would Kiakhta have become? Would Siberia have flourished differently? Would it have spun off and become its own independent state as Potanin had once advocated?

How had the Bechstein survived the chaos, I wondered, when so little else had made it through? If all the assumptions were true, this was a piano that carried the musical ambitions of a rich merchant family. It was also a direct connection to the vision of those brilliant exiles of 1825 who spread their European culture through a region that still feels fundamentally Asiatic – fenceless steppe country imbued with Buddhist history, where there are as many churches as there are Buryat invocations to the spirits evident in the blue and yellow ribbons tied to trees. The Bechstein was an instrument invested with so much desire, I was ready to believe almost any version of events as Siberia's past and enigmatic present pulled me in. 'From Baikal onwards, the poetry of Siberia begins,' wrote Chekhov to a friend: 'Before Baikal it was all prose.'

6

The Sound of Chopin's Poland:
Tomsk

I N A SMALL VILLAGE east of Lake Baikal, in a tiny church hidden behind a Soviet candy factory, I went to meet a priest, Sergei Paliy, who I had been told had a good piano. His coarse beard, which forked in the wind, reached down to his belly button. His long black cassock had a solemn weight to it, and fell slightly too high on the ankle. He belonged to the Old Believers, a traditionalist division of the Russian Orthodox Church that broke off in the mid-seventeenth century when they refused to subscribe to Moscow's liturgical reforms. Around twenty thousand Old Believers chose to commit mass suicide rather than fall into line.

Many of the Old Believers, both clergymen and followers, left Russia for the Polish–Lithuanian Commonwealth on the Empire's western border. A large number went east to Siberia – some voluntarily, others by force. The most famous Old Believer exiled to Siberia was Archpriest Avvakum, who was the only one of the four main dissenters who didn't have his tongue cut out.*

As a means of self-protection, the Old Believers became increasingly closed to outsiders – a habit which continues today. One family retreated so far into the Siberian taiga in 1945, they lived in total isolation in the western Sayan Mountains until a Soviet journalist documented their discovery by a group of prospecting geologists in the late seventies. The family had missed the death of Stalin and the moon landing, which they didn't believe anyway. They thought cellophane was crumpled glass, and had never seen a lemon. They went about barefoot, in birch-bark galoshes and burlap clothes. They possessed a spinning wheel and a Bible, but otherwise entertained each other by remembering their dreams. They kept track of time with methods that predated Peter the Great. There was no instrumental music. As for dancing, it was the devil's art.

Various splinters of these Old Believer communities survive throughout Siberia, their traditions representing some

---

* A religious zealot with a literary bent, Avvakum found time in exile to scribe one of the earliest travel books on Siberia. His pocketbook account describes Lake Baikal covered with so many swans, they looked like snow, and cliffs so high you would crick your neck to see them. Avvakum, *The Life of the Archpriest Avvakum by Himself*, trans. Jane Harrison and Hope Mirrlees (London: Hogarth Press, 1963).

of the strongest examples of Slavic civilization before the Westernizing reforms of the eighteenth century. I encountered opportunists who posed for tourists in gaudy outfits, and those who were still so committed to their secret rituals they refused to talk. I met a piano tuner who no longer observed his parents' religion; he fed me generously with food he could ill afford to spare, yet he didn't share the meal's only knife. Even today, you can tell an Old Believer by the set of crockery and cutlery he keeps to himself – a legacy of their fear of contamination beyond their own closed world.

The Baikal priest was quite the opposite: a good talker, and a formidable collector of Siberian paraphernalia, including a Becker upright piano that had once belonged to a local teacher. It turned out his more interesting story lay hidden inside the church, where he opened up a three-hundred-year-old *Book of the Apocalypse*. It belonged to the community's forefathers, who spent eighteen months from 1765 walking into Siberia from Vietka, a town which was then part of the Polish–Lithuanian Commonwealth. The book's dark images were a premonition loaded with irony given what was to happen next, when the Commonwealth underwent three major partitions during Catherine the Great's reign alone. The territory was divvied up between Russia, Prussia and Austria. What was Poland's loss, however, was Siberia's gain, with significant forced migrations of musically educated Polish rebels – including a significant Jewish population.

In 1795, which was the most dramatic partition of the three, Poland lost its sovereign statehood. Even the country's name was wiped when Catherine annexed the Western Provinces, a region that roughly included Lithuania, Ukraine and

Belarus. Cultural repression contributed to Poland's demise, with Catherine's military confiscating important historic possessions, including magnificent libraries. Poland enjoyed a brief moment of semi-autonomy during the Napoleonic Wars, but that vanished when the Poles actively participated in the French invasion of Russia, and Tsar Alexander I decided the Poles needed to be punished. At the 1815 Congress of Vienna, Europe's borders were redrawn yet again, with the Tsar's brother – the one who needed Chopin to calm his moods – appointed as de facto Viceroy.

It wasn't that the Poles were universally at odds with the Russians. On the one hand, they identified with an imagined national Polish community; on the other hand, they had also partaken in imperial Russian society for some time, with lives played out along the Empire's shifting borders. Over the years, many Russified Poles had risen to powerful positions in Russia, including the Decembrists' prison commander, who had allowed their Siberian academy to flourish. But after the 1815 Congress, the dominant nationalist feeling inside Catholic Poland turned more sharply against the Orthodox empire to the east. Press censorship grew tighter. Secret societies such as Freemasonry were banned.

With their experience of the Reformation and the Enlightenment, the Poles increasingly regarded themselves as the boundary between two profoundly opposed world views, between democratic government's defence of the rights of man, and the autocratic opposite. But it was also a pipe dream to think Poland would be able to shake off the Russian yoke. When the Poles launched their November Uprising of 1830, they were crushed within eight months. Their university was closed, and Warsaw effectively transformed into a barracks for

Russian soldiers. This was a time when the notion of Polish nationality, observed the novelist Joseph Conrad, was 'not so much alive as surviving, which persists in thinking, breathing, speaking, hoping, and suffering in its grave, railed in by a million of bayonets and triple-sealed with the seals of three great empires'.*

This Polish myth of noble martyrdom, prevalent all over Europe, was inflamed by Tsar Nicholas I's predictably vengeful handling of the 1830 rebels. Still smarting from the treachery shown by the Decembrists four years earlier, Nicholas specifically ordered one of the most high-profile Polish insurrectionists, Prince Roman Sanguszko, to travel to his Siberian exile on foot – a brutal and humiliating journey which took the prince a year to walk. There are numerous echoes, in fact, between the story of the Polish rebels of 1830 and the Decembrists. At different prisons and mines in Eastern Siberia, the new influx of Polish prisoners organized lectures, orchestras and a formidable library of books.

Meanwhile, the Polish romance – a nostalgic quest for freedom, which of course ignored the persecution of Russians inside Poland – found significant support in a politically progressive Paris, where around five thousand of the highest ranking rebels managed to escape Russian arrest. Paris was also the city where a twenty-two-year-old Pole called Frédéric Chopin, though not a political refugee himself, arrived in 1831 from Warsaw – via eight months in Vienna – looking for

* Joseph Conrad's short story *Prince Roman – Tales of Hearsay* (New York: Doubleday, 1925) – records the author's boyhood meeting with the elderly Prince Roman Sanguszko, who had survived his exile to Siberia thirty years prior. Conrad describes Sanguszko as 'a man among all men capable of feeling deeply, of believing steadily, of loving ardently'.

work.* He joined several other famous figures in the Polish Romantic movement gathered in France, including the poet Adam Mickiewicz – a friend and confidant of a number of the Decembrists, who later married the daughter of the virtuoso pianist Maria Szymanowska.

Some of the Polish prisoners taken by the Russians were used as soldiers to replenish military garrisons in Siberia. Tens of thousands were subjected to forced penal labour in towns like Tomsk, Omsk, Tobolsk and Irkutsk[†] – a tragedy Chopin sought to capture in his brooding 'Siberian' or 'Revolt Polonaise'.[‡] It opens very quietly, in a low, gloomy register, with the piano's newly invented damper pedal allowing for ravishing variances in mood and texture. The music then explodes – *con forza! agitato! molto crescendo!* – before slipping back into a sense of hopeless defeat, the dark ending of the polonaise evoking the cold and damp of the Siberian mines. According to Robert Schumann, not just this 'Revolt Polonaise' but all Chopin's work in this Polish dance form was

---

* Chopin lived a peripatetic life, travelling widely throughout Europe. In 1838 he wintered in Majorca, where he finished his famous 24 Preludes on perhaps the greatest lost piano of them all. The piano was rediscovered seventy years later by Wanda Landowska, a Polish harpsichordist and Chopin devotee, only to be snatched by the Nazis, and lost again. The full story is told by Paul Kildea in *Chopin's Piano* (London: Allen Lane, 2018).

† The number of Polish people exiled to Siberia in the nineteenth century varies according to where chroniclers drew the Ural line, as well as other factors such as the unreliability of Tsarist records. In *The Mass Deportation of Poles to Siberia, 1863– 1880* (Basingstoke: Palgrave Macmillan, 2017), the historian Andrew Gentes suggests the following: 'The mass deportation of Poles between 1863 and the 1880s was perhaps the largest forced migration of Europeans prior to World War One. It resulted in thousands upon thousands of personal tragedies, a small minority of which were ever documented.'

‡ 'Polonaise in E flat minor'.

expressive of a chivalrous and oppressed people – of 'cannon buried in flowers'.

While the Poles in Paris could protest freely, back home the line of Polish rebels clanking towards Siberia was getting longer and longer, with nearly two thirds of those banished for political offences in the 1830s belonging to a culturally sophisticated nobility. Following the Poles' next notable revolt in January 1863 – at first an under-resourced insurrection of skirmishes and peasant rebellions, which scaled up into a full-blown war   Russia banished another four thousand members of Poland's educated upper classes to the Siberian wastes. While the Russians were ransacking Warsaw, famously tossing Chopin's piano on to a bonfire in the city square, a bright light was being flicked on in Siberia's expanding towns.

When Maria Volkonsky's daughter, Elena, returned to St Petersburg after the Decembrists were granted amnesty, the new Tsar's wife remarked on her excellent French. For a child brought up *'à la Rousseau'*, as her mother described Elena's early years running wild in the Siberian taiga, Elena's sophistication came as something of a surprise to the Romanov court. Elena replied she had been taught by a Polish political prisoner exiled to Siberia. Elena Volkonsky's Siberian education was unusual, but not unique. When the first families of Kiakhta sought piano teachers for their children, they relied upon the Polish diaspora. When Omsk needed an orchestra, it was the Poles who played the clarinet, strings and trumpet.

Thomas Knox, an American journalist travelling through Siberia in 1866, remarked on this erudite presence: 'Siberia has received a great many individuals of high culture in the persons of its political exiles. Men of liberal education, active intellects, and refined manners have been in large proportion among the banished Poles,' he observed. 'The influence of these exiles upon the intelligence, habits, and manners of the Siberians, has left an indelible mark.'

Knox may have been burnishing the miserable reality of the exiles' lives, but his encounters with Polish exiles were still testimony to their influence. Knox wrote about a Pole in charge of the Geographical Society of Eastern Siberia who had been a well-known poet in Kraków, and exiles practising as successful physicians. He also recounted the public execution in Irkutsk of a handsome thirty-year-old Polish pianist and political prisoner, Gustaw Szaramowicz.

When Szaramowicz lost a finger to a stray bullet in the 1863 Polish Revolt, he was said to have looked at his broken hand and remarked: 'Chopin's mazurkas are lost.' Punishment served to harden Szaramowicz's resolve. While working as a penal labourer in the knee-deep snows of Siberia, Szaramowicz led another revolt three years later, this time of seven hundred Polish prisoners assigned to build the road south of Lake Baikal. It is said that when Szaramowicz was being executed by firing squad in Irkutsk, he threw his hat up into the air. *'Vive la Pologne!'* he shouted as he heard the order to fire.

Music disperses easily in big spaces, just like people. Most artists and intellectuals perished in Siberia without so much as a state record of their arrival or their death, whether it was suicide that took them, the typhus-addled way-stations, or the caged barges which carried the exiles upriver into Siberian towns like Tomsk. Their stories were silenced by a penal system which killed off far more people than Siberia ever remembered. Forgetting was also a method of survival. There are records of prisoners who escaped into the taiga and then changed their name to 'Ivan Dontremember' when authorities brought them back in.*

While instruments may not have been among the luggage of the deported (though certain ranks were allowed to travel by cart with whatever possessions they pleased), the sound of music would have formed a strong connection to the Poles' former homeland. Writing in 1846, the exiled nobleman Rufin Piotrowski – one of the most famous political prisoners to escape Siberia, his disguise a home-made goat's-hair wig – said the only music he heard in thirteen years was Poland's national song, which rang out across the Siberian steppe: 'I forgot my chains, forgot my past life, my future destiny, forgot everything.'

What would have definitely been present was the sound of the piano in a nineteenth-century Polish exile's head. In mid-nineteenth-century Warsaw, the piano was 'reigning like a despot in the drawing rooms', reported one local newspaper. 'There is almost no house where the thumping of a piano is not heard,' claimed the *Warsaw Courier*: 'We have pianos on the ground, first, second and third floors. Young ladies play the piano, mothers play the piano, children play the piano. The piano has become a family piece of furniture, the family talents' touchstone.' These social habits migrated into Siberia as the century progressed and Polish exiles intermarried with

---

* There was also a tradition among convicts who were caught and dragged back to the same prison they had escaped, to take on the the name 'brodiaga', meaning 'origins forgotten'. Prison culture was such that fellow convicts had to keep silent about the returnee's true name. Reveal it, and they could expect to be killed, according to the nineteenth-century Russian journalist Vlas Doroshevich. *Russia's Penal Colony in the Far East: A Translation of Vlas Doroshevich's 'Sakhalin'*, trans. Andrew Gentes (London and New York: Anthem Press, 2011).

A late-nineteenth-century image of a group of escaped convicts in Siberia, one of whom wears a home-made mosquito net.

Russians, with exiles given land plots to help tie them to the country for ever.

The Polish connection, which ran so deep in the nineteenth century, came and went as I travelled through Siberia: in the village east of Baikal, where I met the Old Believer priest with his *Book of the Apocalypse*; in Irkutsk, where many of the people I interviewed claimed direct Polish descent; and in the Western Siberian city of Tomsk, home of Siberia's first university, opened in 1888, where two of the eight founding faculty members were Poles. Tomsk also established one of

Russia's first museums of repression in 1989, occupying the town's former prison. In this windowless vault, the director was gathering the stories not only of thousands of people arrested by Stalin's secret police but also of political exiles of the nineteenth century. He was of direct Polish descent. Half his family migrated to America in the 1860s; the other half migrated from Belarus to Siberia, looking for a better life. 'There is a stereotype that if you find Polish people in Siberia, they are all convicts and exiles,' he said. 'There were free settlers, too, and among them, a great many people who influenced the musical culture of Siberia.'

I arrived in February. The snow had fallen so thickly that in older neighbourhoods a few houses had split under the pressure. Outside the nineteenth-century House of Science – conceived as a foundation stone of Siberian enlightenment, offering free education, regardless of a citizen's creed or background – there stood a crab-apple tree, its fruit ruby-red, like drops of blood. Walking the streets, I imagined Tomsk as it was in the year Chopin's piano was being hurled on to the bonfire in Warsaw. 'The sound of that falling lingers,' wrote Chopin's contemporary, the Polish Romantic poet Cyprian Kamil Norwid: 'Behold – how noble thought / Is trampled by human fury.'

In Tomsk, amnesties came and went. Many Poles returned to a version of home in European Russia. Others stayed on, like the grandfather of the Soviet composer Dmitri Shostako-vich, who was sent to Tomsk after the 1863 January Uprising. Year by year, former exiles moved up through the ranks of Siberian industry, geological exploration and administrative 'society' – a stratum in Siberian prison towns that one Polish prisoner said commanded nearly all the luxury accoutrements of Western civilization.

Nearly. Tomsk was still Siberia, too far away from Europe's musical capitals to concern itself with the debates raging in the West as critics grappled with the musical revolutionaries like Wagner and Liszt. At the dawn of the 1860s, Russia was undergoing its own, slightly lagging cultural shift as music was finally being professionalized under the Imperial Russian Musical Society – a brilliantly ambitious organization, supported at the highest level by the Romanov court, founded in St Petersburg in 1859 by Anton Rubinstein to develop musical taste and talent across the Empire at large. What the Society symbolized was even greater than the sum of its provincial parts: it was a key feature of Rubinstein's wider plan to emancipate Russian musicians from being mere 'entertainers'. He sought to earn them the kind of recognition they had long commanded in Western Europe as professional 'Free Artists' – to give them the dignified status that Liszt had insisted upon in St Petersburg when Tsar Nicholas I had heard him play. The Emperor spoke during a pause and Liszt refused to continue, as if nobility and art deserved an equal footing.

Rubinstein's influence was remarkable. In 1862, he successfully opened the country's first conservatory in St Petersburg, with Tchaikovsky among the inaugural intake. All through the 1860s, the so-called 'Mighty Five' of Russian composers – Nikolai Rimsky-Korsakov, César Cui, Modest Mussorgsky, Alexander Borodin and Mily Balakirev – were busy creating a new, deeply serious national identity for Russian music. All of them were self-taught, at a time when not a single textbook on musical harmony was written in the Russian language.

Meanwhile, in Tomsk, music was being enjoyed opportunistically, with amateur teachers trying to make ends meet as the town expanded with a growing merchant class and an influx of civil servants. This was a time when a Russian version of the *bumjakjak* – a deliciously suggestive word used by nineteenth-century German critics to describe a crude rhythm accompanying folk songs – would have been more common in Siberia's wooden homes than Wagner. But Tomsk was also a growing provincial town hungry for metropolitan culture. By 1885, it had a population of thirty-one thousand people, twenty-six schools, twenty-nine churches, three synagogues and a mosque, while the university was pushing through a stop–start opening as the imperial government responded to suspicions about the town's liberal tendencies.

'A naturally enterprising and promising colony,' is how Tomsk was described by the American journalist George Kennan, who spent September 1885 there with an exiled writer whose wife, an accomplished musician, earned her living teaching music. Kennan reported on the political prisoners. He also documented the city's strangulating censorship, pitiable human misery and prison overcrowding. He predicted a fine future for Tomsk, if only the government would loosen the vice it held around people's throats.

Poor Tomsk – trying to find its dignity, only for Chekhov to condemn its reputation to a national joke when he stayed here five years later. 'The most notable thing about Tomsk is that governors come here to die,' he wrote in a letter to his publisher. In the same lacerating spirit, he wrote a bibliography for a St Petersburg literary journal; the books he cited included *Hedgehog Animal Husbandry: For Glove Manufacturers*, a sixty-kopek paperback on *How to Pinpoint the Universe*, and *A Tourist Guide to Siberia and Environs*, featuring best restaurants, tailors, carriage-builders and coiffeurs, and names and addresses of 'certain ladies'.

In Tomsk, Chekhov made a drunken tour of the brothels with the town's chief of police. He made no mention of music – neither Ukrainian melodies, French *chansonettes*, amateur *bumjakjak*, nor gypsy romances. And yet, even as Chekhov was dismissing Tomsk as boring, the town's musical culture was evolving. The year before he arrived, the first chapter of the Imperial Russian Musical Society opened in the city, its grand piano chosen by none less than Anton Rubinstein's younger brother, the pianist and composer Nikolai Rubinstein. Among the directors of the society was Grigory Tomashinskiy, a Polish émigré to Siberia, who with his wife, Kamila, was among the town's most influential musical patrons, and the host of numerous charitable concerts. Kamila taught piano, basing the musical programme on the founding principles of a special musical school in Irkutsk, also managed by a Pole, where a number of students progressed to the conservatories in Moscow and St Petersburg.

Tomsk might not have experienced pianomania on the scale Liszt had once unleashed in St Petersburg, but the appetite in Western Siberia for the instrument became more and more significant. By 1880, St Petersburg manufacturers were advertising their grand pianos in Tomsk with enthusiasm. Piano tuning was also emerging as a licensed profession, with some of Tomsk's grander families possessing not one but two pianos in their home. Tuners came all the way from Warsaw for the good business that was to be had in Tomsk, where, in 1880, Siberia's first piano shop opened. The owner was Pyotr Makushin, a Russian theology student born near Perm in the Urals, who settled in Tomsk shortly after the Polish rebellion of 1863.

Unlike the Volkonskys, Makushin arrived in Siberia with

Pyotr Makushin and his family, c. 1923.

no financial means. He came instead with the deep conviction that literacy was the key to unlocking Siberia's future, even though a local bishop had tried to warn him off. Tomsk wasn't America's land of opportunity, the priest told Makushin, but a true Siberian backwater. Makushin persisted. A voracious reader, he began with a marketplace stall in Tomsk. Then he bought a horse and cart, and employed a coach driver so that he could distribute his wares to villagers. In 1873, he opened his first bookshop. Eleven years later, he founded Siberia's first national free public library – four months before Moscow's equivalent. He opened an orphanage, a printing house, a museum on Siberian history, two Siberian newspapers, the House of Science and a theatre. He gave lectures in the local prison colonies. In the city's musical circles, a healthy economy evolved as piano classes created demand for sheet music sold not only by Makushin's bookstore – before long as good as any in the capital – but also in a second shop he opened in Irkutsk. As for pianos, Makushin's pioneering store sold more than five hundred instruments in twenty years, including Beckers and Mühlbachs, with ninety per cent of them purchased by citizens of Tomsk.

Not only was piano ownership on the upswing; so was Tomsk's musical talent. Among the town's beloved piano-players of this period was Yadviga Zaleskaya, a young Polish graduate of the Warsaw Conservatory, who moved from Tomsk to the Russian capital in 1893. Seven years later, *Le Figaro* was calling Zaleskaya one of the St Petersburg greats. By the mid-1890s, she had left Russia to perform all over Europe, her enormous popularity epitomized by her performance in Paris in 1900, at which she received two ovations from a sold-out concert hall. Later, her talents took her further afield, to Singapore and Indonesia, before she returned to her native Poland, where she was killed by Nazi SS soldiers in 1944.

One of the town's principal tuners, Anatoly Salaev, agreed to meet me. He was an authority on Tomsk's piano history, and generous with his information. It was Salaev who told me that the music school still contained Makushin's instrument. It stood unused on the second floor. The piano – a Diederichs grand, serial number 6583, dating from 1898 – was originally housed in Tomsk's House of Science.

I went to find it. Under the piano's lid were eight empty butter pots covered in damp silk – a home-made humidifying system for winter. Two strings were missing, said Elena Fefel-ova, who was teaching piano in the same room when I appeared unannounced. According to Elena, who had studied and then worked in Tomsk since 1959, the Diederichs had been owned by the school for as long as she remembered. It wasn't working as it should, she said; the pedals were unstable when it was played. Then she showed me where the case was embossed in gold leaf with Makushin's name.

As we talked, I learned about another alumna of the Tomsk music school, a concert performer and piano teacher called Olga Leonidovna, whom I needed to meet. Olga was living nearby in Bogashevo village. She had played Makushin's Diederichs on numerous occasions, as both a student and a teacher. Olga also had her own special piano, an 1896 Bechstein. Makushin's instrument was of national importance, but Olga's was private property with a unique history. Two women had arrived in Tomsk on a train from Leningrad with the piano in tow during the Great Patriotic War, and sold it to a local for a bag of potatoes. In 1973, about thirty people in Olga's community – friends and neighbours of her parents – clubbed together to help her family buy the instrument.

So I went to visit, and found Olga's Bechstein baby grand in her house – a typical Siberian countryside home with timber walls, the path to the front door cut through metre-deep snow. The piano looked magnificent in the main living room, even though the instrument was cluttered with a grandchild's plastic toys. Only eleven strings in the Bechstein had ever been replaced, she said. Two were faulty, yet the piano still played well enough, with the humidity kept in balance by hanging wet linen in the cottage.

Over a magnificent spread of forest mushrooms, berries and stewed tongue, Olga described her first mentor, a Muscovite bootmaker with a perfect ear who had found her the piano, and persuaded Olga's parents to invest in her early show of talent. It was under the bootmaker's direction that they saved up and bought the instrument. Whenever he came to tune, he would take off his jacket, lean into the Bechstein, and that was it – he would be lost in its music. He loved the piano, said Olga. So did the children in the village, who would gather to watch him work.

'The Bechstein is noble, kind and demanding. It has a kind of magic,' said Olga, picking out a doll from its bed of piano strings as she spoke: 'Every morning, I come to my mother's portrait. I speak to her, and kiss the piano.'

Olga said the Bechstein was suffering a little these days, but it had a proud history. She played a flurry of notes, each sound expanding into the room as if the instrument were sighing, then singing, with relief. For forty-five years the Bechstein

Olga Leonidovna photographed with her 1896 Bechstein at her house in Bogashevo village near Tomsk.

had entertained the Siberian village where Olga's father ran the collective farm. It carried the sacrifices of good friends. It represented the community ethic of Soviet society at its best. For that reason, she was glad I was writing the instrument's story – the best piano in Siberia, she declared, kissing it again – but her beloved Bechstein was not, and never would be, for sale.

7

Home in a Hundred Years:
Sakhalin Island

W HEN ANTON CHEKHOV decided to travel four thousand miles overland from Moscow to the penal colony of Sakhalin Island, he knew he didn't have much to lose. Before he left home, he was already showing the telltale signs of the tuberculosis that would kill him within four years of his homecoming. Nor did he seem to care much about the threat of censorship, having set out to record the horrors of the Tsarist exile system – 'a place of unbearable sufferings, which only a human being, whether free or subjugated, is capable of caus-ing and undergoing'.

Sakhalin Island, about twice the size of Belgium, lies five miles off Russia's Pacific coast, and almost scratches the top of Japan – territory which the two countries have tussled over for centuries. When Chekhov travelled here, the entire island was under Russian control, which lasted until the Tsar lost the southern half to Japan following the 1905 Russo-Japanese War. Not until Japan's dramatic defeat in the Second World War was Stalin able to demand the island's return.

When I visited, Sakhalin's capital, Yuzhno-Sakhalinsk, was pulsing with neon and oil money. The restaurants were busy and the karaoke noisy, the bar music still showing something in common with the description given by Benjamin Howard, a turn-of-the-century British traveller to Sakhalin. With the exception of the Governor's piano, Howard encountered noth-ing but an 'ugly little creature' of a barrel organ, about the size of a sewing machine: 'When the creaky wooden handle was turned, it stirred up rats, cats and puppies.' The entertainment notwithstanding, the modern cut and thrust of Yuzhno-Sakhalinsk felt like the nerve centre of a new universe – the extreme opposite, in fact, of the Sakhalin Chekhov encoun-tered after his long passage east.

Describing the last stages of his journey to the island, Chekhov complained of a disintegrating identity, a loss of Russianness, until the country of his birth felt as unfamiliar as Patagonia. This eastern side of Siberia was a place Chek-hov considered so far from Moscow that he would only be 'Home in a Hundred Years'. His final port of call on the Rus-sian mainland before sailing for Sakhalin was the town of Nikolaevsk (now known as Nikolaevsk-on-Amur). In the 1850s, a journalist for the *New York Times* had stopped off in the same place and thought the scene rather civilized: 'capital dinners', lamps burning with whale oil, coal from Pennsylvania glowing in the grates, newspapers only six months old, and a social club where dancing to the sound of an excellent English piano occurred every Thursday evening. Chekhov acknowledged this brief flutter of polite society: 'apparently the town was no stranger to the humanities, since there was even one occasion when a touring scholar considered it both necessary and possible to deliver a public lecture at the club here,' he wrote.

By the time of Chekhov's visit, Nikolaevsk was down on its luck. The townspeople had taken up the habit of shooting Chinese vagrants, and hunting down 'hunchbacks' – the local term for escaped prisoners, owing to their knapsacks. Here on the edge of Siberia, Chekhov said the locals were ignorant of Russia's history, Pushkin and Gogol. Any lingering connection he might have felt with Moscow was finally severed during a hot week in July 1891 when he crossed the Tatar Strait to Sakhalin Island. He described the steamer's clean, cramped cabins, and an upright piano. Also on board was a baroness, and a prisoner accompanied by a five-year-old daughter who clung to his fetters as he ascended the ship's steps.

Chekhov's port of disembarkation on Sakhalin was the penal settlement of Aleksandrovsk on the island's north-west coast – at the end of the nineteenth century, deemed the most terrible example of the entire Tsarist exile system. I arrived into the island's south, also by boat, so needed to head upcountry to pick up Chekhov's trail. I travelled on a night-train from Yuzhno-Sakhalinsk, sleeping beside oil workers. These were the people Russians describe as 'sitting on their suitcase'. They come to make money, their bag always packed ready to return home.

My cabin share was surprised when I got off at Tymovsk, a dust-blown, back-of-beyond, one-horse-town type of station, where I was met by Grigory Smekalov, a local historian. He drove me to Aleksandrovsk, passing the site of a memorial marking the mass grave of some eight thousand prisoners who died on their marches through Sakhalin's notorious swamp. As we pulled into town, I hadn't expected Aleksandrovsk to be so small, given the size of its sinister reputation. The settlement dribbled out over rising ground above a long beach. Abandoned ships were marooned on its rippled sands, the iron cadavers hollowed out by waves. In the town square, a thin gathering of locals were getting ready to celebrate Russia Day. A rare outsider, I was watched wherever I went.

In one of the only cafés open year-round, Grigory talked me through his work, which revealed his own deep sense of moral justice. His father endured a labour camp in Chukotka, north of Kolyma. Grigory was interested in repairing reputations – not just those of forgotten individuals who suffered repression, but places blackened by historical events. He said he wanted Sakhalin to be known for more than Chekhov's withering report. 'It is essential to restore Sakhalin's history, to show that heroes existed,' he said. He and I agreed to trade some research. In return for help looking for pianos in this former prison colony, I would dig into the archives at the Scott Polar Research Institute in England. Grigory was researching Captain Robert Scott's dog handler, Dmitri Girev, who was born in Aleksandrovsk and joined the British explorer's 1911 attempt on the South Pole.

Girev was the son of a female convict. He was brilliant with husky teams, a talent Scott's right-hand man, Cecil Meares, spotted when he came to Siberia to purchase dogs strong

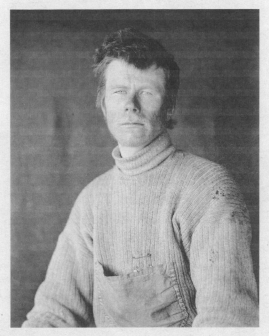

Dmitri Girev, photographed in 1912. In Russia, Girev often travelled long distances to hunt and fish using his family's dog team.

enough to drag the British expedition across the Antarctic ice. If only Scott had trusted a Sakhaliner's tenacious capacity to survive some of the harshest conditions known to man. Some four hundred miles short of the South Pole, Scott sent Girev and his dogs back to base. Girev survived, along with some of the Sakhalin huskies.*

Nobody knows about Girev's Sakhalin history, said Grigory, nor the role these Siberian dogs played in one of the most

---

* Girev was in the search party that found the dead explorer. His favourite dog, Osman, lived out the rest of its life in a New Zealand zoo, according to a Wellington newspaper. *Free Lance* (August 1916).

One of Captain Scott's sled dogs, Chris, listening to a gramophone on the ice, c. 1911. In total, thirty-three dogs were taken on the expedition, a large proportion of them purchased from Sakhalin and the Amur River region with money donated by English schoolchildren.

iconic polar journeys of the twentieth century. They only know Chekhov's version of Sakhalin's story, he said, which clanks with the sound of iron manacles. From the open windows of Chekhov's lodging, the rare glimmers of music he described included the tireless whistling of canaries, and soldiers rehearsing on flutes, bassoons and trombones. They were practising for a parade to welcome the Governor General.

'In the General's garden there was music and singing,' wrote Chekhov. 'They even fired a cannon – which blew up. And yet, despite such gaiety, the streets were dismal. No songs, no accordions, not a single drunk . . . A penal colony illuminated by Bengal flares is still a penal colony, and music, when heard from a distance by a man who will never return to his homeland, brings on only a deadly yearning.'

Chekhov's readers wanted drama, said Grigory – yellow-skinned lunatics, tales of corrupt officials, Dostoevsky and Gogol. They wanted to hear the gruesome stories, like the one about the governor murdered in the bakery, who fell into the trough and stained the dough with blood. They wanted their writers to tell gory tales about people eating each other, and feeding on rotten pieces of wood. Chekhov gave plenty of lurid detail – the bodies turned crimson with bruising, and the chattering teeth of a prisoner who bit his glass cup compulsively whenever he was given his medicine – while also

Chekhov's 1890 photograph of the notorious thief Sonka the Golden Hand being chained by her jailers on Sakhalin Island. Sonka – real name, Sophia Bliuvshtein – was a renowned con woman, remembered for charming wealthy men into giving her vast sums of money. Intense public interest resulted in a Russian movie serial about her exploits being produced in 1914.

gathering histories of the most famous prisoners, some of whom Chekhov later turned into fictional characters in his work.

Despite the contemporary public's appetite for sensational detail, Chekhov's portrait of Sakhalin wasn't entirely devoid of 'civilized' society. In one prison colony, Chekhov described a doctor who had amassed a 'luxurious' zoological collection over his ten-year sojourn on Sakhalin; in Chekhov's opinion, the doctor's elegant specimens would have made for an excellent museum. Usually Chekhov's remarks were more acerbic. At another settlement, he described a governor's wife sitting in the garden 'majestic as a marquise' with her daughters 'dressed up like little angels'. They talked in soft words and pleasant tones while surveying their watermelons, tended by a convict who guarded the fruit deferentially.

As for Aleksandrovsk, Chekhov depicted the town as the centre of Sakhalin society, made up not only of prisoners but also engineers, clerks, free settlers and military personnel. The ladies could purchase fashionable summer hats, along with stars for epaulettes, and Turkish delight. There were jewellers, upholsterers and watchmakers, with officials able to take on as many prisoner-servants as they liked.

According to Grigory, one ex-murderer who 'made good' when his sentence was up became so successful in the construction trade he could afford to import Sakhalin's first ever Ford motor car from America – a status symbol that before long would become a greater indicator of wealth than a piano in the parlour. There were a number of merchants who became members of Sakhalin's nouveau riche; they would have almost definitely owned an instrument, said Grigory, who talked me through some of Aleksandrovsk's forgotten biographies.

Unfortunately, little of that world survived. In a single week of anarchy in 1905 during the Russo-Japanese War, the convicts burnt down the colony's two prisons, as well as the Governor's Residence. It is hard to say how many instruments were lost to those flames, said Grigory. But there had been music in this prison colony, of an unexpected kind.

The scene is described by Vlas Doroshevich, one of imperial Russia's most celebrated journalists, who followed in Chekhov's footsteps in 1897. 'Penal labourer E's wife' was 'a miniature young woman, nearly a child', who had voluntarily joined her suitor in exile when he was sentenced to twenty years' hard labour for murdering a friend. When they were married in Aleksandrovsk, the ten-minute wedding feast was celebrated drinking tea at the doctor's house, where E's wife stayed. Her husband was then returned to his shackles, and taken back to jail. When it was discovered that she had been a student at the conservatory in St Petersburg, her life became unbearable. Local officials in Aleksandrovsk dragged her out to play piano at evening events. The doctor's family, who worried about her exhaustion, tried to stop her, but she feared officials would retaliate by making her husband's prison term even worse if she didn't perform to demand.

'[T]he poor woman's heart was obsessed by this one idea. She continued to play,' wrote Doroshevich:

> The good administrators' families considered it improper to shake hands with a 'convict's wife' so she, arriving in the evening to play 'as a courtesy,' would give a curtsey to everyone and slowly sit down at the piano to await orders. 'Play!' One relentlessly cheerful figure especially pestered her – the chancery's head

clerk, already mentally ill at the time and soon to be sent to a madhouse. 'Listen to how you play!' he'd say with typically saturnine pomposity. 'You're not playing right! Not so fast! Play slower. Now play happier! Devil knows what you're playing!' She wept and played; played hunched low over the keys so her tears wouldn't be noticed.

Mrs E's luck changed when an influential member of St Petersburg society arrived in Aleksandrovsk. The official recognized her from a past encounter back home as she stood beside the piano. He kissed her hand. The wives, who had spurned her before, became immediately solicitous. Her husband was released and put in charge of the meteorological station. In their apartment stood 'a splendid piano' that her relatives had sent from Russia, its whereabouts now unknown. It stood close to a garlanded portrait of her teacher, Anton Rubinstein. 'Music – it is all that beautifies her life during long, long Sakhalin winter evenings,' wrote Doroshevich, 'when outside a blizzard whirls and moans and her wretched husband sits and draws or writes poems. Disciplined classical music is her only happiness, after her child – and she plays it as perhaps no one else can. Only very unfortunate persons can play very well. There is so much suffering, grief, torment and tears.'

I took the road from Aleksandrovsk to nearby Dué Post, where the coal mines used to be. I passed by the high promontory where Chekhov liked to walk, and looked out from the old lighthouse on to the smudge of Russia's mainland, which was close enough to see. I passed Voevodsk Chasm, a sunken mine-pit beside the coast road. During Tsarist times, the pit had been turned into a prison yard. Back then, it had also functioned as a kind of hideous entertainment zone where prisoners were executed, the spectacle watched from all sides by convicts and exile-settlers. 'The condemned man is delivered in fetters,' wrote Doroshevich, 'In fetters, he listens to his sentence. Then they unshackle and put the shroud on him, and loop the lard-greased noose over the shroud.' The gallows stood next to a hole where some of the 'wheelbarrow-men' worked. These recidivist offenders – the runaways and murderers – were chained to their wheelbarrows by their hands and feet for the rest of their sentence. They remained cuffed to the wheelbarrows even as they slept, with their instruments of torture placed beneath them in specially adapted bunks. In the rare event that a wheelbarrow-man was released from his burden,

The wheelbarrow-men of Sakhalin Island, photographed in 1903.

he was so broken, said Chekhov, he couldn't hold a cup without slopping tea.

Where the executions had once taken place, there was now a banana-yellow car sitting in the adjacent lay-by, and the smell of smoke from charred kebabs. On the beach below, a couple were holding hands as they took in the summer sun, lying on their backs. It was a bright June afternoon. The sky was cloudless, which did nothing to help the coast throw off its grey pall. The strand was strafed with driftwood, the tideline of flotsam and jetsam marking the edge of an ocean as dead as standing water in a sink.

'A dreadful, hideous place,' wrote Chekhov, 'wretched in every respect, in which only saints or profoundly perverse people could live of their own free will.' 'Perhaps the most foul hole as exists on earth,' wrote Doroshevich. By the turn of the twentieth century, when a British anthropologist called Charles Hawes visited Dué, he said there wasn't a girl over the age of nine who was still a virgin. Dué represented the ultimate depravity of the Tsarist regime, which at the end of the nineteenth century was under dramatically mounting pressure to change its ways. Exiled liberals, the impoverished peasantry and an exploited workforce were feeding the support base of organized radicalism. The turmoil, including strikes and public protest, culminated in St Petersburg in January 1905. 'Bloody Sunday' left a hundred and thirty peaceful protesters dead – a violent response on the Tsar's part which triggered further unrest in the provinces.

Even Russia's musical culture was drawn into the political flux. In 1905, the composer Nikolai Rimsky-Korsakov signed a resolution written by leading Moscow musicians calling for political reform. 'We are not free artists,' they declared, 'but like all other Russian citizens, the disenfranchised victims of today's abnormal social conditions.' Performances of Rimsky-Korsakov's work were turned into political events. 'Down with autocracy!' shouted someone from the back of the auditorium at one of his St Petersburg premieres. After Bloody Sunday, the legitimacy of the Tsar's reckless regime was disintegrating fast. It was under these circumstances – with the architects of the 1917 Revolution, Leon Trotsky and Vladimir Lenin, now politically active – that Bolshevism was able to gain such rapid ground.

The approach road to Dué Post wasn't promising. The route separating the foreshore from a steep, treeless slope was still inscribed with the scars of the coal tracks used by the Dué mines. There was no coal glinting in the scree, as there was when Chekhov visited. Every fragment of fuel had been used up. All that was left was scavenged earth. Dragonflies with crisp, see-through wings milled about flowering weeds. Outnumbering all the other insects were hungry mosquitoes.

As for Dué itself, the carcass of an old coal store and landing stage marked the end of the beach, where a group of young men were lolling about drunk. Around me stood the mangled footings of topsy-turvy buildings overwhelmed by storms. Industrial machinery had long ago been stripped of anything that could be used. Gone were the 'white spick-and-span cottages' belonging to the prison governor, priest and officers described by early visitors. The wooden homes were caving in, their frames as tilted and bewildered as the teenagers pickling themselves in alcohol.

The further down Dué's single street I ventured, the more tenebrous the feeling. The ground was being picked over by dogs with tails clamped between their legs. Two children ran across the street in flapping shoes. In concrete buildings, even the layers of graffiti had been licked by fire. Along the stretch of track where the road ran out entirely, there were a couple of apartment blocks. Pinned to their walls were a clutch of satellite dishes, and on the corner, some freshly painted white tyres sunk into the ground to mark off a sitting area. This was Dué's social club.

I poked around for signs of life – in the last stop on my last day in the most feared Tsarist penal colony in Russia. A woman looked at me, then closed her door without dropping her stare. I watched an old man slip his head out of an upper window, then close it again like a badly played stage direction. When I found a coarse, pot-bellied fisherman sorting his nets outside a garage of scattered car parts, I asked if there was anyone with a piano. The man grunted a half-answer and pointed to the apartment block behind.

At the corner, a woman with blonde cropped hair was tending some flowers planted in two old tyres. My interpreter and she got talking. The woman – plump, smiley, dressed in leatherette leggings and a leopard-print top – said there was one person left in Dué who could help me. So we followed her past a puttering Russian flag into one of the apartment blocks. The main door to the stairwell was propped open with a child's sledge. The woman clacked up the lightless steps, passing doors which looked like they hadn't been disturbed in a while, the air heavy with cigarette smoke.

The woman took us inside her mother's flat. There were three rooms: a bathroom, a main room and a small kitchen with an iron oven, three tin bowls and two tin mugs, a kettle and a single electric burner. Bread was lying on the sideboard, and six onions in a string bag hung from the wall. The main room was furnished with two beds, which doubled as sofas in the day, a cabinet, a chest of drawers and two chairs. A television was playing in the corner. On the wall hung a carpet, a Russian Orthodox cross and a torch. On the table sat a TV guide, an ashtray, various medicines and a simple glass vase of purple lilacs. In the middle of this modest flower arrangement stood the strong stem of a fresh narcissus.

The lady was called Lidiya – a woman as thin as a bird, her tracksuit bottoms hanging loosely off narrow hips. At first, her raisin eyes flickered between attention and trepidation. She moved around the room nervously, lost as a ghost, as if she had wanted to remember something, then had forgotten what it was. She rearranged an icon on the cabinet. She turned off the TV – the sound of a Russian game show replaced by the drone of a sleepy fly – then sat down on the edge of the sofa. She moved restlessly, rocking back and forth. Her back was hunched, her whole body arched over her rib cage, as if to protect her from too much breathing. When we explained the reason for my visit, the woman pulled herself closer. Bit by bit, she started to talk – fluidly, intelligently. She ran her hand through her hair, as if to help arrange her memories until bit by bit something inside her started to unfurl.

She said she lived in this apartment with one of her unmarried sons, though her roots were in Ukraine. Her grandfather had been a rich peasant, or *kulak*. He had wanted to move to Siberia, but his wife didn't want to leave so he threw her from the top of a bell tower. Lidiya didn't know in which town. She paused and began to rock more nervously. She waved off any attempt to be mollified, then started up again, talking more quickly than before.

Her grandfather disappeared – she didn't know whether he survived prison, or Siberia, or even the journey there – but he left behind a son born in 1908, who was taken in by a woman who had no children of her own.

'That was my father,' said Lidiya: 'In the thirties, he left Ukraine and came to Dué as a free settler looking for work. He came to cut wood.'

Her father played all sorts of instruments, she said. He was self-taught on the mandolin, conducted a trumpet orchestra, a string orchestra and a male and female choir. A younger version of herself started to show, Lidiya's joyful telling caught up in wet lungfuls of air. She didn't remember a piano; instead she talked about the instruments her father had made when he was living in Western Russia. He would take hair from horse tails at night, then use it to string a wooden frame. In Sakhalin, he became the director of the club at Dué, which used to occupy a wooden building near the shore, close to the railway which took away the coal. Soon he was producing all the amateur performances. How marvellous they were, Lidiya recalled. She remembered one in which the musicians wore different costumes for the different republics of the USSR. She vividly described the brightly coloured outfits lined up backstage, as if they might still be hanging there now.

At home, when the radio was playing and music came on, her father would tell his children to stop talking. With his mandolin, he would play the same music he had just heard, repeating it by ear. He would often fix and tune the instruments that belonged to the local military station. Everyone in the village knew and respected her father, she said.

Back then, before the coal mine closed, there were five thousand people living in Dué. These days, there were only thirty-eight families left. The old club was gone, along with the house Lidiya had been brought up in – a wooden home built by the Japanese before the war. Its corridor had papered walls printed with flowers and beautiful girls in kimonos.

'We tore down the paper and cut out the images and kept them,' she said. 'We loved the Japanese pictures, and the doors made of glass, which were too heavy for me to open.'

It was a happy childhood. Lidiya's mother worked in the coalhouse. The sea provided them with fish. Her father netted herrings, which they carried in cotton bags her mother stitched. They sold the surplus, along with the crabs they collected at low tide. When there were heavy storms, the sea would throw sharks on to the shore. They took the liver, she said; she remembered how well they all felt whenever they drank the fish oil.

She went to the cabinet and pulled out a plastic bag of photographs. Among them was a crumpled black-and-white picture of her father in 1953. He was posing with employees of the club. His smile was wide, creasing his cheeks. He also had a slight squint, from an artificial eye.

'My father had a great sense of humour,' she said. 'He gave us that. We like singing. We like parties.'

Lidiya was fifty-three when her father died. He was buried in the cemetery above the village. Then she stopped talking and started rocking again with her hands to her head, her face slightly flushed. My interpreter stopped asking questions. I let the silence hang, to ease the story out of a room of memories where only ex-Soviets can go.

Several Japanese people who lived on Sakhalin chose to

Employees of the Dué House of Culture, a kind of Soviet clubhouse – described as a 'symbol of the state's attempt at "enlightenment" and edification' – in 1953.

stay after 1945, said Lidiya.* She talked about one man who taught them how to collect crustaceans from a sea cave – a delicacy unknown to Russians – and an edible green fern from the forest. The Japanese man spoke bad Russian, and lived in Dué. He was kind, gentle, polite. Lidiya's father shared his fish with him.

Lidiya was still rocking. She seemed stressed, perhaps with the memory of those she had loved and lost resurfacing in the room. I couldn't tell if the Japanese man was a secret,

---

* Following Japan's defeat in the Second World War when they lost control of Sakhalin to the USSR, the repatriation process began from South Sakhalin, which had been under Japanese rule since 1905. Around 400,000 people left. The Japanese inhabitants who stayed on became known as the 'remaining' or 'unreturned'. Taisho Nakayama, 'Japanese society on Karafuto' in Svetlana Paichadze and Philip A. Seaton (eds) *Voices from the Shifting Russo-Japanese Border* (London and New York: Routledge, 2015).

a stowaway. He was not. She was sad simply because happier days were gone, her grief perhaps more acute given it was Russia Day – a holiday soaked in nostalgia, and a reminder of the fall of the Soviet Union, when the whole country pays tribute to their nation. She said the Japanese man was buried in Dué's old cemetery, in an unmarked grave. He lay near her father, and her beloved husband. Then her body crumpled, like that of an inconsolable child, the divide between her experience and mine as huge as the line of Solzhenitsyn's: 'Can a man who's warm understand one who's freezing?'

Lidiya agreed to show me the way to the old Dué graveyard. We drove past the burnt-out home that her late husband had refused to leave. He had died of a heart attack four years before, when most of Dué's last hangers-on left the community entirely, or retreated into the newer apartment blocks. Then we turned up a stone track that wound through the taiga behind the sea. In Chekhov's time, this was where women used to sell their bodies, and where escaped convicts would ambush the foolish. Not many people passed by any more. The undergrowth was too thick, the path treacherous with ruts.

At the cemetery, Lidiya took me to the graves of her father and husband. Both were marked by the same fresh narcissi I had noticed in her home. Both were clean, unlike the abandoned headstones on every other side, or the pits and hillocks Doroshevich described – graves of the unknown, marked with wordless sticks.

Lidiya pointed to a stately tree bursting like a shuttlecock out of the ground. Somewhere beneath its canopy were the bones of the Japanese man who had been their friend, rooted into the place that had been his home, living among the progeny of exiles and communist believers in a godforsaken place on the edge of a scum-scuffed sea. I had come to Sakhalin wanting to find Mrs E's Becker, or at least something which spoke of Chekhov's time when Russian piano culture had been thriving across the Empire. I had found love and humanity instead – in the last house at the end of the last street at the dead end of Russia, where at one point in history, there had been killing on the darkest scale. I left Dué in extreme discomfort from ravaging mosquito bites. I said goodbye to Grigory Smekalov, who on my drive back out to the train station said that people had been seen following me around town. Yet in spite of everything sinister about Sakhalin, I felt a profound affection for the image of a fiddle made with stolen horsehair, and Lidiya's precious narcissus standing strong in a shaft of Siberian light.

PART TWO
Broken Chords
1917–1991

'Reality is incomprehensible and abhorrent, but there is always the hope that it is nothing but a filthy covering behind which is a high mystery. Perhaps the occasional glimpses of beauty in Nature, man and art are simply mysterious pointers towards something which exists eternally in some other sphere and beckons man to itself, filling him with hope?'

– Anatoly Lunacharsky, *On Literature and Art*

'I am not sure that in the kind of world in which we are living and with the kind of thinking we are bound to follow, we can regain these things exactly as if they had never been lost; but we can try to become aware of their existence and importance.'

– Claude Lévi-Strauss, *Myth and Meaning*

'And someday in the future, this Archipelago, its air, and the bones of its inhabitants, frozen in a lens of ice, will be discovered by our descendants like some improbable salamander.'

– Aleksandr Solzhenitsyn, *The Gulag Archipelago*

8

The Last Tsar's Piano:
The Urals

I N ST PETERSBURG DURING the first winter of my search, I had gone to find a mid-nineteenth-century oil on canvas by Georg Wilhelm Timm depicting the 1825 Decembrist Revolt. Completed in the reign of Tsar Nicholas I to commemorate loyalist regiments, it was stored in the Hermitage Repository, a vast overflow of the state collections, in the city suburbs. Walking through dull grey corridors with security codes and cameras, I reached room B5, where the painting stood against the wall, surrounded by images of well-fed burghers, grey-hounds and glossy thoroughbreds.

You could taste the savage cold in the canvas. The sky was brooding grey. Snow was being kicked up by horses galloping for the Senate, the public jostling for a view of the cavalry, including a man in a fur hat with a violin sticking out from his coat. The violence, however, was kept off stage. Timm's painting depicted the Romanov regime as majestic, elegant and above all legitimate, the crowd patriotically doffing their hats to the Tsar's protectors.

On my way out, the curator took me into his office, where paintings were piled in stacks. On the floor was a full-length portrait of Tsar Alexander II lying on its side. His face had been vandalized in the ferocity of the 1917 October Revolution, and never restored. I counted the bayonet holes in the canvas: one in his right eye, three in the forehead and a pierced throat. The violence was visceral and well preserved, each stabbing driven into the painting with an intent both utterly unknowable and profoundly present, a reminder that Russia could no more escape its past than I could escape the victim's stare.

The end of the Russian Empire came more quickly than anyone could have predicted in a country creaking under the pressure of economic, military and political collapse. The 1905 Russo-Japanese War had cost Russia dearly. Pogroms – the organized killing of Jews in Russia and Eastern Europe – were running out of control in the Pale of Settlement, a giant ghetto in Russia's Western Provinces where Jews had been forced to live under discriminatory laws since Catherine the Great. Russia's 'Little Father', as Tsar Nicholas II was known by the devout, had earned himself a new nickname, 'Nicholas the

Close up of the mutilated portrait of the last Tsar's grandfather, Alexander II. The State Hermitage Museum, St Petersburg.

Bloody', in response to his violent suppression of a peaceful protest in January 1905. This event stirred dissent on an unprecedented level. As a result, the 'soviet', or council, appeared, representing the rights of workers. A year later, Nicholas was forced to make concessions by opening Russia's first elected assembly, the State Duma, even if this turned out to be more like lip service than a truly significant shift in power.

Politically weak-minded, the Tsar's popularity fell even further the more his family pulled towards the Siberian 'holy man' and faith healer Grigory Rasputin – the Romanovs' reviled confidant, who had risen to power through an uncanny ability to alleviate the discomforts of the Romanov heir, the Tsarevich Aleksei, whose haemophilia was so debilitating that even a carriage ride could trigger fatal bleeding. Rasputin had such an intensely intoxicating effect on the Tsarina, people feared his sinister influence all over Russia. Yet the Romanovs, still living in their gilded bubble, kept Rasputin closer to them than the country's newly elected ministers until his murder in December 1916.*

Two months later, on 23 February 1917, more mass protests broke out in the capital – a people's uprising driven by drastic food and fuel shortages compounded by Russia's involvement in the First World War. On 2 March 1917, Nicholas was forced to abdicate. The imperial family were at first confined to their palace outside the capital, until the provisional government and its rival for power, the Petrograd Soviet, made the decision to remove the Romanovs from the gathering revolutionary ferment. On the morning of 1 August 1917, Nicholas, his wife, four daughters, the sickly Tsarevich, and forty-five retainers began their journey to Siberia. They travelled in a first-class carriage of the same company that operated the luxurious Trans-Siberian tourist trains, to spend the autumn and winter of 1917 under house arrest at the Governor's House in Tobolsk.

Stuck in Siberia, the last Tsar therefore didn't witness the October Revolution, nor Lenin and the Bolsheviks' seizure of

---

* The British historian Orlando Figes tells a curious story about how Rasputin's embalmed body, originally buried in the grounds of the Tsarskoe Selo palace complex outside St Petersburg, was dug up after the Revolution, carried off in an old piano, and taken into the forest to be burnt by soldiers. *A People's Tragedy: The Russian Revolution* (London: Jonathan Cape, 1996).

The last of the Romanovs, photographed in 1913.

power from the provisional government. The family's concerns turned towards their narrowing domestic world instead. The Tsarina played the piano. The Tsar cut wood in the garden. For fresh air, the children sat outside on the roof of their prison.

As the Bolsheviks' power increased, the family's few remaining privileges were removed. Cases of wine sent from Petrograd were emptied into the river beneath Tobolsk by guards. The Tsar and his son were no longer allowed to wear their epaulettes. Visits to church were banned. As winter began to lock in Tobolsk with the seasonal freeze, the children put on plays, dreaming up fantastic worlds as news from outside became harder to come by under the darkening skies of a country's violent disintegration.

Back in Petrograd, the American journalist John Reed described the meltdown of civil society. He wrote about electricity shortages, robberies, breadlines and servant problems.

The imperial family taking fresh air on the roof at the Governor's House in Tobolsk.

Waiters who had joined the class struggle were refusing tips. Revolution wasn't the time to be eating out. Nor was it a time for music. 'I know nothing greater than the *Appassionata*, I'd like to listen to it every day,' wrote Lenin to the author Maxim Gorky. 'It's beautiful, superhuman music . . . But I can't listen to music too often, it affects the nerves, makes you want to say kind, silly things, to stroke the heads of the people who, living in a terrible hell, can create such a beauty.'

As political chaos spread out of the capital, instruments were being stolen, sold to foreigners or burnt as firewood. Noble families were saving what they could, huddled up around their few remaining possessions, including instruments too big to move. Grand pianos were being driven around the city on the back of trucks to propagandize 'live' to the masses. 'Drag pianos out onto the streets,' exhorted the poet Vladimir Mayakovsky as the new ideas began to spread: 'Beat them until they fall to pieces.'

The nineteenth-century piano factories, which were already faltering due to a dramatic fall-off in demand during the First World War, came to a standstill. Becker ceased output. The Diederichs factory was reduced to ten men – a situation compounded by trade embargos imposed by European countries during the civil war, when production fell through the floor. Musicians were fleeing Russia, apprehensive of the shifting social order. Sergei Rachmaninoff, the country's most prestigious composer, left for the United States in December 1917, and Sergei Prokofiev emigrated to America in May the following year.* Out of necessity, some musicians kept on performing for new audiences of workers and civil servants. Many more fell silent. 'We are all either consumed by ceaseless activity, or else we retreat into ourselves, in order to find an interior equilibrium that will allow us to stand firm in all the confusion about us,' wrote the music publisher Mitrofan Belyayev.

It is astonishing that not everything was destroyed in these dark days of revolution. This was because of the immediate, prescient actions taken by Lenin to protect the country's enormous cultural wealth. On day three of the October

---

* There were many musicians who supported the Bolsheviks, only to regret their decision later. The Futurist composer Arthur Lourié stayed and joined the revolutionary cause full of hope; in 1918, he was appointed head of the music division of the People's Commissariat of Enlightenment. But when he went to visit Berlin in 1922, Lourié never returned home. Prokofiev, on the other hand, returned to Russia permanently in 1936.

Revolution, Lenin appointed the critic and playwright Anatoly Lunacharsky as Commissar of Enlightenment – an Orwellian-sounding title for a sensitive, artistic man whose numerous roles as head of the Soviet Ministry of Arts included shoring up the country's cultural treasures. Lunacharsky needed to stem the flow of instruments out of Russia; he needed to nationalize them, like the piano factories, making them state rather than private property.

Before long, a young cellist called Viktor Kubatsky was lending Lunacharsky an enthusiastic hand, making house visits to gather the best instruments in private ownership. Kubatsky was given his own train and soldiers to help him execute orders. His sweep included a cello made by Nicolò Amati, which was discovered in a derelict mansion in the Crimea, and four Stradivarius violins confiscated from an old count; they were handed over only after the count performed one last melancholy solo dressed in his ceremonial military uniform. These state treasures now form a significant part of Russia's two principal collections of musical instruments. Remarkably, not a single piece in either collection has since been lost, not even during the Nazis' Siege of Leningrad, when the number of civilian casualties ran to nearly four times more than the total of bombing victims in Nagasaki and Hiroshima combined – a siege so devastating not even the city's cat population survived.*

For the Romanovs languishing in Siberia, it was hard to know what might happen to them as the country lurched from

---

* Cats provided a food source for a starving populace during the Leningrad Siege. The Hermitage cats, however, were saved in order to keep the treasures of the museum safe from mice.

their old regime to its extreme opposite. The Bolsheviks – by now the dominant political power in the capital following the October Revolution – became increasingly concerned that for as long as the royal family remained alive, factions among pro-royalist Whites had a rallying call in the Tsar to draw popular support. On 26 April 1918, Nicholas, his wife and their third daughter, the eighteen-year-old Grand Duchess Maria, were escorted from Tobolsk to Ekaterinburg in the Ural Mountains and placed under much stricter bondage inside a new place of house arrest. Because the Tsarevich was too ill to travel with his parents, he followed three weeks later with the rest of his siblings and a few remaining loyal retainers. This time, the family's guards were commanded by the hard-line Ekaterinburg Soviet, who were much less sympathetic than the family's Tobolsk jailers.

The family were locked inside the Ipatiev House in Ekaterinburg's city centre. In its early days, before it was renamed the House of Special Purpose by their Bolshevik captors, it had been home to Pyotr Davydov, a dramatic tenor and graduate of the St Petersburg Conservatory. Later it was bought by Nikolai Ipatiev, a private railway contractor of considerable wealth. The family were assigned four rooms. The rest of the building was occupied by their guards. Heavy iron bars had been fastened across the windows, and the plate glass painted out white so the prisoners couldn't even see a bird flying. The Romanovs were allowed to breathe fresh air for an hour or less each day in the small garden to the rear, which was surrounded by a high, hastily erected fence. Food was scant: black bread for breakfast, while all the Empress ate was macaroni.

At least there was a grand piano – an ebony instrument

noted in an inventory taken by a Soviet official on 27 April 1918 just before the imperial family's arrival. The piano occupied the drawing room, although it was later moved upstairs to the commandant's room. It was still there after the Tsar and his family had been executed, according to a report by Nikolai Sokolov, the Whites' criminal investigator into the Romanov assassinations, who picked over the evidence when the killers fled Ekaterinburg. He noted that a Russian-made Schröder had been pushed into the right-hand corner of the room. On top of the piano were several boxes, a scent bottle, sewing threads and a type-lined office ledger. Downstairs in a narrow basement, bullet holes from the executions still marked the walls – scars betraying little of the magnitude of events when three hundred years of Romanov rule came to their final, cataclysmic end.

It occurred soon after midnight on 17 July 1918. Tsar Nicholas II, his wife Alexandra, their five children and four remaining retainers, including the family doctor and a maid-servant, were herded into the basement. They were faced by three principal executioners, and seven guards. The Tsarevich, who was sick, and his mother, who complained, were given chairs.

The Bolsheviks shot the Tsar first, striking him in the chest before unleashing a fusillade of bullets which filled the room with smoke. One of the murderers vomited. Another was injured in the arm by a ricocheting bullet. The executioners let the smoke settle, then shot the Tsarevich. The boy crumpled from his chair to the floor, broken but still breathing. When the bullets didn't appear to penetrate the other children's bodies, the executioners resorted to knives and bayonets, slipping about a room pooled with blood. It took a full twenty minutes to kill them all. The youngest daughter, Anastasia, was the last Romanov to die, her skull crushed by rifle butts.

Unbeknown to their executioners, the girls' corsets had been tightly sewn with jewels before they had left Petrograd. The diamonds protected them like bulletproof vests, with fragments of jewellery later found scattered in a Urals mineshaft a few miles to the city's north-west, where the bodies were first interred. Precious stones and pearls, hacked and tarnished by fire, had been trampled underfoot, along with splinters of glass from the Empress's spectacles, the family doctor's false teeth, and eggshells from the executioners' picnic. Of the Romanovs' entourage present that night, the only survivor was the Tsarevich's spaniel, Joy. The dog turned up a few days after the execution. It was standing half-starved in the Ipatiev House courtyard. As for the family's other lapdog, its head had been smashed with a rifle, just like Anastasia's, and thrown into the same disused mine as the family, deep in a Urals forest.

After the slaughter, the Bolsheviks tried to destroy the evidence before abandoning Ekaterinburg ahead of the Whites who were rapidly gaining ground. Sokolov's report described the scene. The Ipatiev House had been ransacked, the fireplaces littered with everything deemed not worth stealing. Papers, plates, even the Tsar's precious epaulettes, which he hadn't been allowed to wear during his imprisonment, were thrown into the flames. But neither the cake of soap, nor the sheets bearing the imperial monogram were destroyed – and neither was the last piano the Romanovs ever played.

*

That's why I came to Ekaterinburg – to see if I could track down this instrument because of its profound relevance at the time of the assassinations when the Russian Empire died and the Soviet state was born. This city on the brink of Europe and Asia felt too significant to pass through on a train, too much of a geographical and historical turning point. Then I entered the station cafeteria, and was so unnerved by an encounter with a bearded priest, I wanted to leave in the same moment I arrived. He crossed himself every time he caught my eye. He smelled of mould, and was followed by a silent wife in a black headscarf and full-length tunic. She had the deadest skin I had ever seen on a living human being. Whenever he spoke to her, she tautened and withdrew, as a snail into its shell.

It was as if the city was contaminated: the mangy dogs with ribby coats, the parking lots where not even weeds seemed to put out any shoots, the hotel elevator where the air felt too close to share it with a troupe of Russian weightlifters. I was quick to judge, but then my interpreter was reluctant to come. She had spent her childhood in Ekaterinburg. During perestroika, her mother, a laboratory assistant, sold cigarettes one by one in a booth at the tram stop. These were deadbeat, joyless years, when heroin took hold in their community. She described the glazed eyes and foot-shuffling on her journeys to and from school. She described how lives were worn thin by a city she considered innately cruel. It made complete sense that Ekaterinburg was the place of the Romanov executions, she said; its spirit had always oppressed her.

There were times, however, when the imperial murders were considered a feather in Ekaterinburg's cap. Within a decade of the killings, the Ipatiev House was turned into a

Tourists and officials visiting the cellar of the Ipatiev House in 1927.

Museum of Revolution, which told the Bolsheviks' narrative of the Romanov deaths.

In 1977, when a cultural institute occupied half the building, a local theatre group staged a play in the Ipatiev cellars. It was a private performance for family and friends. The play was *The House of Bernarda Alba* by the Spanish writer Federico García Lorca in which an entire family lives in the shadow of a domineering mother, until one of the daughters hangs herself. In a group portrait taken in 1977, the eleven actors pose beside a noose-like contraption.

Although the very room where the blood was spilt was not used, looking at these pictures through the lens of what we now know happened to the Romanovs induces a powerful response: the composition of the photograph is still haunted by the image of the cellars as a place of execution – a story the

The basement of the Ipatiev House after the executions.

Rehearsals for a private performance of The House of Bernarda Alba *in the Ipatiev basement, photographed in 1977 by Vitaly Shitov, a photojournalist who spent forty years researching the story of the Ipatiev House.*

Soviet authorities first extolled when they turned the Ipatiev House into a kind of shrine and renamed it the House of the People's Revolt. Later, as Russians came to mourn the royal family, the Soviets did everything they could to excise events from national memory, even wiping the executions from history books. But regicide isn't easy to forget. So when the Ipatiev House was being cited as the location of the Romanov murders in propaganda by anti-Soviet circles in the West, the authorities ordered the house to be destroyed.

Even if the house was gone, I still hoped the Ipatiev piano might be somewhere in the city, its keys holding on to the memory of the last of the Romanov melodies described by the guards, who recalled sacred songs and women singing. They remembered secular pieces, too, which were always melancholy.

The demolition of the Ipatiev House in September 1977, photographed by Vitaly Shitov. He was the only person, aside from officials inside the cordon, to photograph its destruction. He used a hidden camera, recording events from a bus some twenty metres away.

The music was different in the commandant's room, where the drunk guards made a racket banging on the instrument (the piano was moved from the hall, according to Nicholas's diary). The jailers chose music which was deliberately offensive: songs like 'You Fell as a Victim in the Struggle', or 'Let Us Forget the Old World'. Prince Lvov, the first prime minister after the Tsar's abdication, was in Ekaterinburg at the same time as the Romanovs. While not a reliable witness, Lvov told a more sinister version of events: in the evenings, the guards bullied the Tsar's daughters to play the piano. This claim was later substantiated by a peasant woman who lived with one of the soldiers.

But what of the instrument they played? My most promising lead was a local tuner who had been trying to make enough money to restore the piano he believed was in the Ipatiev House at the time of the murders: a Bechstein grand piano pushed up against the back wall of his dusty Ekaterinburg warehouse. Together we extracted a date from its keyboard frame – 8 April 1921 – and the signature of a tuner well known in the city at the time. The words 'House of Revolution' were written in black ink.

At Ekaterinburg's newly constructed Church on the Blood, built on the site of the Ipatiev House, there was a Becker grand piano, serial number 15177, in the museum's conference hall next door. The museum's official guide said he believed that the Becker had come with the Romanovs to Siberia all the way from Petrograd. He said a member of the Austrian royal family gave it to the Tsar. It ended up in the Siberian city of Tobolsk, where the Romanovs were incarcerated, before it was sold to the church by a vet. The story was compelling, but I couldn't verify it. There was no evidence of a piano leaving

Petrograd on the imperial train – not a whiff of music, in fact, beyond a portable gramophone, and the piano Nicholas mentions in a diary entry. The instrument belonged to the steamer the family used for the last part of their journey to Tobolsk.

When I repeated the claims of the official guide to a city archivist, he scoffed: 'Our church loves beautiful legends.' When I told it to an Ekaterinburg antiques specialist, he tipped back in his chair and sighed. He couldn't lead me to the definitive piano – possibilities, yes – but he could show me a plate purchased from descendants of a cleaner who worked in the Ipatiev House during the Romanovs' imprisonment. The cleaner's husband, a Bolshevik sympathizer, had wanted to smash the crockery. That wouldn't happen now, he said. The Romanovs were fashionable again; there were some useful principles in Russia's imperial history that suited the present political culture. 'Revolution. Civil war. The Great Patriotic War. The migrations of people. It's surprising that out of all that history we can save a single atom,' he said, 'but ideas have survived.'

'I can find you many, many pianos from the Ipatiev House,' said one of the city's museum directors. 'The only thing that was saved on the day the house was destroyed was the fireplace and a stair rail.'

And bricks, said one of his colleagues. Someone who witnessed the mansion's demolition took a brick from the site. He cut it into little pieces, and sold them off as relics.

The director warned me to be cautious. 'In Pompeii tourists take away pieces of stone as keepsakes,' he said. 'I read somewhere that the Italians bring these stones in on lorries and scatter them to protect the true relics.'

Not long after this conversation, when I was about to give up on Ekaterinburg, I received news that the man who had first discovered the Romanov remains in the forest outside the city had agreed to meet me. His name was Aleksandr Avdonin. I had been told he knew more about the end of the Romanovs than anyone else – expertise I had originally pursued in the hope it might extend to the lost piano. An academic in geological and mineralogical science, he kept a low profile. My interpreter, who had pressed hard for the meeting, supposed music must have appeared a relatively neutral approach.

Aleksandr Avdonin lives in an attractive wooden cottage beside a river, not far from the city outskirts. You can tell the home belongs to a geologist. In a kitchen as tidy as the cabin of a sailing boat, there is a collection of rock crystals, chunks of malachite, and a bowl of sky-coloured marble stones polished into the shape of eggs.

Galina, Aleksandr's wife, showed me to my seat at the kitchen table. As she made a large pot of tea, I explained I was looking for a specific piano – the Ipatiev grand.

Galina said she used to have a piano – a Soviet-made Red October instrument, serial number 48 if she recalled correctly, but she had given it away a few years ago.

But what did she know of pre-Revolution instruments?

The old pianos had almost all gone, she said as she cut the ham into thick slices, arranged small pastries on a paper doily, and Aleksandr entered the room. He wore a cream roll-neck sweater with a white Adidas sports jacket. He had white, thinning hair and was clearly weary. He had recently been ill, said his wife.

We ate spoonfuls of berries from the woods, which were just like the pickings of wild strawberries Aleksandr collected before breakfast when he was young. He loved the Urals, he said; it was the region where he was born, in 1932. He came from a poor family of five. In his childhood, they lived in a railway workers' barracks close to the station in Ekaterinburg where the Romanovs had disembarked from their final train journey – a mild and tender family is how people described them when they witnessed their arrival in the city. Aleksandr was interested in this history, but with the official silence around the Romanov murders, he kept his curiosity to himself.

When I asked Aleksandr if he knew where the Ipatiev piano might have ended up, the conversation digressed. He looked out of the window as the light cast a golden glint across the table on to the bowl of jam. All the rivers in the Urals flow east, he said. But not the one that runs close to their house. In March the river is frozen. Only after the melt does the river flow hard and fast to the west. There was something he liked about this fact, about living on the great Eurasian divide. He talked about Magnitogorsk, another city in the southern Urals. When he was younger, they watched the cinema in Europe, and had dinner in Asia. He turned to his wife.

'You remember that?' he asked.

Aleksandr said he had visited the Ipatiev House before it was destroyed. As he was growing up, he had also met and talked to people who had been present in Ekaterinburg shortly after the executions. He had spoken with a local man who as a fifteen-year-old boy had taken part in a search for traces of the royal family, carried out under the aegis of the Ekaterinburg District Court after the White Army had occupied the city.

Aleksandr had also read a book which had slipped the censors' net – a bibliographical rarity called *Last Days of the Romanovs*, written in 1926 (then withdrawn and destroyed) by the chairman of the Ekaterinburg Soviet during the period of revolution. Although the chairman did not participate directly, the circumstances of the massacre would have presumably been well known to him. This report said that Sokolov failed to find the grave of the Romanovs because what was left of the corpses, which didn't burn, was buried in a site which investigators didn't excavate. Then there was a poem by Mayakovsky, which hinted at the real site of the bodies: 'nine versts', or six miles, past Iset mines and cliffs. Mayakovsky, it seemed, had been shown the site by a member of the City Executive Committee, who had acted as the poet's tour guide in 1928.

These leads indicated that Sokolov's original report may have been wrong when he had first described the place where it was assumed the bodies were disposed of – a mineshaft at Ganina Yama, nine miles outside the city. Among other fragments, Sokolov found the Empress's emerald crucifix, two pieces of skin and a severed finger, but no substantial remains. Sokolov concluded the bodies had been dismembered, burnt and dissolved in sulphuric acid there and then in an attempt to destroy the evidence.

Sokolov, it turned out, had based his original conclusion on a number of assumptions. The bodies were initially thrown down the Ganina Yama mineshaft on the night of the assassinations as Sokolov more or less described, but the hole was shallower than the killers had thought. Two days later, the murderers had in fact moved the bodies three miles to the west, to a swampy meadow near Railway Crossing 184 on the Old

Koptyaki Road, also known as Pig's Meadow. This was where the murderers attempted a second cremation, and used sulphuric acid to do away with the evidence. What was left, including the skulls, was buried in a shallow grave under railway sleepers. This is how the alternative version of events goes – a version revealed by a chain of discoveries that began to unravel in the 1970s.

It started with a meeting in Ekaterinburg during the summer of 1976 with a nationally famous screenwriter, Geli Ryabov, who was also a press officer at the Ministry of Internal Affairs. According to Aleksandr, Ryabov suggested they should look for the Romanov remains. Aleksandr was a good person to lean on; his work as a geologist meant he was deeply familiar with these Ural forests. Discretion, however, was paramount. Sensitivities around the Romanov story were running high. Only a year after this meeting, the Ipatiev House was bulldozed to the ground. If the party was so quick to destroy evidence of the Tsar's place of execution, then there would be more trouble if another burial site was identified.

On 1 June 1979, the secret search party began to dig at Pig's Meadow. They removed the railway sleepers and dug out three skulls. As Aleksandr talked, I couldn't stop thinking how it must have felt to touch this history; forever after, it must have been like sleeping in the presence of unquiet ghosts. Galina said that her husband was so stressed by the discovery that he didn't speak for a couple of months.

Two skulls went with Ryabov to Moscow for expert examination. One stayed in Ekaterinburg. The investigation was highly secretive, wrapped up in all sorts of feelings I found hard to pull clearly out of the conversation, given the layers of

One of the murderers, Pyotr Ermakov, photographed in the twenties standing on railway sleepers in the forest where the Romanovs were buried. It's not known who took the image, nor who wrote the words on the back of the picture: 'Place where the Romanovs were burned.'

meaning too untouchable for an outsider to understand. Then a year later, in July 1980, all the findings were returned to their swampy grave. The discovery was locked back down with the gravity of what they had found lying heavily upon their conscience for another nine years. Occasionally, Aleksandr would walk past Pig's Meadow to see if anyone else had dug. No one was to speak of it: it was still too dangerous. As for all Aleksandr's notes, he didn't dare keep them at his home, so took them to the house of a trusted friend for safekeeping – a detail given in the book he later wrote, documenting every part of the search. It is an important testimony given the controversy which was unleashed in 1989 when the discovery at Pig's Meadow was leaked to a Russian newspaper, and this dramatic switch of burial place ricocheted through every stratum of the country's political, civil and religious society.

The news seemed to divide everybody: the Orthodox faithful, royalists, journalists and scientists trying to make sense of this unfinished chapter in Russia's violent history. Boris Yeltsin – born near Ekaterinburg, and by this time a member of the Politburo, the Soviet Union's ruling body – argued for the rehabilitation of the Romanovs. Forensic DNA specialists, both foreign and domestic, got involved. Further investigations were made, revealing many new findings and yet more family remains, with an official state exhumation of the Pig's Meadow site in 1991. The Russian Orthodox Church, however, couldn't agree that the discoveries were conclusive. There were arguments over the Romanovs' canonization status and how to remember and glorify the dead. Books were written. Documentaries were made. Everyone had an opinion – they still do.* In 2001 the Church then built a grand monastery and place of pilgrimage at Ganina Yama – effectively committing to the simpler version of events that went by the original Sokolov report, which asserted that Ganina Yama was where the bodies had dissolved into the earth.

Galina got up from the table and went to fetch Aleksandr's book from a shelf. She also handed me a handwritten card, cut from a box of tea bags, on which was written a simple

* My last correspondence with a spokesman for the Russian Orthodox Church in March 2019: 'The Church is ready to wait for the results as long as it might happen. For us the most important thing is that the results are accepted by everyone, so they don't divide the Orthodox believers into those who accept and those who do not accept the remains.'

sentence: 'A scientist defends his invention* when he is absolutely certain or sure in the correctness of his research.'

'The rest,' she said, 'is pseudo-scientific ignorance.'

I had come to the Urals to find the Tsar's last piano. Instead I had found myself trying to make sense of a bizarre knot in the nation's relationship with its past. I wanted to listen to Aleksandr talk, an elegant, erudite man who said he didn't make the investigation out of a desire for fame, wealth or political gain. I found myself wanting to understand his motivations.

'The truth was a burden I felt from childhood,' said Aleksandr. 'Historical truth had not been established, and it needs to be finished.'

Over one more cup of tea, I told Aleksandr I had found three instruments with possible ties to the Ipatiev House. I described the Bechstein carrying the signature of the well-known Ekaterinburg piano tuner, with the words 'House of Revolution' written on the soundboard.

Aleksandr shook his head. He thought the piano I had found was interesting, but he believed it belonged to a different place. He started to talk again about how the forest was a place of sorrow. He was also exhausted. As I watched Galina take his hand, I realized we all need them in the end. Pivots. The fixed point on which a mechanism depends. The person or thing on which something hangs. Like a piano, movement is dependent on the stability of its fixed parts. When a key on a grand piano is pressed down, it sets in motion a small pivot movement that throws a felted hammer upwards to strike a

* It could say 'intention' or 'invention'. The handwriting is unclear, but the meaning is not.

string, or strings. Only with a stable pivot will the music ever sound.

The next day, before I left Ekaterinburg, I visited Ganina Yama with Nikolai Neuimin, head of the Romanov Memorial Hall, which is a branch of the city's regional history museum. Neuimin was present at another excavation at the Pig's Meadow site in 2007, when the remains of two of the missing children, the Tsarevich and his sister Maria, were found some seventy metres from Aleksandr Avdonin's original discovery. At the entrance to the Ganina Yama complex, we refused an official guide, and instead walked among the chapels dotted about the forest, their green roofs and golden crosses glinting through the trees.

There was scaffolding surrounding new additions, and a bronze sculpture of the five Romanov children wearing crowns. Groups of visitors came and went, including families on walking tours with priests. They stood by the sinkhole where the imperial family was first thrown, the depression's snowy surface stippled by the drip of water from overhanging boughs. The devout crossed themselves and prayed in an expression of religious conviction that my companion, Nikolai, didn't share.

Moving away from one of the tour groups, Nikolai started to talk about Pig's Meadow.

But someone had been listening.

Nikolai was pulled aside.

A church official warned him not to speak of the second grave.

We drove to the Pig's Meadow site nearby. At the end of a path which had been swept to the graves, Nikolai pulled out a set of photographs from his bag, including a black-and-white image of some of the remains as they were originally discovered.

We stood beside the simple metal cross above the railway sleepers, which was strung with a white, red and pink plastic wreath. At the base of the cross someone had hammered a small bronze plaque: 'The Children. Good Night. God Bless.'

In the snow, I could see the colour of Aleksandr Avdonin's hair, which Galina said turned shock-white two days after the discovery of the skulls. In the quivering forest, I could hear the shouts of the killers and the victims. Beneath the Urals' black soil, I could feel the questions reverberating deep inside Russia's conscience, like the last working key on the Ipatiev piano hitting a broken pivot and not making any sound. My conscience also hummed and hawed. Something in me found it violently exciting to have stepped so close to the end of the Russian Empire; every hint of a lost piano encouraged my ambitions, as if the historic instruments with state stories somehow carried a deeper timbre. I also felt ashamed, as if I had joined the ranks of the early nosy parkers, the 'amateur Sherlocks or Pushfuls', which were the words the British journalist Robert Wilton gave to the people thirsting for information about the murders in his controversial account written soon after they had occurred. As Galina had pointed out when we had met, my search for a piano was different to the kind of search a scientist undertakes. I had come looking for a specific instrument, but I was also interested in the symbolic connections of my quest. Now as I stood beside the cross, I was struck by an overwhelming sense of sadness. Even if I had found the Tsar's last instrument, how could such a piano ever sing again? There was too much tragedy in it. I knew I was chasing the impossible, looking for an object with clear, undisputed provenance in a country where Ipatiev crockery is fought over, bought and sold, where in spite of an abundance of facts, not even the location or identity of the Romanov remains are a universally accepted truth. Just find a piano with a pure sound, I told myself, something humble, human and loved.

9

The End of Everything:
The Altai Mountains

AT ONE OF THE most southerly points of Siberia, where the border crumples up against Central Asia's great belt of mountains, four countries converge: Russia, China, Mongolia and Kazakhstan, close to a plateau which locals call 'the End of Everything'. At some point in my search I needed to survey a route out of Russia into Mongolia. With a successful piano discovery, the Altai Mountains might provide a possible exit route. Aside from the border at Kiakhta, this was the only road into Mongolia open to foreigners.

I was feeling optimistic. Not only was my work with local radio and TV raising possibilities, but other research had thrown up reassuring traces of European piano culture making it out this far. In 1848, an English couple, Lucy and Thomas Atkinson, travelled through the Altai. Among their charming descriptions of frozen Winsor and Newton paints, and encounters with the Decembrists, they said the town of Barnaul was alive with pianos. The instruments belonged to the new industrialists cashing in on the Altai's nineteenth-century silver mines.

History showed that these mountains had also proved happy hunting grounds for those prepared to look. In 1825, the eminent German biologist Carl Friedrich von Ledebour, a narrow-faced plant-hunter with a slightly forward stoop, ventured into the Altai and extracted an impressive cache: forty-two chests of plants and seeds, and five hundred insects. Henry J. Elwes, a British naturalist remembered for his booming voice, made another significant haul. He gathered close to a thousand butterflies when the sun shone, and when it rained, he hunted the region's *Ovis ammon*, or Altai argali sheep, instead. But it was Russia's Prince Elim Pavlovich Demidoff – the richest man in the world – who made perhaps the biggest killing after he spotted some of the Altai's most alluring quarry in a London taxidermist's shop. In 1898, he bagged thirty-two of the largest wild sheep on the planet, each animal weighing more than two big men, a single horn if it were uncoiled measuring almost two metres in length.

Given their rugged isolation, the people of the Altai Mountains had a reputation for being confidently self-sufficient. With some good country for farming, it had a long history of attracting hardy migrants with their pot-bellied horses and

Clement St George Royds Littledale, a member of Demidoff's Altaian hunting party, trying out a yak for size.

cows tied to the tails of wagons. The region had also proved a good place for Russians to find refuge from the civil war, which ravaged the country from around the time of the Tsar's execution until 1922. I therefore reasoned that any pianos that had made it all the way out here were less likely to have been destroyed in a place where a quiet frontier spirit still endured. This was especially true of the region's edges, in the shadow of the Ukok Plateau, which holds some of the deepest layers of Siberian human history known to archaeologists. I wanted to explore this neck of mountains near the Altai's southern edge – specifically, a village called Ust-Koksa a couple of hundred miles from Ukok. There was a former Aeroflot navigator living here who had collected forty-one pianos and distributed them among local children living in the mountain communities. Like the Decembrists, he wanted to spread culture and education through Siberia's backcountry.

The collector was an enthusiastic bibliophile called Leonid Kaloshin. I thought it heroic that he had brought in not only tens of thousands of books, but also pianos from Moscow – all at his own cost – having been lured here by the esoteric philo-sophies of the Russian author Nicholas Roerich and his wife, Helena, whose spiritual writings drew him in even more. The Roerichs had spent the summer of 1926 in the Altai as part of a four-year painting and ethnographical expedition at a time when the graves of Red soldiers were still fresh from the coun-try's civil-war upheavals.

Nicholas Roerich, born in St Petersburg in 1874, was one of Russia's great twentieth-century polymaths. He first rose to prominence as an archaeologist, then as a set designer for the composer Igor Stravinsky, and Sergei Diaghilev, the impres-ario and founder of the Ballets Russes.* Roerich was a brilliant painter. His wife, Helena, was a talented pianist (her uncle was the Russian composer Modest Mussorgsky, who was one of the so-called 'Mighty Five'). The Roerichs were also deeply unconventional. When they ventured into Siberia, walking into the Altai Mountains accompanied by Wagner's music and a portable gramophone, they were searching for the mythical kingdom of Shambhala – the earthly paradise in Tibetan Bud-dhism. The couple's writings still bring followers here nearly a century later, people who not only share the Roerichs' belief in the existence of Shambhala, but also in the notion, much

---

* Their production of *The Rite of Spring*, which premiered in Paris in 1913 with Roerich's stage sets, was deemed scandalously avant-garde. It caused all sorts of trouble, with rumours of police being called to stop the hurling of missiles from the audience.

like the Decembrists, that only with the assistance of high culture, distributed beyond the city's elite theatres, concert halls and galleries, will humanity thrive. In the nineties, when Russians were suffering a crisis of faith, people began to migrate to the Altai from all over the country with the conviction that the Roerichs were right – that this region was some kind of Shangri-La, or Promised Land.

Paradise, however, has never been an easy place to get to. Ust-Koksa, where the Aeroflot captain lived, was a three-day journey from Novosibirsk, travelling through imposing territory with narrow saddles, chiselled cliffs and dangerous roads. The Altai was also a geopolitical hotspot. The Russians were building a new gas line through the region, linking Western Siberia to China. There was nervous talk among ecologists and locals, who were intent on ensuring any kind of developments steered clear of sacred ground. Wildlife and conservation activists were under scrutiny from authorities. An English writer poking around for pianos in these parts might look suspicious. At Biysk, a town midway on my Altaian journey, I therefore took advice, and picked up 'security'.

'Security's' name was Uncle Vitya – a geologist with friends in useful places, who knew a great deal about Roerich. Uncle Vitya was also acquainted with the Aeroflot navigator. He knew the criminals who once ran amok in the mountain villages. In the nineties, he had survived an attack when bandits attempted to knife him. I was travelling in January, which is a month of deep snow and road closures. I needed someone who knew the lie of the land.

I liked him immediately. Uncle Vitya sported a gnome-ish woollen hat from beneath which his thick curls constantly escaped. He waddled rather than walked, and wore sturdy glasses. Sitting in the car, his belly spread so wide that it was difficult to work the gear stick. There was something calming about his presence – a happy-go-lucky man with a generous double chin and cheeks that wobbled when he laughed. Uncle Vitya would become important to my travels in Siberia, like a kind of lucky charm. Whenever Uncle Vitya was with me, I felt safe. Whatever Uncle Vitya said, I trusted. He was warm and witty, his stories mixing myth, Soviet history and various random metallurgical observations.

We stopped every now and again to make offerings to the spirits – near springs, high passes and holy cairns – with Uncle Vitya's lulling voice the only thing I could hear across plains that spread out so far and wide, the roads vanished in the distance. We talked about scattered Soyuz rockets, and in the absolute whiteness of winter, how Siberia must be a perfect hunting ground for meteorites. If the stones lay on top of the snow cover, they could only have fallen from the cosmos. Uncle Vitya used to spend large amounts of time as a geologist in the field, which was when he first saw a yeti. These days, he lived in a housing block in Biysk, a town that once processed rocket fuel for the Russian cosmodrome in Kazakhstan, just across the border.

Isolated spots of the Altai are peppered with metal scraps jettisoned by Soviet spacecraft. There is one such piece, photographed in the Altai Republic in 2000, which stands upright like a chesspiece in a field. The image depicts two men on top of a crown of crumpled metal photographed at the very moment a butterfly storm is taking place. The creatures are swarming in a thick cloud of beating wings, the butterflies as white as snow. The image thrums with vibrations in the air, a rushing whirr against the Altai's summer flush of grass. The

Altaian space junk, shot by Norwegian photographer Jonas Bendiksen in 2000. The men in the image are collecting scrap metal from the crashed spacecraft. The white flecks are butterflies.

landscape feels like a kind of paradise, a throwback to an untamed planet – raw and unpopulated, the rocket the poisoned apple in a field of blooming life.

The farther we went into the mountains, the more insistent the feeling of nature's plenitude. The landscape had a thrumming, superabundant energy as we headed towards Belukha, among the highest peaks in Siberia. In Boris Pasternak's autobiography, the writer of *Doctor Zhivago* described the Russian composer Aleksandr Scriabin at the piano and 'the pitch of an unheard-of blending' – music that could also describe the colours of the Altaian landcape. The snow crust creaked when I waded into drifts as deep as my thighs. We crossed narrow bridges strung with baubles of snow dangling off scoops of wire. Above the skirts of forest which draped the mountains, the sky turned from white to pink. When snow began to fall, the flakes looked like diamond dust, then splinters of trembling gold. The Altai is a wild and secretive place, said Uncle Vitya. He talked about a group of Freemasons rumoured to be building 'Moon Cities' in the mountains, and how he, too, was filling his dacha's basement up to its roof with potatoes to see him through the Apocalypse. He talked of Roerich again, who considered the Altai a kind of 'melting pot of nations'.

The Russian belief in mysticism can get to you sometimes, especially on the edge of Siberia where superstitions seem to lurk under every boulder. *A piano, a piano*, I kept telling myself; I needed to keep the object front of mind, not the symbolism Russians can read into every experience, which was pulling me in with the same ease as Uncle Vitya's stories. If a photographer could come upon a piece of space junk in the Altai at the very moment a butterfly storm was taking place, then surely I would find an instrument for Odgerel.

'Of course you'll be successful,' nodded Uncle Vitya with conviction: 'You'll not only find music in the Altai,' he said reassuringly, 'but a universe beyond perception.'

We entered a river valley shrouded in winter – a slumbering landscape threaded by a stream. When crystals fell from the feathered branches, it felt like I was walking into a cloudburst. We crossed high-altitude plains and zigzagged down switchbacks – in Russian, nicknamed 'a mother-in-law's tongue'. We passed ancient standing stones that marked our slippage from modern Russia. Familiar place names gave way to different sounds as we travelled towards an older, Turkic etymology, in words which revealed the extraordinary layers of ethnic history in the Altai, where a Bronze Age civilization developed some three thousand years ago and began to spread outwards with man's mastery of the horse.

The Altai's roots run as far back as the Pazyryks, a Scythian tribe who invented saddles, said Uncle Vitya, as well as the Huns, Uyghurs and Mongols. The stories of human prehistory in these mountains make the Altai another cradle of mankind. In caves hollowed out like honeycombs, scientists have discovered relics of a subspecies of human more than a hundred thousand years old. A finger bone here, a child's tooth there. In all, just four tiny specimens of 'Denisovan Man' have ever been found.

That this relic DNA endures not only in Altaian bone fragments but also in modern-day Oceania is spectacular testimony to the extent of hominin migration, and the fact different subspecies of prehistoric humans likely interbred. The discoveries also underline the advantages of Siberia's remoteness, implying how much more is still left uncovered. Then there is Siberia's protective permafrost. The land functions like a dry freezer, preserving the mummies of early nomadic tribes which scientists keep uncovering from the Altai's *kurgans*, or underground tombs. These chambers, filled with objects to support the deceased on their next journey, are treasure troves of story, with the best of them the Ukok Princess, a Scythian mummy buried some two thousand five hundred years ago with the conviction that her death was a continuation of her life. Six horses were found on top of her funerary chamber. Beside her head, there was a meal of mutton still smelling of the cooking juices. The Ukok Princess – found lying sideways 'like a sleeping child' – had been sent on her way with a bag of cosmetics, a yellow silk top with maroon piping, and flakes of gold. She shouldn't have been disturbed, say local naysayers;

it was a profane meddling with worlds we don't understand. The Altai's mummies are still of this world, which is why every time an ice-plugged tomb is opened up, earthquakes seem to follow. We are interfering with a lost mythology written into the tattoos of these ancient people, each gaunt corpse commanding a presence far larger than skin and bone, weaving together this world and the afterlife. The patterns curl and loop over sinewy bodies the colour of soaked leather: a reindeer here, a bird's wing there; a tiger with claws and stripes cut like a shadow puppet; and the women, beautiful in plumes of silk, who lived and fought like men.

Then another dose of tough Siberian reality. On our way to meet the Aeroflot navigator, we stopped to meet a piano tuner who was also a self-taught rock musician. He owned a Becker grand, dating from the 1890s, which he had picked up after a flood in a local music school. Descended from Old Believers, he was fixing the piano up to sell. We talked about Freddie Mercury, while sharing bread and pickles in a room short of seats. He talked about the Led Zeppelin records that got him into music in the first place. When American rock was hard to find during Soviet times, 'we listened to it hidden-ly', he said.

Hidden-ly. The word seemed to describe the heart of the Altai, like the vibration inside the butterfly storm, or what the English poet Shelley called the 'gleams of a remoter world'. *Hidden-ly* was a way of life in these mountains, said Uncle Vitya. It was why Leonid Kaloshin, the Aeroflot navigator, came to live here in the first place, in a cabin on a hill at the head of Ust-Koksa village.

Leonid seemed pleased to see me when he bounded down the steps to the door. He was burly, with a slim bandana which kept his unkempt hair off his vigorous face. His handshake was firm and matter-of-fact, and his eyes a twinkling grey. He was charismatic, over seventy years old, but looked fifty as he leapt back up his rickety stairs to the warren of rooms and corridors of his house.

A kitchen and bed were squeezed in among piles of books. Shelves curled out of the main living area past a small stove into a back room with narrow walkways. There were novels, poetry, history books, an 1837 edition entitled *Activities of Peter the Great and Wise*, a 1902 copy of Byron's works, and an illustrated collection of Oscar Wilde's *Fairy Tales*. Among the shelves stood a picture of a passenger jet, a wooden sculpture of Helena Roerich in the lotus position, and a portrait of Ernest Hemingway. On the windowsill, geranium

Leonid Kaloshin photographed in his library in Ust-Koksa village in 2017.

leaves released the sweet, oily smell of summer. The rooms, however, were freezing. Leonid, who had run out of money to buy fuel, hadn't had a chance to replenish his stocks. Whenever he ran short, Leonid went to collect his own wood from the forest using a rusty UAZ van – a Soviet classic, in gunmetal grey – parked up beside his house.

For twenty years, from 1969 to 1989, Leonid had worked as a flight navigator on Aeroflot passenger planes. He had flown nearly eleven thousand hours in his career, criss-crossing the USSR. Then one day in 1984, he went to an exhibition of Nicholas Roerich's paintings in Moscow. Leonid was entranced. Ever since, he had attached himself to the idea that the Altai was the spiritual heart of Russia.

'I left my job to move to a place I'd never been,' said

The first passenger flight from Novosibirsk to Moscow in July 1957 pulled Siberia closer to European Russia than the Trans-Siberian Railway had half a century before. This is an airport waiting room in Siberia in January 1964.

Leonid. 'I got some work with air traffic control in Ust-Koksa, which I did for four years until perestroika. I brought my books. I lent them out to my neighbours. I started to catalogue them. I wanted to open a community library.'

Part of me thought it was odd that this man had left all the security of a successful Soviet career because of the promise of some kind of Siberian Shambhala. Another part of me knew it made sense, given his view from the library of some of the most beautiful country on Earth. As for Leonid's interest in music, that came later, when he encountered a little boy in Uymon Village – the same settlement where the Roerichs stayed when they travelled through the Altai and lived with a family of Old Believers. The child who inspired Leonid's piano quest was trying to play a wooden table painted with a keyboard.

'When I saw how strongly he wanted to hear music, I went to Moscow and bought him an instrument,' said Leonid. 'Nothing special; it was one of four pianos an old man was selling off cheaply from his garage. I've done the same ever since, bringing pianos to the Altai.'

Leonid was now building a concert hall at the back of his house with the help of friends and volunteers. Soon he would need to find a grand piano for performances. The concert hall would have perfect acoustics, he said, for around seventy people. He said he couldn't sell any instrument, not for now; all those he had brought to the Altai were simple uprights given out to children, or purchased by local families at a very low price. But if I found a good grand piano suitable for his hall – the Old Believer's Becker sounded interesting to him – then he would be very grateful if I could find the money for it. He didn't have much; he lived on a small Aeroflot pension, but he usually found a way of working things out. In fact, would the Mongolian concert pianist like to come and play here when his concert hall was completed?

'But this place is so remote,' I remarked, feeling the tables turn: Leonid was asking me to find him a piano, rather than the other way around.

'The world is very remote,' he said, his grey eyes alight: 'We are at the centre.'

10

The Moscow of the East:
Harbin

Eᴀʀʟʏ ᴏɴ ɪɴ ᴍʏ travels in Siberia, I had come across the memoirs of Thomas Preston, the British Consul to Western Siberia during the Russian Revolution. A consummate pianist, Preston was living in Ekaterinburg when Tsar Nicholas II arrived in the city as the Bolsheviks' prisoner. It may have been a country falling apart with the end of the old regime, but it was also alive with the nineteenth-century musical greats, evidenced by all those moments in Preston's narrative when he says more about the likes of Tchaikovsky and Alexander Glazunov than he gives astute political insights into the disintegrating social order. 'A passport . . . particularly in Russia,' is how Preston describes music. I was drawn to what Preston noticed – specifically the image of pianos flowing out of Siberia on the last trains out as chaos took over.

Preston saw the car drive past that took the Romanovs to the Ipatiev House, which was located a few doors down from the British Consulate. After the executions, Preston also witnessed the Whites and the Reds converging in the Urals, and the people of Ekaterinburg rushing to escape. On a hot day in July 1919, he described some fifty, sixty trains backed up on a single line of railway, and citizens fighting for space on the trains' roofs and buffers. Those with the means bought entire rail coaches, ramming them full of safes, expensive furniture and grand pianos. Everyone was headed in the same direction, including Nikolai Sokolov, the Whites' criminal investigator into the Romanov assassinations. Sokolov was travelling with three suitcases and a small wooden box containing his official report on the murders, along with bullets, splintered jewels and a finger – likely cut from the hand of the Empress in order to retrieve a ring.

The trains went first to Omsk, then to Chita via the Trans-Siberian Railway. They then took the branch line south via the Chinese Eastern Railway to Harbin – these days a Chinese metropolis, but at that time in history a Russian city across the Siberian border in Qing-controlled Manchuria. Known as the Moscow of the East, Harbin was bubbling and cosmopolitan, swollen with floods from the Songhua River. There was a brittle glamour to the city, with cabaret nights, rampant prostitution and banditry. But at least life felt free. As early as 1907, plays censored by Tsarist Russia premiered in Harbin. Against the brutality of the Russian Civil War and the rise of

Bolshevism, Harbin's libertarianism was appealing, the city full of pianos which had belonged to brilliant early jazz artists who gave Harbin its swing in one of the stranger twists in the musical history of Eurasia.

Harbin's evolution had been a curious one – a freak Russian settlement in Chinese territory established in 1898 when the Tsar struck a deal allowing Russia to run a railway through Manchuria to the Pacific. Within a decade of Russian engineers arriving, the little village swelled into a city, bolstered by an influx of Russian Jews escaping the pogroms in the Pale. Recuperating Russian soldiers, waylaid on their return home from the Russo-Japanese War, also chose to stick around. Before long, European-trained architects were finding work designing mansions for the city's nouveau riche.

A flooded street in Harbin, 1932.

Around the time of the October Revolution, Harbin had a population of about a hundred thousand Russians, and twice that number of Chinese. Those numbers soon surged due to refugee arrivals from the Russian Civil War. Newspapers were being published in Russian, Chinese, Ukrainian, German and Yiddish. During festival weeks, Russian *drosky* drivers in brightly coloured silk shirts drove their jangling horses up and down Harbin's wide boulevards. Some of the buildings looked as if they had been lifted straight out of St Petersburg, their blue onion domes puncturing the sky. 'It was like a dream of old Russia,' wrote a *New York Times* journalist in 1923, 'beauty in a place raw and unbeautiful.'

The same journalist described an intimacy coupled with suspicion in the way the city's huddled souls eyed each other with hunger and distrust. (Former White Russians who became Soviet citizens in Harbin during this period were known as 'radishes': 'red on the outside, white on the inside'). Other first-hand accounts described the half-starving women who disembarked the trains. They became prey to Harbin's white-slave traders and 'underworld gentry' in a city where racketeers and smugglers literally got away with murder, and bodies swung from telegraph poles. This was a town where the law was tenuous and the nightlife, wrote a wide-eyed, twenty-year-old White Guard, was devoid of all pretence to either modesty or temperance. Champagne flowed among desperate characters thrown together by war, with any fear about tomorrow lost in a drunken fog of gaiety and nervous tension. There were two operas, six theatres, and music halls in full blast. Not only did numerous instruments appear in Harbin during this tumultuous period, but a completely new style of music.

In spring 1917, the first jazz record ever made was released in New York. Four years later, jazz was seeping into Siberia with the American Expeditionary Force that occupied Vladivostok at the end of the Russian Civil War. Gramophone records began travelling along the seams of the Trans-Siberian Railway, this new music spreading nationwide by the thirties as Russian jazz developed its own unique sound.

In Harbin, musicians became celebrities, playing in the Railway Club, restaurants, cinemas, theatres and hotel ballrooms. Artists made the covers of magazines and established their names before moving on to the glamour of Shanghai, where the French, British and American appetite for jazz in the city's foreign concessions kept many a Russian musician in employment. The anarchic freedom of improvisation fitted with contemporary Russian culture in the Far East, where big bands and ragtime struck dramatic *carpe diem* chords in refugee communities. The Harbin Symphony Orchestra included principals who had been soloists in major Russian orchestras. The First Harbin Musical Academy was among the top conservatories in Asia. Some thirty music schools were flourishing in the city.

Amateur musicians, inspired by the beautiful cacophony, included a young Siberian engineering student from the Trans-Siberian Railway town of Chita: Oleg Lundstrem, whose family had left Russia for Harbin in 1921. When Lundstrem stumbled on a recording of 'Dear Old Southland' by Duke Ellington, that was it: the swing was on. In 1934, Lundstrem founded what was to become the world's longest existing jazz band. Oleg played the piano. His brother, Igor, played the saxophone. In Harbin and then Shanghai, where the siblings moved in 1936, the appetite for this Russian-embellished style was so significant that within six years of forming his nine-piece orchestra, Lundstrem was nicknamed the 'King of Jazz in the Far East'.

For Harbin's entertainers, these were glittering times. There was first-class cabaret and ballet, with artists from Moscow's Bolshoi later moving to Paris for careers at the Folies Bergère. White Russian 'princesses' worked as dancing girls alongside gypsy performers (the less attractive Harbin women, observed an American journalist in 1933, tended to work in dentistry). Theatre, film and opera were on fire. 'Here in Harbin, the whole house rocked with "Bravas!"' observed the *New York Times*. The era's biggest voices – Sergei Lemeshev, Aleksandr Vertinsky, Fyodor Chaliapin – all toured here, performing at the art nouveau Hotel Moderne, founded by the magnificently rich, somewhat controversial Russian-Jewish owner, Josef Kaspe, who had arrived in Harbin around 1903. During the Russian Civil War, it is thought Kaspe made his fortune trading in émigré jewels. Whatever the truth of it, his wealth was so significant that he brought in craftsmen from Europe to build his Harbin empire. He opened a chain of theatres and a cinema, and hired an entire philharmonic orchestra to accompany the silent movies.

For a brief moment in time, the Moderne became the main stage for the Oleg Lundstrem Orchestra. Where was that piano? I wondered. The Moderne was also where the hotel owner's younger son, Semion Kaspe, was booked to perform in 1933. A talented concert pianist trained at the Paris Conservatory, Semion returned to Harbin in order to give a series of recitals – a plan which went tragically wrong when on a hot day in August he was kidnapped on his way back from a party. When his father refused to pay the ransom – it is unclear if Josef Kaspe was calling their bluff, or simply couldn't afford the vast sum being asked of him – the kidnappers sent the old man his son's ear lobes in an envelope.

'Finish it quickly,' Semion wrote in a letter to his father: 'Do not forget that human beings have limited strength.'

When his father still refused to cooperate, the kidnappers killed the young pianist. When Semion's body was recovered, it was so mutilated from torture it is said that Josef Kaspe lost his mind.

The motivations for the murder were political, not just about greed. At the time of Semion's kidnapping, a French flag was flying on top of the Hotel Moderne because Kaspe had transferred ownership to his two sons, who held French citizenship. Kaspe had hoped this would give the hotel immunity from the Japanese, who had invaded Manchuria in 1931

The concert pianist Semion Kaspe, pictured in 1931.

and established the puppet state of Manchukuo. The Japanese wanted to get their hands on the hotel, which was the most iconic symbol of the city.

White Russian fascists working as proxies for the Japanese were among the suspects accused of Semion's kidnapping. However, the judge was murdered a week after the sentencing. The suspects were retried several years later, and found not guilty. The liberal atmosphere of Harbin may have been creatively exciting, but it was also plagued by a hostile clash of ideologies, corruption, terror and violent anti-Semitism.

As Japanese influence increased across the region, the habit for kidnapping and extortion became something of 'a cottage industry'. During the decade-long occupation, which only ended with Japan's defeat in the Second World War, the tensions ran so high that more than twenty thousand Russian residents in Harbin chose to be repatriated into the USSR. Natalia Spirina was among them – a disciple of the Roerichs who managed to take her beloved upright piano back with her from Harbin to Novosibirsk. The 1910 Schröder, serial number 36494, survives in Siberia to this day.*

A large proportion of *kharbintsky* – ethnic Russians from Harbin – met less than salubrious fates. They returned to the USSR, only to perish in the Gulag because of their connection to the Whites in the Russian Civil War, or because of an alleged collaboration with the Japanese. Others felt tricked by Soviet propaganda when apartments they had been promised weren't ready. The returnees were abandoned in the middle of nowhere with their baggage, including the odd piano left to spoil in the Siberian rain. Russian Jews, Harbin's

---

* In the Nicholas Roerich Museum in Novosibirsk.

second-largest community in the early twenties, fled to Australia and Palestine. Some also made it out to California, others to South America. Sticking around wasn't much of an option. From 1936 to 1945, the Japanese turned a Harbin suburb into a centre for biological-weapons research, where thousands of prisoners, including Chinese, Koreans and Russians, were subjected to grisly human experiments.

These days, Harbin is one of the newest megacities of the People's Republic. The city blinks with multi-lane highways, super-modern hotels and a world-class opera house in flashing silver. Harbin's enormous wealth flows out of the nearby Daqing oil fields, each pumping elbow of iron moving in a constant, syncopated rhythm as China's high-speed trains fly past like snub-nosed planes. After Siberia's rib-thin settlements, where the train gropes through the empty steppe, the hurry of Harbin feels like a shock to the system.

I spent four days looking for a living Russian connection to Siberian pianos in this city of over ten million people. Instead, I discovered the Kaspe files were still locked shut by the Chinese government. Any significant first-hand sources connected with the Russian diaspora had already perished or fled many years ago. The only direct connection to one of the early émigrés I was able to track down was an eighty-five-year-old half-Russian, half-Chinese woman who agreed to meet, then backed out. I sought help from an Israeli academic, Professor Dan Ben-Canaan, the Founder of the Harbin Jewish Culture Association who taught at the city university. He had written about Kaspe and the Jewish story in Harbin. He had also done much to try and protect the old architecture.

Still, Harbin's Russian buildings weren't what they used to be. All but a handful of the turn-of-the-century dachas where the Russian train managers had once lived were now demolished. The Orthodox Cathedral of St Sophia, whose bells had once echoed through Harbin's streets, had been turned into a museum. The old synagogue – a rare architectural survivor, given around eighty per cent of Harbin's fifty churches and synagogues were ravaged during Mao's Cultural Revolution – was now a concert hall. Harbin's only working Russian Orthodox church functioned out of the back of an old shop, next door to a dental surgery; it was presided over by a Chinese priest, and on the day I visited had a congregation of thirteen. As for surviving Russian pianos, I learned that Mao Zedong's widow, who was fond of piano music, didn't quite manage to save the instrument from its unpalatable Western reputation. 'During China's Cultural Revolution,' writes one leading historian, 'the piano was likened to a coffin, in which notes rattled about like the bones of the bourgeoisie'. In 1966, Mao's Red Guards smashed instruments to pieces, raided music schools, and locked keyboards shut. Their campaign of terror drove soloists to suicide.

These days, there are plenty of Russian music teachers working in China. Russia's pedagogy has value in this country; China's brilliant virtuosos continue to be the beneficiaries of a migration of Russia's intellectual capital. But it seemed strange to me that in a country which now counted piano talent as one of its most important cultural exports, there was only negligible evidence of the wonderful old Russian artists who did so much to turn the Chinese ear to piano music in the first place. There was the occasional reproduced photograph in a museum display or hotel lobby. I found a piano shop, a tuner, but no traces of old instruments. In all my days of looking, the only antique piano I uncovered (but wasn't allowed to touch) stood in a restaurant serving borscht to tourists.

Then a promising lead. I received word from a Russian musicologist about a collection of survivors in a small museum put together by a committed Chinese academic. I visited the pianos in a new building designed to look like something out of imperial St Petersburg – a tactful nod, I was told, to an ongoing economic warming between these countries. One or two of the instruments were Japanese, but most of the display rooms were occupied by Russian pianos. Of the pre-Revolution instruments, nearly all of them carried the same provenance: 'Harbin Musical School'.

It was my story's Room 101.* As I wandered through the salvaged remains, I couldn't find a piano attached to an individual's past, whether the ghost of Lundstrem, Kaspe or any of the humble Russian teachers and performers who gave this city its brief and glittering place in Eurasia's musical history. It was as if there was no past before Mao, no individual before state property. Above all, it was as if there were no spectacular refugees who had brought with them (and left behind) that brilliant early sound of jazz as piano music began to seep out of the hands of the intelligentsia to inspire new strata of society both inside and beyond Siberia's borders. The collection

---

* ' "You asked me once," said O'Brien, "what was in Room 101. I told you that you knew the answer already. Everyone knows it. The thing that is in Room 101 is the worst thing in the world."

. . . "The worst thing in the world," said O'Brien, "varies from individual to individual. It may be burial alive, or death by fire, or by drowning, or by impalement, or fifty other deaths. There are cases where it is some quite trivial thing, not even fatal." '

George Orwell, *Nineteen Eighty-Four* (London: Secker & Warburg, 1949).

was significant, given what little remains of Russia's true history in China, but there was also much that was missing. I longed to know who had played this or that instrument, whose fingers had expressed the love or pain of their Harbin exile. The sense of dystopia struck me forcefully, how an object can lose its meaning when it has lost its owner's story, like a body detached from its soul, or a refugee from his homeland.

11

Beethoven in a Red *Chum*:
The Yamal Peninsula

IN HARBIN, LIFE WAS a fluid, bubbling improvisation, like a brilliant, unpredictable jazz set feeling its way to the next note. The dazzle of a sequin, the shimmy of a skirt, the sight of a pretty ankle in the dance clubs were enough to make you think life was worth living, at least for today. In Harbin, Russians didn't have Stalin sitting behind them as he sat listening to Shostakovich in his box at the Bolshoi Theatre in Moscow. 'Muddle instead of Music' was the story that ran in *Pravda* two days after Stalin heard Shostakovich's popular opera *Lady Macbeth of Mtsensk* in 1936 and walked out halfway through.

The USSR of the thirties, while leading to better living standards and greater opportunities for the general population, also resulted in trauma on an unprecedented scale. With his policy of mass collectivization, Stalin created huge state farms, once again chaining peasants to the land in what has been called Russia's 'second serfdom'. Alongside the agrarian revolution, rapid industrialization pulled the country into the twentieth century, but with astronomical human costs that included famine and ecological devastation. In Ukraine, an estimated 3.9 million people died from starvation in the early 1930s alone.

All sorts of incongruities developed in the musical arts during 'The Great Retreat', as the Soviet historian Nicholas Timasheff described Stalin's policies of the thirties. Music splintered into a spectrum of innovations, sometimes random, sometimes of true musical value, as Soviet culture locked itself in. Replacing the comparative artistic freedom of the twenties were the aesthetics of socialist realism: a return to a romantic musical language, sometimes aggressive nationalism, and a strong resistance to the avant-garde. A new genre of mass song evolved, with state interference – sometimes implied, other times overt – helping to turn music into a powerful ideological tool. With tight censorship causing artists of every kind to be terrified about where in Stalin's hierarchy of ideas their work might be filed, all that composers had to protect themselves was the innate ambiguity in music: you can hear in it what you like. This was one of the reasons musicians were comparatively less affected than other artists by Stalin's secret police, the NKVD. Musicians were also protected by the Soviet virtuoso's propaganda value at home and abroad. That said, the toughest years of repression still led to an escalation of attacks on music that didn't align with Soviet values. (Shostakovich, for example, always kept a suitcase packed with necessities on the basis he could be arrested at any time.) In the thirties, threats were omnipresent: the whisper of a neighbour, a hint of Western inspiration, a flurry of defiant notes could lead to the labour camps.

In this single decade, the number of prisoners in the Gulag doubled, then tripled. Historians argue about the relevance of the assassination of the top party official Sergei Kirov in 1934: was this the trigger Stalin needed for his fear of counter-revolution to spiral into paranoia?* By 1936, the clampdown had escalated into the Great Terror – a two-year assault that saw charges of treason and terrorism brought against some of the Politburo's most powerful figures. No one was safe. The culture of suspicion affected every kind of citizen – worker, peasant, pianist or senior official, with several new orders made in 1937 to widen the net for arrests.

During this intense period of change, people also began to move around the USSR in search of security and opportunities. As a result, Siberia underwent its most dramatic shift in history, its population swelling by three hundred per cent in the thirties alone. Incomers included forced labourers sent to Siberia to work in the Gulag system, victims of famine seeking a better life, tens of thousands of Poles and other repressed ethnic groups in targeted deportations, and Russians drawn by the sudden economic growth of Siberia's

---

* This is a whodunnit that continues to this day, and divides historians. There has always been speculation that Stalin himself ordered the hit on Kirov and, by doing so, created a reason for any possible 'enemy of the state' to be hunted down.

industrial cities. The influx helped to break up Siberia's previously cohesive ethnic groups. While the USSR's 'friendship of nations' supported multiculturalism, it was strongly controlled from Moscow. Stalin rearranged the country's autonomous republics and administrative regions in a way that further divided Russia's indigenous people – many of whom were resistant to the ideologies of the regime, their new Soviet-approved identities, and the precedence being given to the Russian language.

For people like the Nenets, who traditionally moved about the Arctic with their reindeer herds, special state boarding schools were created to teach them to read Russian and be good communist workers. The Nenets still live on the Yamal Peninsula, which sticks up like a crooked finger where the Urals peter out inside the polar circle. Even today, a proportion of Nenets travel some eight hundred miles on an annual round-trip migration in pursuit of lichen to graze their reindeer. Under Soviet power, the young were separated from their traditions, as well as from their families. The Nenets' education in music changed, too, now they were no longer as close to the lullabies of their mothers. In addition, propaganda brigades turned up in the tundra with all sorts of new ideas about the Soviet way of life. The brigades installed musical instruments in cultural stations, which were founded to provide basic social services while encouraging a new settled existence around collective reindeer farms. Where there were no fixed meeting places, the brigades travelled with their ideas instead. In the Yamal Peninsula, music floated out of Red *chums* – the traditional reindeer-skin tents shaped much like tepees – which moved about the tundra with film projectors and crank-operated gramophones. These portable schools, while few in number, brought benefits, including veterinary and medical assistance. They also functioned as a Soviet experiment in acculturation.

Those who wanted no part of the changes took their native shamanism underground. They migrated to more remote pastures. Unwilling to adjust to collective rules during this period of 'galloping Sovietization' – including industrial development on an unprecedented scale – the Nenets began to sabotage Soviet trading posts, and team up as best they could in uprisings, with the heaviest years of repression, from 1937 to 1938, regarded by some groups of Nenets as a war.

The change from nomadism led to purposelessness, which tipped easily into alcoholic chaos. Others were thoroughly seduced by what they saw and heard, like a Nenets woman I met who described how odd these Red *chum* visitations were, at least in the beginning, when as a child she watched a tank charge at her on the screen put up inside the tent. She and the other children, terrified by what they could only think was magic, were desperate to look behind the screen to see who or what was making the menacing sound. The music was baffling to them until, bit by bit, they not only got used to the new arrivals, but yearned for more. In the settlement club, this same Nenets child used to warm a coin in her hand and put it against the frosted window to make a peephole for looking through the ice to watch the adults' film. How that tiny kopek-sized hole in the window expanded over time – bringing together Russians with very different cultural histories – seemed to me a powerful parable of what had happened to Siberia over centuries of complex assimilation. I was fascinated by it, and while I didn't expect to find a surfeit of pianos in the tundra, I wanted to know if there might be any evidence remaining – even just one eccentric outlier to capture the imagination.

Salekhard is the Yamal Peninsula's main settlement, on the rim of the Arctic Circle. It is near the mouth of the River Ob, which is the world's longest estuary. The peninsula reaching north extends far beyond where the firs run out, where the frayed edge of north-west Siberia extends into the Arctic Ocean. Up here, the sky is 'a deep blue, like a water-sky', which was the description given by the explorer and scientist Fridtjof Nansen when he came to Yamal in 1913. Nansen, famous for his 1895 attempt on the North Pole, travelled to Siberia by sea from Norway to explore the potential of a northern trade connection with the Siberian interior, reached via the Arctic. I came on the train from Moscow, the last stages of my journey hugging the Polar Urals.

When I left Salekhard to travel even further north into the tundra, a snow-squall was gusting, the blizzard moving in drifts of smoke as we crossed the River Ob by amphibious truck. During the Second World War, German U-boats slipped into these waters as part of an ambitious Nazi strategy called Operation Wunderland to command Siberia's Arctic sea lanes. Despite its strategic importance then and now, Salekhard remains isolated. There is still no bridge over the Ob between the train station at Labytnangi and Salekhard, which is on the opposite side of the river. In summer, Salekhard is reached by ferry. In the mid-season melt, when the river is clogged with chunks of ice, locals use a helicopter.

The further north we went, the more the sun seemed to nudge the surface of the Earth. Where the snow had been blown off pools of frozen water, the ice was the colour of

Getting around the Yamal Peninsula before helicopters became common. Then, as now, the Yamal is hard to penetrate. Decommissioned tanks are used, their caterpillar tracks ideal for the tundra when the ground turns to bog in summer.

pewter. We passed abandoned skeletons of iron – diggers, lorries and drilling machines stuck in hollows of land from Yamal's vast natural gas fields. As the day turned to dusk, the territory became lonelier. This wasn't 'the land of the future', as Nansen called Siberia; it felt closer to the start of time.

Nansen loved his Russian voyage – the flushes of sunset, the sea's billowy surface, the darting skuas skimming a leaden ocean. He described listening to the whine and hum of the ship's radio, and the splash of water against the boat at midnight, which was easily mistaken for the sound of surf on an illusory shore. For entertainment, he took a gramophone. The Nenets told Nansen they had heard better music in Salekhard.

It was probably true, since pianos had already reached this pocket of Siberia, with one instrument in particular making an unusual journey around the Yamal Peninsula at the end of the nineteenth century. In 1893, a Victorian spinster called Helen Peel played the piano for sailors on the *Blencathra*, a British ship tasked to deliver rails for the new Trans-Siberian Railway. The piano was brought to accompany a Mr Popham on violin, and a Mr James on flute. Miss Peel, whose ambition of eating strawberries at the Pole was never realized, returned home overland through Siberia, but the ship stayed on.

Nansen wrote how this tough little vessel made several further voyages to Siberia's River Yenisei before disappearing without trace in 1912 after getting caught in ice off the Yamal Peninsula. Nothing was heard of the ship or crew for a year. Nansen thought there was an outside possibility that rather than having sunk, she might still be locked into the pack ice and was floating somewhere in the north of the Arctic Ocean. Nansen had no idea that fourteen crew had in fact abandoned ship and were using a map copied from one of his previous books, *Farthest North*, to find their way home across the frozen water – a journey only two men survived.

Where was the lost ship's piano now? I pictured the instrument drifting in a polar sea, its ivories washed up among a colony of seals, the notes entwined with the clicks and trills of a beluga whale. I wondered if the instrument might one day reappear beside the stove in a fisherman's cabin, or as a piece of soundless furniture stripped of its wires to make snares for Arctic hare. The further I travelled into the whiteness, the stranger it seemed that people might choose to live all the way out here. Then towards the end of the day's drive, a settlement next to a church appeared at the head of a smooth white plain.

The church, which stood on a squat hill, was surrounded by small chapels painted in the cartoon blue of a Californian swimming pool. The encampment was girdled by a cluster of golden crosses and a hem of trees. This was where the Nenets author and advocate for native rights Anna Nerkagi had founded a community school. She came out to meet me – a tiny bird-like woman who stood no taller than my shoulder. The children gathered behind her full skirts, their cone-shaped hooded capes fashioned from reindeer fur – diamonds of white and brown, the designs like one of Picasso's harlequins. Anna's brother wore a kind of cassock and thick leather belt strung with a sheathed knife and a pouch of snuff. Other men in the community wore long, thigh-high boots, or *pimy*, gartered in colourful bands strung with pom-poms. Some of the younger men wore army fatigues and tracksuits.

In the nineties, Anna had led protests against the industrial invasion of the Nenets' territory. When roads were put through Yamal, they brought gas fields and well heads which interfered with the Nenets' old migration routes. These days, she has accepted the changes. But then adaptability is in the Nenets' history; without it, they would never have survived. Anna's endeavours – to teach young Nenets the traditional methods for living in the tundra – is among her best attempts to help her people hold on to some of the last of the old ways. She encourages the community to make money with a modest tourist operation. She is also a committed Christian, who corralled various resources in order to get the church built.

We settled in for hot tea inside the *chum*. Anna offered me frozen fish cut into slivers, and reindeer meat as chewy as leather. There were significant lulls in the conversation as we got used to each other's presence, as if everybody was waiting on someone else to break the silence. As we shared the food being passed around the tent – the women seated on one side, men on the other – I asked Anna about music.

Conservationist Aleksandr Batalov measures the tiger's footprints in the snow at the start of my Russian journey.

Standing on a frozen lake close to the Mongolia–Russia border. I spent a day travelling to the head of this remote tract of water, where I found an old Russian piano.

A Steinway belonging to Ulaanbaatar's opera house – one of a handful of venues for classical music performances in a country four times the size of Germany.

*Arriving into Irkutsk
train station in winter.*

A typical cabin on the shores of Lake Baikal.

Sergei Paliy and a member of the Old Believer community I visited outside Ulan-Ude.

Wearing my summer protection against Siberia's mosquitoes in the abandoned town of Kadykchan.

Inspecting a nineteenth-century piano in the Selenga Valley where the Decembrist exiles Mikhail and Nikolai Bestuzhev eked out a living after their hard-labour sentences were up.

'The only music you will hear in the tundra,' Anna snapped, 'is the kettle whistling on the fire.'

I had been too abrupt with my questioning, and needed to find a different, gentler way in. I knew that Anna was brave and respected by her people. I also knew the Nenets had *some* musical history. I had read about how their oral traditions were closely bound to elemental sound – the scratch of fire and wood, the whoosh of wind, a metal pike driving a hole into a frozen lake. I had heard recordings of Nenets who could imitate birdsong. In their childhood, they sang to help with hunting. The children lay in the snow with their feet in the air to trick other birds into thinking their legs were the necks of geese. This attracted inquisitive birds, which the men then netted or shot. Musicians in Salekhard told me how song – the Nenets' beautiful, yearning voices – could be heard in their lullabies, shamanic rituals and ecstatic rites. In Yamal, music played a part in survival, like the presence of a friend. It was a way to endure extreme monotony in an empty place. Just as music allowed Maria Volkonsky to hang on to the threads of her European culture during her Siberian exile, song helped the Nenets cling on to the one part of their identity that the Soviets couldn't destroy when they attacked their traditions and persecuted their shamans.

Had it all disappeared? Would I hear anything of their rare song tradition that so fascinates musicologists – a tradition which bears 'not a single trace of Western influence'? Where were the magic drums? The stretched reindeer-skins beaten with antlers? Maybe I had to accept that I was at least a century too late, the Nenets' belief system already destroyed by Tsarist missionaries, then by the state's massive attack on religion in the thirties. Because when I tried to ask Anna once again about music, she was crystal clear: her community lived by its Russian Orthodox principles. In her opinion, music and dance were pastimes for lazy people with city lifestyles. Pianos out here were a wishful leap too far.

Later on, as we started to get to know each other, Anna took me to a nearby hill covered with flinty stones. With the tundra spread out around us, she said the stones concealed the entrance to the *chum* belonging to the Sihirtia – trolls, or magical people, who the Nenets believe are their predecessors. The Nenets say they pushed them off the land until the Sihirtia retreated and started living underground. Occasionally, the Sihirtia come out at night, in a mist or a sea fret, but otherwise they're elusive. As I struggled to understand how the Sihirtia, a cornerstone of the Nenets' culture, lined up with her Christian beliefs, Anna explained it thus: these sacred rocks were God's unfinished altars and churches, she said.

The more Anna opened up, the more I began to understand how the community's Orthodoxy seemed to blur with the Nenets' residual conviction that the landscape was instilled with an ancient spiritualism not even Stalin could stamp out. When I spent time with Anna's brother fishing, then herding the reindeer, it was if he could read the landscape in a different way to other people I had encountered in Siberia. He took me to the cliff edge at the head of another valley.

'I've been to the end of the world,' he said, describing journeys north to the Kara Sea, 'but I've never been to Moscow.'

A Nenets boy had told me the Sihirtia were huge, with white fur and ferocious teeth. Anna's brother said no, the Sihirtia were small.

I asked Anna's brother if he could explain to me the contradictions between shamanism and the presence of the church, between the music that belongs to the Nenets culture and the Russian culture which had been overlaid. I wanted to know when the Sihirtia were last seen.

'Best to ask Anna,' he said. 'My main thing is fishing and reindeer.'

The ridiculousness of encountering a piano among these people became clearer the more I learned about the Nenets' way of life: it wasn't just Anna's version of Russian Orthodoxy that forbade instrumental music and dance; the absence was a true feature of the Nenets' original culture. Given the sparse economy of the Nenets' way of life, their lack of instruments was entirely logical. They harvest nothing more than they eat, and own nothing more than they use.

On my last night in camp, I listened to the church bells – the only music I heard in three days. When I walked beyond the ring of trees, everything was blanketed in white. It was hard to tell if the hunched mounds were dogs or sledges or clumps of stones and Sihirtia tombs. The tundra was skinned with ice, hiding the life beneath the surface. I watched the sun sink. Soon the sky turned black except for the prick and pulse of satellites and stars. The church bells stopped ringing. The footsteps fell still. A glimmer of green light appeared as the aurora borealis began to dance over the plain.

I swapped the stars for streetlights on my return to Salekhard to find the celebrated Nenets composer Semion Nyaruy. Like Anna, he was a figurehead of Nenets culture – a man whose expressive, syncopated songs unshackled the Nenets from any feeling of shame about their native language or cultural heritage. In the sixties, his talents took him to the Leningrad

Conservatory. His songs were distributed throughout the country's radio stations. He also owned a piano, or so I was told.

When we met, Semion was a very old man living with his wife in the city outskirts in a wooden house with tundra views. When I knocked on the door, he was watching TV. He sat on the stool beside his instrument, a Tyumen upright, serial number 31116, which was covered with the flag of the Russian Federation. He was too delicate to stand up, his frailty barely concealed under a purple satin robe (a *malitsa* in Nenets culture) cuffed in white Arctic fox. He had a beard like Lenin's, which suited his pointed face, and a bald pate, like a tonsured monk. His eyebrows were strongly arched, and his hands, which looked arthritic, had a violent shake. His wife brought tea and sweets while he played with a black puppy on his lap.

He loved dogs. He said he had eight when he was a boy living in the tundra. He talked about the instrument he used at his boarding school, where he wasn't allowed to speak his Nenets language. He struggled at maths and Russian, but when his perfect pitch was recognized, he won a place at a music college in Tyumen. He talked about his mother, who died when he was twelve. His father, a party member, used to move the Red *chums* through Yamal on a sledge, setting them up for government doctors, teachers and cinema operators.

'I would listen to Beethoven in the Red *chum*,' says Semion. 'Whenever I heard Beethoven, I disappeared inside his music.'

Semion described the projector, the books, and the portraits of Stalin and Lenin his father transported about Yamal. His father was a wonderful singer. There was never a piano, he said; it would have taken twenty reindeer to pull a piano through the tundra.

Semion's wife, who knew by heart every song he had ever composed, was a linguist, a specialist in the Nenets language.

'Like music, our words go deep inside ourselves,' she said. 'Our language is like cell memory. We have many words for snow and wind, but nothing for physics.'

Semion was drifting from our conversation when the outside door opened and closed. I asked him if music belonged in the tundra. He looked up.

'You should ask the sun how the oxygen appeared,' he said.

A minute or so passed. Semion looked exhausted. Then, upon the arrival of his son in the room, a smile broke out on his face.

I asked Semion if his first instrument was the one behind him, and if he would play one of his songs.

'My fingers won't listen to me. And my head won't either,' he said.

With his son's gentle urging, Semion agreed to sing. They performed one of his compositions – mother, father and child in melodic unison, their bodies linked in a close-knit triptych with Semion seated at the piano stool. Sometimes he seemed a beat behind. Sometimes it was as if he had forgotten the words. Sometimes the puppy put him off. Then his wife handed him a china reindeer, which he gripped with both trembling hands. His chest rose boldly. *Hey hey hey*, he called, partly singing, partly chanting, his hands holding up the ornament like a priest might an icon. He delivered his Nenets song – part lament, part gleeful celebration, with nothing familiar or European to its melodies – as if he wanted all the world to know the tundra was the soul of the planet.

Semion wouldn't, however, be persuaded to play the piano – an instrument he encountered for the first time in his boarding school. He said the Tyumen was out of tune. He talked instead about a German-made piano he had bought forty years ago. He loved how each note would stay in the air. His wife said she thought the German piano may have come from the Salekhard theatre – one of the ones used by construction workers on Railway 501. In the nineties, she had handed it on as a teaching piano to a local music school.

It was a curious moment: in pursuit of an instrument that carried the melodies of an indigenous people's song, I had in fact tripped up on a different story. Railway 501 was one of the most notorious white elephants of the entire Stalinist regime: in 1947, Stalin ordered the construction of a new railway linking Salekhard in the west to Igarka a thousand miles further east along the polar circle. It was a brutal idea – part of what Stalin called his Great Plan for the Transformation of Nature – through treacherous Arctic territory.

To make up the workforce – which in 1950 included around ten thousand paid labourers – thousands of convicts were gathered out of the Gulag camps. In July of that year, the total number of prisoners feeding the railway construction was an estimated seventy-five thousand – for the most part 'politicals', including engineers, teachers, scientists, composers, famous musicians, and Japanese prisoners of war. Time would be taken off sentences for extra work, which encouraged construction crews to shore up the railway with light trees instead of rock to advance the line's progress. Within two years, labour gangs of up to fifteen hundred prisoners were working from camps based no more than four miles apart. On top of the starvation rations and scalding freeze, there were cases of prisoners being tortured in unfathomable acts of sadism. A geologist, accused of giving information on the territory to a group of escapees, was tied to a birch with wire, attacked first by nesting ants, then by vicious tundra mosquitoes until he finally lost consciousness.

At the height of the build in the spring of 1953, nine miles of track were being laid every month – in temperatures dipping to fifty degrees below. The workers' hair froze on to their neighbour's skin as they slept close to keep warm. Advance parties made beds in the open snow using branches for mattresses. Frozen bread was cut with a saw, as if each loaf were a piece of wood. By the time Stalin died, so many thousands of people had perished in the building of Railway 501 that the track was renamed Dead Road. His plan was then abandoned with just a few hundred miles to go.

'Do you know what I dream about now?' said Lyudmila Lipatova, a historian in Salekhard who started researching this story in 1988: 'A bridge over the Ob, which would help complete the railway Stalin almost finished. It was a crime to start such a construction after the Great Patriotic War, when our country was in the condition it was in. But to stop when so close to finishing? That was a crime even worse.'

Lyudmila, who had interviewed survivors from the railway construction, found evidence of extreme human resilience. A Greek poet studied higher maths by writing numbers in the snow. A travelling arts troupe of some two hundred prisoners was formed, including set painters, singers and ballet dancers. There was also a symphony orchestra forty members strong. Among them were Russian musicians captured by the Nazis in Stalingrad – prisoners of war whom Joseph Goebbels, Minister of Propaganda of Nazi Germany, had commandeered for

217

performances at camps in Germany. On their release, Stalin re-arrested his own Red Army soldiers as traitors and sent them to Railway 501.

With a cheap thirty-kopek ticket, everyone could afford to hear the travelling operettas. The railway's chief of construction considered theatre necessary to raise their spirits in the dark polar nights – not only for his workforce, but also for the free working people of the Far North. He requested the transfer of some of the best musicians from other Gulags, including a conductor of the Odessa Opera, as well as pianists and singers he knew by name.

If it weren't for the barbed wire, guards' towers and prison slang, the troupe's performances would be as good as anything heard in the capital, remarked one of the artists, who remembered the sound of waltzes floating across Arctic marshes under the glance of prison lights. If there is dark irony in this remark, it's hard to determine the desperate depths given the complex nuances, censorship and fear of reprisal (the musicians also commented on the better living conditions they enjoyed, and clean sheets). Lyudmila described how the ensembles and their instruments travelled throughout the region, the backs of their trucks functioning as concert stages. They moved up the rivers when the summer melt arrived, performing at several dozen construction camps along the advancing line of rails. They also performed in Salekhard, their repertoire hosted on two main stages: the House of Culture – a Soviet community hall for art instruction and entertainment – and a stage at the local fish factory. In one of these fixed venues, there would have been a piano, said Lyudmila. They functioned like municipal theatres, giving performances for the free people of Salekhard.

A prisoner sings for Gulag officials.

A Gulag orchestra is marched to a local village to perform. These two drawings are taken from Drawings from the Gulag by Danzig Baldaev © FUEL Publishing. Baldaev worked as a prison guard in the USSR from 1948, allowing him to record an unflinching portrayal of the labour camp system.

I called the music schools in town, but there was no trace of the German instrument Semion's wife recalled. Evidence of Railway 501 was also almost gone. Lyudmila drove me to a clump of sagging buildings on the other side of town. She showed me an old railway workers' barracks. Go in there, she said, and get a sense of what Salekhard was before.

I entered a long, dank corridor. It was windowless, with duckboards sitting on bare earth. Outside a closed door, which was partially felted to keep out the cold, there were two oil drums filled with water. Above them ran loops of electrical wire. The ceiling was peeling paint. The herringbone wood and plaster walls were caving in. I knocked on a door at one end, and a wheezing couple let me in. There were two tiny rooms, barely a window, three cats, one dog, a TV, a small table where one person could sit if the bed were moved, and a carpet hanging on the wall. They didn't want me to take photographs. They were people I couldn't place – Ukrainians, Tajiks, Nenets, I wasn't sure.

'If you want to understand people, you have to go deeper, and live among them a long time,' said Lyudmila. 'When I came to Salekhard, the stories were thick as a forest. I started to make my research, and I got caught in the thought: Who are we Russians? Why don't we know our roots? We know the names of Greek gods, but not our own Slavic history. But people like the Nenets know more; their stories go back further. They know why the forests and the sun have a soul.'

'I am Orthodox, a believer,' she said, 'but we all grew out of paganism. I think we will all grow back to it again. We will go back to nature to understand the depth of what is happening and what is going to be.'

In another part of Salekhard, Lyudmila took me to see a

few remaining sleepers from Railway 501, revealed when she scraped away the snow with her foot. This tiny patch of history, which betrayed nothing of the railway's epic sorrow, felt like a stark moral prompt to engage with the extreme opposite of music. Confronting memory and repression, I knew that however hard I wanted my piano hunt to celebrate all that is magnificent about Siberia, much of what I was looking for was tied up with a terrifying past. I needed to heed the warning I was given by a brave Russian journalist early on: you have to know why you're ignoring things you don't want to hear, what should be remembered, and why people fall silent and try to forget.

12

Music in the Gulag Archipelago:
Kolyma

MY FIRST GLIMPSE OF the Sea of Okhotsk, the steel-coloured cul-de-sac of water between Russia's eastern edge and the Kamchatka Peninsula, was from the foot of a woolly mammoth cloaked in a North Pacific drizzle. The sculpture, made from scrap cogs, chains and pipes, was cartoonish. It felt out of synch with the dismal human history of the place. Its backside faced the water of Nagaevo Bay, where prisoners began arriving in the early thirties to complete their sentences in a string of Gulag camps scattered through

Kolyma. The mammoth's tusks faced the former Soviet convict town of Magadan.

Nearby was a half-moon of gravel fashioned into a plinth of artificial beach. On concrete foundations stood metal sun umbrellas, which were out of proportion – the small caps on long stalks incapable of casting any shade, even if the sun did appear. A ship's carcass was snagged in the shallows beside a web of cranes. Even in July, one of only five months of the year the Sea of Okhotsk isn't frozen, there were no vessels coming in or out of the harbour. It was a raw landscape: bald, scarred, austere. On the tourist map I had picked up, the city was surrounded by areas marked 'undersized vegetation'. It was as if there were nothing to hold the town in place: no roots, no pilings, no foundations. The jetty looked as if it were finally slipping into the sea, and there weren't any people. Something was missing. It was like my hotel, where there was no second floor, just a first and a third.

An Okhotsk sea fog moved in until I could barely see the grey stillness of the bay where Stalin's Gulag ships had offloaded their human cargo, including Russians, Poles, Lithuanians, Latvians, Hungarians and Volga Germans, Koreans, Japanese, and Spaniards 'rescued' by the USSR during the Spanish Civil War.* Among them were political dissidents, hardened criminals, recidivist killers, invalids half dead with dystrophy, poets, pianists, and starving women with skinny clavicles – 'half-human, half-bird creatures', as they were described by one Kolyma survivor.

---

* British historian Robert Conquest details the Spanish presence in Kolyma: some five thousand young children, first taken to the USSR as a 'humanitarian gesture', were brought up in orphanages then fell into crime. *Kolyma* (London: Macmillan, 1978).

The ships travelled to Nagaevo Bay from three ports on Russia's Pacific seaboard: Vladivostok, which marked the eastern terminus of the Trans-Siberian Railway, Nakhodka Harbour, and the coal port of Vanino. This was where the Leningrad violinist Georgi Feldgun remembered playing for criminals in one of the transit camps: 'Here we are on the edge of the world, and we are playing eternal music written more than two hundred years ago, we are playing Vivaldi for fifty gorillas.' Feldgun experienced music as a means of torture. For others, such as the Lithuanians singing their hymns from the ships' holds, music was an act of defiance, a collective comfort as the steamers left the mainland, sailed past the southern end of Sakhalin Island, and into the narrow strait dividing Russia from Japan. The Kolyma-bound ships then swung north towards Magadan.

During the Stalin years, everyone who lived and died in Kolyma made the journey from the Russian mainland via the Sea of Okhotsk – unconfirmed thousands transported in American, Dutch, British and German-built vessels. An unknowable number of prisoners perished on these ships. Typhus, hunger and cold were the predictable enemies on voyages that took anything between five and thirteen days. The prisoners were also susceptible to the capricious, virtually unlimited power of the Soviet authorities. Guards used hoses of freezing water to push their wards back into the holds, which were stuffed with four-tiered bunks, the bodies layered tight, like anchovies in a tin. Other ships were crammed with prisoners cooped up in cages. Muscles atrophied. Skin turned white. Witnesses described the grinding of the ships' engines. They also remembered the sound of 'wild laughter', the entreaties of women, and the caterwauling. A Polish survivor, Janusz Bardach, described the hard-core criminals, the *urkas*, laughing, talking and groping each other as if they were on some kind of holiday cruise. In such a twisted reality, every noise took on a sinister meaning.

'The boat moved off to the sound of the mournful singing and dancing and the noise of retching,' wrote one female prisoner. 'In the darkness hands reached out towards me from all sides.' The same prisoner described a doctor's assistant, a Polish Jew, who helped her when he could: he played softly on an accordion, 'a melody which was grey like the sea, like our ship, like the fog'. When one of these ships ran aground on the shores of Japan, rescuers managed to retrieve only a handful of survivors from the pile of over six hundred prisoners battened down beneath the hatches. As well as the drowned, they found convicts who had chosen to cut their own throats rather than wait for the rising water.

Foreign shipyards made the convict ships sold to Stalin. When repairs of Gulag vessels were being undertaken in America, workers remembered the horrid stench still rising from the holds. In 1939, the *New York Times* reported that the Soviet ship which foundered in Japan, drowning seven hundred, was carrying fishermen from Kamchatka – a piece of misreporting based on a staggering system of Soviet lies. In 1944, the American Vice-President Henry Wallace visited Magadan. At the time, the West was the principal buyer of Soviet gold, with Kolyma's mines a major source. Local authorities went to great lengths to deceive their visitors. The watchtowers that lined the road into Magadan were taken down. The shops were stuffed with luxury items hitherto unknown in the region. Wallace bought a bottle of perfume and, for entertainment, was taken to the Magadan Theatre, where he watched a play performed by prisoners.

The US Vice-President Henry Wallace, pictured in Kolyma in 1944. Instead of meeting actual Gulag labourers, Wallace was introduced to a group of 'big husky young men' – members of the Young Communist Organization dressed up as miners.

I came to Magadan knowing that there had been pianos played by the Gulag's performing troupes. I intended to travel along the Kolyma Highway, a rough road pockmarked with old labour camps, stretching twelve hundred miles from Magadan to Yakutsk, the largest city in the world built on permafrost and the capital of Yakutia. During the Gulag period, Kolyma's number of camps and its extreme remoteness made it feel like 'a whole separate continent of the Archipelago', wrote Solzhenitsyn; it was the place beyond the *materik*, or mainland. According to a Polish historian and Gulag survivor writing in 1949, over three million prisoners were exiled to Kolyma, of whom only five hundred thousand made it through.

Among them was the composer Vsevolod Zaderatsky, a graduate of the Moscow Conservatory who had worked as the last Tsarevich's piano teacher. In 1915, he travelled once a week, almost every week, from Moscow to the royal household in St Petersburg. In Kolyma, Zaderatsky convinced his camp overseers to give him a few scraps of paper, promising that he would never write words, only musical notations, at a time when just being caught with a pen and paper was asking for a death sentence. From 1937 to 1938, Zaderatsky composed a cycle of twenty-four preludes and fugues for piano on telegraph forms and two small notepads. In a letter home to his family, the Muscovite director Leonid Varpakhovsky, who kept a copy of a Handel concerto under his pillow, wrote about playing in the camp's wind orchestra: 'My comfort is the music into which I immerse myself, so that I forget the world.'

For some musicians, however, picking up an instrument in the camps was a travesty of the brave creative life they had known before. They resisted cultural programmes for the 're-education' of prisoners. For many musicians, it was performance by brute force; for others, it was indescribably sad. Kolyma survivor Yelena Vladimirova described an orchestra of Kolyma prisoners tasked to provide culture to fellow convicts in a frozen landscape – how it was a 'travesty of freedom' performed by 'people half alive'.

In the Magadan archives there is a picture of a grand piano sitting centre-stage in an empty theatre in the forties. The instrument, which would have been played by the town's convict-musicians, was photographed in the main hall on the second floor of the Magadan State Music and Drama Theatre – a building constructed by prisoners as the Kolyma camps were being developed. There had been amateur theatre before, at two local venues, but with the arrival of talented prisoners, performance standards improved, and so did the facilities. According to the theatre archives, the town's first professional play, staged in 1933, was called *Utopia*. Among the new venue's most important patrons was Eduard Berzin, the first commander of Dalstroi, the pseudo-corporation founded in 1931 to develop roads, settlements and mines in north-east Siberia, which relied upon Gulag labour. A graduate of the Berlin College of Fine Arts, Berzin had a fondness for European culture.

With the city's population of free workers and Soviet officials, the Magadan Theatre evolved into a lively centre for music and entertainment. Solzhenitsyn writes about the famous Soviet tenor Vadim Kozin performing in the venue. How Kozin ended up here was quite another story. He was born in St Petersburg in 1905. In the twenties, he made his way in Western Russia by playing the piano in cinemas. Throughout

A piano in the performance hall of the Magadan State Music and Drama Theatre, c. 1940.

the thirties, he toured the Soviet Union as a tenor, becoming so famous that mounted police were needed to keep the concert fans at bay.

In 1944, three years after his mother and sister had perished in the Siege of Leningrad, Kozin was arrested and sent to Kolyma with a combination of charges, including sodomy. When he was released in 1950, his career looked set to pick up again. In 1956, he bought a piano from Kamchatka, a modest Red October upright, serial number 113075, delivered to Magadan by boat. Then he was arrested a second time in 1959 when he was on tour in Khabarovsk. Released a few months later, Kozin stayed on in Kolyma and lived in an apartment in Magadan. He wrote songs about the town, which became his adopted home. Its citizens celebrated Kozin's presence, once again lauding his performances. Kozin's surviving diaries, however, reveal a man tortured by the hypocrisy of Soviet society.

I visited Kozin's Kamchatkan Red October upright, which survives in his former one-room flat on the fourth floor of a bleak, rain-scoured housing block.* But it was the grand piano in that black-and-white archive photograph I wanted to find. There was something enigmatic about its presence, like a black crow about to take flight from a public entertainment hall in one of the most feared Gulag zones in the USSR – a piano played by a run of both free citizens and persecuted musicians.

Was this the piano which accompanied Kozin at his inaugural performance in front of the Gulag commanders? Was it the same instrument I saw in a photograph of a short, hollow-eyed Kozin standing beside an orchestra on the Magadan

* Kozin's flat is now a small museum at 1 Shkolnaya Street, Magadan.

stage? Solzhenitsyn's account describes how Nikishov, another Dalstroi chief, interrupted Kozin's applause: ' "All right, Kozin, stop the bowing and get out!" ' Another account described Kozin's rapturous reception, then the chief's thundering voice as he stood up and called him a pederast.

I visited the Magadan Theatre when it was under renovation, half expecting to find the original plaster relief of Stalin on the rear wall of the main auditorium. It is one of the weirder features in twenty-first-century Russia that, in spite of all the unfathomable acts of mass murder, Stalin is consistently voted by Russians as the greatest man who ever lived. Statues of Stalin aren't unusual in modern Russia, some having been erected only in the last few years.* In Magadan, however, Stalin isn't the local hero: on a hill above Nagaevo Bay, there is a statue glorifying Berzin.

Everything disturbed me about Magadan: the city's fairground at night, its big wheel creaking in the Pacific fog; the garden ornaments for sale in the market, which looked half alive; the graffiti depicting a child's teddy with stitched wounds to its head. Then I met the Tatar caretaker in Magadan's

---

* Smack in the middle of Siberia, a long way from any mitigating oceanic climate, there is the bitterly cold diamond town of Mirny. When I visited in the summer of 2016, I paused at a crossroads in the town centre. On one corner stood a newly installed statue of Joseph Stalin, and on the second corner a Russian Orthodox Church featuring an image of the last Tsar of Russia, his head haloed in gold. On the third corner, there were flags promoting President Vladimir Putin's United Russia party. Close to the fourth corner, or thereabouts, stood a children's school of art, with numerous modern grand pianos partly paid for by the diamond company that employs much of the community. Standing here felt like being at the centre of a whirlwind: how can Putin, Stalin, the last Tsar and big business all coexist like this, as if the past and future are in harmony? The confluence seemed to me bewildering, made all the more haunting by the music playing out of the loudspeakers in every street.

Vadim Kozin performing in Madagan in the late forties. According to Solzhenitsyn, Kozin tried to hang himself after his first performance in Kolyma but was taken down out of the noose.

Cathedral of the Holy Trinity. He had a young face with bright eyes, black hair and a long white beard that fell over his sternum. He showed me a picture on his mobile phone: a blue flash of light in front of an icon. An angel, he said, a little miracle.

Don't think it's all bad here, said a mining executive I accosted for help on the street. In Magadan, he described a lively contemporary culture. In the city's Philharmonic Hall he showed me a brand-new Kawai grand piano made in Japan, serial number 2605001, pushed back among the scenery props. In 2010, this concert grand was shipped from Japan to Finland, then to Riga in Latvia, and on to St Petersburg, where it was unloaded and taken to Moscow. Here it boarded an Aeroflot Tu-204 jetliner and was flown to Magadan. The piano's journey covered two thirds of the Earth's circumference. A direct route from Japan across the Okhotsk Sea would have been ten times shorter, but the port customs proved too forbidding – ironic given the ease with which human cargo arrived into Magadan during the Gulag period.

Despite all the benevolent townspeople willing to help me, there was still something rotten about Kolyma. Gone were the buoyant post-Stalin years when government subsidies kept the working people in reasonable comfort. Among the region's former draws was Kadykchan, a town along the highway built up around an old Gulag coal mine. This was where the poet Varlam Shalamov was sent to complete his hard-labour sentence under Stalin. After the camp system started to be dismantled in the late fifties, Kadykchan's population swelled when a number of Russians moved to the region, lured by salary bonuses for workers prepared to live this remotely.

By 1986, there were around ten thousand people living in Kadykchan, and a functioning community. A cinema was built called 'The Miner', and a restaurant opened called 'The One Who Lived Near the North Pole'. There was a local Kadykchan newspaper, a TV station and even a municipal ice rink – unusual for Soviet times, but a way to attract free workers to the middle of nowhere. In the late nineties, the coal mine closed down – an event linked to an explosion, a dramatically altered perestroika economy, and according to one impassioned local historian, a foreign conspiracy to monopolize the gold trade. Soon after, the town's boiler system also stopped working and the town emptied out, leaving just a hundred and thirty-eight families. Now there was no one, or at least no one I could find. Kadykchan was simply too cold to carry on without hot water. Savage nature had pulled the buildings into ruin. Grids of housing blocks had been evacuated and plundered to the last few panes of glass. Bridges had collapsed over rivers. In Kadykchan, the only remnants of music were broken pianos in a practice room in the town's abandoned school, the instruments' innards strewn about the floor.

Kadykchan was one of the largest of the Kolyma towns which emptied out after the collapse of the USSR. These days, there are only a handful of small settlements still clinging on. In *Kolyma Stories*, a semi-fictionalized account of his Gulag experience, Varlam Shalamov wrote about the region's summer greenery – how it grew with a kind of wild rush, as if to catch the briefest of temperate seasons. I came in July and the landscape was still a dull brown pit decorated with the white balls of dandelions, the colour gone, their ghostly seeds clinging on to stalks. Some days, a thick, wet mist hung so low that headlights didn't shine but bled a smudged yellow. Other days, in the dry heat, dust clouds ballooned along the road whenever a rare vehicle came into view – dust I couldn't shake off my shoes. More than anything, the land flanking the main Kolyma Highway felt like a place where people didn't belong. Walking through Kadykchan's ruins, the absences unnerved me: the numbered coat-hooks without any coats; the rolls of film curled up like wood shavings in looted apartment blocks; a Pushkin mural peeling off a schoolroom's walls.

In the settlements we passed through, I found a few sad instruments. In a garage there was an upright piano stored with rotting rubber gas masks; another in a disused cinema; and an ill-sounding Red October, serial number 154273, in a music school standing among portraits of Beethoven and Tchaikovsky. In this same building, in the town of Ust-Nera, where the Kolyma Highway branches south for Yakutsk, there were also pictures of brilliant students who at one time in Kolyma's past had thrived under the Soviet musical education system. The Gulag may have been filling up under Stalin at an appalling pace, but at the same time, literacy rates in the USSR nearly doubled by the end of the decade. In the thirties, when Kolyma was being mined by a constant supply of prisoners, new departments at the Moscow and Leningrad conservatories were bringing music students from peasant and worker backgrounds into the academic fold.

In a town called Susuman, a mining community with a small guest house tucked inside an apartment block, I sank into a smelly bed. Dogs cried through the night. Some late arrivals pulled their bags up the stairwell – truck drivers, geologists and miners who still scratch about in Kolyma for gold. There was a groaning from heating pipes, but otherwise nothing but a hollow silence. In *Kolyma Stories*, Shalamov described sour sweat embedded in the clothes that survivors took from the dead. The poet said it was a good thing there was no scent to the convicts' tears. As I lay awake staring at the ceiling, waiting for a water droplet to break, Kolyma felt like the saddest place on the planet. It was too far from anything I might ever understand. A week later, the road too difficult to travel, I was eager to fly out. I left in a small plane, my eyes mapping the close-shaven fat on a man who sat in a seat in front, the texture of his skull like a brain exposed. The image stayed with me, along with the sight of a handgun in our driver's glove compartment, the swellings in the land from mass graves, and the statue of Lenin in Kadykchan with half his face shot away.

13

The Siberian Colosseum:
Novosibirsk

'**M**ETRONOME' COMES FROM THE Greek *metron*, meaning 'measure', and *nomos*, meaning 'rule' or 'law'. It is an instrument of inevitability, a musician's measurement of time. During the Leningrad blockade, which ran for nearly nine hundred days from September 1941 to January 1944, Soviet authorities mounted hundreds of loudspeakers through the city's streets. Music was a way to keep the people's spirits up. The authorities also broadcast the tick-tock of a metronome – at first to signal an air raid, the pulse speeding up with the approaching enemy, then to fill the silences in programme intervals. To Leningraders, it was a well-documented adage that the rhythm of the metronome took on the feeling of a heartbeat.

For many living through the Leningrad blockade, their hearing adjusted to a different soundscape as curfews set in, along with the roar and scream of enemy bombardment, and the silence which comes with death and dystrophy. The Soviet poet Vera Inber said Leningraders got so adept at listening they could separate the sounds of an air raid like the orchestral parts in a Tchaikovsky concert. Another diarist, a fifteen-year-old student at the Leningrad Conservatory, described stepping over the entrails of a trolley bus into her ruined apartment, where her grand piano stood in a cold room: 'Music makes me fearless; shell fragments hit upon the roof, but I play. The plaster begins to fall down but I go into the melody.'

For the composer Dmitri Shostakovich, his siege experience may have been brief – the blockade started on 8 September 1941, and Shostakovich left the city in October – but it helped him repair his reputation after the disastrous review of *Lady Macbeth of Mtsensk* as 'Muddle instead of Music'. Shostakovich's famously stirring and patriotic Seventh, or *Leningrad* Symphony, was music which tore at the world's heartstrings: 'Your song tells us of a great singing people beyond defeat or conquest who across years to come shall pay their share and contribution to the meanings of human freedom,' wrote the American poet Carl Sandburg. As a piece of psychological warfare, it was brilliant – a calling card for the USSR about the urgency of their fight against the fascist advance. It used music as a political instrument of war, just as the Nazis announced their victories on German radio with a broadcast of Liszt's *Les Préludes.*

'My weapon was music,' wrote Shostakovich: 'I sat at my piano and worked, fast and intensely. I wanted to create a piece about our lives, about these days, about the Soviet people, who would go to any lengths for the sake of victory.' Moscow's Bolshoi Orchestra, which had been evacuated ahead of the Nazi advance, gave the world premiere of his *Leningrad* Symphony in the city of Samara on 5 March 1942. The score was then flown to Moscow, where it was performed three weeks later. Sometime in the late spring, it was taken out of the country on microfilm via Tehran, Cairo and Casablanca in a heroic evacuation route, then on to London and New York. When it made its premiere in the US on 19 July 1942, Shostakovich was turned into an international celebrity, the composer's rapturous reception earning him the cover of *Time* magazine.

From inside a besieged Leningrad, the Soviet authorities knew the music would be at its most powerful. But there was only one ensemble left that could possibly play this hugely ambitious work. The city's best orchestra, the Leningrad Philharmonic, had already been evacuated to Novosibirsk in Siberia, leaving behind a starving, lower-rank alternative. The Leningrad Radio Orchestra comprised a hundred members before the war. In the middle of the siege when the orchestra was ordered to re-form, the list of members made for dismal reading: there were numerous names crossed out (known to be dead), and others marked up in red to indicate they were on their way out. At the first rehearsal fewer than twenty musicians turned up, so military commanders called on soldiers to make up numbers. In late June, Shostakovich's score was airlifted into the besieged city and the improvised orchestra – playing in layers of old clothes, described by one participant as 'dressed like cabbages' – began to prepare as best they could.

The drummer perished on his way to work, wind players fainted for lack of food, while musicians were pulled out mid-rehearsal to go fight fires. When a date was finally fixed for the Leningrad premiere, Soviet artillery targeted German guns within range of the Philharmonic Hall, where the performance would take place, to ensure that Nazi bombers wouldn't be able to overwhelm the music. The city already had seventeen hundred loudspeakers in situ; in the run-up to the Leningrad performance, many more were erected to broadcast the symphony across German lines.

In the falling afternoon light of 9 August 1942, the city's hungry populace fell silent for one of the most dramatic moments in an incomprehensible war. '[W]e were stunned by the number of people, that there could be so many people starving for food but also starving for music,' said the trombonist: 'Some had come in suits, some from the front. Most were thin and dystrophic.' When it was over, not only Leningraders but also German soldiers listened to the half-hour standing ovation given by a people on its knees.

As Leningrad suffered, Novosibirsk – the de facto capital of Siberia, sitting almost a third of the way between Moscow and Vladivostok – was doing rather better: it wasn't under bombardment, and could therefore function as a kind of Siberian safe house during the war. Once known as the 'Chicago of the Soviet Union', Novosibirsk is still home to the largest opera house in Russia, founded under Stalin in the thirties. The so-called Siberian Colosseum dominates an empty square frilled with Soviet statuary. The dome, almost twice the size of the cupola belonging to St Paul's Cathedral in London, heaves itself out of the city's skyline. The building may not be conventionally beautiful – the façade's tall columns and stunted concrete pediments seem to obey no discernible law of classical harmony – but there is no denying its grand intention: a panoramic theatre so huge it could accommodate a column of tanks above the orchestra pit, the scale so significant that Soviet tractors could be driven from the street to the stage. The original decor was equally extravagant: crystal chandeliers, red velvet drapes, faux-Roman statues and Victorian bric-a-brac. Built into the basement, according to local rumours, was one of Stalin's bunkers.

In order to complete this mammoth project, the wartime factories of Novosibirsk, many of them evacuated from Western Russia, contributed specialist expertise, including aviation engineers who assembled the mechanics for a ninety-tonne stage curtain that came up out of the floor and shut like a

The Novosibirsk Opera and Ballet Theatre under construction in the 1930s.

crocodile locking its jaw. Novosibirsk's opera house became one of the boldest, most defiant expressions of Soviet ambition yet. While it was being built, more than twenty-four million Russians, both soldiers and civilians, perished in the Great Patriotic War. That was enough dead to sell every ticket in its auditorium nearly twenty thousand times over – the equivalent of a full house every day for fifty-five years.

The Novosibirsk Opera and Ballet Theatre, which officially opened on 12 May 1945, carried another layer of heroic significance: it was where the Soviet Union's cultural treasures – including musical instruments – were evacuated for safekeeping during the Nazi onslaught. It was used as the main storehouse for some of the greatest works of art in Russia's possession, delivered from both Moscow's Tretyakov Gallery and Leningrad's Pavlovsk Palace and State Hermitage Museum.

Packing was done in a hurry. Some three thousand pieces were sent from the Tretyakov, including the string instruments that had been gathered with such enthusiasm after the October Revolution. The largest canvases were transferred on to rolls – including Vasily Surikov's famous nineteenth-century painting depicting the Old Believer and religious martyr Boyarina Morozova being carried off in an exile's chains. The collection was then loaded on to railway wagons bound for Siberia, followed by another two thousand works, and fifty museum employees and their families.

Owing to the speed of the Nazi encirclement, the evacuation of artworks from a besieged Leningrad was even more frantic. As the noose tightened, Pavlovsk Palace – a centre of musical culture in Russia ever since the late eighteenth century – became a target for German guns. Museum staff buried what they could in the palace grounds. Leningraders boxed the

Siberian painter Vasily Surikov's Boyarina Morozova *being returned to the walls of the Tretyakov Gallery, Moscow, in 1945 after its wartime stay in Novosibirsk.*

porcelain toilet set, gifted to the Romanovs by Marie Antoinette, in freshly cut grass. They wrapped up breakables in imperial dresses. A member of Pavlovsk's staff made sketches of how the interior looked before it was abandoned, as well as the swagged curtains of the Tsar's baldaquin bed. Priceless treasures too large to extract were abandoned where they stood, including Maria Feodorovna's late-eighteenth-century Clementi upright grand piano.*

It was Andrei Zhdanov – the Leningrad boss and Stalin's heir apparent, nicknamed 'The Pianist' by rivals mocking his

---

* The Clementi is among Russia's most significant lost pianos. It was possibly taken by the Nazis or by the Spanish, both of whom quartered divisions at Leningrad's Pavlovsk Palace, where the piano was last seen.

musical abilities and cultural ambitions – who issued the order to extract the city's historic treasures. When Leningrad's first museum trains departed in July 1941, they were filled to bursting. The armoured cars pulled out of Leningrad with several thousand pieces from the Hermitage Museum, as well as another forty-two boxes from Pavlovsk – including 'Crate 63', containing Catherine the Great's precious 1774 Zumpe *piano anglais*.

Until November, the Zumpe was kept in Gorky outside Moscow, where it was placed under guard in a city church. When German aircraft closed in again, the piano was evacuated first to Tomsk, then to Novosibirsk, with the onward destination of each train revealed to the museums' keepers only as the cavalcade reached a new station.* On the long, two-month journey to Siberia, the convoy encountered hostile railway workers, brutal weather conditions and a fire from a stove. To escape bombardment, one of the trainloads hid for two weeks in a forest siding. Another attack, which directly targeted the Zumpe train, sent the museum workers running for shelter. Despite all these hazards, Catherine's precious square piano was finally offloaded in Novosibirsk at the end of December 1941 in a staggering winter low temperature of minus fifty-five degrees.

The Novosibirsk opera house was where the Zumpe stayed until the end of the war, cared for in the same half-finished building that the museum workers made their home for over two years. The Tretyakov employees slept in a dormitory in the make-up rooms. The Pavlovsk workers occupied

---

* A number of Hermitage treasures were stored in the Ipatiev House for safekeeping during the war. This is ironic given that so many of the evacuated objects used to belong to the imperial family, who were murdered in the same house in 1918.

Packed boxes of paintings from the Tretyakov Gallery stored at the Novosibirsk Opera and Ballet Theatre in 1944.

the basement, where they slept on one of the rugs salvaged from the Romanovs' last family home.

The evacuation plans had been executed almost perfectly – including the safe extraction to Novosibirsk of Yevgeny Mravinsky, conductor of the Leningrad Philharmonic. Like the artworks, Mravinsky and his orchestra made a circuitous journey to dodge enemy bombardment, and on 4 September 1941, arrived in Novosibirsk with their instruments. Mravinsky travelled with his mother, wife and several domestic cats.

Over the next three years, Mravinsky's orchestra went on to play more than five hundred concerts in Siberian exile, with the city's radio stations broadcasting the Philharmonic's music across the Soviet Union. Sometimes they performed in Novosibirsk's still-unfinished opera house. The Philharmonic also travelled to various Siberian towns, with concert standards, said Mravinsky, equal to the orchestra's Leningrad appearances. This included the biggest event of all: the Novosibirsk premiere of Shostakovich's *Leningrad* Symphony on 9 July 1942, which the composer went to Siberia to hear, going straight from the railway station to Mravinsky. Swept up in the patriotic fervour, museum staff put on an exhibition entitled 'Treasures Saved from the Germans' featuring a selection of works from Russia's outstanding cultural heritage in safekeeping in Siberia.

'Not one of the orchestras that have performed my work has attained such a perfect fulfilment of ideas,' wrote Shostakovich of the Leningrad Philharmonic-in-exile. An article in the newspaper *Soviet Siberia* described the fearful horror in the music, and how deep inside there was this animal-like howling. Shostakovich was rather pleased with the result: 'Far off in the middle of Siberia, one suddenly felt so much the

An exhibition of Russian artwork in the Novosibirsk Opera and Ballet Theatre during the Great Patriotic War. In the foreground, an art expert measures the room's humidity.

Leningrad milieu one has been familiar with and which one misses so much. During the rehearsals and concerts, I again experienced that creative process – that noble musical culture that is so characteristic of the city of Lenin.'

That noble musical culture. The concert grand used by the Leningrad Philharmonic during the siege years would be a prize to find – a piano which understood music as an expression of continuity and defiance. If the true instrument survived – the one revealed in a two-second flash of a piano lid in grainy film footage, as well as in the descriptions of an instrument which accompanied the Philharmonic's celebrated Glazunov Quartet – it seemed one of the likely possibilities was a nineteenth-century Steinway concert grand, serial number 45731, standing unused in an organ room at the Novosibirsk Conservatory. Instruments such as this aren't common in Siberia, said my source, Vladimir Biryukov, the president of the Siberian Piano Tuners Association and head tuner at the Novosibirsk Philharmonic. He believed the Steinway had first come to Siberia with or for Mravinsky's Leningrad orchestra. His reasoning was simple: the concert grand was too spectacular to have had any purpose other than to service the most important venue and musicians of the period.

I tried to trace its history by contacting the Leningrad Philharmonic as well as Steinway archivists in New York. Identifying the piano's serial number, Steinway said the piano was an iconic Model D Cherry with German legs, completed on 16 May 1881, shipped without its finish coating to Hamburg, and thence to the father of Sergei Rachmaninoff's publisher and friend, Alexander Gutheil of Moscow, on 24 February 1882. Then the trail went dead: there seemed to be no knowing how or when it had arrived in Siberia. There was one man, however, who might be able to shed some light: a piano tuner

Vladimir Biryukov, the president of the Siberian Piano Tuners Association and head tuner at the Novosibirsk Philharmonic, with the Steinway grand he believes was played by the Leningrad Philharmonic-in-exile.

called Igor Lomatchenko. I had been told he was full of know-ledge, and had a roomful of instruments in the basement of the Novosibirsk Opera and Ballet Theatre.

I arrived in Novosibirsk on the day of the Epiphany, a January holiday which Russians celebrate by immersing themselves in holes cut in the ice of frozen lakes and rivers. Down on the Ob, a festival spirit prevailed. Tough Siberian men, bellies folded over their pants like dough, queued to get into the water and receive blessings from a priest. Some of the women wore bikinis; others wore long nighties with high necklines. With breasts sagging and arms folded in for warmth, they looked like pupae, their fragile bodies vulnerable in encasements as thin as paper. There were young men in tight swimmers enjoying the jocularity of stripping down and a morning off work, and friendly *babushki* pleased to see a foreigner among the festival ranks. Among them was a thoroughly defeated young woman with hollowed cheeks and faraway eyes. As she stood dripping water, the tiny red roses in her cotton gown clinging to her skin, she had the look of someone who no longer remembered if she'd ever laughed.

In the centre of Novosibirsk, the opera house was lit by a pink dawn. At the stage door, musicians came and went for rehearsals. I passed by a run-through of a Verdi opera, then headed into another curl of corridor with stage scenery stored on either side. There was a tiered wedding cake large enough to conceal a small troupe of ballerinas, a Trojan horse, and two huge elephants on wheels. Communist red stars and oriental lanterns hung from ropes. A girl in a black tutu stretched out on a creaky bench.

Igor was in the basement of the opera house practising his cello in front of a wonky music stand. He was middle aged, almost bald, with a jolly face and slightly protruding ears. He had a wide smile, big hands, broad shoulders and a stocky build. He was a member of the opera house orchestra, and the principle tuner responsible for all its pianos. Since 1978, he had occupied Room 1037, a room as hot as an oven in the same

247

basement where in the middle of the war the Tsar's carpet was rolled out and used as a makeshift bed. More like the inside of someone's soul than a workshop, Room 1037 was swollen with unexpected possessions that were gathered, layered and piled into corners, hanging from pegs, and stuffed into any available mug or disused paint pot.

The muddle was both commonplace and magnificent – a magical place where a rare musical artefact might lurk, or an astonishing sound be hidden by the limbs of other, less remarkable instruments. A pink snout poked out from behind an upright piano – the papier-mâché head of a suckling pig on a platter, which looked like it had drifted in from a *Nutcracker* set. A tuxedo hung from the ceiling, the suit ironed until its fibres had taken on a silvery sheen. There was some of the outdoor camouflage that Russian hunters use in the taiga, and a table stacked with boot polish, a collection of mechanical clocks, and stubby paint brushes washed until they were almost bald. The walls were decorated with pictures of bears, Lenin and Louis Armstrong. Various cellos, some missing their fronts, were lying against pianos. A full-size punch bag was suspended over a concert grand in the middle of repair, the precision and the improvisation of Igor's craft hidden among the pliers, lacquers and copper-wound bass strings, the tuning pins, hinges and wooden ribs. It was as if all the niche skills which had created the early piano industry had ended up here, in a basement in Novosibirsk: the belly-men (who worked with the sounding-board makers), the chipper-ups (the men who gave the instrument its pre-tuning), the key makers, polishers and action finishers.

'It's not much,' said Igor, 'but it is my life.'

Igor said it was hard to know which instrument most

deserved his attention: the Becker brooding in a corner, the Schröder with the tinny top notes, or the unnamed pianos stored too close to each other for anyone to be able to play a note. He talked about how every piano has its own voice: rich, mellow, strident, glassy, warm, thin or cool. Generally speaking, the voice dulls and flattens with age and wear. The hammers harden, strings relax. Soft tones shrivel then vanish. He showed me the modern Steinway concert grand played by Denis Matsuev whenever he was in town, which had its own humidity-controlled storage room. Back in his workshop, he pointed out a sturdy upright in the corner, regarded as one of the best upright pianos ever built – the one I had noticed because of the papier-mâché pig.

'A 1930s Grotrian-Steinweg,' said Igor. 'It's a German piano, with a tender sound. But then it has seen a great deal. I can hear it in the way it plays.'

Novosibirsk was a city full of interesting instruments, he said. He agreed that the Steinway in the conservatory – the one Buryikov suspected had belonged to or was played by the Leningrad Philharmonic – was indeed superb. He could trace the piano's movements in Novosibirsk from the seventies, when he believed it was transferred from the city's opera house to the musical comedy theatre. But he couldn't track its history any further back in time. He then talked about various pianos that his son was restoring for a local piano collector.

'You need to meet my children. We're not one tuner in my family, but three,' said Igor, his crab-apple cheeks burnished pink with pride.

We arranged to reconvene at the same place in two days' time to talk some more. Except when that day came, Room 1037 wasn't the same place at all. Everything had been tidied up: pianos organized, tools sorted. The boxing bag was no longer suspended over the grand piano. The coffee rings had been wiped away, the sheet music put into piles. New seats had been arranged and each one assigned to a Lomatchenko family member. The only other day of the year on which they ever gathered like this was Stalin's birthday – the same birthday as his, said Vasily Lomatchenko, with a beaming grin.

Vasily was Igor's father. Despite his eighty-three years, he had an almost lineless face, laughed gaily and sometimes danced on the spot. Vasily wore a freshly pressed pale blue

The Lomatchenko family, from left to right: Kostya, Evgeniy, Fyodor, Igor and Vasily.

shirt with the top button done up, a woollen sleeveless pullover and polished shoes. Igor's youngest son, Evgeniy, was shy and slim; he preferred restoring the cabinetry of pianos to tuning. Evgeniy's brother, Kostya, was in his early forties. He was unusually tall, with boyish blond hair – like a polar bear, said my interpreter. Kostya – joined by his seven-year-old son, who also wore a bow tie – was both a tuner and a restorer. He talked about some of the instruments he knew about or had worked on over the years: a French-made Gaveau thought to have come from a German U-boat, and a concert grand taken back from the Germans at the Battle of Moscow in 1941. Kostya wanted to attend the crème de la crème of tuner training: the C. F. Theodore Steinway Academy in Hamburg. He dreamed of starting a Russian piano factory to manufacture some of the best instruments in the world. He was sensitive, warm and extraordinarily enthusiastic – a tender giant with a kind of bright, child-like soul. When we had first met, he cried. When I asked him why, he said it was because a stranger had come out of nowhere and told him she was interested in his work. When I asked my interpreter to help me understand his response, she said later: 'Every piano for Kostya is unique. He knows it, and even when he describes how a piano sounds, the beauty touches him deeply. It's as if he is sensitive to different vibrations to those which you and I can feel.'

But it was Kostya's grandfather, Vasily, who held the room's attention as he began to talk about how his ancestors had ended up in Siberia. Vasily's father had belonged to the wave of emigrants who left Ukraine at the turn of the twentieth century. They travelled to Siberia by horse cart, and settled in a village called Dovolnoye, about a hundred miles from

Novosibirsk. Vasily sounded it out slowly: *Dov-ol-noy-ye*, which meant something like 'Pleasant Village'. Vasily's father, whom he described as a quiet, unaffectionate man, fought for the Whites in the Russian Civil War. At least, they think he did, but Vasily's father never spoke of it. He was marked out as a *kulak*, or rich peasant, by Stalin's regime – an arbitrary process which effectively reallocated wealth based less on formal criteria than the whim of neighbours, local officials and Soviet activists. He was sent to work in the mines for ten years. When he finally returned home, he was despatched to Moscow to fight the Nazis.

In 1953, Vasily also did his military service. He joined a train packed with some four hundred Siberians and set off for Sakhalin Island. Two years later, he went to live in Kuzbass, Siberia's coal-mining region, where he made do with a tent for the first twelve months. He drove lorries in the Sayan Mountains near the Mongolian border, using dangerous roads which looped up and down the region's steep ridges. He kept a sack of salt under the seat of his truck which stopped the windows misting up; the salt absorbed the humidity of his breath. Although he liked the solitude of the road, he couldn't stop wanting future generations of Lomatchenkos to live a different life.

Vasily married and had a son. In 1961, he sold the wooden house he had built during his first winter in Kuzbass, and moved his family to Akademgorodok. This was Siberia's new science city going up in the forest outside Novosibirsk, an elite Soviet utopia founded in the fifties as a progressive hothouse to attract some of the country's best brains. Like the university in Tomsk, it was a proud, ambitious institution which gave Siberia enormous credibility – and still does. Vasily found work with the town's construction crews, while his wife got a job in the canteen at the House of Scientists, Akademgorodok's main social club.

Despite funds being short, Vasily used a quarter of the money from his house sale to buy a piano from a local second-hand shop. Although he had not received a musical education himself, he bought the instrument in 1962 when his son was five years old in the belief that a cultured life would change the family's fortunes. Around this time, the musical education system in the Soviet Union was beginning to peak. In the early sixties there were over four hundred thousand primary-age children enrolled in elementary music schools, and twenty-four college-level conservatories. Opportunities were open to all, regardless of status, as musical education was systemized even in the smallest towns. It was a broad cultural transformation supported by all the inexpensive instruments which were being manufactured and distributed more widely than at any other time in Russia's history. Igor, who played the piano, focused on the cello. He was talented, said Vasily, but as Igor got older there were the usual distractions with football and girls. When Igor quit, his father didn't argue. Vasily was a man of older Soviet times, who knew how tough life could get. He found his son a job in a concrete factory, where Igor worked until his hands bled – an experience Vasily knew would turn his son back to music.

Six months later, Igor started learning how to tune pianos, and in 1978, landed a job at the Novosibirsk Opera and Ballet Theatre.

I asked where the instrument was now – the one Vasily had bought with the money from the sale of his house.

'It's over there,' said Igor, pointing at the piano used like a platter for the papier-mâché pig: 'I showed you yesterday. A 1930s Grotrian-Steinweg.'

Kostya chimed in. 'I need to show you all the peculiarities,' he said. 'Heavy, powerful hammers. A basic, strong construction. Original ivory-covered keys, which would last another hundred years. It's not the grandest, but the full sound it produces is something unique.'

When the piano's top was opened, the instrument smelled as if it hadn't breathed for a while. Igor took out the top door to reveal the serial number: 63216. The back frame of the piano, the classic model 120, was star-shaped, a bit like the British flag – a Grotrian-Steinweg signature, which made these pianos about as good as an upright ever got. The firm bracing allowed the soundboard to vibrate freely, its solidity helping to ensure a tonal stability up and down the octaves.

'It's a long-liver,' said Igor, 'a robust piano with a bright voice.'

The Grotrian-Steinweg had ivory keys. I pressed a few; a muddy note, a clacking action, then in the higher register, a singing tone, and a light, responsive touch. It could use some tuning pins, said Kostya, which needed to come from Germany, but the hammers were good and strong. They needed some refacing and toning, he said.

As the Lomatchenkos talked between themselves about the superiority of German engineering, I could hear the advice from an English piano manufacturer, Brian Kemble, who was guiding me through the technicalities of my search.

'It's simpler than you think,' said Brian. 'If you find a piano everyone likes, it's missing something; it's too generic. You want to find the instrument somebody is passionately in love with.'

The instrument's piano maker had an impressive pedigree. Friedrich Grotrian, born in Germany in 1803, first learned his craft when he lived in Moscow at the height of the nineteenth-century Russian piano boom. Friedrich was in Russia, making pianos, when all the great virtuosos passed through, including Liszt. When Friedrich returned to Germany in 1854, he worked for Theodor Steinweg whose father, Heinrich Steinweg, emigrated to the US in 1850 where he changed his name and founded Steinway & Sons three years later. In 1865, Theodor Steinweg went to America to join the family. Back in Europe, Friedrich Grotrian bought out his former employer to operate the Grotrian-Steinweg factory in German Braunschweig. The firm is still in the hands of Grotrian's fifth- and sixth-generation descendants.*

Finding records would be hard, as I was soon to discover. The Grotrian-Steinweg piano factory in Braunschweig was bombed by the Allies during the Second World War, destroying the archives of seven thousand Grotrian-Steinweg pianos, including, it would seem, evidence of this piano's original owner. Much later in my travels, I then saw a name that had been inscribed into the instrument itself: the lowest key of the piano was marked with a tuning date of 20 October 1944, and the name of the *Klavierstimmer*, or piano tuner, Carl W. Aug[xx]t,† based in the town of Allenstein in the former East Prussia. That tuning date, scratched in pencil, was just ninety-four days before the Red Army marched into town. Seven months

---

* In the seventies, after a drawn-out legal tussle, Grotrian-Steinweg were forbidden from disclosing the Steinway family connection to the American market. Grotrian-Steinweg therefore dropped the Steinweg name when they exported pianos to North America, where the brand is known as Grotrian.
† The surname is not entirely clear owing to the smudged ink.

later, Allenstein was effectively scrubbed off the map. What was left was handed to Poland at the end of the Second World War and renamed Olsztyn.

The Soviet advance on East Prussia from 1944 to 1945 may have been brief, but it took a heavy toll, inducing a massive panic migration. Aleksandr Solzhenitsyn, then an artillery captain stationed in East Prussia, described the looting in Neidenburg thirty-odd miles from Allenstein, in his narrative poem, *Prussian Nights*:

> *And through the fires, the smoke, the soot,*
> *The Conquerors of Europe swarm,*
> *Russians scurrying everywhere.*
> *In their trucks they stuff the loot:*
> *Vacuum cleaners, wine and candles,*
> *Skirts and picture-frames and pipes,*
> *Brooches, medallions, blouses, buckles,*
> *Typewriters (not with Russian type)*

While Solzhenitsyn mused about the rights and wrongs of his own desire to take three hundred Faber-Castell pencils from a ruined post office, other Soviet officers – permitted to send ten kilos of stolen goods home every month – were bolder. What they couldn't post, they stuffed into the interiors of their tanks; furniture and even livestock were taken. The vanquished behaved similarly on their way in and out of enemy territory, with Hitler's determination throughout the war to obliterate a nation's cultural memory one of the most uncompromising in history. Rather than let their treasures fall into Soviet hands, priceless collections were also burnt or looted by civilians before the Red Army arrived. But somehow this little Grotrian-Steinweg had survived, even if the how, why or where remained entirely unclear. It was a mystery, the piano's roots – where exactly they fitted in to this place and time in history – shackled to a time of chaos.

'When you hear it, you cannot say it's very dry, or very glassy, or very metallic,' said Kostya, as he stroked the piano's case, who knew only his family's history with the instrument. 'It's balanced, full, a rounded sound. And see the frame? It's cast iron. It has an integrity, which deserves proper restoration. We need to get some new tuning pins, which hold the strings, restring and make the tunings. If I get those new parts in from Germany, it will take two or three months to fix up.'

I asked Kostya what he thought might be the right finale for the Grotrian-Steinweg, not knowing it for myself.

'The word "finale" means end. An instrument must be played. It will feel good when that instrument is working again,' said Kostya as he gently closed the piano shut.

14

Vera's Mühlbach:
Akademgorodok

W HEN VASILY LOMATCHENKO first moved to Akademgorodok, he was among seventy thousand construction
workers who believed they were building some kind of Soviet
paradise. A bold new science city made profound economic
sense in the ideological thaw that followed Stalin's death in
1953, with part of its purpose to help the new First Secretary
of the Communist Party, Nikita Khrushchev, develop the
technology to exploit Siberia's vast potential. Siberia may
have been home to only a small proportion of the country's

population, but it was also home to up to ninety per cent of the country's natural resources.

On paper, Akademgorodok looked spectacular. The spirit of optimism would be articulated not just in the city planning – a beach beside an artificially flooded River Ob, an ice rink, cycle paths and meandering forest walks – but in the social clubs, cafés, theatres and music societies. Laboratories and libraries would be world-class. Senior members of Akademgorodok's scientific elite would each get a detached woodland cottage to live in rather than a flat in a Soviet apartment block. Even the city hotel would be a cut above the rest in order to host some of the country's most brilliant minds.

It was a powerful idea that appealed to just about everyone, leading to the creation of what was later described as 'the little town with probably the biggest I.Q. anywhere'. For the country's intelligentsia with a renegade bent, the far-off location of Akademgorodok meant their work might be less shackled to the party's chain than the equivalent institutions in Moscow. Then there were the dreamers who would have chased utopia wherever it showed up. The challenge was to manipulate these mixed motives (and the state's uncertain funds) in order to construct a viable, lively community with scientific excellence at its heart.

Within a decade of breaking ground, Akademgorodok had fifteen functioning research institutes. An Institute of Cytology and Genetics was opened – 'a miracle', wrote the geneticist Raissa L. Berg, given that not long before, the study of genetics had been banned by Stalin, who considered genetic inheritance ideologically opposed to Marxism. In deep Siberia, the academic elite found more freedom to work. Houses had electric ranges and fridges, and benefitted from subsidized utility bills. The higher the ceiling, the higher the salary, Berg observed. Scientists benefitted from superior grocery rations. Musicians, artists and poets arrived, along with everyday Russians in support of this dazzlingly inventive city where the mushrooms were bountiful, and the mosquitoes horrid.

Within this close-knit community lived a French-born concert pianist, Vera Lotar-Shevchenko, who settled in Akademgorodok in 1966 and lived there until her death in the early eighties. I was told about her story by Memorial, a human rights organization in Moscow. One thing led to another and now Anastasia Bliznyuk, a beautiful, outstandingly educated violinist in the Akademgorodok chamber orchestra, was helping me look for Vera's last instrument: a pre-Revolution, Russian-made Mühlbach grand piano.

Vera Lotar-Shevchenko was born Vera Lautard on 2 October 1899 in the Mediterranean resort of Nice in France. People who knew her described her as stout, round-shouldered, with arthritic hands and stubby fingers. She had short nails, clipped or bitten down to the quick. The red joints of her fingers were gnarled from labour. She wore a backwards hat and old jumpers. Later in life, she dyed her hair an orange colour. She made friends easily, with a French accent and gravelly voice that never left her. She showed little interest in everyday domesticity, and would let her dinner burn while she practised the piano, forgetting about the pan until neighbours complained about the smoke. She would eat a tin of fish for lunch, liked cheap Bulgarian 'ox heart' red wine, and Russian Camembert cheese from Moscow. She also liked astronomy. She used to say the magnitude of the stars kept life's trifles in perspective.

According to one of her friends, Vera described her early

childhood as bourgeois, presided over by a socialite Spanish mother and a tough English governess who made her take cold showers – a regime Vera hated, even though she later said it helped her survive some of her toughest years in the USSR. Vera's father was said to have been a brilliant, hot-tempered mathematician who worked as a professor at Turin University. He also loved to gamble, his card losses eventually forcing the family to move from a grand villa into a cheap hotel on the Côte d'Azur.

Taught piano from a very young age, Vera showed signs of exceptional musical talent, and advanced rapidly. There is confusion as to where she trained, and under whom. One account leads back to the Franco-Swiss pianist and composer Alfred Cortot, whose technique was so impressive that even Vladimir Horowitz, one of the twentieth century's most iconic classical pianists, approached Cortot and asked him to reveal his secret. Another source cited her teacher as the Italian Ernesto Consolo. Whatever the truth of it, Vera perfected a spectacular 'velvet' playing style. By 1920, her profile was significant enough for the French newspaper *Le Figaro* to describe Vera's performances of Liszt as 'rare brilliance'.

Vera's personal life, however, was unhappy. When her first marriage to a Frenchman failed, she fled to Rome in 1930, where she met her second husband, a Russian engineer called Vladimir Shevchenko whom she had encountered at the salon of a Russian émigré duchess. In the most romantic telling of their love affair, Shevchenko used to arrive with a violin tucked under his arm. Shevchenko, however, wanted to go back to the homeland his family had fled in the early twentieth century. In 1939, the couple moved to Leningrad, where Vera found work as a performer. Then Shevchenko was arrested, accused of acting as a foreign spy. He was sent to a Gulag in Zlatoust in the Urals.

When Vera travelled to the town to try and prove his innocence, she, too, was arrested. In February 1943, Vera was sentenced under Article 58.10, for 'anti-Soviet agitation and propaganda', and sent to a labour camp not far from Ekaterinburg.

What happened to Vera's husband in the Gulag is unclear. Some said Shevchenko was diagnosed with schizophrenia, then dystrophy. Other accounts claimed he was shot. A few said he jumped out of a window. Vera believed none of them and continued to write letters to him deep into her eight-year incarceration. It was to no avail. By the time she came out of the Gulag herself, the man she loved had been taken from her, leaving her nothing but the music inside her head. She didn't even have her husband's violin, which was eventually delivered to her. Unable to look at the case, which she said resembled a small coffin, she gave the instrument away to rid herself of the memory.

Vera couldn't, however, give up music altogether. She adored Bach, and she admired Chopin's Preludes. To Vera, music was like breathing. In prison, the female prisoners had seen how badly she had pined for her piano, so they carved a keyboard into her wooden bunk with a kitchen knife so she could practise silently at night. Another account gives her Gulag piano as a kitchen table. Yet another said her playing in prison was limited to a one-off encounter with a piano in a village house. Where the stories do converge is in 1950: the first thing she did on her release was walk on to the streets of the local town, Nizhny Tagil, to find a music school. Still wearing her convict's quilted pea coat, she asked to play the piano.

Vera sat at that instrument for one, maybe two hours (typically of Vera's story, there are others who say far longer). She played without stopping, laughing and crying, the recall of her repertoire note-perfect as her stubby fingers behaved with the same exhilarating precision as they had before her arrest. Teachers and students who were listening at the door were dumbfounded by this magnificent squall of Chopin, Liszt and Beethoven. It was as if every part of Vera's being were lost to the power of music, as if she could see everything all at once, the '[n]othing that is not there and the nothing that is'.

The face of Vera Lotar-Shevchenko on her gravestone in Akademgorodok.

Vera didn't leave any memoirs. She was a charismatic introvert who lived deep inside herself, except when she played the piano with a divine intensity which seemed to draw people in. There is an old recording of Vera playing Beethoven's Sonata No. 32, Op. 111. Listen to the music and, despite the crackle, the effect is mesmerizing. She plays with a fevered urgency, each note brimming with the strength of her character, as if playing the piano is a kind of therapy.

After her Gulag experience, Vera never recovered her international career. She didn't return to France. On her release, she got a job at the Railway Club Theatre in the Urals city where she had first walked out of prison. By 1965, she was working in Barnaul in the Altai. This was where the Soviet journalist Simon Soloveychik happened to hear her play to an audience of fifty-three people in a hall for five hundred. On 19 December 1965, Soloveychik wrote about her performance in the Soviet newspaper *Komsomolskaya Pravda*. Describing her extraordinary sophistication, poetry and ambitious French repertoire, he cited the world-class virtuoso Sviatoslav Richter and a Beethoven recording by Artur Schnabel. He said listening to Vera induced the same feeling – that he was hearing piano music for the first time. He called it an encounter with beauty at its very limit.

Endorsed by that article, Vera was hired as a soloist by the Novosibirsk Philharmonic and moved to Akademgorodok at the invitation of the city's academics. The Soviet scientist and computer pioneer Alexei Lyapunov, who became one of her Akademgorodok patrons, hosted intimate concerts in his home. It seemed as if Vera had found her safe house, a place where she could focus on the music she lived for, even if there were still moments when she remained tainted by her Gulag past. On a cold Tuesday night during the winter of 1966, she played in the Novosibirsk Opera and Ballet Theatre. The concert had barely been advertised. There was only a single poster pinned up inside the theatre beside the cashier. When Vera arrived on stage, there were two instruments: a Steinway concert grand – was this the same instrument I had tried to trace back to the Leningrad Philharmonic-in-exile? – and a dilapidated Soviet-era Estonia. The Steinway was locked shut, in what felt like a deliberate snub. Vera cried a little. She asked her friend for a shot of vodka, then walked back on stage in a borrowed, ill-fitting concert dress to play the Estonia so spectacularly that everyone from the coat-check to the kitchen staff was spell-bound. Vera refused an encore, telling the audience how hard it had been to perform on the Soviet piano when beside it stood the greatest instrument of them all.

Anastasia, the violinist helping me with Vera's story, was among those who had heard Vera play during her Akademgorodok years. Anastasia's family had lived in the same apartment block. Whenever she practised, Vera would open the door to her flat and leave it slightly ajar. People would gather on the stairwell to listen to her rehearse – a concert hall on the third floor of a Khrushchev-era flat fash-ioned from sixties prefabricated concrete.

Anastasia took me to the city's South Cemetery, where Vera was buried in a quiet grove of birch trees. On the way, she pointed out the town's public sculptures, which included a computer start-up button and a lab mouse on a granite plinth knitting a double-helix string of DNA. There was a tidy order to Akademgorodok, as if everyone knew their pur-pose. Slender black shapes moved slowly through the wide, quiet streets, nobody touching or talking, their bodies pressed slightly forward into the cold. There were barely any cars, yet the town's traffic lights seemed to pause longer than in other towns, as if someone had decided to give Akademgorodok's citizens more time to think.

At a stonecutter's shop beside the cemetery gate, new headstones were layered up like sheaves of paper. Inside the cemetery, the tips of graves nudged out of the snow like stone buds. The academicians' grand memorials lined the main, well-kept boulevard, as if the same lead scientists who benefitted from favourable grocery rations in life also merited a better plot than regular citizens when their time was up.

Anastasia led me to Section Six in the cemetery, where Vera's coffin had been draped with a home-made French tricolour flag and lowered into the Russian earth. I had paid for her grave to be cleared of snow, which revealed a headstone decorated with an etched portrait of Vera as an older woman, her hair cropped to the ears and her eyes downcast. On the headstone was written: 'Life in which there is Bach is blessed.' As I stood in front of the memorial, I wondered what part of Vera's story she would have wanted to be remembered, and if she would have been glad of my search for her last piano and the story it told of the cultural landscape which opened up with Khrushchev's thaw.

During the construction of Akademgorodok, restrictions on freedom of expression began to relax throughout the USSR. On 25 February 1956, Khrushchev made a 'secret speech' to delegates at the Twentieth Communist Party Congress – an event which had a cataclysmic effect, not only in denouncing a system that by the time of Stalin's death was entirely totalitarian, but by destroying Stalin's cult of infallibility. Some of Stalin's most feared labour camps were abolished, with large numbers of political prisoners granted amnesty, or 'rehabilitated' (a process which exonerated victims of their alleged crimes, often posthumously). More overt signs of renewed confidence and tolerance spread into Russian society. There was even a tentative melt in Cold War relations. In 1958, the Texan pianist Harvey Van Cliburn won the International Tchaikovsky Piano Competition in Moscow – with Khrushchev's approval.

A year later, in July 1959, Richard Nixon, then Vice-President of the United States, flew to Novosibirsk. He visited the city's opera house, comparing Novosibirsk's hunger for culture with that of nineteenth-century San Francisco. The audience of two thousand, observed a *New York Times* journalist, were 'dressed as if ready for a football game'. On the same trip, Mrs Nixon went to a Siberian fashion show.

In this busy period of de-Stalinization, hope for some kind

Nikita Khrushchev congratulating the American pianist Harvey Van Cliburn.

of freedom was a very real possibility. In 1962, Solzhenitsyn's *One Day in the Life of Ivan Denisovich* was published in the Soviet Union, giving a first-hand account of the Gulag experience. This was an extraordinarily significant moment, indicating a new transparency on the past. Then in 1964 the USSR's new leader, Leonid Brezhnev, ousted Khrushchev and began his eighteen-year tenure as General Secretary when the Soviet Union shifted gear again. His anti-reformist stance gave the USSR stability and prestige – as well as the world's fastest, deepest submarine, and a functioning space station – but it also induced an era of political, cultural and economic stagnation.

In Akademgorodok, however, there were citizens who behaved as if none of this was happening, as if they considered themselves somehow immune to the renewed ideological clampdown. In May 1968, the city's House of Scientists hosted a Festival of Bards. The event was announced with a banner over the door to the concert hall: 'Poets! Siberia Awaits You!'

Locals queued enthusiastically for tickets to the festival's main act: the pianist, guitarist and underground poet Alexander Ginzburg, or 'Galich', as he was known. Galich was used to performing his satirical work behind closed doors. This would therefore be the first open concert of his career. When the day came, Galich sang 'Clouds', about a former Gulag prisoner who got drunk in a bar, and 'Pasternak in Memoriam', which described Pasternak's funeral at a time when his masterpiece, *Dr Zhivago*, remained banned.

At first, Galich's lyrics were met by stunned silence. Then all two thousand people in the audience rose to their feet in applause.

As word spread through Akademgorodok, Galich was fetched from the city hotel for a 2 a.m. encore at the movie theatre to perform for the students of the Physics and Mathematics School. In Galich's provocative rendition, Russians were hearing the truth about Soviet doublespeak in a public auditorium – and they couldn't get enough of it. But the honeymoon wasn't to last. For a while, some of the party faithful had been concerned that the town's outspokenness represented a danger to the status quo. Then, in the same year as the Festival of Bards, a leaked petition – signed by forty-six Akademgorodok researchers denouncing the closed trials of political dissidents – sent shockwaves through the system. Not long after came the most dramatic expression of the changing times: three months after Galich's performance, Soviet tanks rolled into Czechoslovakia to put an end to the Prague Spring.

Now all that remains of Akademgorodok's Galich story is pushed into a corner of a private home on the felicitously named No. 4 Truth Street in the heart of Akademgorodok – the armchair which sat on the stage during Galich's famous 1968 performance.* The chair is part of a precious collection of memorabilia – a kind of private museum filling the four-room, ground-floor apartment belonging to Anastasia. I visited for tea. Among the treasure trove of objects and photo albums, there was one image which stood out among the rest: a woman in a Mary Quant-style minidress on a set of weighing scales. The photograph recorded a beauty contest in Akademgorodok. A year earlier, the same contest was won by a man in drag.

'My father,' said Anastasia; 'he had beautiful legs.'

When Anastasia's family arrived in Akademgorodok, the

---

* Galich was effectively hounded out of the Soviet Union in June 1974. Some years later, he was found dead in Paris, electrocuted when he tried to plug in a new tape recorder. His story is told in Alexander Galich, *Songs and Poems*, trans. Gerald Stanton Smith (Ann Arbor: Ardis Publishers, 1983).

city was still being built. Back then, the only way to make a telephone call was by travelling on one of the two daily buses, route number eight, to Novosibirsk. Anastasia's father, who worked as a scientist-engineer in the Research Institute of Automation, was nicknamed the city's Minister of Bizarre Affairs. He was one of the earliest members of the irreverent social club, Under the Integral, which organized the Festival of Bards.

Anastasia made tea, weaving in and out of the city's cultural history. She told a story about Arnold Katz, among Russia's most important twentieth-century conductors, and his performances in the House of Scientists. I listened, ate sweets and flicked through an old telephone directory. Vera Lotar-Shevchenko's name stared back at me with a curious matter-of-factness. Her six-digit number was still there: 65-98-29. The simplicity was beguiling, as if I could just pick up a phone and ask to pop round to hear her play in her apartment, the door half ajar.

I hung around for a while in Akademgorodok, coming and going, looking for people who remembered Vera. The hotel I stayed in was once the highest building in the city, but only just. In 1959, when Khrushchev visited to check on progress, he instructed the city's architects to keep their ambitions in check. On the plans, the top four floors of the projected twelve-storey hotel were quickly lopped off.

I liked the city's pace. Sunday morning in Akademgorodok felt like a sleepy morning in any university town, with its farmers' market spread along the sidewalk. On the bonnet of a dove-grey Lada were buckets of berries, pickles, pumpkins, persimmons, and a tub of plump porcini mushrooms, their silky russet tops dusted with frost. The emerald picket fences around the academicians' cottages were neatly painted, just as they were at the time of the town's founding. The aero-modelling club established in the sixties for the children of engineers was also still active. At Akademgorodok's House of Culture, I listened to the town's chamber orchestra tuning up. Among the string musicians, there was a geology professor who had played with the orchestra since the sixties. He remembered Vera and the balmy early years when Akademgorodok was created.

Anastasia found what I was looking for: Vera's last piano was in the care of the University's Physics and Mathematics School, where Siberia's cleverest children are sent to boarding school. This is the super-cell of the prodigious Russian brain, each school place dependent upon highly competitive Olympiads designed to harvest talented future scientists out of Siberia and the Russian Far East. The instrument was a Mühlbach grand, serial number 8250, dating from around 1905, when the factory was producing two hundred and fifty grand pianos a year. The German maker was among the foreign artisans who moved to St Petersburg in the nineteenth century, and did a good trade until the factory closed after the October Revolution. In its time, Vera's instrument was a bestseller: a seven-octave *kabinetnyi*, or mid-size boudoir grand.

Anastasia's discovery had got the school's staff so excited that a Novosibirsk TV crew was invited to attend the unveiling of the piano, which had clearly seen better days. From descriptions of Vera's playing, it was easy to imagine how the varnish had worn off, as if Vera had leaned in so hard against the instrument she had blunted its edges. Now it smelled of old age. There was an interview on the evening news. It was during this hullabaloo that I noticed a man standing silently in the background, using a window ledge to prop himself up as he watched the scene play itself out. My interpreter went over to talk with him. She knew who he was: Anastasia had called him a few days before and had been hoping he would turn up.

His name was Stanislav Dobrovolskiy, a tuner, jazz pianist and professor who had taught advanced piano at the Novosibirsk Conservatory for forty years. He looked like a poor pensioner. Even bulked up with a thick coat and trapper's hat with the ear flaps down, he resembled a sheet of tissue that might blow away in a wind. His wispy moustache, which extended out beyond the width of his thick-rimmed spectacles, belonged to a different time and place. He was short and frail, reminding me of the story I had heard in Novosibirsk about some new pianos imported from China: the humidity and temperatures were so low in Siberia in winter that the instruments were condemned before they arrived, the moisture sucked out of the pin blocks which meant that the strings couldn't hold any tension.

Stanislav had come along because he had tuned the Mühlbach several times in its history. It was a noble instrument, he said. He ran his hands over the strings. This was a piano which needed to be played, he said. He talked about how it was made by artisans who took their time to let the wood adapt. Thirty, forty years it takes to get the raw materials right, he said; Vera's piano was produced the old way – an art which predated the Revolution.

It soon became clear that Stanislav knew the Mühlbach's history better than anyone else in the room. Various sources told me that the piano had been given to Vera by her patron Lyapunov, and then bequeathed to the Physics and Mathematics School upon her death. Only later did I learn that the black-and-white portrait the university staff had placed on the piano for the TV cameras wasn't a picture of Vera at all. Dead for less than forty years, and her story had been replaced by a stranger's. It was an error, nothing more – given her lack of memoirs, nobody could be exactly sure of what Vera did or did not look like as a younger woman – but it was also symbolic of the speed and ease with which someone's history can disappear.

I arranged to meet Stanislav again, partly because of his relationship with the Mühlbach and also because Stanislav worked as one of the federal experts who analyses the value of a piano. He explained how every instrument has to be sent for an evaluation. During the troubled years of perestroika, Stanislav had also come up with a plan for Soviet customs officers on how to frisk a grand piano for drugs. A piano, he said, was a better place for hiding heroin than down the bell of a trombone. More than anything, I wanted to see him again because of a passing comment he made about surviving the Siege of Leningrad. The way he wore this monumental experience so lightly made for an uncanny feeling in his company.

We met a couple of times over the next few days, and while his physical strength was failing, his face always wore a slight smile, as if he, too, didn't quite know why he had lived this long. He brought with him envelopes containing photographs of pianos, his federal certificate, which allowed him to evaluate historic instruments, and his medals for surviving the most devastating siege in recorded history – a relentless assault which he said tuned his ear to music in the first place. To keep him occupied during the blockade, Stanislav's mother gave him a hand-cranked phonograph, which arrived on his fifth birthday in August 1942, and two hundred records. His mother had acquired them from friends, including musicians in the orchestra which performed the Leningrad premiere of

Shostakovich's Seventh. There were recordings of Italian operas, as well as Soviet singers like Vadim Kozin, and Klavdiya Shulzhenko, 'Russia's Vera Lynn' who performed hundreds of concerts for Soviet troops defending the besieged city. Stanislav said he played each piece of music so often that even now he would be able to perform every single melody from memory. As for the records he didn't like, they had another use. When there was electricity, he sat on the oven with a record between his bottom and the stove top. The records slowly melted, the heat seeping into his bones.

'Music was all I cared about,' said Stanislav.

Stanislav was the only child of a single mother. During the siege, he described how familiar streets started to appear strange to him. Leningrad's most iconic structures were camouflaged to confuse German pilots. St Isaac's dome was dulled with grey battleship paint, and the spire of the Admiralty scaled by mountaineers so it could be hidden under canvas. One night when his mother moved them from their home in the suburbs to a safer address, he remembered the sharp glances of hungry, frightened citizens as he passed under the city's gloomy bridges. Nearly eighty years later, the scene still broke into his dreams. The young Stanislav was confused by people sleeping on the streets, their bodies swept with snow. Only later did he realize they were corpses.

It was cold, always cold – the winter of 1941 to '42 one of the bitterest in Russia's twentieth-century history. In his kindergarten, where children tried to warm up around the only furnace, he described how badly he wanted to touch the fire, even if it was just with a single finger. He remembered being loaded into a truck to join an evacuation convoy of children being taken across Lake Ladoga on the city's north-eastern

Victims of the Leningrad Siege being brought to the city's Volkovo Cemetery in October 1942.

flank. A seasonal ice road crossing the lake was the last route out of the besieged city – and a lethal one when the Nazis took to bombing the evacuees. Lagoda's ice held for six months during the first winter of the siege, allowing for the escape of half a million people. But the *blokadniki*, as siege survivors came to be known, also knew the 'Road of Life' by another name: the 'Road of Death'. During the Lake Lagoda evacuations, hundreds of trucks fell through the ice. As for Stanislav, his mother pulled his little body off the back of an exiting convoy just in time. She wanted to keep her only child close to her in the belief it was his best chance of survival.

Inside the city, the bombardments mostly happened in the early evenings, and shuddered on until nightfall. Some attacks Stanislav remembered more clearly than others, like the bomb which took out the house next to where he was playing with friends. The buildings lost their façades. In one flat there was a grand piano, its legs caught on masonry so the instrument dangled over the street.

You got used to a way of doing things, said Stanislav, who learned to count the fifteen-second gaps in gunfire when you could run for safety. Most of the time he was left home alone. He remembered cakes made of milled sunflower, fashioned into slabs so tough you had to cut them with a chisel or drive in a nail. His mother would queue for twenty-four hours in breadlines for an eighth of a loaf. You did anything to survive, he said. One of their family friends suspended a piece of sugar from the ceiling. She hung it there because the thought of it made everything else taste that little bit sweeter. His mother cut the bark from birch trees and put it through a mincer. She made cutlets by mixing the pulp with carpenter's glue, which contained protein from fishbones. Once his uncle came home with a rabbit. They ate the meat and boiled the rest down to soup. It turned out they had eaten a cat – a lie Stanislav never forgave.

But in all this horror there was a curious redemption to be found in Stanislav's soundscape. He described Uncle Pavel, a neighbour sharing the same Soviet apartment. A violinist with the Orchestra of the Leningrad Radio Committee, Uncle Pavel asked Stanislav to sing whenever he was at home. Stanislav, who was shy, would lie on his back under the bed with the covers drawn up over his head, his fingers beating out the rhythm on the springs as if it were a guitar. Uncle Pavel was fond of birds. He had a captive bluethroat – a pretty, robin-like bird, too small to be eaten – with an outstanding skill. Uncle Pavel would play on his violin while the bird sat in a cage covered with a dark cloth. After several repetitions the bird would remember the melody. When Uncle Pavel removed the cloth, the bird was then given the few crumbs they could spare as a reward.

One summer, a friend of his mother's taught him how to wire up a bottle to find a radio wave. Then she got her hands on a trophy radio set, made by Telefunken, taken from the Germans.

'It was jazz I got interested in once the blockade was over,' said Stanislav. 'I would listen to different music, picking up banned radio waves from Europe and America. After three or four years, I got quite good at gathering radio parts and fixing them. I had a German radio book to help me. *Empfänger-Schaltungen der Radio-Industrie*. I made money doing up these machines for other people. That's how I earned three thousand roubles to pay for part of my first grand piano; the rest my stepfather paid for. I was about eighteen years old. I found the instrument myself, in an antiques shop, but I only understood its uniqueness later. It was a pre-Revolution grand, with a very delicate upper register, produced by Carl Rönisch. I've always liked German engineering.'

Rönisch was a manufacturer from Dresden who opened a St Petersburg workshop in 1897. The Rönisch action lasted well in extreme conditions; it was strong enough to handle the trials of shipping, which is one of the reasons Rönisch pianos sold well in the Spanish and British colonies, as well as in Russia. Rönisch tweaked the seasoning and finishes for the Russian climate, and along with Jacob Becker became one of the market leaders who distributed grand pianos to settlers moving into towns along the Trans-Siberian Railway. Stanislav talked about how Rönisch's instruments were popular with the

The Lost Pianos of Siberia

founder of the Imperial Russian Musical Society, Anton Rubinstein. The more he talked, the less Stanislav's remembering focused on the siege than on the music that punctuated his past. He was using pianos in the way J. Alfred Prufrock measured out his life with coffee spoons.

Stanislav progressed rapidly through the city's elite musical institutions, winning places at the St Petersburg State Academic Capella and the Leningrad Conservatory. As the city recovered from the war, he started listening to Voice of America. From 1946 onwards, Willis Conover presented an hour of jazz between 11 p.m. and midnight. In 1959, the *New York Times* estimated that thirty million people outside America were listening in.

'I can still hear his voice,' said Stanislav. 'My mother switched on the radio to help me sleep. She thought I was a good boy, going to bed on time. Really, I was just wide awake listening to Benny Goodman, Glenn Miller and the Casa Loma Orchestra. The music kept playing in my head.'

In 1960, Stanislav started teaching at Kirov Music College. This was also when he had to give up his beloved Rönisch because it wouldn't fit into his Soviet dormitory. Five years later, he moved to Novosibirsk. He joined a jazz band and supplemented his earnings with piano tuning now and again, while also working as an expert for the Russian customs authorities.

Every historic instrument should carry a passport, he said, denoting its status in the Russian national heritage. Mühlbach, Diederichs and Stürzwage were brands the Russian Cultural Ministry tended to keep in the country. But there were a few exceptions, he said. There were many Beckers in circulation before the factory was nationalized. He called

Becker the Russian Steinway. He reminded me that German engineering was rooted in Russia's piano-making history – that despite the war the two countries were closely bound.

When his mother saw German prisoners of war at the end of the siege, she said they looked even more starved than the Leningraders – eighteen-year-old boys who had no more asked for a war than the Russians whose bodies his mother was dragging on sledges from the hospital to barges on the River Neva. In the fifties, Stanislav worked as a tour guide for Leningrad's permanent collection of musical instruments. He took a delegation of Germans to visit the Russian Museum. The group stopped at a siege painting. It was the colour of lead and depicted a frozen Neva clogged with bodies.

'I will never forget the silence,' he said. 'The Germans stood with their arms against their bodies, tears running down their faces.'

Stanislav told a story about a German boat that saved his life. When he was a young boy, he was out on the water sailing with his mother at her yacht club when a storm blew in out of nowhere. She quickly bundled him into the cabin below before the boat flipped. The yacht, which was German-made, was strong enough to right itself, with a keel which didn't snap.

'Look for a piano with good German engineering,' he advised me. 'The most reliable in the world.'

From that day on, Stanislav Dobrovolskiy had never lost his respect for German design. The Germans saved him from drowning. The Germans taught him how to wire up a radio. The Germans showed him how a good piano should be made to stand the test of time.

PART THREE

Goodness Knows Where
1992–Present Day

'Often the object of desire, when desire is transformed
into hope, becomes more real than reality itself.'

– Umberto Eco, *The Book of Legendary Lands*

''Tis wonderful how soon a piano gets into a
log-hut on the frontier.'

– Ralph Waldo Emerson, *Society and Solitude*

'There are many kinds of endings – triumphant and tragic,
poetic and laconic, funny and melancholic, majestic and
expiring. We find endings that present a final conclusion and
others that leave things open. Open endings, as in Schumann's
"Kind im Einschlummern" or Liszt's "Unstern" (Disaster) point
into the unknown and the mysterious, unseal an enigma.'

– Alfred Brendel, *A Pianist's A–Z*

15

A Game of Risk:
Kamchatka

IN 1986, THE LEGENDARY Soviet pianist Sviatoslav Richter took a piece of cardboard bearing a map of the USSR, and with a dark-blue marker drew a route through Siberia, filling in the names of all the places he wanted to visit. He put the plan into his suitcase and set off to achieve his goal – a journey from Moscow to the Pacific and back again, travelling partly by road and partly by rail, stopping often to perform piano recitals. On this epic tour he was accompanied by his friend the philologist and writer Valentina Chemberdzhi, who subsequently published her recollections of the journey.

Richter was aware of the intensive foreign tours made by Franz Liszt – and the comparison is enlightening. Both men endured endless bumpy potholes to get to where they wanted to play. They also both made do with whatever instrument they were presented with, Liszt performing on a rattling Tompkinson upright in an Irish hotel sitting room, and Richter on all manner of Soviet equivalents in the small towns scattered through Siberia. Contrary to popular myth, Richter didn't bring with him his favourite Yamaha ('it's hard to imagine a grand piano in a yurt or in the taiga!' observed Chemberdzhi). 'In deepest Russia, I didn't always have these fine instruments – far from it; but I paid no attention,' said Richter. 'In any case, there have been times when I've played on terrible pianos, and played extremely well.'

Richter, who hated flying, visited Khabarovsk, Chita (where he looked for the Decembrists' pianos, and failed to find them), Ulan-Ude, Irkutsk, Krasnoyarsk and Barnaul, as well as numerous settlements in between. In Abakan on the Yenisei River, a local article described the Richter frenzy: for the first time, Siberians could hear him perform live. Venues included local music schools and concert halls. Richter's programmes – even those scribbled on pieces of paper and posted shortly before the event – always sold out fast, sometimes in less than thirty minutes. '[T]hrough word of mouth the hall would be full. That's not done in the West,' he once remarked. With Richter, simplicity was the point. He liked to play in the dark so that the audience would focus on the music, not the performer. 'All that matters is that people come not out of snobbery but to listen to the music,' he said. Reading

Chemberdzhi's account, it seems Richter's Siberian audience understood: her spirited descriptions reveal the people's genuine appreciation for a live musical art, which was exactly as Denis Matsuev had described Siberia to me early on in my search.

Still, it must have been a strange time to be on the road in the USSR. A few months before Richter set out, an explosion at Chernobyl caused the largest nuclear-power-plant disaster in history – an event which could be squarely blamed on a long-standing lack of state investment. The centrally planned economy, on the verge of bankruptcy, was dependent on the price of exported oil, which was falling through the floor. The new leader of the Soviet Union, the General Secretary of the Communist Party Mikhail Gorbachev, travelled to Nizhnevartovsk, a Siberian oil town on the River Ob, where he got a measure of the country's socio-economic doldrums. 'In tsarist Russia's last years, the average number of people in prison was 108,000. In 1986, ten times more. And we call that socialism!?' remarked Gorbachev at a party meeting in September the same year.

Gorbachev proposed a series of changes with the policy of glasnost, or openness, to encourage a more questioning press and consultative government. This unravelling of the old order continued through the perestroika years as Gorbachev began to restructure the Soviet Union's economic system. On the one hand, there was plenty to celebrate. There was access to hitherto forbidden experiences, from the taste of an American burger – the extraordinary queues on the day McDonald's opened in Moscow in January 1990 symbolizing everything tempting about Western life – to the explosion of music in youth culture. In Leningrad, rock surged out of illegal clubs and electronic synthesizers. Punk and heavy metal fed audiences hungry for artists' subversive, often political, lyrics, which began to spread via self-published records.* On the other hand, all the old securities of the socialist system disappeared when, on 25 December 1991, Gorbachev announced that the Soviet Union would be dismantled once and for all, heralding a new era of free elections, free press and freedom of worship. The economy went into freefall. For Russians already struggling to make ends meet, everything fell apart, from reliable salaries to subsidized holidays. To have capitalism come along and offer Russians a completely novel (and hitherto despised) economic model was like turning around and questioning all the sacrifices every family had endured one way or another: Marxist revolution, the Great Patriotic War, Stalin's Terror. It was too much, too soon, the slump into national poverty and panic an indignity too far. By 1992, queues outside food stores had returned to city streets, with rising prices and dramatic shortages. The memory of this experience was one reason why not only Putinism but Russian Orthodoxy was thriving when I was travelling in Siberia. Twenty-five years after perestroika, Putin was giving a form of highly charged national pride back to his country, while the Church was providing a powerful belief system to fill the vacuum lingering from the changes. Although Putin had created a new regime under controls that chilled me every time I picked up a newspaper back home in England, it was still attractive for most Russians, who remembered the unpaid salaries, rapid rise of gangsterism and a corrupt new oligarchy.

One of the regions which emptied out most dramatically

---

* Since 1964 there had been only one official record label in the Soviet Union: Melodiya. Foreign music was strictly regulated.

A fan of the Russian punk group Miracle Yudo, photographed by Igor Mukhin in 1986. The image comes from the photographer's book I've Seen Rock'n'Roll, *which documented the new generation of Soviet musicians unleashed by glasnost.*

A queue to buy food in St Petersburg in 1992.

after the dissolution of the Soviet Union was Kamchatka, a place so out of the way it has always been significantly subsidized by Moscow. Kamchatka is in the same time zone as Auckland, nine hours ahead of Moscow. On its eastern edge lie the Commander Islands, a short distance from the Aleutians, which are US sovereign territory. At its southern tip, the Kamchatka Peninsula peters out into the Kuril Islands. Arctic in the north and subtropical in the south, this bewitching archipelago curves in an arc around the eastern boundary of the Okhotsk Sea, until it almost touches the tip of Japan.

Getting to Kamchatka has also always been challenging. Eighteenth- and nineteenth-century accounts are riven with complaints. For most visitors to Kamchatka, their spirit if not their body had already been broken by the overland journey from European Russia to the Pacific along the Yakutsk–Okhotsk Trakt. They moaned about corduroy roads made from logs laid across sunken pilings. They feared the bogs and anthrax, which obliterated strings of pack horses as they picked their way through swamp, forest and mountain ravines. Bears and escaped convicts added to the threats. On reaching the Sea of Okhotsk, the Kamchatka-bound traveller would then have to pick up a ship.

'[H]ere there were not what we call roads,' wrote Lyudmila Rikord, wife of the newly appointed chief of Kamchatka, Pyotr Rikord, in 1817: 'the horses wander at will, choosing paths in various directions.' But despite the challenges of the journey from St Petersburg, Lyudmila wasn't to be relegated to the back of beyond without the musical sophistications associated with a woman of her elevated rank. Her instrument, made in the imperial capital, was brought to the peninsula as a gift by a Russian admiral called Vasily Golovnin – a man of action who had come to survey the Kuril Islands in 1811 only to be captured by the Japanese. He languished in captivity for two years until his friend, Lyudmila's husband, busted him out. The piano was a thank-you for this act of gallantry, the instrument travelling in a Russian man-o'-war from St Petersburg through the Baltic and North Sea, south to Cape Horn in South America, then across the Pacific, finishing its passage to Kamchatka in 1818. When it got close to the peninsula's main harbour, Golovnin's sloop was unable to reach the shore. For three days the settlement was locked in by fog. Sea ice pulled the ship from her anchor, but Golovnin persevered. 'I consider myself particularly fortunate that I could provide some pleasure to this most worthy lady by bringing to Kamchatka a pianoforte' – 'delivered in good condition', Golovnin noted with pride. He added: '[T]he pleasure of playing the piano in such an isolated spot, for someone who loves music, is immense!'

Golovnin's seaborne piano delivery had taken eight months and eight days to complete. Even today an overland journey would be close to impossible. There is still no road connecting the neck of the Kamchatka Peninsula to the rest of Russia. The Sredinny Range, a spine of ice caps and lava plateaus, runs down the centre of Kamchatka in a line of volcanic cones. Off these peaks flow short, fast-moving rivers which flood alluvial plains. Wildlife has the upper hand, thriving in a hostile landscape where geysers burst into the air. Pools of chocolate mud bubble and steam, while up above, the sky is often draped in rainbows – double, even triple half-moon crescents of splintered light. There is jeopardy in the whorls of molten lava glowing red at night, and the petrified forests which stand like fields of stubble, the scorched birch as thin as matchsticks.

Boris Pasternak's remark that Kamchatka was the place at the back of the classroom where the worst-behaved kids would be sent still resonates with Russians. Among Westerners, however, the word rings with a different association: in the board game Risk, Kamchatka is ideal territory for launching an invasion of North America, which isn't far from the truth. During the Cold War, the entire region functioned as a highly militarized zone closed to foreigners. But when the Soviet support machine dried up with perestroika, the military also shrank. One in ten of Kamchatka's population left for what they thought would be an easier, more affordable life on 'the mainland'.

On the day I arrived, the sky was bruised with rain. It was lunchtime and the canteen in the capital, Petropavlovsk-Kamchatsky, smelled of grease. The server dumped a piece of battered fish on a plate and moved me along, past sugared puddings in a glass cabinet and cold soups which looked as appetizing as the leftovers of a party from the seventies. The cashier, who didn't smile, had fingers as fat as sausages. I sat down, disappointed that my first view of Kamchatka's capital, famously nestled beside a rim of volcanoes, was concealed by thick Pacific weather.

The fish, it turned out, tasted better than it looked. I remarked on this with an enthusiastic gesture to the stranger at the neighbouring table. There was an exactitude to him – neat grey hair, a leather jacket with squared-off shoulder pads, and a gold pin fixing his red tie. He pulled out a photograph from his bag, a picture of him and his friend Mikhail Kalashnikov, a Siberia-born military engineer who invented the AK-47. I asked my new acquaintance if he, too, was in the military. The Russian army is still a major employer in Kamchatka – something I was aware of from pianos I had been told about, the instruments passed from one military family to another as postings changed.

Another diner was listening to our conversation – a woman in white ankle boots with stubby heels, a white silk shirt with a high neckline, and a matching white belt cinching her waist. With her hair combed into place under a fawn mohair hat, she looked like a woman in a French café painted by one of the Impressionists.

'You are talking with our most famous Kamchatka poet,' she announced.

I asked what she did for a living.

'I clean. Four floors, five toilets, three rooms, every day,' she said, her coffee cup elegantly pinched between her forefinger and thumb.

I mentioned a rendezvous I had with Valery Kravchenko, a teacher and performing pianist who had been living in Kamchatka since 1968. Kravchenko was also a journalist and a photographer, and the person who had told me about Golovnin's piano delivery to Rikord's wife. I had been in touch with him ever since he had first emailed me the picture of a piano sitting at the foot of Gorely volcano at the beginning of my search. Valery had many more stories to tell about pianos in Kamchatka, he said, as well as something special to show me – a nineteenth-century Ibach grand brought here in the thirties. I asked my new café acquaintances if either of them knew the man I was talking about.

The woman put down her mug with exaggerated condescension. The poet rolled his eyes.

Of course they knew Valery Kravchenko, they said.

'Kamchatka is a very cultured place,' said the woman.

She talked about Inspirations – a club she had been going to for years, where they liked to sing. The man recited one of his poems: 'I am very useful to this Earth, to this very fairy-tale Earth.' My local guide – a tall, athletic seventy-year-old who claimed direct descent from one of Napoleon's soldiers left behind in Russia after 1812 – joined the conversation. He said Valery Kravchenko was a friend. Together they had travelled into the mountains with pianos in tow, as if this were the most natural thing in the world.

The poet gave a high kick, which probably wasn't as high as he had hoped for, but was impressive all the same.

The cashier with the sausage fingers smiled.

Petropavlovsk-Kamchatsky, or Petropavlovsk for short, is unlike any other Russian city. At night, there is something of San Francisco to the pinpricks of light curled around the hills, dips and shoreline. The horseshoe-shaped Avacha Bay lies out in front, the lid of water heavy, as if it is a bowl of liquid mercury. By day, the city returns to being utterly, unapologetically Soviet. Housing blocks crawl up the hillsides. Winds burnish the statue of Lenin, his long coat seeming to fill like a sail in a Pacific gale. In Kamchatka, they say spring, summer and autumn pass so quickly, it is as if they are a single season. Locals also know the rules. In summer, when Kamchatkans collect berries in the woods close to their homes, they occasionally take a wrong turn; if not found within three days, they are usually assumed dead.

In Kamchatka, you can lose a lot of time waiting for the weather to clear. On one visit, I didn't see further than the brake lights on the car in front of me on a four-hour drive. On

A Chechen separatist plays the piano in the republic's capital, Grozny, on 27 December 1994.

Exactly one month and a day later, a Russian soldier plays an abandoned piano in the same city.

another visit, in one of the village houses where I stayed, I spent days watching the rain fall in long, strong lines. In the plot opposite, a woman tended her ground as if she relied on this small piece of black Kamchatkan sod for more than just the potatoes it yielded. Her whole bearing was downturned, her drooping shoulders hunching her to the earth. In a corner of her plot stood a blue tractor. At the back was a greenhouse. Each morning she deadheaded her purple dahlias with a delicacy that didn't feel like it belonged to her. Her sadness was present in every slow step, in her mournful journeys back and forth across her little square of earth. When I mentioned the scene to my host, she said her neighbour used to work on the collective farm nearby, which was now in ruin. She understood the old woman had lost one of her sons – a soldier who fought for the Russians in the Chechen war in the mid-nineties, when the poorly paid, post-perestroika Russian army was fighting for a country exhausted by reform.

I wanted to go and talk to the old woman, but whenever I walked by her gate, a fierce dog drove me away. The dog also scared off a pony, which wandered the street like a community pet. Its owner was a young boy who led the animal home each day, the child tiptoeing over puddles so as not to dirty his shoes. He didn't bother to stop at the garages where the other local kids hung out – sea containers, which lay higgledy-piggledy along one side of the unpaved street. One of the neighbours had converted his box into a local bar; in another, a group of teenagers stretched themselves out on cast-off sofas with exposed springs. The kids unnerved me at first – the red-headed twins, and the creepy gas mask one of them always wore. After a while, we became familiar.

These masks were staples in the Cold War – originally made in case an attack from America took place. In the second half of the nineteenth century, however, the Russian–American relationship was fuelled by a very different propaganda. Russia was being called 'America's best friend'. The country's two leaders were being favourably compared in the press – Tsar Alexander II for abolishing serfdom in Russia, and Abraham Lincoln for outlawing slavery in the United States. America was consumed by 'Russia Fever'. The American entrepreneur Perry Collins declared Siberia to be anything but a 'waste space on the map of the globe'. This enterprising New Yorker, who had already followed the Gold Rush to California, saw a lucrative future for America with a new trans-Siberian telegraph – a cable which would snake up the coast of British Columbia, across the narrow Bering Strait between Russia and Alaska, then skirt the northern edge of Kamchatka before slipping south and straight for Moscow. This plan to bind the Pacific – a bold collaboration in a race against the transatlantic cable being laid between America and Britain – brought American adventurers, as well as pianos, deep into the Kamchatka wilderness.

George Kennan – who poured a bucket of cold water over 'Russia Fever' a quarter of a century later with his bestselling indictment of the Tsarist exile system – was a member of Collins' first exploratory party, which made landfall at Petropavlovsk in 1865. He writes about the captain of the port, who owned a Russian-made piano, the collection of German, Russian and American sheet music testament to the captain's refined musical tastes. In 1866, a swashbuckling Thomas Wallace Knox, who made his name as a war correspondent during the American Civil War, described the simplicity of a

Kamchatkan home with its stove, table, simple chairs and 'an occasional but rare piano'. In Ghijiga, a truly cut-off settlement tucked inside the western armpit of the Kamchatka Peninsula, an American gold prospector encountered a piano some thirty years after the US telegraph crew. He sat down and struck up the 'Washington Post' march: 'Evidently, many of those rough but kindly people had never heard anything like it in their lives, and, as the Russian is musical to his heart's core, I felt pleased to have added my mite to the evening's entertainment.'

Of all these accounts, one of the most intriguing was the bathhouse piano spotted on a hunting expedition in 1900, when Prince Demidoff, the Russian hunter who had already shot his way through the Altai, travelled to Kamchatka to bag some *Ovis nivicola* – a relative of the snow sheep. It turned out to be a journey rough beyond reckoning. In Kamchatka, 'classical concerts were replaced by the howling of sledge-dogs'. Even the horses streamed with blood from the mosquito bites. There were, however, glimmers of what he called 'civilization'. At volcanic mud baths in the shadow of Vilyuchinsky volcano, the party encountered a villa with taps running on hot water from the geothermal springs, a drawing room with a sprung sofa, and an old, stained piano.

When I met the pianist Valery Kravchenko in Petropavlovsk and told him about these nineteenth-century sightings, I was looking for his help. He was a petite man with glasses, a slight stutter, and a warm voice. He looked a bit like Liszt, with white hair cut into a bob, which he swept off his face with a modest flourish.

Valery took me to hear the Ibach grand piano he had been telling me about for a while: an instrument which was poorly

Prince Demidoff with his wife and St George Littledale in Petropavlovsk, taken from Demidoff's 1904 work, A Shooting Trip to Kamchatka.

lacquered, with a surface crumpled from water damage, but still in possession of its original strings and hammers. It occupied an attic at the top of a writers' club overlooking some sleepy port buildings. Dating from the 1850s, the Ibach was the most interesting survivor in Kamchatka, said Valery. In 1936, it had travelled to Petropavlovsk from Moscow with David Lerner, an artist of the Moscow Philharmonic tasked to bring music to the citizens of Kamchatka.

'Lerner said it was the equivalent of taking a piano to the moon,' said Valery.

The journey took about three months, travelling first by train to Vladivostok, then on a boat. The Ibach was played on the radio and heard all over the peninsula. Then in 1937, Lerner was arrested and accused of 'counter-revolutionary' activities. He was released two years later. At the age of eighty-six, Lerner was named a People's Artist of Russia. He and Valery became close friends.

'Music, nature – there are no borders to its effects,' said Valery.

He opened the Ibach's lid to play some Chopin, the piano's warm depth of tone made all the more melancholy by the purple sky outside.

I followed through on my attempt to find the bathhouse piano spotted by Demidoff's hunting party. The next day, I ventured off in a snowmobile to the foot of Mutnovsky volcano, where Demidoff had roamed, looking for his sheep. I had marked up a

Valery Kravchenko playing the Kamchatka Ibach, 2017.

map in an attempt to identify the volcanic pools where the hunters rested up, though it was difficult to be exactly sure of their
stopping points, given the number of springs and tributaries
of the Paratunka River half described in Demidoff's account.
All I encountered was a babbling stream and two Russians sun-
bathing on plastic camping mats. They wore their swimmers – he
in tight blue briefs, she in a black bikini – while a bear on the
other side of the valley walked the edge of the snowline.

When I returned to the city, Valery and I talked some more
as he came and went from his kitchen with tea, and white bread
laden with juicy beads of caviar. He wasn't born in Kamchatka,
he said, but on a beach on the Caspian Sea during the Great
Patriotic War. With his father away fighting, his mother fled the
region where Nazi SS execution squads were shooting, hanging
and burning communist partisans. He learned to play the piano
because of an army wife who had set up a music school in the
barracks where Valery's family had gone to live after the war.

It wasn't until the sixties that Valery was drawn from
Western Russia to the country's Far East. The Soviet journalist
Vasily Peskov – the same man who had written about the family of Old Believers living in isolation in Siberia – gave such
alluring descriptions of Kamchatka that when a job came up
teaching piano in Petropavlovsk's music college, Valery leapt
at the opportunity. Like his friend David Lerner, who brought
the Ibach to this peninsula, Valery's role was to spread piano
culture to the farthest boundaries of the USSR – to take
Chopin to the back of the proverbial classroom.

We watched a short film about the piano expeditions
into the wilderness which Valery had helped organize every
summer for the last decade. The footage showed a piano being
carried on a palanquin up the slopes of Gorely volcano. Valery

urged me to return to Kamchatka for an expedition with his friend Vladimir Shevtsov – an alpinist who introduced heli-skiing to the region when Gorbachev's reforms opened the slopes to foreigners. It was Shevtsov's idea to take a piano to Gorely. The volcano had a natural amphitheatre, said Valery. Shevtsov envisioned people sitting on its slopes listening to classical music. The first year, the instrument was delivered to the cave in an off-road truck. Thereafter, it was carried by local volunteers on home-made litters.

'It's a private thing,' he said, 'but if strangers should happen upon a performance, it gives intense pleasure.'

Valery encouraged me to keep on with my search. He said the stories were as good as gone if I didn't try to grab their disappearing parts.

'I do not think some ideas are impossible,' he said.

He told me about a brand new Primorskii piano he was the first to play in the Commander Islands in 1969, in the main settlement's wooden club. But it wasn't music that pulled him all the way out there, he said; it was the seabirds.

Valery reached for a book – a grey, hardback volume, *The Edge of the Earth*, which he kept wrapped inside a bag. He flicked to a page showing a black-and-white photograph – the silhouette of a seagull standing on the shoulder of a child. Called 'The Boy and the Bird', it was a true story told by the journalist Peskov.

The boy finds an injured bird on the beach and nurses it back to health. Every time the boy returns to the seashore, the bird flies out of the colony and sits on the boy's shoulders. The bird and the boy become friends. Valery Kravchenko grew so fond of the story that he wrote to the boy, using just his name on the envelope. The address line was 'The Commanders' – no house number, nothing.

The boy and the bird, photographed by Vasily Peskov, March 1966.

'We corresponded for a number of years,' said Valery. 'I sent him camera film, which he couldn't buy on the islands. We finally met when I arrived in the Commanders to perform.'

We ate more caviar. Valery smoked one half-cigarette after another on his balcony. We looked at a photograph of Valery playing the piano to television cameras in the sixties, and one of him in a trench coat, standing face to face with a bear on its hind legs.

We flicked through images of his father in flying goggles in 1939, and another of him playing a guitar, one foot propped up on a park bench. He told me about how his real father had died in the war, and that he had been brought up by another man. Valery didn't know this had happened until years later when he chanced upon some papers in one of his mother's

Valery Kravchenko, photographed with a bear in the Kamchatkan village of Esso in 1975.

cupboards, which revealed the truth about the switch in fathers he had been too young to recognize for himself.

'Whenever I play Chopin's Nocturne No. 13, Op. 48, I devote it to the father I didn't know,' said Valery; 'It is impossible to get rid of the past. That is a very important feeling for artistic people.'

Back at my hotel, I gathered my bag's contents spread about the floor of my room – a muddled heap of books on piano history, Demidoff's hunting notes, and the numerous pieces of red-tape paperwork which Russian authorities make a habit of for foreigners. Water beads had dried on my coat, leaving spots of salt. Pieces of sea-wrack clung to my boots. I was excited about this next stage in my travels. The Commanders are a sensitive border area still tightly wrapped in special permits. I would then travel south through the Kuril Islands, where permission to visit can be hard to obtain. I was joining a tourist birding cruise, taking one of just a handful of ships out of Kamchatka that make this journey each year. I hoped there might be one or two instruments, given the islands' position as a staging post on the old sea route from Siberia to America. By now I also had two good leads: Valery Kravchenko's Soviet-era upright which he had played fifty years ago in the settlement's wooden club in Nikolskoye village on Bering Island, and an instrument I was tipped off about by a former soldier who had been posted to the Kurils. He remembered a pre-Revolution piano on Kunashir in the archipelago's southern reaches. He last saw it inside an old boat, which stood on the foreshore. He even played it, back in the eighties. It will still be there, he wagered. Once on the Kurils, always on the Kurils, went the conversation, as if there were no other place left to go.

16

Siberia's Last Piano:
The Commanders to the Kurils

I N 2011, THE BRITISH author Horatio Clare began a hunt across Europe's wetlands to find a small, possibly extinct bird, the migratory slender-billed curlew. As it happened, Clare never got a glimpse of the bird's thin, down-curving beak, but if there were any of these creatures left, they might be in Siberia. *Orison for a Curlew* is Clare's elegant prayer for an outside chance – that this delicate little creature, teetering on the brink of extinction, is still alive in the taiga beyond the sight of man. Clare argues with unassailable conviction that 'too much certainty is a miserable thing'. I clung to the same idea when I joined a ship of birders with whom I had nothing in common other than the desire to find a rarity.

At the end of May, our ship, built as a scientific research vessel, left Petropavlovsk to sail east for the Commanders. They are made up of two main islands, Bering and Medny, and a clutch of smaller islets. The ropes from the pilot boat creaked as we slipped out of the slender neck of Avacha Bay to cross the northern tip of the Kuril–Kamchatka Trench. In the nineteenth century, this oceanic gully was the deepest on record, measured using a mechanism fashioned from piano wire. If there was a hint of nonsense in this method of sounding the depths of the North Pacific, there was also a shiver of darkness: piano wire was also used by the Soviets to hang traitors during the Second World War.

We crossed the line where the Asian continental shelf rubs up against the Pacific's mighty sea trough, the pressures of subduction inducing all manner of restless waters, freak waves and unpredictable eruptions. Bleeping dials flickered on the ship's bridge, which was furnished with phone receivers, screens and buttons marked with Cyrillic script. At the back of the bridge, the first mate worked with protractors and rulers to mark our line on a paper map pooled in light. Someone had written in pencil 'Whale' in the fold-line, as if it were always there – a Moby Dick forever loitering in the chasm.

Two days later we made landfall at the Commanders. Sitting at the western end of the Aleutian chain, they hang like a string of beads between Russia and Alaska. We anchored off Medny first. Darkly alluring, this is about as far as you can go in Russia – the silent, final ellipsis at the end of this vast country's turbulent story. It is Siberia's last frontier, a tiny continental fragment where sea and land fight against each other in a state of constant tension and unease. Medny is where Eurasia runs out entirely, a high-walled, fortress-like rock some two hundred miles off America. Deep-water channels both here and in the Kurils provide corridors for submarines to patrol the North Pacific's lower latitudes.

With thin evidence of any significant human habitation, I pinned my hopes on the skipper's proven success rate in uncovering the last possibilities at Russia's limits – be they one of the rare species the birders were after, or in my case, pianos. Rodney Russ, the New Zealander who had chartered our Russian ship, was a Nansen-like character: attractive, broad shouldered, with weather-creased eyes. He spent half his year in the Southern Ocean, the other half in Russia. He was rarely out of his orange waders, and his small cabin was filled with the finest English-language books I had yet found on Siberia outside the British Library. In twenty years of travelling Russia's Pacific and Arctic fringes, Russ had undertaken vital scientific research. He had made important sightings of North Atlantic right whales (fifteen years ago, it was thought only several dozen of these creatures remained). He and his colleagues had also identified a new breeding site of the critically endangered spoon-billed sandpiper. The bird is exceptional, its long, slim beak tipped with what looks like a black ace of spades. Current research suggests there are no more than two hundred and fifty nesting pairs left in the world, making this discovery of sandpiper eggs in a field of cloudberry tundra akin to finding life on another planet.

Everyone on the ship knew about the sandpiper story: a

birder who used to collect policemen's helmets; a man who was another of the expedition's 'big-listers' (number thirty-something in the world, whispered his nemesis); a former schoolteacher who made a career change to give him more time to bird. They conversed in a private language. They talked about 'gripping off' (showing off about a find another birder missed), 'stringing' (pretending you have seen a rare bird), 'dipping' (when you travel to see a rare bird, and miss it), and 'twitching' (a twitcher chases a rare bird for his 'list', including one-off vagrants, which is different to a birder, who makes a sighting in a bird's natural habitat). Each evening the group compared notes in the ship's bar. Petty jealousies, barely concealed under a thin layer of civility, erupted into accusations of bad etiquette. Before long, two travellers weren't talking to each other over some incident of sabotage, or 'flushing', when one birder spooks another birder's quarry. Both men told different versions of the same event.

Initially, I avoided people's direct questions about what I was doing here; I didn't want to be too friendly in order to give me time to write. It turned out I had nothing to fear from my fellow travellers' attentions. When I eventually revealed my true motives for making this journey, I realized my piano quest lay so entirely off the birding spectrum that no one but Mary, my eighty-year-old cabin-share, wanted to sit next to me at mealtimes anyway.

Mary and I got along like a house on fire. When we were at sea, we would both rest in the cabin. She would kill time organizing her list, familiarizing herself with the new species she hoped to find, their images detailed in her heavily annotated book on birds of the Russian Far East. I would do the same, my list comprising all the instruments I had already ticked off during my travels, each brand's history explained by my field guide to Russia's great piano makers.*

By now, I had a shortlist of about fifteen possibilities. Among them were the pianos I needed to scout out further, like the Kiakhta Bechstein. Then there were the 'extinct' pianos – the truly lost, like the Magadan grand, which I kept on my list *just in case* because I found its presence in that photograph so compelling. There were three or four instruments simply weighed down with too much history – among them, the Bechstein from Ekaterinburg marked up with 'House of Revolution' on its soundboard, and Vera's Mühlbach grand. These were the untouchable treasures belonging to Russia's national history, which I was glad I had found, if only to draw attention to their memory. I had a list of pianos which were never going to be cleaved from their owners, like Olga's Bechstein, originally bought for a bag of potatoes. In return for all the time they had given me, I owed these people some of my reporting, which included information I would later glean from foreign piano factory archives.† Then there was the longlist: plain pianos, often with an untrustworthy provenance, most of them tracked down by my occasional appeals on Siberian media. Not all of them were successful. It was one of these media pushes which had led to a run of pest calls from a man who claimed to be calling from inside a Krasnoyarsk prison. Highest on my list were two instruments I kept on

---

* Anne Swartz, *Piano Makers in Russia in the Nineteenth Century* (Bethlehem: Lehigh University Press, 2014).
† One of the most interesting results was Tobolsk's Erard piano – serial number 75796, damaged on 22 March 1988 by a burst hot-water pipe. My research in the factory archives led back to an 1896 buyer in Poland.

coming back to: the Novosibirsk Grotrian-Steinweg upright in Igor Lomatchenko's Room 1037 in the Novosibirsk Opera and Ballet Theatre, and a fascinating Stürzwage grand in Khabarovsk which I still needed to dig into further.

As I surveyed my findings, I saw all the surprises my search had thrown up – and how each piano had reduced Russia's illimitable size to a human scale. Drawn in by the Siberians who play, tune, keep, fix, break, love and live with pianos, it was difficult for me to cross their half-finished stories off my list. I longed to find the true history of the Novosibirsk Steinway which the Leningrad Philharmonic-in-exile might have played. As I sailed south, I obsessed about the instruments I hadn't tracked to their reliable beginning. I complained to Mary that while her list was building, mine felt incomplete. I wanted to find more of those people who had allowed me to make trespasses into their homes: Russians like the tiger protector in his forest who showed me the tuft of golden hair; the Aeroflot navigator building his concert hall of Siberian larch; or the jazz pianist I met in the Altai, whose rich American rhythms disturbed the snow on his dacha's roof until it slipped off in slabs to the fright of the dog outside. I tried explaining to Mary how Siberia's humps of snow, like funerary barrows, conceal everything and nothing, how humble village houses hold stories no one will ever know. That was the part of me I had lost to Siberia – the distracting knowledge that there is always further to go.

The nineteenth-century philosopher, writer and ecologist Henry David Thoreau criticized such esoteric adventuring in his private journal: 'By another spring I may be a mail-carrier in Peru, or a South African planter, or a Siberian exile . . . But what of all this? . . . Our limbs, indeed, have room enough, but it is our souls that rust in a corner. Let us migrate interiorly without intermission.' I knew I needed to sit still, to read beside a porthole and watch the skies moving past. I needed to allow myself the indulgence of being sucked back into other writers' literary adventures in Siberia, taking me to all the places I couldn't get to – the islands of the Laptev Sea, Chukotka, the Putorana Plateau. I wanted to capture that moment in history when I most wish I had been a traveller in Russia: the second half of the nineteenth century, when Chekhov was on the road, and the nation's pianos were in full voice. The stories from this period are of course troubling, given the brutality of the exile system, but they are also full of wonder. Among them is one book I adore: *On Sledge and Horseback to Outcast Siberian Lepers* by Kate Marsden, a spinster nurse who left England for a leper colony near Yakutsk in the same year as Chekhov. On her hand-drawn map, the path she took from St Petersburg to Yakutsk is marked up as 'accomplished'; her other route, a line over the top of Siberia into Kamchatka's narrow neck, is marked with a wistful 'contemplated'.

Marsden claimed she was going to find a Siberian herb that might cure leprosy. Before long, however, the magic herb all but disappears from her account. Telling asides in her memoir reveal her to be a Victorian adventurer trying to escape the shackles of her time and gender. She endures the slights of men – 'of course, it was quite natural for the gentlemen to remark that, like most of my sex, I wanted to get at the end of the journey before setting off'. She also does the burgeoning feminist movement back in Britain no favours as she occasionally slips into asides the 'lady tourist' might want to hear, with eulogies about her Jaeger stockings: 'Even my own

The English nurse Kate Marsden 'dressed' for Siberia.

attention, I must confess, was diverted from the lepers for a moment in thinking what to wear.' Still, her Siberian journey is one of the toughest on record. She enters a prison cell of twenty murderers, and remarks on the politeness of the convict who takes her by the hand to show her through the darkness of the jail. She challenges a local paper-mill magnate, who is polluting a river. She describes an outcast leper child who died alone, with clay in his belly, unable to scavenge anything to eat. I found much to admire in Marsden's story – most of all her courage. But I also had to heed the warning bell she sounded loud and clear: the more this English nurse was taken in by Siberia, the more she lost sight of the object she had come to find.

My cabin-share, Mary, had no time for self-doubt. What an adventure this is, she said every time I offered her a hand getting up and down the stairs in a lurching Pacific swell. She explained that a birder never closes their list; it is a life's work, because no list can ever be definitive. In the ornithology world, there is a phenomenon called 'extralimital' species to describe birds at the very limit of their range. There will be a score of far-fliers that may occur up here in the North Pacific, she said. Then there are the 'escapees' – exotics which have flown their cage to start a rogue population in a place where they would never normally migrate. That should give me hope, she said, that there might be the musical equivalent of a blue canary nesting in the bluffs.

I adored Mary. She laughed in her sleep. She talked about blossom nomads – birds that chase the nectar – and the call of the eastern spinebill; back home in Canberra, one came into her garden to sing every day. 'He brings his wife,' she said, 'but she's not quite as brilliant as him.' Mary was also mischievous. At breakfast she told the most competitive birder on the ship he had missed a 'lifer' (a new species he could have added to his list), which flew right past the ship's bridge when he was on its stern. When we were back in our cabin she said she had been pulling his leg.

She showed me the travellers, the migratory giants, who come this way to feed on upwellings from the ocean trench where the Sea of Okhotsk mingles with the warmer waters of the Pacific. These were the evolutionary champions, she said, travelling halfway around the world to get here, answering a hidden pull to do with the sun and the stars and the Earth's magnetic field. Most of all I wanted to see the bar-tailed godwit, the concert grand of shorebirds. Tall and long-legged, the bar-tailed godwit is now thought to make the longest unbroken migration of any bird species on the planet. A wader with a broad-bean-sized brain, it is able to predict the weather forty-eight hours before a change in the wind. It can cover close to seven and a half thousand miles along the western side of the Pacific in nine days flat. It travels between the northern tip of New Zealand and north-east Siberia, the godwit's monumental crossing almost double in length to the land-and-sea journey made in the eighteenth century by the explorer Vitus Bering, whose wife, Anna, left some of the earliest evidence of a clavichord in Siberia.

In July 1741, Bering made landfall on Kayak Island in the Gulf of Alaska, only to founder on the shores of the Commander Islands on his way home. He perished within a few weeks of the shipwreck, his death recorded by George Steller, the expedition doctor and naturalist who survived nine months marooned on the Commanders living off the local manatees. Steller described these creatures as over seven metres in length, six metres in circumference around the belly, with meat which tasted like beef. They produced milk and buttery fat like a cow's, a single manatee able to feed forty hungry sailors for two weeks. The so-called Steller's sea cow was one 'discovery' on Bering's trip;* the other was the American continent itself, which gave the Tsars the basis for later laying claim to their US possessions,

---

* Unwittingly, Steller also helped to bring about the manatees' demise. Just twenty-seven years after his discovery, these toothless giants, which grazed peacefully close to shore moving at a 'half-swim, half-walk', were rendered extinct by incoming fur-hunters after an easy meal.

The Medny fur trade, still going strong, c. 1930.

from California to Alaska. In 1867, this territory was then sold to America in its entirety; but for reasons not altogether clear, Tsar Alexander II left the Commander Islands off the inventory. The oversight proved lucrative. The Commanders possessed healthy rookeries of northern fur seals, sea otters, and shores bristling with blue Arctic foxes. When Bering's surviving crew returned to St Petersburg with their harvest of skins, wide-eyed fur trappers were not long in realizing the islands' potential.

When we arrived at Medny, winter's mantle of sea ice had melted away, allowing us to anchor on the edge of a submerged caldera close to where a volcano had once exhaled. Surrounding the ship were high cliffs funnelled with waterfalls and crowned in milky fog. For a moment, this could have been

Hawaii – the velvet greens, the moody swings of sun and shade, the sea a lumpy stew on one side of the bay and a glossy mirror on the other. Scores of northern fulmars skimmed across the undulating swell, using the ocean's updraughts to help them fly. The birds wheeled in broad arcs, breasting the wind. Common guillemots lined up in rows, swooping off the cliffsides. The tufted puffins, with bellies like barrels, were silent at sea, but when they were nesting, they grumbled like old men.

Using rubber dinghies, we landed on a beach of stones tinted copper-green. Among the driftwood were vertebrae from seals. The carcass of an Arctic fox was curled up on the edge of the grass like a dog waiting for its owner to return. Seeing the few tumbledown buildings, I wondered if the Russian border guards who once lived here might have demanded a piano for entertainment at some point in their history. Distractions of any kind would have been a necessity for survival, not least to dim the sound of the rattling windows in Pacific storms.

The birders headed off to where nesting colonies streaked the cliffs. I walked the other way. A few brave flowers were showing – pale lemon primulas and anemones. The smell of seaweed rose from the tideline whenever the wind fell away. Abandoned machinery, oxidized by the weather, lay within three roofless buildings behind the shore.

From 1826 until 1970, this was a village with a score of houses, a small church and a wooden cutter boat, the population including indigenous Aleuts originally imported from the Aleutian Islands to harvest the pelts. Then, in the Soviet era, descendants of these same indigenes were relocated to neighbouring Bering Island, which now has the

Commanders' only settlement, where around six hundred people live. Even Medny's border-patrol post had been abandoned, following the hard winter of 2002. That year, twelve soldiers ventured out to find driftwood – the only source of fuel in this treeless place. They walked for days, roped their haul on to a raft, and floated themselves and the wood towards camp. But a storm pushed the raft out to sea in one of the last tragedies connected to this island's lonely past.

Once, this desolate speck of ground had given a good living. In the late nineteenth century, an American trading company leased the islands from the Russian government to harvest its sea otters. The fur trade on Medny was significant enough to merit the import of gravestones from San Francisco for employees. I stumbled upon marble blocks amid topsy-turvy crosses struggling to stand tall in the marsh. Disturbed earth revealed man-sized humps in the ground, including a stone memorial where two Aleut sisters had been interred together not far from where the island's cheek toppled into the sea. Surf pushed up through holes in the rocks below. There was something magnificent about this brink of land, something mesmerizing about the churning power of the ocean below.

Then out of nowhere, one of the birders came up behind me. He was carrying a small speaker, which rang with a recorded birdsong.

'It's how you pull them in,' he said.

He waited for a while for a living bird to respond.

'Get good at this and you can bird by ear.'

Back in my cabin, I checked with Mary if you could mark a bird off your list on the basis of hearing its song.

'Aw, no,' she said in her slow Australian drawl. 'I don't tick a bird unless I see it. Like anyone, I like a good song, but you gotta see a bird for it to mean anything.'

We sailed on to Bering, where Valery Kravchenko came in 1969, his performance advertised on a billboard in front of the explorer's statue on the shorefront of Nikolskoye village. Back in the sixties, times were good. There was a thriving mink farm, salaries were high, and the Soviet support-machine was beneficent. Valery's recital took place in the House of Culture when the town's population was more than twice the size it is now. He brought Chopin's music to the island's tiny community, just as his friend, David Lerner, had done in Kamchatka thirty years before when he had arrived in Petropavlovsk with the Ibach in tow.

Since perestroika, however, things hadn't been the same. The wharf was cluttered with broken boats. In Nikolskoye's lower village, the soccer field was fringed with legless seats. On a windowsill of a semi-abandoned home, even the silk flowers had shed their petals. So fragile were some of the buildings, it was as if it would take only a moderate storm to remove the last remains. It had happened before when the tail end of a tsunami caught the island off guard. Here, on the storm-chafed shore of Bering Island, Valery left the piano in the settlement's wooden club.

I visited the newspaper offices in Nikolskoye. The editor, who knew nothing of Valery's instrument, said she would put out a notice in the next edition. I hurried up the hill to the new part of town and its modern House of Culture; there was little time, given the ship needed to press on with its birding itinerary rather than wait for me to find an instrument. The director said there was only one music teacher on the island, the wife of the priest. There were no old pianos, she said. Then I found a woman who remembered Valery's instrument. There had been an electrical fire – maybe it was November, sometime in the eighties. She said the piano had disappeared, but Valery's legacy remained. She used to listen to classical piano music on any records she could lay her hands on all the way out here, in these tiny blips of land separating Russia from America.

We left the Commanders to sail south beyond the nose of the Kamchatka Peninsula, passing occasional shipwrecks, their hulls tossed aside in storms. Close to shore, the ships' carcasses were wrapped in ghostly fog. We were headed for the Kurils. The northern islands are fierce. Angry squalls rip the top off the ocean to create spray like bursts of smoke, the sea rolling around basalt cliffs. The southern Kurils are more benign. They are covered with cedar forests, hot springs and groves of whispering bamboo.

I had ten days ahead of me, weaving through this chain from top to bottom in the relative warmth of June. In winter, my journey wouldn't have been quite so easy, said a former sea captain on Sakhalin Island, who had spent fifty years sailing a fishing trawler in the Sea of Okhotsk and the North Pacific. The ship would spend six months at sea, sometimes longer. In order to fill their time, the captain persuaded his crew to buy a piano – everyone chipped in with a share of their bonus – which then travelled into the Bering Sea, up and down the Kurils, even as far as the Russian Arctic. He talked about the pleasure the instrument gave them, and how he was a self-taught pianist. Once he spent nine months at sea without ever touching land. In winter, he said the storms could be so brutal that water would freeze to the side of the ship until it developed a dangerous tilt.

Even in summer, our plans were dictated by capricious weather. We failed to land at Atlasov Island, the tallest volcano in the archipelago, because of a powerful northerly. We couldn't get close to Matua because of a Notice to Mariners about a new exclusion zone. Every two hours our captain checked in with Russian authorities. This has always been sensitive border territory, with ownership of these islands oscillating in different sovereignty claims between Russia – the Kurils' existence on Russian maps first drawn by the Tobolsk map maker Semion Remezov in 1700 – and Japan. During the Pacific War, Matua was turned into a labyrinth of trenches. The Japanese strike force set sail from the island of Iturup to launch their attack on Pearl Harbor. Even now, the sovereignty conflict bubbles on in the southern islands: Russia and Japan still haven't signed a peace treaty since the cessation of hostilities at the end of the Second World War, when Stalin got the Kurils back from Japan and sent in new cadres of Russians to populate the land.

While I was on the ship working my way through the New Zealander's Siberian library, my interpreter was on Sakhalin Island, where I would meet up with her again a couple of weeks later. She was working the phones and local media, and also trying to trace the soldier's instrument on the Kuril island of Kunashir. Eventually, a photograph of it arrived depicting the piano as it was now. All that remained was the instrument's iron frame, a moribund piece of scrap metal drowning in the summer's new bamboo. It was a Czech-made Rösler with a serial number dating the piano to before the October Revolution. The soldier said it had belonged to a

Soviet musician who had come to the islands in the fifties. I contacted a local museum archivist, but no one recalled the pianist, from where he had come, or even his name. His story had passed into oblivion in a place Soviet historians used to call 'the end of the world', the *finis mundi*.

We sailed south. The islands' conical peaks appeared and disappeared. Sometimes their rocky spires were ribbed with snow, and sometimes they were bruised from lava. Then the mist closed in again and I could barely see more than a few metres in front. There was the smell of sea kelp, and malodorous gases from hidden volcanic vents. Tsunamis are common in the Kurils, when the Pacific sucks in its breath and swallows up whatever gets in the way of its killer waves. New islands are constantly being formed. Others are toppling, sagging and shifting their stance as the seabed groans thousands of metres beneath. The turn-of-the-century British fur-hunter Captain Henry James Snow described the sensation of being out at sea and below deck when his ship began to quiver. Then came a series of muffled booms which continued for two hours, even though the surface of the sea was barely agitated.

I was standing alone on the ship's foredeck when we seemed to stop moving altogether. It felt like a fermata, the moment in a piece of music when a note, or rest, is held longer than usual. The sea was flat, and a mysterious calm prevailed. Everything grew sad and dull, as if the ship were stuck in some kind of hole. Out of the silence, a gull looped in, wings stretched, coral-pink feet luminous in the melancholy glow. The bird almost struck me with its wing, before it tipped back into the gloom of the Pacific Basin, its wingbeat fading into a part of the world so remote that there have been times when the Kurils didn't even make it on to the map.

In the eighteenth century, the French explorer Jean-François de La Pérouse said the Kuril Islands' only purpose was to provide a refuge for the shipwrecked. Franklin D. Roosevelt valued them as so utterly irrelevant, he signed over their switch from Japanese to Soviet rule during a session at the 1945 Yalta Conference that lasted for less than the time it took Winston Churchill to smoke his cigar. At one time in history, these far-off islands had been overseen by a prison governor in Irkutsk, with the arm of the Tsars still long enough to overwhelm the indigenous Ainu, who were ultimately pushed out or culturally absorbed either by Russians moving down from the Kamchatka Peninsula, or by the Japanese travelling up from the south. Hunters came for furs, reducing the Kurils' sea-otter population to near extinction. Tens of thousands of seals, their skins peeled off like wet socks, were slaughtered in the Kurils' breeding grounds.

On the seventh night we anchored off Yankicha Island, halfway down the so-called 'Fog Archipelago'. The anchor's chain rattled into the sea. On the other side of the headland stood a cluster of lonely rock stacks. A pod of killer whales seemed to warn us off, circling close to our inflatable boats when we tried to enter a sunken caldera. Birds were starting to fly in under a dusky light. There were hundreds of thousands of them – first the crested auklets, then the whiskered auklets – floating on the water until the surface turned black. They swirled up in thick, balletic curls, like swarms of bees, to find their burrows away from the island's poisonous fumaroles bubbling out of the beach. It was a mesmerizing show of life – a deafening cacophony inside the caldera's walls, the swarms so thick they blocked the sun's last light. This was nature without men, thriving on an island which was still being formed.

The following day we continued to an island that felt like the opposite of Yankicha's hidden Eden. Simushir was a former Soviet submarine base concealed inside a half-sunk caldera, the narrow opening to the sea plugged with a thick bank of fog. Once inside, the sky was clear and the turquoise water as still as a millpond. Military detritus littered the shore.*

Receding into the land behind was a long run of three-storey housing blocks missing their windows, the glass blown out so they resembled skulls with empty eye sockets. A fuel depot had leaked oil. Vehicles and barrels picked up by storms had been tossed into hollows in the land and drowned in thickets of brush. Metal guts were hanging out of the rusted bonnets of military jeeps.

I went looking for clues about the people who might have lived here. But in all the clutter, there were no human faces. Nothing. Neither a cutting from a newspaper, nor a photograph forgotten in a drawer. I stumbled into what must have once been the hospital, with vials of powders and broken beds. I stepped around a dentist's chair, among film reels and leather boots. A mural of a red sickle was peeling off the wall. Another fading image with bubbled paint depicted the Simushir caldera with a rocket launcher to one side. In what must have been a military briefing hall, a lectern stood above a room of toppled chairs as if the audience had just got up and left, tossing their seats to one side.

I could hear the silvery music of songbirds. Trees were starting to grow through the crevices, their russet-coloured

---

* In 1931, the American aviators Charles and Anne Lindbergh were towed to Simushir in their floatplane by a Japanese ship after making an unscheduled landing on a flight from New York to Nanking. Otherwise the island's existence has gone by more or less unnoted in Western sources.

roots and branches reaching for clefts of light. Wild roses broke out of patches of disturbed concrete. Some nutcrackers were nesting in a corner, the young hatchlings safe in a bed of catkins and electric wires.

Back on the ship, Mary told me about a Siberian ruby-throat she had found panting on the deck a few yards from where she stood. Tired from its journey, this tiny red-breasted robin was using our ship as a raft. It tickled her, that this little vagrant was hitching a free ride. She thought it marvellous that it had found us when it was flying so many miles off course. Mary was how I wanted to grow old. She was doing this trip with five clumsy stitches across a knee she had slashed in a fall two days before we sailed. She didn't think my piano quest was lunacy. Nor did it matter that she couldn't scramble up to the puffin nests. She may have even fibbed a little on the application form about her physical abilities in order to book herself a place on this cruise. But above all, Mary refused to shrivel up into a closed and diminished world. Listening to her chuckle in her sleep, I knew she understood better than anyone why we were both here, that even in a place as difficult as Siberia, there might be something magical hiding in the fog. My piano hunt and Mary's vagrant robin had more in common than it first appeared: neither of us had come for the certainties, but for the outside possibility that a little marvel might appear.

17

Provenance Regained:
Khabarovsk

A T THE BEGINNING OF my search, shortly after being dazzled by the burning orange of the tiger in the snow, I had a night to kill in Khabarovsk before making my way home to England. On that dead, wintry evening, I met up with the only piano tuner I could find in the city. He was stiff, even a little anxious. In an attempt to win him over, I invited him to a piano recital advertised at the city's Philharmonic – a hall Richter played in (and complained about) during his Siberian tour in the late 1980s.

The Khabarovsk recital I had bought tickets for was no Richter sensation. It was musically thin and indifferently attended. The concert hall had no more than the first few rows filled, mostly with neatly attired women smelling of fur and talcum powder. In the hum of conversation in the foyer, I felt insincere looking for music in a sleepy place a long time after Lisztomania had first swept through Europe. During the recital's second half, I listened to a crooning version of a Rod Stewart classic. In the seat next to me, the tuner's eyelids lowered, until I suspected he had nodded off. Only when we were parting did my gentle prodding generate anything like a lead.

The tuner knew of one interesting Russian grand piano: a nineteenth-century Stürzwage built by a maker of Finnish descent, Léopold Stürzwage, who opened a Moscow workshop in the same year Liszt made his Russian debut. The piano maker had entered a ready market. For sixty years, the factory whirred and banged to keep up with demand. Then Stürzwage's heir, also called Léopold, born in 1879, abandoned the family business for a career in painting. In the early twentieth century he left Moscow for Paris, where he changed his name to Léopold Survage, worked as a tuner at the Pleyel concert hall in Paris to help make ends meet, and trained with Henri Matisse. He exhibited his musically inspired 'colour symphonies' with Marc Chagall and Wassily Kandinsky, and got employment designing stage sets and costumes for Sergei Diaghilev's Ballets Russes, where Nicholas Roerich had also worked. He designed fabrics for Coco Chanel, and shared a studio (and drinking habit) with the painter Amedeo Modigliani. In a 1918 Modigliani portrait of the Russian émigré, one of Survage's eyes is smudged. When Survage asked why he had been given only one eye, Modigliani replied: 'You regard the world with one eye, and with the other you look inside yourself.' For an emigrant watching the October Revolution tear the old order asunder, those words must have resonated with a deeper kind of ache, echoing the sentiment given by the literary critic Edward Said in his description of the exile's divided psyche. 'Exile is strangely compelling to think about but terrible to experience,' he writes.

> It is the unhealable rift forced between a human being and a native place, between the self and its true home: its essential sadness can never be surmounted. And while it is true that literature and history contain heroic, romantic, glorious, even triumphant episodes in an exile's life, these are no more than efforts meant to overcome the crippling sorrow of estrangement. The achievements of exiles are permanently undermined by the loss of something left behind forever.

The Stürzwage piano fascinated me – partly because I had always loved that Modigliani portrait but had never taken heed of the sitter's identity, and partly because somewhere deep in the piano's past I could picture the elegant fingers of the artist fixing its strings – the disillusioned piano maker who had left his father's business to train as a painter.

With the tuner's help, I eventually found the piano's owner: a local philanthropist called Valery Khidirov, an Ossetian originally from the Caucasus Mountains. Khidirov was attached to the instrument, even if he didn't play himself. In the early nineties, he had bought the Stürzwage for his daughter for less than a hundred dollars.

Valery Khidirov's daughter, Anna, photographed with the Stürzwage piano in the family house in Khabarovsk.

Every time I passed through Khabarovsk, I visited the Khidirov family, who fed me generously and helped with my attempts to trace the Stürzwage's provenance. The piano was glorious, and very, very old. It was a baby grand with its original strings and a shallower than usual depth of touch. The mechanical action was the lighter Viennese type, as opposed to the heavier English version. It lacked the sophisticated over-stringing that revolutionized piano technology in the 1850s, which gave pianos greater resonance.* There was no serial number to date the instrument accurately, nor the signature of the individual maker, which is occasionally found written in pencil on the side of the white keys.

Valery Khidirov remembered the piano's previous owner being a teacher, and the rough direction of the Khabarovsk suburb where she lived. But that was in 1991, more than twenty-five years ago. He said he didn't know what I would find now. Nor could he remember the name of the school where the piano had sat for years. Besides, in a country as big as Russia, people move about. What he did recall was an interesting history: the piano first came to Siberia by sledge, travelling from St Petersburg to Tobolsk.

On my second visit to Khabarovsk a few months later, I took a taxi to knock on the door of one of the kindergartens in the neighbourhood Valery had described. I negotiated my way into the principal's office, where I was met by a woman with a droopy beehive hairstyle and a face as blank as putty. She had never heard of such a story, reminding me that there were a great many people who had sold everything they owned to survive the dark days of Russia's near-bankruptcy. As she peered at me across her desk, I could tell she thought I had lost my mind. There would be other Stürzwages, I told myself. So I put the piano behind me and focused my energies elsewhere until I returned to Khabarovsk a third time towards the very end of my two-year search.

I made an appeal to find the Stürzwage's original owner on a TV news channel broadcast throughout the Russian Far

---

* English piano manufacturers say 'over-strung'; US piano manufacturers say 'cross-strung'. I have generally used the English piano industry's terminology.

East. Two days later, I got a call – from a man who said he remembered the piano from the perestroika times. It had belonged to his ex-wife. The man then rang back with her telephone details.

I called the number. The woman who picked up the phone was suspicious at first. She wanted to know how I had found her. When I explained, she went silent. Then: 'He's still alive?' she asked.

The woman's name was Irina Zhdanova-Kamenska. She agreed to meet me, along with her eighty-six-year-old mother, Nina Alexandrovna. They lived together on the third floor of a Soviet-era block on the outskirts of Khabarovsk, in the same general direction where I had looked before, but about half a mile off. An arsenic-green staircase led to the two-room apartment with six cats or more curled up on the wardrobe and linoleum floor. In a small bedroom, Irina introduced me to her mother, who sat on a swivel chair, her feet swinging from the seat like a child's. Her cheekbones looked sharp from the way her hair was pulled back from her forehead. Her eyes were hollows, sunk into the back of her head. She was blind, she said. She wore a floral suit jacket, matching skirt and thick woollen socks. Her smile was warm and kind.

Nina began to talk, her emptied eyes belying a sharp recollection of detail about the piano she had been given by her aunt, who in 1970 had sent the instrument to Khabarovsk on a train from Tobolsk. Except when the piano arrived at Nina's address in the Russian Far East, she couldn't fit it through the narrow corridor of her flat. So Nina talked to the director of her children's kindergarten, and asked them to take care of the Stürzwage instead. But they abused it. They put flowers on it. The water damaged the piano's case.

'So one day I went in there and grabbed it,' she said. 'I pushed it into the apartment, and forced my girls to learn how to play. Then when times got tough, my daughter sold it.'

'That piano is the story of my childhood,' said Nina.

I took off my coat.

One side of Nina's family was descended from exiles. The other branch was of noble birth. In the nineteenth century, they made their mark as prominent educators in Tobolsk. This was the family the piano came from.

Nina's great-grandfather had three children. The oldest died of starvation in the Leningrad blockade, which Nina remembered from a letter the family received in 1942; it described how when a woman gave birth to a child in the hospital, others made a rush at her and ate the afterbirth. The second son, who was an officer on a ship in the 1905 Russo-Japanese War, was killed in action. The third child was Nina's grandmother. She had married the son of a Pole captured during one of the later Polish revolts. She had met him at the Governor's House in Tobolsk, where the Tsar and his family were later incarcerated. As Nina talked me through the family tree, it started to feel as if all the fragments scattered throughout my piano hunt were finally coming together like Russian dolls in one neatly organized, close-fitting stack.

Nina's grandfather was a well-regarded academic among the citizens of Tobolsk. He was executed during the Revolution by the Reds because, as city treasurer, he had refused to hand over the keys to Tobolsk's coffers. In December 1920, he was shot in the prison at Tyumen, then thrown into a hole cut into the ice of the river. At least that is what they think happened to him, based on witness accounts.

Nina Alexandrovna's ancestors, photographed in 1899. In the centre is her great-great-grandfather, Illarion Slavuta. In front on the right is her father, Aleksandr Ternovskiy, aged four. On the left is Nina's Aunt Lena.

Nina's father, Aleksandr, escaped any further revenge by the Bolsheviks. He fought for Russia in the First World War. After the Revolution, he went to work as a geologist in the goldmines in Yakutia. He later transferred as a free worker to Kolyma.

Living in such extreme locations worried Nina's mother, who by now had children to raise. So in 1932, the year after Nina was born, Nina was sent to live with her widowed Aunt Lena in Tobolsk, who was a biologist and musician. Aunt Lena had ordered the Stürzwage baby grand from St Petersburg before the Revolution, and had it delivered by sledge from the train station at Tyumen to Tobolsk, which was one hundred and sixty miles north of the main Trans-Siberian Railway. Aunt

Lena had lost three sons in a week in 1920 to a typhus epidemic; it was decided she could care for Nina while her parents settled in Kolyma. From that day on, Nina, her beloved aunt and the Stürzwage were tightly bound.

'On the day I arrived in Tobolsk, I cried and cried,' said Nina. 'Then they pressed my baby fingers on the keyboard. Apparently, only the noise from the piano would calm me down.'

The piano sat in the dining room of the family home, which looked up at the escarpment where the Tobolsk priest used to do roly-polies when he was training at the seminary. The piano was shaded by a huge pot-plant – a fig tree Nina's aunt had grown from seed.

'It was like a jungle,' said Nina. 'The top board of the piano looked like the shape of the African continent. Which is why we named the piano Africa.'

Nina had only a few toys, including models of monkeys, birds and crocodiles, which were placed on top of the instrument. On Sundays the arrangement was cleared away, the lid opened up and Aunt Lena played. There was singing and dancing. There was Mozart, Chopin, Tchaikovsky and Beethoven. They invited other children to listen, including a Tatar family who lived in poverty opposite their house. She described exploring a river meadow close to where the Cossack adventurer Ermak Timofeevich is said to have drowned. She remembered being alone in the forest, listening to the cuckoos.

'I loved animals,' she said. 'I always have. When I was a child, we had a map called "Animal World of the USSR", which we hung above the piano. I knew the territory where each animal belonged.'

In 1946, Nina was sent to join her parents. To get to Kolyma, she had to wait with her mother in Nakhodka, one of the ports that also processed the Gulag ships. The families were given flour, but no stoves to cook on. They slept in canvas camps, waiting for transport to Magadan. When the first ship caught fire, killing more than a hundred people and causing the sky to rain oil, they waited for an alternative ship to make safe passage across the Sea of Okhotsk. She described the campfires pinpricking the hillside, her mother making pies, and the suck and croak of frogs. She remembered how, in the middle of the night, a chicken's hysterical cackle woke everyone up just in time to prevent thieves stealing from their luggage.

Nina's mother brought the chicken with them to Kolyma. When the family settled in the gold-mining town of Susuman – the same stop on the Kolyma Highway where I had spent a sleepless night in a bed that smelled of other people's sweat – they fed the chicken cockroaches. Nina's mother gathered them by slathering a bowl in fat. When the cockroaches came to feed in the night, they got stuck in the grease.

The family home in Susuman was small: two bedrooms and a kitchen. There was only one piano in the entire settlement, located in the House of Culture. Nina heard the singer Vadim Kozin when he came to perform. She remembered how nothing would grow, and the coldest winter, which hit minus sixty-two. She remembered swimming in spring in the icy river, and the freezing burn. She imagined being Tom Sawyer and moving along the Mississippi in a boat. She wanted to know what people lived for: love, society, Stalin. She wasn't sure herself. She learned *Eugene Onegin* by heart. She wrote poetry, and still does. She became a zoologist, specializing in fish. All she wanted to do was travel – an interest inspired by the map of Africa laid out on the top of the Stürzwage at Aunt Lena's house in Tobolsk.

'I travelled all over the USSR. Magadan, Novosibirsk, Barnaul, Khabarovsk, Tyumen, Perm, Ekaterinburg, Astrakhan, Kharkov, Yaroslavl, Ussuriysk, Vladivostok, Yuzhno-Sakhalinsk, Ulan-Ude, Ust-Barguzin . . .' The words kept rolling off her tongue, the litany as alluring as when I had first looked over a map of Russia. Since then, I had run into numerous people in Siberia who had little to say about a place where they didn't intend to remain. I had also met plenty others who didn't want to remember why they had come. Repression. Migration. Conflict. So much of what happens, happens without trace. Siberia can feel like a country within a country. Sometimes, however, the truth is more banal than all of this, and Siberia is like anywhere else – a place where people get bound to the territory, not knowing quite when, why or how. There were times when I came to think of Siberia not only as a physical location, but also as the word to describe what happens if you stay too long in a place that is not your own, sticking around for one winter too many until you realize you have gone too far to turn back. But now I'd spent more time here, I realized that there was more to it than loveless migration, that when it came to the best of people – the staunch, steadfast Russians who had helped me with my search – Siberia was really something else. There had been the Lomatchenko family in Novosibirsk, the singing priests in Tobolsk and the siege survivor in Akademgorodok. And now Nina – this blind, bent, brilliant old woman, who was so frail and vulnerable, yet so full of fire for the things she loved. Nina was an encyclopaedia of twentieth-century Russia, who said there was only one thing she hated about her life. When she was a child in

Kolyma, her father would punish her bad behaviour by making her sort through jars of sand. She would have to sit at the table and pick through the grains for flakes of gold while her friends played outside. It was agony to Nina; all she wanted to do was run wild, to jump into the water, even in the fearful Kolyma cold. As she talked, it was as if there was a kind of burning heat inside her, a glow behind her hollowed eyes. To Nina, Siberia was no heart of darkness: it was the *Appassionata* – an experience of such intensity, it had worked its way deep into her magnificent Russian soul.

Epilogue

'You cannot fathom Russia with the mind . . . You can only believe in it.'

– Fyodor Tyutchev

'I never choose a piano and don't try them out before a concert. It's useless and demoralizing. I place myself in the hands of the piano tuner. If I'm on form, I can adapt to no matter what instrument, whereas if I'm in doubt, I never succeed in doing so. You have to believe, more than St Peter, that you'll walk on water.'

– Sviatoslav Richter, *Notebooks and Conversations*

'Siberia is an extensive and chilly land. I go on and on without seeing an end to it. I've seen little that's interesting and novel, but on the other hand I've felt and experienced a great deal . . . I've had the kind of sensations you wouldn't undergo for millions of roubles in Moscow. You ought to come to Siberia! Ask the Public Prosecutor to exile you here.'

– Anton Chekhov, Letter to his brother, June 1890

Epilogue:
The Orkhon Valley

A STAY OF SEVERAL WEEKS on Sakhalin Island will bring on a kind of rheumatic sickness, wrote Anton Chekhov, the effect of so-called 'climatic influences' inducing 'Febris Sachalinensis'. A contemporary Western authority on the Russian Far East, John J. Stephan, makes note of how during the Second World War, Japanese soldiers defending the Kuril Islands complained of 'Kurilitis' to describe an affliction brought on by being stuck too long in an isolated place and a cruel climate. The master of twentieth-century Siberian nature writing, Valentin Rasputin, remarks on another kind of illness induced by Siberia – an opening up of expanses you never knew were there.

> Siberia has the virtue of not startling or astonishing you right away but of pulling you in slowly and reluctantly, as it were, with measured carefulness, and then binding you tightly once you are in. And then it's all over – you are afflicted with Siberia. After malignant anthrax [*sibirskaia iazva*, literally, 'Siberian ulcer'], which apparently doesn't exist anymore, this is Siberia's most famous disease: for a long time after being in this land a person feels hemmed in, sad, and mournful everywhere else, tormented wherever he goes by a vague and agonizing sense of his own inadequacy, as if he's left part of himself in Siberia for ever.

I had only five days left on my visa when I headed home to England from Khabarovsk. I flew over the Yenisei River and Lake Baikal. Once I hit Irkutsk, my flight retraced the line that the nineteenth-century blind traveller James Holman followed out of Siberia on his way back to England. Despite his blindness, Holman's presence in Irkutsk had put him under suspicion that he was acting as a British spy. He was quickly and forcibly escorted from Siberia on the orders of the Tsar. Poking around Russia's terra incognita was problematic then, and it still is now.

When Chekhov made his journey to Sakhalin, he claimed he was writing a thesis to support his medical career. He also said he was undertaking a census measuring the convict colony's household groups. Suspicion was inevitably aroused.

One prisoner, who had killed his wife with a hammer, thought Chekhov was counting convicts in order to send them to the moon. 'My main aim in conducting the census,' admitted Chekhov, 'was not its results but the impressions received during the making of it.'

When I applied for my Russian visa in London, I told the consulate my purpose of travel was to look for pianos in Siberia.

The woman at the desk glanced at me as if I had lost my mind. As I left, another applicant held the door open for me.

'That was the worst story I ever heard,' he said.

'Why are you going?' I asked.

'Football,' he said.

My original motives were genuine, but they had also kept expanding. 'I'm interested to be where I was not,' Richter told a local journalist, who was as bemused as anyone to find a Soviet megastar touring the Siberian back country. I shared Richter's curiosity, to which I added a foreigner's naïvety: I was interested in seeing those parts I had never known existed in the first place, which in an over-travelled world makes Siberia stand out. Catherine the Great had once reasoned that her Empire had expanded so dramatically under her rule because of the Russians' 'proclivity for adventure'. What she probably meant to say was the Empire had swelled so effectively because of the Russians' love of a good fur, but still, I understood her point: Siberia is a very fine place indeed for travellers in pursuit of the adrenaline which truly adventurous travel imparts.

Was it all just a grand romance? A nostalgic, picaresque quest for the exotic? A chase for the object of desire rather than its achievement, marked by marvels, monsters and eccentric diversions? Or was it just another contribution to the annals of travel into the Siberian absurd? There was a good tradition in them. James Holman's *Travels through Russia, Siberia, Poland, Austria, Saxony, Prussia, Hanover, &c. &c. Undertaken during the Years 1822, 1823 and 1824, While Suffering from Total Blindness*; John Dundas Cochrane's 1825 *Narrative of a Pedestrian Journey through Russia and Siberian Tartary, From the Frontiers of China to the Frozen Sea and Kamchatka*; and *Vagabonding at Fifty*, written by two sedate, middle-aged American women, Helen Wilson and Elsie Mitchell, who made a baffling journey into the Altai in 1925. They came from the suburbs of Berkeley, California, dressed in khakis and panama hats, and were accompanied by a pet fox terrier. Their purpose was to join an international brigade of communists in Siberia, but when factory life wasn't quite as they had expected, they took to the mountains for a holiday instead.

I knew the entire endeavour had been inflected with a measure of madness. But then, if I had paused to read every dreadful story, real or fake, written about Russia, I would never have got on a plane to Siberia in the first instance. If I had let anxiety take hold, I wouldn't have seen the many, many places which found a place in my heart, but not in the pages of this book. There was the magical Lake Numto, where I stayed with a family of forest-dwelling Nenets. There was the buzz of Tyumen, where I watched the oil men come and go with the kind of swagger you would expect in Moscow. There were the numerous musical performances from Novosibirsk to Khabarovsk – some very good, others as familiarly parochial as those I know from my own rural community on the sleepy English coast. And there was the outright weirdness of Birobidzhan, a Soviet experiment on the Russia–China border conceived in the 1930s to function as the USSR's 'Jewish

Autonomous Region'. There were roadsigns in Yiddish, one rabbi, and no Jewish musicians I could find, aside from a visiting theatre group from Israel.

In all these meanderings, one of the biggest challenges had been keeping on the right side of the authorities. Aside from working with local news channels to find pianos, I had been more or less successful in flying beneath the radar until I reached the Altai Mountains. I was called in by an FSB official to go over my paperwork. He worked for the state security service. He talked about Somerset Maugham and Joseph Heller, conversing in perfect English with a nimble intellect and a disquieting familiarity.* He knew my education, I assumed, from my visa application. His fascination with my time at Oxford made me suspect that we both saw each other through the prism of a James Bond movie. To me, he was the Russian baddie; to him, I was the entitled Englishwoman who might work for MI6.

The next night my interpreter received a late-evening call from the same official. His continued attention was unnerving, as if he didn't believe I was in Siberia to look for piano stories. I think the FSB man thought I was a little odd. I was confident I had the correct paperwork to be in this region, so when we parted, I decided to press on for the border post near Kosh-Agach, one of the last settlements before Mongolia.

I wanted to spend a couple of days looking at this

---

* The British anthropologist Charles Hawes had a similar experience when he was taken in for questioning by Russian authorities on Sakhalin Island at the end of the nineteenth century. Like me, he was circumspect. Like me, he was also surprised by the eloquence of his interrogator: 'A highly educated man, speaking English, French and German, besides his native tongue, he was surprisingly au courant with English literature.' Charles H. Hawes, *In the Uttermost East* (London and New York: Harper & Brothers, 1904).

potential route out of Siberia – to see how good the road was, since this border crossing was one of only two in Siberia open to foreigners en route to Mongolia. I also wanted to immerse myself one last time in the landscape before abandoning it completely. The Altai was too beautiful not to see more of the mountains. Having encountered a tiger at the beginning of this journey, I had it in my head that it was worth trying to find a snow leopard. My book's theme – a far-flung search for Russia's remarkable survivors – turned around the rare and disappearing, which was enough to justify the diversion.

My interpreter and Uncle Vitya made the necessary arrangements. My paperwork was signed off by the local officials. I hired a heavy-duty, off-road truck furnished with a stove and bunks. I would be accompanied by two wildlife rangers and a couple of snowmobiles. Uncle Vitya checked my wardrobe and insisted on some extra purchases. The temperature was dipping to minus twenty and below.

That's what I was doing – tipping off what felt like the End of Everything, every part of my body clinging to a gold-toothed wildlife ranger on the back of a snowmobile – when my luck slipped into free fall. From the top of a bald hill I could see Mongolia. A flock of argali sheep were moving across a treeless valley beneath me. The sheep were huge, their extravagant curled horns twisted like corkscrews and swept backwards as if bent by the wind. For a few long minutes, we pursued the flock through a whiteness that rolled out in every direction. Then out of nowhere, four armed border guards in white camouflage appeared on snowmobiles. While I had been following the sheep, they had been following me; they said that I had to go with them back to Kosh-Agach.

The interrogation lasted the rest of the day. When I thought it was over, I was put in the back of a van, taken to the customs police, and fingerprinted. When I scrubbed my fingers, which were stained with ink, I looked at the whorls on my thumb and thought of the tattoos on the Altaian mummies. I stood against the wall. All I could do was press the small of my back into it to stop my body shaking.

I had stepped across a line in a place I wasn't meant to be. My questioners were polite. They were professional. They were cold as ice. They said I had trespassed into the wrong border territory, without permission. They fined me – I had committed an 'administrative violation' – and warned me that one more error and my visa allowing my return to Russia could be revoked. But when I found those rare argali sheep, I also experienced the thrill of discovery. There seemed to me something important about not letting anything scare me off from the quiet corners of Siberia to which pianos had come. Still, that incident also changed things for me: I needed to be careful.

In February 2018, two years after deciding to take on this search in one of the most remote places on Earth, I started making enquiries about a piano for Mongolia. I did this with the help of the Novosibirsk tuner Kostya Lomatchenko. His family instrument – the Grotrian-Steinweg I had first encountered in the basement of the Novosibirsk opera house along with a papier-mâché pig – had drawn me in immediately, despite the broken sounds and missing keys. The Grotrian seemed to have everything 'right' about it, at least by the time I had worked out what 'right' might be: the instrument was private rather than state property; it carried an intimate meaning rather than national significance; it was one of the best uprights ever made, and more transportable than a grand. Eventually, I found space in our growing friendship to ask if the Lomatchenkos would let it go – the instrument bought by Kostya's grandfather from an antiques shop in the sixties with the sale of his house.

The Lomatchenkos agreed, since they all tuned instruments but no one really played. Under Kostya's direction, Odgerel's patron, Franz-Christoph Giercke, and I would buy the specialist parts from Germany, and a system to stabilize humidity in order to protect the piano in the dry air of Mongolia. Kostya and his father would then spend three months restoring the piano, which they did in the basement of the Novosibirsk Opera and Ballet Theatre. Stanislav Dobrovolskiy, the tuner who had survived the Leningrad Siege, would help advise on paperwork for the relevant authorities. In return for his time and assistance, he had asked that I send him a copy of a 1958 vinyl record he was keen to hear: *England's Greatest Combo . . . The Couriers of Jazz!* by Tubby Hayes and Ronnie Scott.

In April 2018, I received news from my interpreter, Elena Voytenko, that the Grotrian-Steinweg, its action now able to withstand anything a dazzling virtuoso could throw at it, was ready to travel. By way of thanks, Franz-Christoph Giercke and I also agreed to pay for Kostya to pursue his dream: to fly to Germany and complete his advanced piano tuner training at the Steinway Academy in Hamburg. If successful, and accepted on to the course, this would help make him one of the best-trained piano tuners in Siberia. I gave Kostya my word: if he could get a piano to Mongolia, then I could surely get a Siberian to Steinway.

On 18 May 2018, the Grotrian-Steinweg was packed with mattresses, ropes and foam to start its two-thousand-mile-long journey by truck and trailer from Novosibirsk to the Orkhon Valley in Mongolia. The delivery from Novosibirsk took eight days, via the River Yenisei and Lake Baikal, then through the Kiakhta border crossing between Russia and Mongolia. The Russian despatch party comprised Kostya Lomatchenko, Uncle Vitya – my lucky talisman and 'security' detail, who wanted to come along for the ride – and my Russian interpreter, Elena, whose extraordinary determination throughout my quest had made this final journey possible. The driver, Igor, was an athletic, blue-eyed subway operator from Novosibirsk.

Unfortunately, the political climate had changed dramatically during the last few months of this book's writing. Tensions were running high between the UK, the US and Russia. For this reason, I met the piano in Mongolia. I was joined by my friend the photographer Michael Turek and my twelve-year-old son, Danny. I had been feeling jumpy given my visa was marked. Perhaps I was being paranoid, but I was disappointed not to share fully in this closing mission when for good or for bad I had sought to transcend the notions of fear that exist around the idea of Siberia.

I was equally despondent about the fact I was missing out on one of the great road trips of Central Asia: after making their drop-off in the Orkhon Valley, the Russians would return home through western Mongolia and the Russian Altai to complete a month-long circuit of three and a half thousand miles. I was envious of the fun they would have, with a third of this journey spent travelling roadless open steppe (they got lost twice and saved two German tourists headed to the 2018 FIFA World Cup who got stuck in a Volkswagen in a Mongolian river). My disappointment at not being part of this expedition soon faded, however, when the piano was finally unloaded into the *ger*. For a couple of days, Kostya worked privately with the piano, getting it to the tuning standard he wanted. It was during those days, when the piano was opened up, that I noticed the stamp of 'Allenstein' on the wooden key. Then finally, as the sun was going down on a crisp night in May, we heard Odgerel Sampilnorov play.

The occasion was deeply moving. A group of herders gathered to listen to the premiere. Odgerel, who was nervous that she and the instrument might not get along, played the work of a contemporary Mongolian composer, Byambasuren Sharav. She immediately pronounced the Grotrian-Steinweg superior in sound to the Yamaha baby grand. Kostya Lomatchenko wept. Uncle Vitya shared his moonshine and his stories about yetis. Franz-Christoph Giercke brought out silver cups and gave Uncle Vitya, whom he adored, his English Lock & Co. black felt fedora hat. Igor collected flowers from the river to present to Elena, with whom he had fallen thoroughly in love.

For the next few days, all of us came and went through the *ger*'s low door to listen to Odgerel play some more. It was like eavesdropping on two people getting to know each other for the first time. This was music at its best: intimate, pure and true. Russian, Mongolian, German – it didn't matter whose; the music flowed so effortlessly it was as if it were revealing a shared and noble truth. Kostya and I would lie on our backs on the tent's yak-hair floor. Both of us liked listening in. Sometimes Kostya cried, sometimes he smiled, overwhelmingly proud about the piano's sound he had spent months repairing. I felt proud, too, not because I had put any trust in my musical judgement, but because all the searching had come together in this single moment – and powerful conviction – that people basically want the same thing: harmony, beauty, continuity.

Throughout my journey, I had been asking myself: what is the point of music? Now we were all together in Mongolia, what was Kostya, with his extreme sensitivity, thinking about as he lay there with his eyes closed? Did he, too, wonder about the piece of green felt draped over the piano's case? It had come with the instrument – a sort of slip laid over the keyboard to protect the ebonies and ivories. The felt was embroidered with flowers – stitched by one of the Grotrian-Steinweg's previous owners before the Lomatchenkos had bought it in the Novosibirsk antiques shop. It was a personal memento – a kind of coat to protect something that had been dearly loved by someone, somewhere, its history still unknown. Who was this person? Would they be glad to be weaving these invisible roses in the lives of those who came next? Was there someone still alive who remembered learning to play their first scales on this Grotrian-Steinweg before Europe was torn apart? Or was the piano's wartime story a false trail? If only the threads could lead back. If only someone one day might claim this piano's early history, there might be another chapter left to write.

Next year, declared Giercke, we all needed to return to Mongolia to listen to Odgerel play the piano in concert with the horsehead fiddle, or *morin khuur*. He would organize a recital, he said – a grand performance in a clearing on a rocky outcrop in the steppe, a holy place which he had first encountered twenty years before. He said it was a day's drive away from where we stood, with a small Buddhist temple at its top and the most perfect acoustics he had ever heard. With that final flourish of the beautiful eccentricity that had got me into this Siberian piano hunt in the first place, he sent us off with Kostya to make a sound check.

'Tell me if I haven't been hearing things,' said Giercke. 'The acoustics are so perfect, you can hear a pin drop.'

We went, got the car stuck, listened to Kostya test the acoustics with a whisper, and all marvelled that Giercke was right: the sound rolled around the bowl of rock in the purest air imaginable. That night, which was to be our last all together in Mongolia, we made firm promises to each other – the most important oath being the one Odgerel gave to Kostya that his gift of a piano would be loved, and if there was ever a problem with it, or she could no longer care for it, she would be back in touch. We toasted each other late into the night. We said our goodbyes knowing there would be more toasts to come. The subway driver was falling deeper in love. Uncle Vitya again told his story about the yeti. The next day, Elena, Igor, Kostya and Uncle Vitya departed, their empty trailer enveloped in a plume of dust.

Odgerel now performs solo recitals in Mongolia's Orkhon Valley during the summer months. To my knowledge, the Grotrian-Steinweg, which she otherwise keeps under careful, humidity-controlled conditions at her apartment in Ulaan-baatar, is the only piano of its kind in Mongolia, and continues to sing with one of the most beautiful voices I ever heard in two years of searching. Cantabile, Odgerel calls it, after its singing voice: tender, smooth, vulnerable and full of feeling, with a rich, warm bass and a silver treble, the hammers delivering keen, precise blows to achieve a perfect clarity. She keeps Rachmaninoff and Liszt for the Yamaha, and Chopin and Debussy for the sweet, voluptuous colours of the little upright. Her touch connects with the piano's inner resonance, like an alchemist might turn stone to gold. '[John] Field did not so much play his own nocturnes, but dreamed them at the piano,' observed Liszt of the Irishman who had first set Russia's hearts alight. That was how it felt listening to Odgerel on the Grotrian-Steinweg. It was as if she were revealing the singing heart of the instrument that had affected so many lives through the centuries, its voice reaching all the way back to Bartolomeo Cristofori's magnificent invention when the fortepiano's trembling notes first filled the palace of a glittering Medici prince.

On their drive back to Novosibirsk through the Altai, the Russians stopped in to visit Leonid Kaloshin, the Aeroflot navigator. Elena then spent a week helping him improve his vegetable garden. Igor, the subway driver, assisted with a local piano delivery on Leonid's behalf.

Semion Nyaruy, the Nenets composer I had met in Yamal, died on 4 April 2018. His widow hopes that the Salekhard Department of Culture will build a museum exhibit in his honour, and that Semion's Tyumen upright will be preserved there. In the short term, the piano may be sent to Semion's alma mater, the Tyumen music school.

The captain of the fishing ship, Valentin Lekus, who got his crew to club together and buy a piano to assuage the long months at sea in the North Pacific, also died before this book was published. He sang a song for me when we were together – the 1939 classic 'We'll Meet Again', made famous by Vera Lynn during the Second World War. It was like listening to a man's heart stripped bare – a gentleman who had given his best years to a hard life on Soviet ships in one of the toughest climates on the planet. When I write this now, the song stays with me as one of the most affecting moments during my time in Siberia, along with the image of a fiddle made with stolen horsehair and Lidiya's narcissus standing tall in a pool of light.

I received further news about the Bechstein I had found in Kiakhta, which confirmed the piano had been delivered to Kiakhta Museum in 1979 from the capital of Buryatia, Ulan-Ude. I received no information attributing it to the tea merchant family. So I contacted Bechstein's archivists instead, and found a fascinating glimmer of a deeper past: in 1874, the piano was despatched to a 'Nikolai R.' in Moscow – one of several delivered to the same person that year. Could it have been Nikolai Rubinstein, who had chosen the piano for the Imperial Russian Musical Society in Tomsk?

Nina Alexandrovna isn't in good enough health to see the Khabarovsk Stürzwage again in person, but she and the Khidirov family have struck up a close friendship. They often visit Nina in her apartment. They, too, like listening to Nina's stories about her early childhood in Tobolsk, when the piano was covered in a map. The piano has also now been restored. In the winter of 2018, the Khidirov family arranged for a professional pianist to play the instrument, and then brought Nina a recording of the music. 'Sometimes an old person cannot die because his or her soul aches or feels pain about something; they need to wait for something in their story to finish,' wrote my interpreter, as I was finishing up the last few sentences of this book: 'Nina's soul is calm. She likes listening to the Stürzwage, knowing that the piano is now with a generous and outstanding family in a house full of love.' In Nina's last days, she listens to the music of her childhood.

It is worth noting that I never made it deep into the Russian Arctic to follow Fridtjof Nansen. I found a polar specialist who could fly me via helicopter close to where I wanted to go in Siberia's Severnaya Zemlya archipelago. However, my application for a permit was rejected by the FSB a few weeks before we were due to depart. It contained several reasons for refusal, namely 'Refusal of territorial security authorities in special permit to enter the border zone for foreign citizen.' I guess the authorities had given up believing I was looking for a piano in the equivalent of outer space, which in many ways, was fair enough. As it happened, the helicopter I was due to fly in crashed on the very charter I would have joined.

On 9 August 2017, despite my encounter with authorities in the Altai, I was issued with a second year-long writer's visa to continue my work in Siberia. This was a huge relief to me. Then, on 29 November 2018, I received news that the Russian Ministry of Foreign Affairs had rejected my application for a third year of work. Among other things, I was planning to fill in some gaps in my reporting in Krasnoyarsk, an important city on the River Yenisei where, in the last years of the nineteenth century, George Kennan had encountered one of the finest drawing rooms in Russia, replete with paintings by well-known European artists, and, of course, a grand piano.

Hearing the news was like discovering that the person you are obsessed with is as unlikeable as all your friends had suspected. There was an 'I told you so' echoing back through my journey which I didn't want to accept. It felt as if I were effectively being exiled from an exile's land. After falling for Siberia, I was now unable to return. Something in me felt depleted. But a far larger part of me knew that in spite of everything difficult about Russia, there was also powerful redemption in its extremities. What this country endured is hard to fathom, and that was in the bloody twentieth century alone. Siberia may be on the periphery of our consciousness. It may hold some of the bleakest stories of human cruelty.

There may be numerous difficulties to uncovering truth and testimonies, and to accepting the extent of Russia's calamitous past. But in spite of everything, Siberia is fundamentally life-giving all the same – a wellspring of culture, humanity and moral courage in the last place on Earth I expected to find it, revealed to me by people who not only opened their pianos but also their homes and hearts to a stranger. This book remembers their kindnesses, but above all, the music and memories they shared.

August 2019

To see more of this story in Michael Turek's pictures, listen to recordings by Odgerel Sampilnorov, and find out more about the search, visit www.lostpianosofsiberia.com.

A Brief Historical Chronology

1587 The Western Siberian town of Tobolsk is established. Over the next hundred years, it evolves into the biggest fur centre in Siberia.

1639 Russians reach the Pacific Ocean for the first time, travelling overland across Siberia.

1700 Bartolomeo Cristofori, instrument maker to a Florentine Medici prince, produces a new invention that plays soft (*piano*) and loud (*forte*).

1703 Tsar Peter the Great establishes Russia's new capital, St Petersburg, in the image of a European city, earning it the moniker 'Venice of the North'.

1730 Russia begins building the Great Siberian Trakt – an overland trade route from Moscow to China.

1741 Vitus Bering reaches Alaska from Russia – extending the Empire into what will become known as 'Russian America'.

1762 Catherine the Great becomes Empress of All Russia following the death of her husband, Tsar Peter III, in a palace coup.

1774 Catherine commissions a piano in London. Over the next three decades, the instrument undergoes rapid changes in technology.

1782 Wolfgang Amadeus Mozart and Muzio Clementi 'duel' at Emperor Joseph II's court in Vienna. Construction begins on Pavlovsk Palace – a centre of Russian musical life throughout the nineteenth century.

1784 John Broadwood in London is now making more pianos than harpsichords.

1789 The French Revolution, which lasts until 1799, destabilizes the monarchies of Europe – and attracts the interest of Russian liberals.

1795 Beethoven begins composing his thirty-two sonatas, reinventing the genre of solo keyboard music.

1796 Catherine the Great dies. The harpsichord and organ no longer dominate orchestras as the piano gains in popularity.

1801 Clementi publishes the first ever piano method book, *Clementi's Introduction to the Art of Playing on the Piano Forte.*

1812 Napoleon invades Russia. In September, the Battle of Borodino becomes the bloodiest single day of battle in recorded history, not surpassed until the first day of the Battle of the Somme in 1916. Napoleon succeeds in capturing Moscow but is quickly forced into a retreat made desperate by the brutal Russian winter.

1821 French piano maker Sébastien Erard patents the 'double escapement'. With a note able to sound repeatedly without the key having to return to its full height, a new explosion of virtuosity is unleashed.

1825 The Decembrist Uprising results in the exile of more than a hundred high-profile Russian aristocrats and gentlemen revolutionaries to Siberia.

1830 By this time, the piano resembles the modern instrument we play today. This is the beginning of the Romantic period, and the golden age of virtuosos. In this same year, Russia crushes the November Uprising in Poland; nearly two thirds of those Poles banished for political offences in the next decade belong to a culturally educated nobility.

1842 Franz Liszt makes his blistering Russian debut.

1848 'The Spring of Nations' – the most widespread revolutionary wave in European history – brings down numerous absolutist regimes, but not Russia's.

1853 One of the most remarkable years for the piano industry: Steinway & Sons is established in New York, Blüthner in Leipzig, and Bechstein in Berlin.

1855 Alexander II becomes Tsar. A year later, he grants amnesty to the Decembrist revolutionaries, allowing survivors to return from Siberia to Western Russia.

1861 Serfdom is abolished by Tsar Alexander II, four years before slavery ends in America. Around this time, Fyodor Dostoevsky publishes *The House of the Dead*, inspired by the four years he spent in Siberian exile in the 1850s.

1862 The St Petersburg Conservatory opens – the first school to professionalize music in Russia.

1863 The January Uprising in Poland, crushed by the Russians, results in a new influx of political exiles to Siberia.

1867 Russia sells Alaska to America for US$7.2 million.

1872 The Empress of Russia, Maria Alexandrovna, receives a Steinway concert grand, serial number 25000.

1877 The phonograph, or record player, is invented, although it won't be until the 1910s that the device begins to replace the piano as the primary source of music in the home.

1881 Tsar Alexander II is assassinated by revolutionaries in St Petersburg.

1891 Work begins on the Trans-Siberian Railway.

1894 Nicholas II becomes Tsar. George Bernard Shaw declares 'the pianoforte is the most important of all musical instruments; its invention was to music what the invention of printing was to poetry'.

1896 Piano manufacturing hits boomtime in America.

1897 Lenin is exiled to Siberia for three years, along with other leaders of the Union for the Struggle for the Liberation of the Working Class. Lenin's noble status means his experience of exile is far more comfortable than that of his poorer comrades.

1903 Joseph Stalin is first exiled to Siberia. Between now and 1913, Stalin is exiled seven times, managing to escape on six occasions.

1904 The Trans-Siberian Railway opens.

1905 Tsarist authorities respond violently to a peaceful protest on 'Bloody Sunday'. Russia loses the southern half of Sakhalin Island at the end of the Russo-Japanese War.

1908 Henry Ford introduces the Model T motor car. In the West, it won't be long before the car overtakes the piano as a show of status.

1913 Tsar Nicholas II celebrates the three-hundredth anniversary of the Romanov dynasty.

1914 The First World War begins. Germany and the Austro-Hungarian Empire declare war on Russia.

1917 The February Revolution takes place. Tsar Nicholas II abdicates, and the imperial family are taken to Siberia. The October Revolution establishes Lenin's power. The Russian Civil War begins.

1918 The Tsar and his family are murdered in Ekaterinburg. Lenin introduces the Soviet system of forced labour camps.

1922 Vladivostok falls to the Red Army, and the Russian Civil War is finally over. Shamanism, animism and totemism are officially banned.

1924 Lenin dies, making way for Stalin, who will become one of the most powerful, murderous dictators in history.

1929 'De-kulakization' and rapid industrialization begins in the USSR, signalling the end of private land ownership and the start of widespread famine.

1936 Stalin's Great Purge begins.

1939 The Second World War effectively halts piano building worldwide. Materials and manpower are in short supply.

1942 Dmitri Shostakovich's Symphony No. 7 in C Major premieres in Leningrad during the Nazi siege.

1953 Russian piano manufacturing increases tenfold, from now until 1970. Nikita Khrushchev is in power – a period of 'de-Stalinization'.

1958 American pianist Harvey Van Cliburn wins the inaugural International Tchaikovsky Piano Competition in Moscow, indicating a thaw in Soviet–US relations.

1964 Leonid Brezhnev is in power. An ideological clampdown begins.

1969 From quiet beginnings, Japan now manufactures more pianos than any other country.

1985 Mikhail Gorbachev is in power. Perestroika begins a political movement to transform the Communist Party of the Soviet Union, which leads to the dissolution of the USSR in 1991.

1986 Russian pianist Sviatoslav Richter travels across Siberia. Vladimir Horowitz makes a homecoming trip to the Soviet Union, travelling with his concert grand Steinway & Sons Model D piano.

1991 The Soviet hammer and sickle is taken down from the Kremlin and replaced by the new tricolour flag of the Russian Federation.

2000 Vladimir Putin wins his first presidential election.

2016 The search for the lost pianos of Siberia begins.

Selected Bibliography

The Notes give a clear indication of the books I have relied on for their scholarly expertise. This selected bibliography focuses on the literary, adventurous and sometimes eccentric first-hand accounts from travellers past and contemporary, which are currently available in the English language (aside from Valentina Chemberdzhi). I have also included fiction, and one or two critical historical texts that readers interested in Siberia might consider essential reading. Also listed: some expert music books for those with a keener interest in this side of the story, and a small selection of relevant films.

Valerian Albanov, *In the Land of White Death*, trans. Alison Anderson (London: Random House, 2010)

Dmitri Alioshin, *Asian Odyssey* (New York: Henry Holt & Co., 1940)

Anne Applebaum, *Gulag: A History* (London: Penguin, 2004)

Vladimir Arseniev, *Dersu the Trapper*, trans. Malcolm Burr (London: Secker & Warburg, 1939)

Avvakum, *The Life of the Archpriest Avvakum by Himself*, trans. Jane Harrison and Hope Mirrlees (London: Hogarth Press, 1963)

Glynn R. Barratt, *Voices in Exile: The Decembrist Memoirs* (Montreal and London: McGill-Queen's University Press, 1974)

Daniel Beer, *The House of the Dead: Siberian Exile under the Tsars* (London: Allen Lane, 2016)

Anton Chekhov, *Sakhalin Island*, trans. Brian Reeve (Surrey: OneWorld Classics, 2007)

Valentina Chemberdzhi, *V puteshestvii so Sviatoslavom Rikhterom* (Moscow: M. RIK 'Kul'tura', 1993)

Anthony Cross, *In the Lands of the Romanovs: An Annotated Bibliography of First-hand English-language Accounts of the Russian Empire (1613–1917)* (Cambridge: Open Book, 2014)

Selected Bibliography

Galya Diment and Yuri Slezkine (eds), *Between Heaven and Hell: The Myth of Siberia in Russian Culture* (New York: St Martin's Press, 1993)

Fyodor Dostoevsky, *Notes from Underground*, trans. Richard Pevear and Larissa Volkhonsky (New York and London: Alfred A. Knopf, 2004)

Orlando Figes, *Natasha's Dance* (London: Penguin, 2003)

Ian Frazier, *Travels in Siberia* (New York: Farrar, Straus & Giroux, 2010)

Andrew Gentes, *The Mass Deportation of Poles to Siberia, 1863–1880* (Basingstoke: Palgrave Macmillan, 2017)

Eugenia Ginzburg, *Into the Whirlwind*, trans. Paul Stevenson and Manya Harari (London: Persephone Books, 2014)

V. D. Golubchikova and Z. I. Khvtisiashvili (eds), *Practical Dictionary of Siberia and the North* (Moscow: European Publications & Severnye Prostory, 2005)

Janet M. Hartley, *Siberia: A History of the People* (New Haven: Yale University Press, 2014)

Charles H. Hawes, *In the Uttermost East* (London and New York: Harper & Brothers, 1904)

A. J. Haywood, *Siberia: A Cultural History* (Oxford: Signal Books, 2010)

Alexander Herzen, *My Exile in Siberia* (London: Hurst & Blackett, 1855)

James Holman, *Travels through Russia, Siberia, Poland, Austria, Saxony, Prussia, Hanover, &c. &c. Undertaken during the Years 1822, 1823 and 1824, While Suffering from Total Blindness, and Comprising an Account of the Author Being Conducted a State Prisoner from the Eastern Parts of Siberia* (London: Geo. B. Whittaker, 1825)

Jacek Hugo-Bader, *Kolyma Diaries* (London: Portobello Books, 2014)

W. Bruce Lincoln, *The Conquest of a Continent: Siberia and the Russians* (Ithaca: Cornell University Press, 2007)

Kate Marsden, *On Sledge and Horseback to Outcast Siberian Lepers* (London: Record Press, 1892)

James Meek, *The People's Act of Love* (Edinburgh: Canongate, 2005)

Fridtjof Nansen, *Through Siberia, The Land of the Future*, trans. Arthur G. Chater (London: William Heinemann, 1914)

Selected Bibliography

James Palmer, *The Bloody White Baron* (New York: Basic Books, 2011)

Sooyong Park, *The Great Soul of Siberia*, trans. Jamie Chang (London: William Collins, 2016)

Vasily Peskov, *Lost in the Taiga*, trans. Marian Schwartz (London: Doubleday, 1994)

Susanna Rabow-Edling, *Married to the Empire* (Fairbanks: University of Alaska Press, 2015)

Valentin Rasputin, *Siberia, Siberia*, trans. Margaret Winchell and Gerald Mikkelson (Evanston: Northwestern University Press, 1996)

Varlam Shalamov, *Kolyma Stories*, trans. Donald Rayfield (New York: NYRB Classics, 2018)

Aleksandr Solzhenitsyn, *One Day in the Life of Ivan Denisovich*, trans. H. T. Willets (New York: Farrar, Straus & Giroux, 2005)

—, *The Gulag Archipelago*, Volumes I, II & III, trans. Thomas Whitney (London: Harper Perennial, 2007)

Richard Stites, *Serfdom, Society and the Arts in Imperial Russia* (New Haven and London: Yale University Press, 2005)

Willard Sunderland, *The Baron's Cloak* (Ithaca and London: Cornell University Press, 2014)

Christine Sutherland, *The Princess of Siberia* (London: Quartet Books, 2001)

Sylvain Tesson, *Consolations of the Forest*, trans. Linda Coverdale (London: Penguin, 2014)

Paul Theroux, *The Great Railway Bazaar* (London: Hamish Hamilton, 1975)

Colin Thubron, *In Siberia* (London: Chatto & Windus, 1999)

Piers Vitebsky, *Reindeer People* (London: Harper Perennial, 2005)

Stephanie Williams, *Olga's Story* (London: Viking, 2005)

Christian Wolmar, *To the Edge of the World* (London: Atlantic Books, 2014)

Alan Wood, *Russia's Frozen Frontier: A History of Siberia and the Russian Far East 1581–1991* (London and New York: Bloomsbury Academic, 2011)

Selected Bibliography

Music

Cyril Ehrlich, *The Piano: A History* (Oxford: Clarendon Press, 1990)

Marina Frolova-Walker and Jonathan Walker, *Music and Soviet Power 1917–1932* (Woodbridge: The Boydell Press, 2012)

Marina Frolova-Walker, *Russian Music and Nationalism from Glinka to Stalin* (New Haven and London: Yale University Press, 2007)

Amy Nelson, *Music for the Revolution: Musicians and Power in Early Soviet Russia* (University Park, Pennsylvania: Penn State Press, 2004)

James Parakilas, *Piano Roles: Three Hundred Years of Life with the Piano* (New Haven and London: Yale University Press, 1999)

Alex Ross, *The Rest is Noise* (London: Fourth Estate, 2009)

Lynn M. Sargeant, *Harmony and Discord: Music and the Transformation of Russian Cultural Life* (Oxford: Oxford University Press, 2011)

Boris Schwarz, *Music and Musical Life in Soviet Russia 1917–1970* (London: Barrie & Jenkins, 1972)

Anthony Storr, *Music and the Mind* (London: Harper Collins, 1992)

Anne Swartz, *Piano Makers in Russia in the Nineteenth Century* (Bethlehem: Lehigh University Press, 2014)

Richard Taruskin, *Defining Russia Musically* (Princeton and Oxford: Princeton University Press, 2000)

Alan Walker, *Franz Liszt,* Volumes I, II & III (Ithaca: Cornell University Press, 1987, 1993 & 1997)

—, *Reflections on Liszt* (Ithaca and London: Cornell University Press, 2011)

Films

Dersu Uzala (1975) directed by Akira Kurosawa (Russian and Chinese language; English subtitles)

Happy People: A Year in the Taiga (2010) directed by Werner Herzog and Dmitry Vasyukov (English and Russian language)

Siberiade (1979) directed by Andrei Mikhalkov-Konchalovsky (Russian and German language; English subtitles)

Acknowledgements

For the numerous people who helped me in Russia and Mongolia, please refer to the book itself. I have not changed any names. My acknowledgements below are for those people who do not appear in a significant way in the main text, or who assisted behind the scenes. Please also refer to the Source Notes and Selected Bibliography. Any errors are unfortunately mine.

I am indebted to a number of specialist readers: Tim Buchen, Junior Professor of History at the Technical University of Dresden, for his knowledge of Russian–Polish relations; Ariane Galy, specialist in Soviet history and owner of History Box; Darya Hoare, for her input on my chapter about the last Tsar, and her professional translations of various Russian texts; John McCannon, Associate Professor of History at Southern New Hampshire University, for his knowledge of arts and culture; and Vladimir Orlov, Associate Professor of Musicology at St Petersburg State University, for his expertise in Russian music and much more besides. Thank you also to Catherine Gerasimov for her friendship on the road in Kolyma and her remarks on modern Russian cultural nuances.

For their help with piano technology, I am immensely grateful to Brian Kemble, the English manufacturer of Kemble pianos and recently retired Managing Director of Austrian piano company Bösendorfer; David Kirkland and Anthony Gilroy at Steinway & Sons; and the expert piano tuner Benjamin Treuhaft, who at one point in his career took second-hand pianos from the US to Cuba. I spent a happy morning at Benjamin's house in Coventry, England, where he showed me the principles of tuning in his garage; years ago, I had worked for his mother, Jessica Mitford, whose advice to write a book took me more than twenty years to act upon. It took another friend, the late Mark Shand, to push me over the edge

364

and give me the nerve to do it. This project is a product of their encouragement.

Thank you also to researchers at Memorial in Moscow; the archives department at C. Bechstein in Berlin; and the C. F. Theodore Steinway Academy in Hamburg for help securing Kostya Lomatchenko's place on a Steinway training course, which he successfully completed in November 2019.

I am indebted to a number of local historians, some of whom I met, and others whose granular research I used heavily: Dan Ben-Canaan, an authority on Harbin's Jewish history and diaspora; Anastasia Bliznyuk, who helped me gather accounts of Akademgorodok; Vasily Khanevich, who charted the lives of the Poles in Tomsk; Lyudmila Lipatova, the Salekhard-based journalist and historian who has written extensively about Railway 501; Anatoly Salaev for his knowledge of piano culture in Tomsk; Tamara Staleva, an authority on Pyotr Makushin; Stanislav Vavilov, a music historian in Tomsk; and Liliya Tsydenova at the Kiakhta Regional History Museum. Their books and pamphlets are all detailed in the Source Notes. What isn't listed is the time many gave so freely.

For guidance with the natural world, thank you to Chris Collins for his knowledge of Russian ornithology; Dale Miquelle, Director for the Wildlife Conservation Society's Russia Programme and Coordinator of the WCS Tiger Programme; and Rodney Russ, founder of Heritage Expeditions and Strannik Ocean Voyages.

For Polish transliteration, thank you to Zuzanna Dyrkacz. For Library of Congress Russian transliteration in my Source Notes and Bibliography, thanks to Ariane Galy. Aside from my principal interpreter and researcher, Elena Voytenko, I was assisted by Ruslan Afinshakov in Khabarovsk, Gabriela Anderson in Yamal, Maria Shilova in Moscow, Yulia Lycheva in Kolyma and Vladivostok, and Arsenii Eremeev and Nadezhda Eremeeva in Irkutsk – all of whom opened numerous doors with their indefatigable research skills.

The historic photographs featured in this book include private heirlooms shared by people I met along the way. Thank you also to Katie Neame and Oliver Grant for their work securing picture permissions and chasing down copyrights.

For their assistance on travel logistics: thank you to Richard Mitchelson at AKE International for his security advice and training; John Birch at Benmar Visa Agency; Rick Fancett at Air Deal; Will Bolsover at Natural World Safaris; Vyacheslav Dmitriev at Baigal Travel; Douglas Grimes and Vladimir Kvashnin at MIR Corporation for their constant support, professionalism and generous introductions (including the bellringer in Irkutsk and Old Believer priest); Martha Madsden at Explore Kamchatka; my PA, Laura O'Sullivan; Boris Golodets, Kseniya Lukyanova and Michael Sadowski at Intrepid Travel; Undraa Buyannemekh, Anand Munkhuu and Jalsa Urubshurow at Nomadic Expeditions in Mongolia; Guy Rubin at Imperial Tours in China; Simon Cockerell at Koryo Group. And the staff at Four Seasons, St Petersburg, and the Ritz-Carlton, Moscow, who gave me space to work and interview.

I would like to thank the following for their help in specific regions. In Akademgorodok: Aleksandr Kandyba, Maxim Kozlikin, Aleksandr Stepanov and Nataliya Timofeeva. In the Baikal region: Vyacheslav Dmitriev, Ksenia Drozdova, Igor Gerasimov, Andrei and Lyudmila Shelkovnikov, Vladimir Shevchenko and Tatiana Starova. In Barnaul and the Altai: Viktor Babushkin, Igor Dmitriev, Grigory Dolgich, Gennadiy Ignatov, Viktor Shvetsov and Nikolai Zhiba. In the Commander Islands: Sergei Pasenyuk and Maria Vozhikova. In Ekaterinburg: Nikolai Neuimin, Vitali Shitov and Sergei Skrobov. In Harbin: Sergei Yuremin. In Kamchatka: Viktor Belyaev, Kirill Kiselev, Igor Sesterov, Vladimir Vyatkin, Viktor Zakharin and Stanislav Zverev. In Khabarovsk: sincerest thanks to the piano tuner, Vladimir Gordeychik; the Khidirov family for their endless hospitality and friendship; Nataliya Kirilenko and Irina Zhdanova-Kamenska; TV journalist Anna Rozhkovskaya; Nataliya Sheremet at Guberniya Media. In Khanty-Mansiysk and the Numto region: Aleksandr Berezin, Lyudmila Matveeva, Alsu Nazymova, Valery Pyak and his extended family, Nataliya Vylla and Vasily Yarema. In Kiakhta: Marina Chagdurova, Aleksandr Kuzkin, Father Oleg and Nataliya Parnyakova. In Moscow: Nadya Eremeeva and Anna Kochetkova. In Mongolia: thank you to all the people who have made the Orkhon Valley feel like a second home to my family – especially Enkhtsetseg

Sanjaadorj and her three children Ich Tenger, D'Artagnan and Kristina-Alegra – as well as Amarzaya Bayarmandakh, Batzaya Bodikhuu, Mendbayar Bold, Enkhdul Jumdaan, Ang Tshering Lama, Dawa Sherpa and Mingma Sherpa. In Novosibirsk: Nina Golovneva, Nataliya Kochergina, Leonid Kolesnikov, Marina Monakhova, Elena Shchukina, Tatyana Sibirtseva and Viktor Titov. On Sakhalin: Valentin Lekus and Rimma Novokreshchentseva. In St Petersburg: Tamara Dubko, and at Pavlovsk Palace, Aleksei Guzanov and Nataliya Kulina, who dug deep into the archives on my behalf to reveal the Siberian tale of Catherine's Zumpe piano. In Tobolsk: Pavel Sidorov and Lubov Zhuchkova. In Tomsk: Aleksandr Adam and Vasily Khanevich. In Tyumen: Nataliya Fedorovna, Aleksandr Shishkin and Larisa Tyurina. In Ulan-Ude: Olga Shaplanova. In Vladivostok: Yuri Shibnev.

Various family and friends endured endless drafts. Thank you in particular to my father, Jonathan Roberts, for his patient and judicious editing; my mother, Anne Roberts; and my sisters, Amy and Flora Roberts. Nicholas Chan impacted the book more than he will ever realize. Thank you also to Alice Daunt, Ben Elliot, Christie Lear, Olivia Lee, Ben Parker and Justin Wateridge. Many, many friends proved to be patient sounding boards and important supporters: Susie Bain, Alex Baldock, Max Baldock, Caroline Barnes, Horatio Clare, Rachel Cobb, Nikki Cooper, Sheila Donnelly, Catherine Fairweather, Liz Fisher, E-Len Fu, Martin Hartley, Derek Henderson, Ken Kochey, Sarah Laird, Kerry de Lanoy Meijer, James McBride, Rosanna Menza, Polly Morland, Martha North, William Jones, Christina Ong, Melissa Ong, the late Willie Roberts, Bels Silcox, Rebecca Smith, James Verner and Janie Woolfenden. Thank you also to Orlando Figes, Marina Frolova-Walker, Inna Krause, Chantel Tattoli and Benjamin Wegg-Prosser for some helpful contacts.

Various magazine and newspaper editors – including Pilar Guzman and Alex Postman – were always supportive and tolerated shifting deadlines. Thank you to Pilar for taking stories on Kamchatka and Baikal, both of which were published in *Conde Nast Traveler*. I would especially like to thank my editor at the *Financial*

Acknowledgements

Times 'Life & Arts', Tom Robbins, who commissioned the article I wrote about a Siberian tiger (a version of which features substantially in this book), as well as stories in Yamal, and a journey to Harbin. The articles are referenced in the Source Notes.

To get this project over the line: special thanks to the chief piano tuner of the Novosibirsk Philharmonic, Vladimir Biryukov; Valery Kravchenko in Kamchatka for his constant encouragement; and Stanislav Dobrovolskiy for his professional assistance and time, which he gave freely; to my agent, Sophie Lambert, and her colleagues at C&W Agency, including Jake Smith Bosanquet, Kate Burton, Alexander Cochran, Emma Finn, Meredith Ford and Dorcas Rogers; Simon Hartley; Michael Brown; Jane Phillips; Michael Turek for his friendship on the road; Dušan Sekulović for his video editing; my US publisher, Morgan Entrekin at Grove Atlantic (without his conviction early on, this book simply would not have happened), and editors Brenna McDuffie and Sara Vitale; in the UK, my brilliant editor Andrea Henry who kept my spirits up and the wheels turning, Doug Young and all their colleagues at Transworld: Tim Bainbridge, Emma Burton, Sarah Day, Phil Evans, Phil Lord, Sharika Teelwah, Viv Thompson, Jo Thomson, Katrina Whone and Sally Wray.

Most of all, I want to thank my colleagues Sam Fry and Serena Strang, who researched and fact-checked for two long years with tireless grace and enthusiasm – any errors in this text are entirely my own, but without Serena and Sam, there would have been many more – and my husband, John. I am lucky to be married to a man who thinks piano hunts in Siberia are not only a valid way of making a living, but an interesting one. Thank you for putting up with my long absences, endless anxieties and, on more than one occasion, agreeing to join me in Mongolia and Siberia with our children.

Picture Acknowledgements

1. Music in a Sleeping Land: Sibir
Page 23: Liszt playing to a Berlin crowd, 1842. Original Artwork: Drawing by Adolf Brennglass. Three Lions/Hulton Archive/Getty Images. **Page 26:** A Russian family with their piano. The Print Collector/Alamy Stock Photo. **Page 27:** Becker pianos at the World Fair. *L'Illustration, Journal Universel*, 1848: 72 (July 1878). Getty Images. **Page 35:** Odgerel Sampilnorov's ancestors. Courtesy of Odgerel Sampilnorov. **Page 35:** Odgerel Sampilnorov's ancestors. Courtesy of Odgerel Sampilnorov.

2. Traces in the Snow: Khabarovsk
Page 44: Nomadic hunter Dersu Uzala. Fine Art Images/Heritage Image Partnership Ltd/Alamy Stock Photo. **Page 46:** Indigenous Siberian fur trapper in Evert Ysbrants Ides, *Three Years Travels from Moscow over-land to China* (London: W. Freeman, 1706). Science & Society Picture Library/Getty Images.

3. Siberia is 'Civilized': St Petersburg to the Pacific
Page 61: Catherine the Great listening to Giovanni Païsiello. Edoardo Matania, 'Giovanni Païsiello and Catherine II of Russia', *L'Illustrazione Italiana*, 39 (September 1881). DEA/BIBLIOTECA AMBROSIANA/ De Agostini/Getty Images.

4. The Paris of Siberia: Irkutsk
Page 70: Travelling on ice in Siberia according to Father Philippe Anvil. John Bell, *A Journey from St Petersburg to Pekin* (Edinburgh: Edinburgh University Press, 1965). Printed with kind permission of Edinburgh University Press Ltd. **Page 71:** The *tarantass. Harper's Magazine* (New York: 1868). Courtesy of *Harper's Magazine*. **Page 77:** Varlam Shalamov. Sourced Collection/Alamy Stock Photo. **Page 81:** Five

Decembrists hanging. Institute of Russian Literature (Pushkin House), St Petersburg. **Page 85:** The Volkonskys. The Picture Art Collection/Alamy Stock Photo. **Page 86:** The Volkonskys' manor house in Irkutsk. Courtesy of the Irkutsk Museum of the Decembrists, Irkutsk.

5. Pianos in a Sandy Venice: Kiakhta
Page 95: Kandinsky's theory of music's relationship to art. Wasily Kandinsky, *Point and Line to Plane* (New York: Dover Publications Ltd, 1979). **Page 98:** Aleksei Lushnikov with his family. Kiakhta Local Lore Museum of Academician V. A. Obruchev, Kiakhta. **Page 99:** The American writer George Kennan. Everett Collection Historical/Alamy Stock Photo. **Page 101:** Aleksei Lushnikov's daughters. Kiakhta Local Lore Museum of Academician V. A. Obruchev, Kiakhta. **Page 101:** The Lushnikov family at the piano. Kiakhta Local Lore Museum of Academician V. A. Obruchev, Kiakhta. **Page 105:** Baron von Ungern-Sternberg. Fine Art Images/Heritage Image Parnership Ltd/Alamy Stock Photo. **Page 106:** The Kiakhta Bechstein © Michael Turek.

6. The Sound of Chopin's Poland: Tomsk
Page 117: A group of escaped convicts in Siberia. GL Archive/Alamy Stock Photo. **Page 122:** Pyotr Makushin and his family. Courtesy of the Tomsk Regional Local Lore Museum of M. B. Shatilov, Tomsk. **Page 125:** Olga Leonidovna © Michael Turek.

7. Home in a Hundred Years: Sakhalin Island
Page 131: Dmitri Girev. Scott Polar Research Institute, University of Cambridge. **Page 132:** One of Captain Scott's sled dogs, Chris. Scott Polar Research Institute, University of Cambridge. **Page 133:** Chekhov's photo of the notorious thief Sonka. Fine Art Images/Heritage Image Partnership Ltd/Alamy Stock Photo. **Page 137:** The wheelbarrow-men of Sakhalin. SPUTNIK/Alamy Stock Photo. **Page 144:** Employees of the House of Culture. Courtesy of a private family collection.

8. The Last Tsar's Piano: The Urals
Page 151: The last Tsar's grandfather, Alexander II © The State Hermitage Museum. Angeli, Heinrich von, *Portrait of Alexander II*. Oil

on canvas, 271×150 cm. Austria, 1876. Inv. no. ERZh. II-693. Photograph © The State Hermitage Museum. Photo by Leonard Kheifets, Yuri Molodkovets. **Page 153:** The Romanov family, 1913. Mondadori Portfolio/Getty Images. **Page 154:** The Romanovs during their imprisonment in Tobolsk, 1918. Sovfoto/Universal Images Group/ Getty Images. **Page 161:** Tourists visiting the cellar of the Ipatiev House. Copy of original image courtesy of the Ekaterinburg History Museum, Ekaterinburg. **Page 162:** The basement of the Ipatiev House after the murders. Fine Art Images/Heritage Image Partnership Ltd/Alamy Stock Photo. **Page 162:** Rehearsals for *The House of Bernarda Alba* © Vitaly Shitov. **Page 163:** The demolition of the Ipatiev House © Vitaly Shitov. **Page 170:** Pyotr Ermakov. Sverdlovsk Regional Local Lore Museum of O. E. Kler, Ekaterinburg.

9. The End of Everything: The Altai Mountains
Page 178: St George Littledale. Courtesy of The Library, University of California at Berkeley. **Page 182:** Altai space junk, 2000 © Jonas Bendiksen/Magnum Photos. **Page 186:** Leonid Kaloshin © Michael Turek. **Page 187:** An airport waiting room in Siberia, 1964. Mario de Biasi/Mondadori Portfolio/Getty Images.

10. The Moscow of the East: Harbin
Page 192: Flooded Harbin © Hulton-Deutsch Collection/CORBIS/ Corbis Historical/Getty Images. **Page 196:** Semion Kaspe. Printed with kind permission of Professor Dan Ben-Canaan.

11. Beethoven in a Red *Chum*: The Yamal Peninsula
Page 208: Travel in the Yamal Peninsula, *c.* 1960. Courtesy of I. S. Shemanovskiy Yamal-Nenets District Museum and Exhibition Complex, Salekhard. **Page 219:** A prisoner sings for Gulag officials. Danzig Baldaev, *Drawings from the Gulag* (London: Fuel Publishing, 2010) © FUEL Publishing. **Page 219:** A Gulag orchestra is marched to a local village to perform. Danzig Baldaev, *Drawings from the Gulag* (London: Fuel Publishing, 2010) © FUEL Publishing.

12. Music in the Gulag Archipelago: Kolyma
Page 226: US Vice-President Henry Wallace in Kolyma, 1944. Courtesy of the Henry A. Wallace Papers, University of Iowa, Iowa City,

Iowa. **Page 228:** The Magadan State Music and Drama Theatre. Courtesy of the Magadan Regional Museum of Local Lore. **Page 231:** Vadim Kozin. Courtesy of the Magadan Regional Museum of Local Lore.

13. The Siberian Colosseum: Novosibirsk

Page 239: The Novosibirsk State Academic Opera and Ballet Theatre. Courtesy of the Museum of the History of Architecture of Siberia named after S. N. Baladin. **Page 241:** Installation of painting, Vasily Surikov, *Boyarina Morozova*, 1887, spring 1945. The State Tretyakov Gallery, Moscow. **Page 243:** Boxes with packed paintings of the Tretyakov Gallery in the Novisibirsk Opera House. The State Tretyakov Gallery, Moscow. **Page 244:** Artist-restorer M. A. Alexandrovsky records readings of temperature and humidity at the Exhibition of Russian realistic art at the end of the eighteenth and nineteenth centuries. The State Tretyakov Gallery, Moscow. **Page 246:** Vladimir Biryukov © Michael Turek. **Page 250:** Lomatchenko family © Michael Turek.

14. Vera's Mühlbach: Akademgorodok

Page 263: Vera Lotar-Shevchenko's grave © Sophy Roberts. **Page 267:** Nikita Khrushchev and Harvey Van Cliburn, 1958. Sovfoto/Universal Images Group/Getty Images. **Page 275:** Victims of the Leningrad Siege. Sputnik/Alamy Stock Photo.

15. A Game of Risk: Kamchatka

Page 287: A Russian punk fan, 1986 © Igor Mukhin. **Page 287:** A queue to buy bread in St Petersburg, 1992. TASS/Ivan Kurtov and V. Chumakov/Getty Images. **Page 293:** A Chechen separatist plays the piano, 1994. OLEG NIKISHIN/AFP/Getty Images. **Page 293:** A Russian soldier plays the piano. Georges DeKeerle/Sygma/Getty Images. **Page 297:** Demidoff with his wife. *A Shooting Trip to Kamchatka* (London: R. Ward, 1904). Courtesy of UCLA Library. **Page 298:** Valery Kravchenko performing © Michael Turek. **Page 301:** The boy and the bird by Vasily Peskov © *Komsomolskaya Pravda* (Moscow: March 1966). **Page 302:** Valery Kravchenko. Courtesy of Valery Kravchenko.

Picture Acknowledgements

16. Siberia's Last Piano: The Commanders to the Kurils
Page 311: Kate Marsden. Kate Marsden, *On Sledge and Horseback to Outcast Siberian Lepers* (London: Record Press, 1892). Courtesy of The London Library. **Page 314:** Medny fur trade. Kamchatka Regional Unified Museum, Petropavlovsk-Kamchatsky.

17. Provenance Regained: Khabarovsk
Page 327: Anna Khidirov and the Stürzwage piano © Michael Turek. **Page 331:** Nina Alexandrovna's ancestors, courtesy of Nina Ternovskaya.

Source Notes

EPIGRAPHS

ix 'Once a certain idea of landscape . . . of the scenery': Simon Schama, *Landscape and Memory* (London: Fontana Press, 1996)

ix 'Objects have always been carried . . . stories that matters': Edmund de Waal, *The Hare with Amber Eyes* (London: Chatto & Windus, 2011)

ix 'My piano is to me what his vessel is to the sailor . . . obeyed my every caprice': Lina Ramann (ed.), *Franz Liszt, Gesammelte Schriften*, Volume II (Leipzig: Brightkopf & Härtel, 1880–83), cited in Alan Walker, *Reflections on Liszt* (Ithaca and London: Cornell University Press, 2011)

AUTHOR'S NOTE

1 **Siberian railway sketches:** This phrase is used by Charles H. Hawes, *In the Uttermost East* (London and New York: Harper & Brothers, 1904)

2 **'diamonds that made one's eyes ache':** John Foster Fraser, *The Real Siberia: Together with an Account of a Dash Through Manchuria* (London: Cassell and Company, 1902)

2 **a Bechstein piano:** See Annette Meakin, *A Ribbon of Iron* (London: Archibald Constable & Co, 1901). Meakin describes concerts aboard the Trans-Siberian performed by 'lady pianists of no ordinary merit'.

2 **'From the shores of the Pacific . . . Europe as well':** Sergei Witte, cited in Simon Sebag Montefiore, *The Romanovs: 1613–1918* (London: Weidenfeld & Nicolson, 2016)

2 **the fancy tourist carriages . . . to stack the dirty dishes on:** See Christian Wolmar, *To the Edge of the World* (London: Atlantic Books, 2014), Harmon Tupper, *To the Great Ocean: Siberia and the Trans-Siberian Railway* (London: Secker & Warburg, 1965), and Lindon Bates Jr, *The Russian Road to China* (New York: Houghton Mifflin Company, 1910). The fat conductor is described by Francis E. Clark, *A New Way Around An Old World* (London: S. W. Partridge & Co., 1901), and the piano as a kitchen sideboard by Michael Myers Shoemaker, *The Great Siberian Railway: From St Petersburg to Pekin* (New York: G. P. Putnam's Sons, 1904).

2 **'Welcome to Siberia':** In the nineteenth century, the only marker denoting Siberia was a stone post (now disappeared) a hundred and fifty miles to

Ekaterinburg's east. 'Europe' was written on one side of the column, 'Asia' on the other. 'No other boundary-post in the world has witnessed so much human suffering, or been passed by such a multitude of heart-broken people,' wrote the American journalist George Kennan (*Siberia and the Exile System*, Volume II (New York: The Century Co., 1891)). For an image of this obelisk, see the painting *Farewell to Europe* by Aleksander Sochaczewski, 1894, Museum of Independence, Warsaw, which depicts Polish prisoners falling at the pillar's foot, desperate and exhausted.

2–3   **There is no dramatic curtain-raiser to the edge of Siberia:** This observation is common to many travellers, past and present, who encounter the Urals and then Siberia for the first time, from John Dundas Cochrane in his 1825 *Narrative of a Pedestrian Journey through Russia and Siberian Tartary* – who describes a 'nearly imperceptible' rise of hills – to Colin Thubron, *In Siberia* (London: Chatto & Windus, 1999). 'I know not why they are so darkly shaded on most of our maps, and made to look like a formidable barrier between the two continents,' observed the Scottish traveller Alexander Michie, *The Siberian Overland Route* (London: John Murray, 1864). I met the Urals for the first time travelling from Moscow to Salekhard, which sits at the northern end of the mountain range.

3   **aside from China, this country has more international borders:** For an explanation of the make-up of the modern Russian Federation, see Robert A. Saunders and Vlad Strukov, *Historical Dictionary of the Russian Federation* (Lanham: Scarecrow Press, 2010).

3   **'land of endless talk':** Alban Gordon, *Russian Year: A Calendar of the Revolution* (London: Cassell & Company, 1935)

4   **'The plain of Siberia begins . . . goodness knows where':** Anton Chekhov, 'Letter to his sister, May 1890', in *Letters of Anton Chekhov to His Family and Friends*, trans. Constance Garnett (New York: The Macmillan Co., 1920)

5   **born from the ashes of a cannibal:** For the full story, see Uno Holmberg, *The Mythology of All Races*, Volume IV (New York: Cooper Square, 1964).

6   **'In matters of translation . . . the equivalent of infidelities':** Franz Liszt, cited in Alan Walker, *Franz Liszt: The Final Years, 1861–1886* (Ithaca: Cornell University Press, 1997)

Part One: Pianomania

9   **'Liszt. It is only noon . . . elbow each other and enter':** Cited in Anne Swartz, *Piano Makers in Russia in the Nineteenth Century* (Bethlehem: Lehigh University Press, 2014)

1. Music in a Sleeping Land: Sibir

12 **Early Arab traders . . . Johann Schiltberger:** See Anatole V. Baikaloff, 'Notes on the Origin of the Name "Siberia"', *Slavonic and East European Review*, 29:72 (December 1950)

13 **'The Rock':** Alan Wood, *Russia's Frozen Frontier: A History of Siberia and the Russian Far East 1581–1991* (London and New York: Bloomsbury Academic, 2011)

13 **falling star destroyed a patch of forest:** See Melissa Hogenboom, 'In Siberia in 1908, a huge explosion came out of nowhere', *BBC News* (July 2016)

14 **'black snow' from coal mining:** See Marc Bennetts, 'Toxic black snow covers Siberian coal mining region', *Guardian* (February 2019)

14 **toxic lakes:** See Andrew E. Kramer, 'It Looks Like a Lake Made for Instagram. It's a Dump for Chemical Waste', *New York Times* (July 2019)

14 **smoke clouds bigger than the EU:** See Jonathan Watts, 'Arctic wildfires spew soot and smoke bigger than the EU', *Guardian* (August 2019)

14 **Every year the shores around Lake Baikal . . . move another two centimetres apart:** The two-centimetre growth rate is given in Tatvana Sailko, *Environmental Crises: Geographical Case Studies in Post-Socialist Eurasia* (London and New York: Routledge, 2014). For more on Baikal's capricious character, see Valentin Rasputin, *Siberia, Siberia*, trans. Margaret Winchell and Gerald Mikkelson (Evanston: Northwestern University Press, 1996).

15 **Fissures in the ice look like the surface of a shattered mirror:** Of all the books on Baikal, there is one I pick up again and again for its magnificent descriptions of the lake, Sylvain Tesson, *Consolations of the Forest*, trans. Linda Coverdale (London: Penguin, 2014). Tesson spent six months living in a cabin on the lake's shores in 2010, observing its ravishing, sometimes frightening changeability in winter, spring and summer.

15 **they filter the top fifty metres of the lake up to three times a year:** Mark Sergeev, *Baikal* (Moscow: Planeta, 1990), cited in Alan Wood, *Russia's Frozen Frontier*

15 **an evolution of ringed seal that swam down from the Arctic:** Fridtjof Nansen, *Through Siberia, The Land of the Future*, trans. Arthur G. Chater (London: William Heinemann, 1914)

16 ***The Gulag Archipelago:*** Aleksandr Solzhenitsyn, *The Gulag Archipelago*, Volumes I, II & III, trans. Thomas Whitney (London: Harper Perennial, 2007)

16 **'cultural education':** See the research made by Inna Klause, 'Music and "Re-Education" in the Soviet Gulag', *Torture*, 23:2 (February 2013): 'Musical

theatres were founded in numerous camps between the 1920s and 1950s. However, an average of only about two percent of the inmates took part in the music and theatre circles.'

16   **you could usually return home:** Anne Applebaum, *Gulag: A History* (London: Penguin, 2004), details a phenomenon called 'wolves' passports', which forbade former political prisoners from returning to the Soviet Union's major cities.

16–17 **Trotsky, Lenin, Stalin they all spent time in Siberia as political exiles before the Revolution:** Lenin's Siberian experience was greatly eased by his access to luxury goods in exile. His family received a number of requests, including one for a pair of kid gloves to protect his hands from Siberia's ravaging mosquito bites. Rolf H. W. Theen, *Lenin: Genesis and Development of a Revolutionary* (Princeton: Princeton University Press, 1973).

17   **'Here was our own peculiar world . . . a house of the living dead':** Fyodor Dostoevsky, *Memoirs from the House of the Dead*, trans. Jessie Coulson (Oxford: Oxford University Press, 2001)

17   **shackles were called 'music':** Cited by Miron Ètlis, *Sovremenniki Gulaga: Kniga vospominanii i razmyshlenii* (Magadan: Kn. Izd-vo, 1991)

17   **to 'play the piano' meant having your fingerprints taken:** Solzhenitsyn, *The Gulag Archipelago*, Volume III

18   **'Truly, there would be reason to go mad if it were not for music':** Pyotr Tchaikovsky, 'Letter to Nadezhda von Meck, 1877', in John Warrack, *Tchaikovsky* (London: Hamish Hamilton, 1989)

18   **'hack[ed] a window through to Europe':** Alexander Pushkin, *The Bronze Horseman*, trans. Alistair Noon (Sheffield: Longbarrow Press, 2010)

19   **with one well-known musical fanatic of Catherine's time:** This anecdote is told in Marina Ritzarev, *Eighteenth-Century Russian Music* (London and New York: Routledge, 2016).

19   **murdered their master by cutting him up into pieces . . . also tasted liberty:** The murderous serfs' revenge is told in Richard Stites, *Serfdom, Society and the Arts in Imperial Russia* (New Haven and London: Yale University Press, 2005).

20   **The German word *Klavier* sometimes referred to a harpsichord:** See Alfred Dolge, *Pianos and Their Makers: A Comprehensive History of the Development of the Piano from the Monochord to the Concert Grand Player Piano* (Covina: Covina Publishing Company, 1911). In *Men, Women and Pianos: A Social History* (London: Gollancz, 1955), Arthur Loesser talks about 'a sloppiness of nomenclature' during this period of the piano's evolution.

20   **'the poor man's keyboard':** Loesser, *Men, Women and Pianos*

20   **'In short, the clavichord was the first keyed instrument with a soul':** Dolge, *Pianos and Their Makers*

21 'Until about 1770 pianos were . . . uncertain in status': Cyril Ehrlich, *The Piano: A History* (Oxford: Clarendon Press, 1990)

21 Within ten years of its invention, versions of this instrument were being made: Dolge, *Pianos and Their Makers*

21 Zumpe couldn't make his pianos fast enough to gratify demand: Charles Burney, cited in James Parakilas, *Piano Roles: Three Hundred Years of Life with the Piano* (New Haven and London: Yale University Press, 1999)

21 certain sweetness when playing a slow *adagio*: In 2016, Pavlovsk Palace Museum released a CD, *And The Old Chords Will Sound*, performed by Yuri Semenov. This is how I heard the Zumpe's sound.

22 'One lady of my acquaintance had carried . . . without inflicting the least injury upon it': James Holman, *Travels through Russia, Siberia, Poland, Austria, Saxony, Prussia, Hanover, &c. &c. Undertaken during the Years 1822, 1823 and 1824, While Suffering from Total Blindness, and Comprising an Account of the Author Being Conducted a State Prisoner from the Eastern Parts of Siberia* (London: Geo. B. Whittaker, 1825)

23–4 Women grabbed at strands . . . a procession of thirty carriages: Most of these details are derived from Alan Walker's stunningly comprehensive biographies of Liszt: *Franz Liszt*, Volumes I, II & III (Ithaca: Cornell University Press, 1987, 1993 & 1996), and *Reflections on Liszt* (Ithaca and London: Cornell University Press, 2011). The story about the German girls making bracelets with piano strings is given in Parakilas, *Piano Roles*.

24 'smasher of pianos': Clara Schumann, cited in Alan Walker, *Franz Liszt: The Virtuoso Years* (Ithaca: Cornell University Press, 1993)

24 Liszt leapt on to the stage rather than walked up the steps . . . : Vladimir Stasov, *Selected Essays on Music*, trans. Florence Jonas (New York: Frederick A. Praeger, 1968). See also Adrian Williams, *Portrait of Liszt, by Himself and His Contemporaries* (Oxford: Clarendon Press, 1990), and Walker's biographies, as before.

24 'Does he bite?': Cited in Patrick Piggott, *The Life and Music of John Field* (London: Faber & Faber, 1973)

24 'the past, the present, the future of the piano': Cited in Wilhelm von Lenz, *The Great Piano Virtuosos of Our Time* (London: Kahn & Averill, 1983)

24 'something unheard of, utterly novel . . . a throne high above the heads of the crowd': Stasov, *Selected Essays on Music*

25 'We exchanged only a few words and then rushed home . . . pouring forth cascades of tender beauty and grace': Ibid.

25 considered the first true 'Russian' opera for its native character and melody: See Richard Taruskin in *Defining Russia Musically* (Princeton and Oxford: Princeton University Press, 2000): 'Through [Glinka],

Russia could for the first time join the musical West on an equal
footing, without excuses, as a full-fledged participant in international
musical traditions, and a contributor to them.' Taruskin, a leading
American musicologist, also sounds a note of caution: 'Measuring the
Russianness of Russian music by its folkish quotient is also a Western,
not a Russian, habit, and a patronizing one that originates in colonialist
attitudes.'

25   'You will find a piano, or some kind of box . . . ninety-three
      instruments and a piano-tuner': ' "Smes": Petersburgskia khronika',
      Literaturnaia Gazeta (January 1845), cited in Lynn M. Sargeant, *Harmony
      and Discord: Music and the Transformation of Russian Cultural Life* (Oxford:
      Oxford University Press, 2011)

25–6 That same year, the London piano maker Broadwood & Sons was one
      of the city's twelve largest employers of labour: David Wainwright,
      Broadwood by Appointment (London: Quiller, 1982)

26   Russian piano-making was thriving: These specific details about the
      Russian piano industry and the state subsidy system are derived from
      Anne Swartz, *Piano Makers in Russia in the Nineteenth Century*
      (Bethlehem: Lehigh University Press, 2014). Swartz helpfully provides the
      cost of a Liszt ticket (fifteen roubles) as well as piano prices of the period
      (from five hundred roubles).

27   'a remarkable bundle of inventions': Dolge, *Pianos and Their Makers*

28   Gobelin tapestries, even Van Dyck paintings, were scooped up: Thomas
      Preston, *Before the Curtain* (London: John Murray, 1950)

28   In 1919, one of St Petersburg's music critics sold his grand piano:
      Nicolas Slonimsky, 'Soviet Music and Musicians', *Slavonic and East
      European Review*, 3:4 (December 1944)

28   Pianos were built with jumbled parts: Preston, *Before the Curtain*

29   'Art belongs to the people . . . feeling, thoughts and desires': Cited in
      Klara Zetkin, *Reminiscences of Lenin* (London: Modern Books, 1929)

33   he handed me a novel by an American author, Daniel Mason: Daniel
      Mason, *The Piano Tuner* (New York: Alfred A. Knopf, 2002)

34   when nomadic pastoralism was replaced with collective herds . . . cut
      up into smaller territories: For a fuller version of events, see James
      Minahan, *Encyclopedia of Stateless Nations*, Volume I (London and
      Westport: Greenwood Press, 2002)

36   'We made our plans in this way . . . not being able to do it': John
      Steinbeck, *A Russian Journal* (London: Penguin, 2001)

36–7 'Even assuming my excursion is an utter triviality . . . I never have
      any money anyway': Anton Chekhov, 'Letter to A. S. Suvorin, March
      1890', in *Sakhalin Island*, trans. Brian Reeve (Surrey: OneWorld Classics,
      2007)

2. Traces in the Snow: Khabarovsk

39 devoured *'with relish'* by hungry convicts: Aleksandr Solzhenitsyn, *The Gulag Archipelago*, Volume I, trans. Thomas Whitney (London: Harper Perennial, 2007)

40 If there was a decent story to tell, I would sell it to a British newspaper: See Sophy Roberts, 'On the Trail of the Siberian Tiger', *Financial Times* (May 2016)

40 These days, professional conservationists are lucky to encounter a wild tiger: See Sooyong Park, *The Great Soul of Siberia*, trans. Jamie Chang (London: William Collins, 2016)

40 Before the Korean tiger researcher and filmmaker Sooyong Park started his work: Ibid.

41 'When this nation becomes better known in Europe . . . prejudices that they have about Russia': Catherine the Great, 'Letter to Voltaire, March 1770', in *Catherine the Great, Selected Letters*, trans. Andrew Kahn and Kelsey Rubin-Detlev (Oxford: Oxford University Press, 2018)

41 When Tchaikovsky met Liszt in 1877: Pyotr Tchaikovsky, 'Letter to Madame von Meck, 1877', in Richard Taruskin, *On Russian Music* (Berkeley, CA: University of California Press, 2010)

41 'Pay no heed to the boasting . . . they would make us pay cruelly for our advantages over them': Astolphe de Custine, 'July 1839', in *Letters from Russia*, trans. Robin Buss (London: Penguin Classics, 2014)

41 De Custine – described as a camp, gossipy travel writer: See Simon Sebag Montefiore, *The Romanovs: 1613–1918* (London: Weidenfeld & Nicolson, 2016)

41 'The Russians have gone rotten without ever ripening!': de Custine, 'July 1839'

41 'There are few places on the earth's surface . . . so little personal knowledge as Siberia': A. F. Spencer, 'Siberia in 1919', *Economica*, 3 (October 1921)

42 'The Siberians were selected . . . resourceful men accustomed to roughing it': Vladimir Arseniev, *Dersu the Trapper*, trans. Malcolm Burr (London: Secker & Warburg, 1939)

43 he gave it ten years before all the sable and squirrel would be gone: Ibid.

43 'the fishskin Tatars': James Forsyth, *A History of the Peoples of Siberia: Russia's North Asian Colony 1581–1990* (New York: Cambridge University Press, 1992)

43 Siberia's population comprised almost a quarter of a million indigenous people: See Janet M. Hartley, *Siberia: A History of the People* (New Haven: Yale University Press, 2014) – an important resource I owe a debt to for information on the indigenous history of Siberia.

44 **outnumbered by indigenous Siberians at a ratio of around three to one:** These numbers are unstable given the difficulty of drawing boundaries around a region like Siberia. I was drawn to the analysis published in Alan Wood, *Russia's Frozen Frontier: A History of Siberia and the Russian Far East 1581–1991* (London and New York: Bloomsbury Academic, 2011). Wood cautions against accepting figures as gospel; the line between who is 'Russian' and who is 'indigenous Siberian' has changed through the centuries according to the prevailing political ideology.

45 **ten per cent of the state income:** R. H. Fisher, *The Russian Fur Trade 1550–1700* (Berkeley, 1943), cited in Wood, *Russia's Frozen Frontier*

46 **earning a copper kettle in return for the equivalent skins:** W. Bruce Lincoln, *The Conquest of a Continent: Siberia and the Russians* (Ithaca: Cornell University Press, 2007)

47 **Sooyong Park, who has written so eloquently about his years sleeping in hides waiting for Siberian tigers:** See Park, *The Great Soul of Siberia* – among the most compelling books I have read about the Russian Far East. I found Park's commitment to tracking tigers profoundly inspiring, especially given the enormous personal privations he underwent to record their behaviour. Another great writer who has documented the region's wildlife is Jonathan C. Slaght, the Russia and Northeast Asia Coordinator for the Wildlife Conservation Society. See his blog, 'East of Siberia', *Scientific American* (2016 and 2017). His fieldnotes are like little missives of poetry documenting the smallest traces of hard-to-find species.

3. SIBERIA IS 'CIVILIZED': ST PETERSBURG TO THE PACIFIC

54 **Ermak's story, both mighty and bathetic:** For more on Ermak see Valentin Rasputin, *Siberia, Siberia*, trans. Margaret Winchell and Gerald Mikkelson (Evanston: Northwestern University Press, 1996).

54 **He expressed surprise to find such a variety of musical instruments:** John Bell of Antermony, *A Journey from St Petersburg to Pekin* (Edinburgh: Edinburgh University Press, 1965)

55 **For exiles, there was also no return:** A comprehensive explanation of Siberia's various iterations of exile is given in Andrew Gentes, *The Mass Deportation of Poles to Siberia, 1863–1880* (Basingstoke: Palgrave Macmillan, 2017) – one of my most important sources on Tsarist exile, along with Daniel Beer's book, *The House of the Dead: Siberian Exile under the Tsars* (London: Allen Lane, 2016).

56 **where the great and good once lived, including Catherine's governor, Aleksandr Aliabiev:** See Rasputin, *Siberia, Siberia*. Rasputin identifies the Korniliev [sic] House as the residence of the governor general, and birthplace of the composer.

57   **had to acquire an instrument, along with other pieces of furniture:**
     Robert K. Massie, *The Romanovs: The Final Chapter* (London: Head of
     Zeus, 2014)

57   **a piano often played by the Empress when she was left by herself:**
     Robert Wilton, *The Last Days of the Romanovs* (London: Thornton
     Butterworth Limited, 1920)

58   **'[I]t's just noise to me':** Cited in Virginia Rounding, *Catherine the Great*
     (London: Hutchinson, 2006). Rounding's riveting book is one of my
     main biographical sources on Catherine.

58   **she was assigned court musicians to tell her when to clap:** Alexander
     Woronzoff-Dashkoff, 'Dashkova: A Life of Influence and Exile',
     Transactions of the American Philosophical Society, 97:3 (2007)

58   **used to scratch on a violin in the imperial boudoir in between playing
     with toy soldiers:** See Simon Sebag Montefiore, *Prince of Princes: The Life
     of Potemkin* (New York: St Martin's Press, 2000)

58   **There was no creature unhappier than herself:** The Tsar's lack of musical
     talent, his cruelty to animals and Catherine's subsequent disgust are all
     observations found in Rounding's *Catherine the Great*.

58   **nothing more than pieces of hollowed wood:** Chappe d'Auteroche, *A
     Journey into Siberia, Made by Order of the King of France* (London:
     T. Jefferys, 1770)

58–9 **perhaps by throttling . . . his death put down to haemorrhoidal colic:**
     See Rounding, *Catherine the Great*

59   **Russian women donned red-heeled shoes:** Woronzoff-Dashkoff,
     'Dashkova: A Life of Influence and Exile'

59   **'being then a new word in St Petersburg, used only by the elite':** Leo
     Tolstoy, *War and Peace*, trans. Louise and Aylmer Maude (Minneapolis:
     First Avenue Editions, 2016)

59   **'the one with little hammers':** *The Merriam-Webster New Book of Word
     Histories* (Springfield: Merriam-Webster, 1991)

60   **cluttered with these new keyboard instruments:** Woronzoff-Dashkoff,
     'Dashkova: A Life of Influence and Exile'

60   **he also taught keyboard:** Anne Swartz, *Piano Makers in Russia in the
     Nineteenth Century* (Bethlehem: Lehigh University Press, 2014)

60   **Another of her lovers – Grigory Orlov, a dashing, music-loving
     officer – made a note of it . . . while he sat playing the harpsichord:**
     This anecdote is told in Jno Hunt, 'The Keyboard Works of Giovanni
     Paisiello', *Music Quarterly*, 61:2 (April 1975)

61   **he required his choir to be with him at all times . . . the field of war:**
     These anecdotes about Potemkin's love of music are given in Sebag
     Montefiore's biography, *Prince of Princes*.

62   **In September 1791, the music-obsessed Russian envoy:** Mark Ferraguto, 'Representing Russia: Luxury and Diplomacy at the Razumovsky Palace in Vienna, 1803–1815', *Music and Letters*, 97:3 (August 2016)

62   **Potemkin's favourite composer was given a village in Ukraine:** See Stuart Isacoff, *A Natural History of the Piano* (New York: Knopf Doubleday, 2012)

62   **or 'clavierland' as Mozart called it:** Arthur Loesser, *Men, Women and Pianos: A Social History* (London: Gollancz, 1955)

62   **'[Clementi's] greatest strength . . . he is a mere machine':** Wolfgang Amadeus Mozart, 'Letter to his father, January 1782', in *The Letters of Wolfgang Amadeus Mozart*, trans. Lady Wallace (New York: Hurd & Houghton, 1866)

62–3 **'make hay while the sun shines':** Muzio Clementi, 'Letter to Frederick Collard, June 1806', in *The Correspondence of Muzio Clementi*, trans. David Rowland (Bologna: Ut Orpheus, 2010)

63   **'slippery' in payments, 'cursedly stingy', possessing 'good ears for sound tho' they have none for sense and style':** Muzio Clementi, 'Letter to Frederick Collard, June 1806', in ibid.

63   **'nothing less than a trumpet could make its way through his obtuse tympanum':** Muzio Clementi, 'Letter to Frederick Collard, August 1803' in ibid.

63   **'keep them some time in a very warm room . . . or any other mischief don't ensue':** Muzio Clementi, 'Letter to Frederick Collard, June 1806' in ibid.

63   **as well as subsidies to help transport pianos into Siberia:** The economic structure of the piano industry is one of the central themes in Swartz, *Piano Makers in Russia in the Nineteenth Century*.

63   **'a lazy dog':** Muzio Clementi, 'Letter to Frederick Collard, April 1807' in *The Correspondence of Muzio Clementi*, trans. David Rowland

64   **'Not to have heard Field . . . sin against art and good taste':** F. A. Gebhard, cited in Patrick Piggott, *The Life and Music of John Field* (London: Faber & Faber, 1973)

64   **'pianopolis':** See Piggott, *The Life and Music of John Field*

64   **'drops of rain that spread themselves like iridescent pearls':** Cited in David Dubal, *The Art of the Piano* (Cambridge: Amadeus Press, 2004)

64   **a hundred-rouble note to light his cigar:** This anecdote and the one following about Field's dogs chewing his earnings are told in Piggott, *The Life and Music of John Field*. Piggott's work is a biographical gem, detailing the life and character of a man much overlooked in history books.

64 sometimes luxurious, often turbulent life Field was to pursue in Russia: My portrait of the disorderly Field is taken from various descriptions of the composer in Piggott, *The Life and Music of John Field*.

64 Polish-born Maria Szymanowska: It is thought she may have been brought with her from Warsaw her treasured English Broadwood – a six-and-a-half-octave grand, serial number 10582. This detail is given by Benjamin Vogel, 'Pianos of Maria Szymanowska', in *The Polish Musicological Yearbook* (Warsaw: Fryderyk Chopin University, 2011).

64 'the velvet paws': Cited in Adrian Williams, *Portrait of Liszt, by Himself and His Contemporaries* (Oxford: Clarendon Press, 1990)

64–5 '[E]verything is full of fire . . . It has a soul': *Journal de St-Pétersbourg* (January 1839), cited in Swartz, *Piano Makers in Russia in the Nineteenth Century*

65 a fairy tale in *One Thousand and One Nights*: Susanna Reich, *Clara Schumann: Piano Virtuoso* (New York: Clarion Books, 2005)

65 'The Russian rouble had a very good clink to German ears': Cited in Nancy Reich, *Clara Schumann: The Artist and the Woman* (Ithaca: Cornell University Press, 2001)

65 By 1810, six Western entrepreneurs had set up piano workshops in Russia: See Swartz, *Piano Makers in Russia in the Nineteenth Century*

65 This single workshop built more than eleven thousand pianos: Ibid.

65 music teachers were paid two to three times the amount: Ibid.

65 'highly respectableising piece of furniture': Frederick J. Crowest, *Phases of Musical England* (London: Remington & Co., 1881)

66 made it through Russia's protective trade barriers: Again, this is explored in painstaking detail – as well as the state subsidy system that enabled the shipping of raw materials for the industry to flourish – by Swartz, *Piano Makers in Russia in the Nineteenth Century*.

66 Tens of thousands of uprights were distributed into small towns: From 1924 to 1934 alone, the Red October factory produced 19,731 uprights and grands. See the entry by Sergei A. Rytsarev, 'Russia – Piano Industry', in Robert Palmieri (ed.), *The Piano: An Encyclopedia*, Second Edition (New York and London: Routledge, 2015).

66 The Red October factory closed in 2004: Swartz, *Piano Makers in Russia in the Nineteenth Century*

66 A piano maker in Kazan turned to coffin-making before going bust: Erika Niedowski, 'Music Fades for Russian Pianos', *Baltimore Sun* (May 2006)

66 it was reported that the last of Russia's piano factories had closed: 'Bor'bu za rynok otechestvennyĭ proizvoditel' pianino proigral', *Kommersant' FM* (March 2016)

4. The Paris of Siberia: Irkutsk

68   **In the Russian State Naval Archives in St Petersburg:** Referenced in Peter Ulf Møller and Natasha Okhotina Lind, *Until Death Do Us Part* (Fairbanks: University of Alaska Press, 2008). This is a compilation of sixteen letters written by Vitus and Anna Christina Bering over the course of 1739–40. It offers in-depth insight into their family life, together with a detailed inventory of the items that Anna brought back to Moscow after Bering's death in 1741, including mention of her clavichord.

68   **took this precious instrument from St Petersburg to the Sea of Okhotsk:** See Susanna Rabow-Edling, *Married to the Empire* (Fairbank: University of Alaska Press, 2015)

69   **recalled the sensation of a finger being dragged across all the keys of a piano:** Prince Peter Kropotkin, *In Russian and French Prisons* (London: Ward & Downey, 1887)

69   **'It is heavy going, very heavy ... flowing into Siberia!':** Anton Chekhov, 'Letter from Siberia', in *Sakhalin Island*, trans. Brian Reeve (Surrey: OneWorld Classics, 2007). This translation is one I have relied on again and again – an annotated collection of notes and letters written by Chekhov to his family, friends and literary associates. The main prize is Chekhov's account of the exile system on Sakhalin Island itself.

71   **'I'm armed from head to foot':** Anton Chekhov, 'Letter to A. S. Suvorin, April 1890', in *Chekhov: A Life in Letters*, trans. Gordon McVay (London: Folio Society, 1994)

71   **'coarse to the touch':** Chekhov, *Sakhalin Island*

71   **caught like a fly in gooey jam:** See Anton Chekhov, 'Letter to A. N. Pleshcheyev, June 1890', in *Sakhalin Island*

72   **Siberia was a place you rarely heard an accordion ... struggle with nature:** See Chekhov, *Sakhalin Island*

72   **'a splendid town' ... as well as 'hellishly expensive':** Anton Chekhov, 'Letter to Chekhov Family, June 1890', in *A Life in Letters*, trans. Rosamund Bartlett and Anthony Phillips (London: Penguin Classics, 2004)

72   **thirteen hundred books to Irkutsk:** W. Bruce Lincoln, *The Conquest of a Continent: Siberia and the Russians* (Ithaca: Cornell University Press, |2007)

72   **A public library went up, designed according to the fashionable European Russian style:** Janet M. Hartley, *Siberia: A History of the People* (New Haven: Yale University Press, 2014)

72   **An orchestra was founded ... five foreign languages:** Ibid. Hartley says German, Japanese, Mongolian, French and Chinese were taught to educuate interpreters and ease trade and administration.

73   **One fifth of all the silk reaching Western Europe . . . China's tea:** For more, see Erika Monahan, *The Merchants of Siberia: Trade in Early Modern Eurasia* (Ithaca: Cornell University Press, 2016) – a helpful resource for understanding the early economic development of Siberia.

74   **like pot-bellied Chinese jars:** Jules Verne, *Michael Strogoff: The Courier of the Czar* (New York: Charles Scribner, 1891)

76   **It was a terrifying symbolic act:** For a re-telling of this well-known Siberian saga, and what it said about Tsarist power, see Daniel Beer's brilliant account in his Cundhill Prize-winning *The House of the Dead: Siberian Exile under the Tsars* (London: Allen Lane, 2016).

76   **who endured four years . . . and taught a fellow prisoner to read:** See Joseph Frank, *Dostoevsky: A Writer in His Time* (Princeton: Princeton University Press, 2009)

77   **the cold that froze a man's spit could also freeze the soul:** Varlam Shalamov, *Kolyma Stories*, trans. Donald Rayfield (New York: NYRB Classics, 2018)

78   **He banned any kind of foreign-printed book:** Charles A. Ruud, *Fighting Words: Imperial Censorship and the Russian Press, 1804–1906* (Toronto: Toronto University Press, 2009)

79   **like a cup of tea nobody wanted to drink:** Nicholas Daniloff, *Two Lives, One Russia* (New York: Avon Books, 1990)

79   **Constantine first heard the ten-year-old prodigy:** Recounted in Moritz Karasowski, *Frederic Chopin: His Life and Works*, Volume II, Second Edition, trans. Emily Hill (London: William Reeves, 1906)

79   **convinced his music calmed Constantine's difficult nerves:** The Chopin connection is told in Alan Walker, *Fryderyk Chopin: A Life and Times* (London: Faber & Faber, 2018).

79   **the First Russian Revolution:** Anatole G. Manzour, *The First Russian Revolution, 1825* (Stanford: Stanford University Press, 1937)

80   **'What a wretched country! . . . how to hang properly':** This anecdote is told in Orlando Figes, *Natasha's Dance* (London: Penguin, 2003).

82   **'All her life was this one unconscious weaving . . . with whom she came in contact':** Leo Tolstoy, 'The Decembrists', in *The Complete Works of Count Tolstoy*, trans. Leo Wiener (Boston: Dana Estes & Company, 1904)

82–3 **When Zinaida threw a leaving party in Moscow . . . wouldn't forget their voices:** See Maria Fairweather, *Pilgrim Princess: A Life of Princess Volkonsky* (London: Constable & Company, 1999). Fairweather tells Zinaida's story.

83   **'a stitched seam' . . . 'the sky-cover to see what is happening on Earth':** See Uno Holmberg, *The Mythology of All Races*, Volume IV (New York: Cooper Square, 1964)

83 **Maria spent her first few months in exile in the town of Nerchinsk . . . :**
My telling of Maria Volkonsky's life in Siberia – where she lived and how,
the travels and location of her clavichord, and the fabulous
resourcefulness of her friend, the French couturier Pauline Annenkov –
rely on the comprehensive research in Christine Sutherland's biography,
The Princess of Siberia (London: Quartet Books, 2001). Sutherland invests
the Volkonsky myth with a level of detail which brings to life the
moving, everyday humanity that helped the Decembrists thrive.

83 **'he would rather deal with a hundred political exiles than a dozen of
their wives':** See M. Kuchaev, 'Stanislav Romanovich Leparskii', *Russkaia
starina*, 28 (August 1880) cited in Jeanne Haskett, 'Decembrist N. A.
Bestuzhev in Siberian Exile, 1826–55', *Studies in Romanticism*, 4:4
(Summer 1965)

84 **large sums of money from home:** In Beer's *The House of the Dead*, the
author describes 'immense sums' of money making it out to the
Decembrists in exile. Of the money officially declared, the men received
355,000 roubles in the decade they spent as state criminals in Siberia,
while the women received 778,000 roubles.

84 **'What remarkable fighters they were, what personalities, what *people*!':**
Alexander Herzen, *A Herzen Reader*, trans. Kathleen Parthé (Evanston:
Northwestern University Press, 2012)

84 **'I have been told . . . improved in their presence':** Tolstoy, 'The
Decembrists'

84 **The Decembrists teamed up to create a small academy:** A fuller
description of the Decembrists' academy can be found in Haskett,
'Decembrist N. A. Bestuzhev in Siberian Exile, 1826–55', and Sutherland,
The Princess of Siberia. Haskett's academic paper is a page-turning
biography-in-miniature of Nikolai Bestuzhev, the Decembrist who
fascinates me more than any other.

84 **a collection that numbered nearly half a million:** See D. I.
Zavalishin, *Zapiski dekabrista* (Munich: J. Marchlewski, 1904), cited in
Haskett, 'Decembrist N. A. Bestuzhev in Siberian Exile, 1826–55'

85 **inventing sea stories about the distant oceans:** Haskett, 'Decembrist
N. A. Bestuzhev in Siberian Exile, 1826–55'

85 **to build a huge Siberian insect collection:** Glynn R. Barratt, *Voices in
Exile: The Decembrist Memoirs* (Montreal and London: McGill-Queen's
University Press, 1974)

85 **benefitted hundreds of Siberian peasant children:** Ibid.

86 **under a sympathetic new governor, who became a visitor to her
musical salons:** Figes, *Natasha's Dance*

86 **she went to the concert, and was given a standing ovation:** One of the
best scenes in Sutherland's stunning biography, *The Princess of Siberia*,

describes this moment when the crowd spontaneously applauds Maria. The author provides numerous other details about how Maria's philanthropy and cultural activism positively affected Irkutsk society in the nineteenth century.

86 **a goose under his arm:** Lucy Atkinson, *Recollections of Tartar Steppes and Their Inhabitants* (London: John Murray, 1863)

86 **'the peasant prince':** Figes, *Natasha's Dance*

87 **During the 1848 Spring of Nations . . . :** For the most part, the Spring of Nations was a false dawn. By the end of 1849, the rebellions had been repressed and punished, and liberals disillusioned by the even more iron-handed rule that the revolts left in their wake. See Michael Howard, 'The Springtime of Nations', *Foreign Affairs*, 69:1 (1989). Still, with hindsight, this was also a turning point in European culture when libertarian thought began to make itself heard.

87 **The Lichtenthal, made by a piano maker who had moved to Russia:** See Richard Stites, *Serfdom, Society and the Arts in Imperial Russia* (New Haven and London: Yale University Press, 2005)

88 **Mozart's favourite maker . . . never break again:** See Hermann Abert, *W. A. Mozart*, trans. Stewart Spencer (New Haven: Yale University Press, 2007)

91 **'The further we moved into Siberia . . . valued their rights more highly':** Cited in Barratt, *Voices in Exile*

5: PIANOS IN A SANDY VENICE: KIAKHTA

92 **when Maria Volkonsky made her last visit to Lake Baikal . . . coming in to drink:** Christine Sutherland, *The Princess of Siberia* (London: Quartet Books, 2001)

93 **depicted by Karl Marx and Friedrich Engels . . . world trade:** Karl Marx and Friedrich Engels, *Collected Works, 1838–42* (London: Lawrence & Whishart, 1975)

94 **the *Baikal*, a British-built icebreaker:** For more on the train's history around Lake Baikal, see Christian Wolmar, *To the Edge of the World* (London: Atlantic Books, 2014) and Harmon Tupper, *To the Great Ocean: Siberia and the Trans-Siberian Railway* (London: Secker & Warburg, 1965)

94 **sometimes took up to a week to make the winter crossing:** R. T. Greener, 'Commercial and Industrial Affairs in Siberia', *US Consular Reports* (March 1900)

94 **Russian artist obsessed by Russian ethnography:** See Peg Weiss, 'Kandinsky and "Old Russia": An Ethnographic Exploration', *Syracuse Scholar*, 7:1 (Spring 1986)

95 **when his relations were living in a taiga village:** Much of the information regarding the Kandinsky family's Siberian history is found

in Vladimir Vladimirovich Baraev, *Drevo: Dekabristy i semeĭstvo Kandinskikh* (Moscow: Izd-vo politicheskoĭ literatury, 1991).

95 **'There was not a lady without a large hat . . . an entire flowerbed':** Letter from Elisabeth von Wrangell to her sisters in January 1830, cited in Susanna Rabow-Edling, *Married to the Empire* (Fairbanks: University of Alaska Press, 2015)

96 **'The Russians, after all that they have borrowed . . . a higher order of life have been engrafted':** Alexander Michie, *The Siberian Overland Route* (London: John Murray, 1864)

96 **Yet once Kiakhta had been so lively . . . :** For these details, I am indebted to two Russian sources: I. I. Popov, *Minuvshee I Perezhitoe. Sibir' I Emigratsiia: Vospominaniia za 50 let* (Leningrad: Kolos, 1924) in the Kiakhta archives, and the research made by L. B. Tsydenova at the Kiakhta Regional History Museum. A wealth of information regarding the lives of the town's merchant millionaires, as well as one of the earliest adverts found for a piano tuner in Siberia, are to be found in Tsydenova's elegantly illustrated book, *HeobyCHAĬnaia Kiakhta* (Ulan-Ude: NovaPrint, 2013).

97 **'Sandy Venice':** Popov, *Minuvshee I Perezhitoe. Sibir' I Emigratsiia*

99 **the Lushnikov house was overflowing with mourners:** Baraev, *Drevo*

99 **'We were very often surprised . . . associations to the civilized world':** George Kennan, *Siberia and the Exile System*, Volume II (New York: The Century Co., 1891)

99 **'Lushnikova the Liberal':** Tsydenova, *HeobyCHAĬnaia Kiakhta*. This text also gives details about the Lushnikov family's impact on Kiakhta society.

100 **one daughter studied sculpture with Rodin in Paris:** Valentin Rasputin, *Siberia, Siberia*, trans. Margaret Winchell and Gerald Mikkelson (Evanston: Northwestern University Press, 1996)

100 **Another daughter went on to sing at the Tbilisi Opera House:** Baraev, *Drevo*

100 **During exile, he relied on colour pigments . . . also posted seeds for the Decembrists' vegetable garden:** Sutherland, *The Princess of Siberia*

100 **A volume of the *Rambler*:** Glynn R. Barratt, *Voices in Exile: The Decembrist Memoirs* (Montreal and London: McGill-Queen's University Press, 1974)

102 **'golden fingers':** Jeanne Haskett, 'Decembrist N. A. Bestuzhev in Siberian Exile, 1826–55', *Studies in Romanticism*, 4:4 (Summer 1965)

102 **He made hats, jewellery from the Decembrists' old fetters . . . cradles and coffins:** Ibid.

102 **'In spite of a frost of twenty-five degrees, it went perfectly':** Cited in Barratt, *Voices in Exile*

102 **Aleksei Lushnikov therefore received one of the most unusual educations . . . newspapers, including *The Bell*:** See Tsydenova, *HeobyCHAĬnaia Kiakhta*

102 **Kiakhta's merchants providing a safe house:** Edward Hallett Carr, *Mikhail Bakunin* (New York: Springer, 1975)

103 **Both the key and the trunk vanished:** These stories about alleged lost paintings, trunks and keys are told in Tsydenova, *HeobyCHAInaia Kiakhta*.

104 **the museum's records of events were deliberately destroyed:** This is according to Stephanie Williams, *Olga's Story* (London: Penguin, 2006) – a book about the author's grandmother, who fled Kiakhta during this period. Williams recounts how the documents were allegedly burnt during perestroika.

104 **the White Army killed some sixteen hundred Reds in Kiakhta:** Tsydenova, *HeobyCHAInaia Kiakhta*

105 **met his death in a baker's oven:** James Palmer, *The Bloody White Baron* (New York: Basic Books, 2011)

105 **frozen to death rather than shot:** Baraev, *Drevo*

106 **split the body in two:** Ibid.

107 **'From Baikal onwards . . . Before Baikal it was all prose':** Anton Chekhov, 'Letter to A. N. Pleshcheev, June 1890', in *Chekhov: A Life in Letters*, trans. Gordon McVay (London: Folio Society, 1994)

6: The Sound of Chopin's Poland: Tomsk

109 **One family retreated so far . . . :** The story of the Old Believers is told in all its mesmerizing detail by Vasily Peskov, *Lost in the Taiga*, trans. Marian Schwartz (London: Doubleday, 1994).

110 **including a significant Jewish population:** See James Loeffler, *The Most Musical Nation: Jews and Culture in the Late Russian Empire* (New Haven and London: Yale University Press, 2010)

111 **Catherine's military confiscating important historic possessions, including magnificent libraries:** Tomasz Nastulczyk, 'Two Centuries of Looting and the Grand Nazi Book Burning', in Flavia Bruni (ed.), *Lost Books* (Leiden: Brill, 2016)

112 **Nicholas specifically ordered one of the most high-profile Polish insurrectionists . . . :** For more on Prince Roman Sanguszko, see Piotr S. Wandycz, *The Lands of Partitioned Poland, 1795–1918* (Seattle: Washington University Press, 1974) and Jocelyn Baines, *Joseph Conrad: A Critical Biography* (London: Weidenfeld & Nicolson, 1960).

112 **lectures, orchestras and a formidable library of books:** See Andrew Gentes, *The Mass Deportation of Poles to Siberia, 1863–1880* (Basingstoke: Palgrave Macmillan, 2017)

112 **five thousand of the highest ranking rebels managed to escape Russian arrest:** Jolanta T. Pekacz, 'Deconstructing a "National Composer": Chopin and Polish Exiles in Paris, 1831–49', *19th-Century Music*, 24:2 (Autumn 2000)

113 **Adam Mickiewicz – a friend and confidant:** Roman Robert Koropeckyj, *Adam Mickiewicz: The Life of a Romantic* (Ithaca: Cornell University Press, 2008)

114 **'cannon buried in flowers':** Cited in David Dubal, *The Art of the Piano* (Cambridge: Amadeus Press, 2004)

114 **nearly two thirds of those banished for political offences:** Vladimir N. Shaidurov, 'On the Emerging Polish Diaspora and Its Development in Siberia in the First Half of the 19th Century', *Journal of Siberian Federal University: Humanities & Social Sciences*, 10 (September 2016)

114 **which scaled up into a full-blown war:** Edward Lewinski Corwin, *The Political History of Poland* (New York: The Polish Book Importing Co., 1917)

114 **Russia banished another four thousand:** Gentes, *The Mass Deportation of Poles to Siberia*

114 **When Maria Volkonsky's daughter, Elena . . . wild in the Siberian taiga:** This anecdote, and Elena's *'à la Rousseau'* upbringing, is told in Christine Sutherland, *The Princess of Siberia* (London: Quartet Books, 2001).

114 **When the first families of Kiakhta sought piano teachers:** L. B. Tsydenova, *HeobyCHAÎnaia Kiakhta* (Ulan-Ude: NovaPrint, 2013)

114 **When Omsk needed an orchestra:** This anecdote is cited in Vladimir Shaidurov, 'The Siberian Polonia in the Second Half of the 19th – Early 20th Century in the Polish Historiography', *Przeglad Wschodnioeuropejski*, 8:1 (January 2017).

114–15 **'Siberia has received a great many individuals . . . has left an indelible mark':** Thomas Knox, *Overland through Asia* (Hartford: American Publishing Co., 1870)

115 **'Chopin's mazurkas are lost':** Cited in Andrzej Solak, 'Legioniści z Sybiru', *Polonia Christiana* (February 2013)

115 **'Vive la Pologne!':** Cited in Knox, *Overland through Asia*

116 **'Ivan Dontremember':** See George Kennan, *Siberia and the Exile System*, Volume I (New York: The Century Co., 1891)

116 **'I forgot my chains, forgot my past life, my future destiny, forgot everything':** Rufin Piotrowski, *My Escape from Siberia* (London: Routledge, Warne & Routledge, 1863)

116 **'reigning like a despot in the drawing rooms':** *The Morning Paper* (1839), cited in Benjamin Vogel, 'The Piano as a Symbol of Burgher Culture in Nineteenth-century Warsaw', *Galpin Society Journal*, 46 (March 1993)

116 **'There is almost no house . . . the family talents' touchstone':** *Warsaw Courier* (1840), cited in ibid.

118 **'The sound of that falling lingers . . . Is trampled by human fury':** Cyprian Kamil Norwid, 'Fortepiano Szopeno', trans. Leonard Kress, in Maja Trochimczyk (ed.), *Chopin with Cherries: A Tribute in Verse* (Los Angeles: Moonrise Press, 2010)

118   **nearly all the luxury accoutrements of Western civilization:** See Piotrowski, *My Escape from Siberia*

119   **the Imperial Russian Musical Society – a brilliantly ambitious organization:** For a deeper understanding of the institution's influence and history, see Lynn M. Sargeant, *Harmony and Discord: Music and the Transformation of Russian Cultural Life* (Oxford: Oxford University Press, 2011).

119   **not a single textbook on musical harmony was written in the Russian language:** See Liliya Shamazov, 'Preface to Piotr Illyich Tchaikovsky, Concise Manual of Harmony, Intended for the Reading of Spiritual Music in Russia (1874)', *Gamut*, 7:1 (2014)

120   **the *bumjakjak*:** See Julia Mannherz, 'Nationalism, Imperialism and Cosmopolitanism in Russian Nineteenth-century Provincial Amateur Music-making', *Slavonic and East European Review*, 95:2 (April 2017)

120   **By 1885, Tomsk had a population of thirty-one thousand . . . liberal tendencies:** Kennan, *Siberia and the Exile System*, Volume I

120   **'A naturally enterprising and promising colony':** Ibid.

120   **'The most notable thing about Tomsk . . . come here to die':** Anton Chekhov, 'Letter to Alexey Suvorin, May 1890', *Anton Chekhov: A Life in Letters*, trans. Rosamund Bartlett and Anthony Phillips (London: Penguin Classics, 2004)

120   **he wrote a bibliography for a St Petersburg literary journal:** Anton Chekhov, *The Undiscovered Chekhov*, trans. Peter Constantine (London: Duckworth, 2001)

121   **Ukrainian melodies . . . gypsy romances:** A more detailed picture of the provincial Russian music scene at this time is given in Mannherz, 'Nationalism, Imperialism and Cosmopolitanism in Russian Nineteenth-Century Provincial Amateur Music-Making'.

121   **the first chapter of the Imperial Russian Musical Society:** Many of the details about Tomsk piano culture in the nineteenth century are derived from local archive work undertaken by A. V. Salacv and L. A. Salaeva, *Iz istorii fortepiannoĭ kul'tury Sibiri: instrumenty i nastroĭshchikii v Tomske (XIX–XXI v.v.)*, Second Edition (updated), (Tomsk: Muzykal'noe obshchestvo Novosibirskoĭ oblasti. Soiuz muzykal'nykh masterov Sibiri, 2013).

121   **Grigory Tomashinskiy:** I use the Russified version of Polish names when the subject settled in Russia.

121   **a Polish émigré to Siberia, who with his wife:** The Tomashinskiys' story is told by V. A. Khanevich, *Poliaki v Tomske (XIX–XX v.v.): Biografii* (Tomsk: Izdatel'stvo Tomskovo gosudarstvennovo pedagogicheskovo universiteta, 2012).

121 **the appetite in Western Siberia for the instrument became more and more significant . . . first piano shop:** See Salaev and Salaeva, *Iz istorii fortepiannoĭ kul'tury Sibiri*

121 **The owner was Pyotr Makushin:** Makushin's biography is comprehensively told in T. Staleva, *Sibirskii Prosvetitel' Pëtr Makushin* (Tomsk: Tomskoe Knizhnoe Izdatel'stvo, 1990) – a source I rely on heavily.

123 **Makushin's pioneering store sold more than . . . citizens of Tomsk:** Salaev and Salaeva, *Iz istorii fortepiannoĭ kul'tury Sibiri*

123 **Yadviga Zaleskaya, a young Polish graduate:** Yadviga Zaleskaya's story is told in Khanevich, *Poliaki v Tomske (XIX–XX v.v.): Biografii*, with other details given by a contemporary local music historian in Tomsk, the academician Vasilov Stanislav.

7: HOME IN A HUNDRED YEARS: SAKHALIN ISLAND

127–8 **'a place of unbearable sufferings . . . capable of causing and undergoing':** Anton Chekhov, 'Letter to A. S. Suvorin, March 1890', in *Sakhalin Island*, trans. Brian Reeve (Surrey: OneWorld Classics, 2007)

128 **'ugly little creature' . . . 'When the creaky wooden handle . . . rats, cats and puppies':** Benjamin Howard, *Prisoners of Russia: A Personal Study of Convict Life in Sakhalin and Siberia* (New York: D. Appleton and Company, 1902)

128 **as unfamiliar as Patagonia:** Chekhov, *Sakhalin Island*

128 **'Home in a Hundred Years':** Anton Chekhov, 'Letter to A. S. Suvorin, September 1890', in *Chekhov: A Life in Letters*, trans. Gordon McVay (London: Folio Society, 1994)

129 **journalist for the *New York Times*:** See 'Manchooria', *New York Times* (August 1858)

129 **'apparently the town was no stranger to the humanities . . . at the club here':** Chekhov, *Sakhalin Island*. The translation I have relied upon by Brian Reeve uses language with such a deft sense of tone, it feels as if Chekhov is in the room throwing around his barbed remarks.

129 **By the time of Chekhov's visit . . . :** Ibid., for the numerous details and anecdotes I give about Chekhov's experience of his journey and stay on Sakhalin Island.

130 **Girev was the son of a female convict:** For Girev's biography, see Vicheslav Innokentievich Yuzefov, 'Northern Sakhalin to the Antarctic: The story of a Russian participant in Scott's expedition to the South Pole, 1910–1913', trans. Ella L. Wiswell, *Polar Record*, 34:190 (July 1998).

132–3 **'In the General's garden there was music and singing . . . only a deadly yearning':** Chekhov, *Sakhalin Island*

133 **a Russian movie serial about her exploits being produced in 1914:** James von Geldern and Louise McReynolds (eds), *Entertaining Tsarist Russia: Tales, Songs, Plays, Movies, Jokes, Ads, and Images from Russian Urban Life, 1779–1917* (Bloomington and Indianapolis: Indiana University Press, 1998)

134 **'civilized' society . . . a 'luxurious' zoological collection . . . 'majestic as a marquise' with her daughters 'dressed up like little angels':** Chekhov, *Sakhalin Island*

135 **'Penal labourer E's wife' was 'a miniature young woman, nearly a child':** This story is told in full in Vlas Doroshevich, *Russia's Penal Colony in the Far East: A Translation of Vlas Doroshevich's 'Sakhalin'*, trans. Andrew Gentes (London and New York: Anthem Press, 2011).

135–6 **'[T]he poor woman's heart . . . so her tears wouldn't be noticed':** Ibid.

136 **'Music – it is all that beautifies her life . . . so much suffering, grief, torment and tears':** Ibid.

137 **'The condemned man is delivered . . . lard-greased noose over the shroud':** Ibid. Doroshevich gives a gory, blood-curdling version of events at Voevodsk Chasm, including a profile of the old executioner, Kamlev.

137 **the 'wheelbarrow-men':** For the full description, see ibid. and Chekhov, *Sakhalin Island*.

138 **'A dreadful, hideous place . . . people could live of their own free will':** Chekhov, *Sakhalin Island*

138 **'Perhaps the most foul hole as exists on earth':** Doroshevich, *Russia's Penal Colony in the Far East*

138 **a girl over the age of nine who was still a virgin:** Charles H. Hawes, *In the Uttermost East* (London and New York: Harper & Brothers, 1904)

138–9 **'We are not free artists . . . today's abnormal social conditions':** *Our Days Gazette* (February 1905), cited in Lynn M. Sargeant, 'Kashchei the Immortal: Liberal Politics, Cultural Memory, and the Rimsky-Korsakov Scandal of 1905', *Russian Review*, 64:1 (January 2005)

139 **'Down with autocracy!':** Ibid.

139 **There was no coal glinting in the scree:** Chekhov, *Sakhalin Island*

139 **'white spick-and-span cottages':** Ibid.

144 **a 'symbol of the state's attempt at "enlightenment" and edification':** Brian Donahoe and Joachim Otto Habeck (eds): *Reconstructing the House of Culture: Community, Self, and the Makings of Culture in Russia and Beyond* (New York: Berghahn Books, 2011)

145 **'Can a man who's warm understand one who's freezing?':** Aleksandr Solzhenitsyn, *One Day in the Life of Ivan Denisovich*, trans. H. T. Willets (New York: Farrar, Straus & Giroux, 2005)

Part Two: Broken Chords

147   'Reality is incomprehensible and abhorrent . . . filling him with hope?':
      Anatoly Lunacharsky, *On Literature and Art* (1932) trans. Avril Pyman
      (Moscow: Progress, 1973)

147   'I am not sure that in the kind of world in which we are living . . .
      become aware of their existence and importance': Claude Lévi-Strauss,
      Myth and Meaning (London: Routledge, 2001)

147   'And someday in the future . . . like some improbable salamander':
      Aleksandr Solzhenitsyn, *The Gulag Archipelago*, Volume I, trans. Thomas
      Whitney (London: Harper Perennial, 2007)

8. The Last Tsar's Piano: The Urals

153   Cases of wine . . . no longer allowed to wear their epaulettes: These
      details are given by Helen Rappaport in *The Race to Save the Romanovs*
      (London: Hutchinson, 2018), a book which traces the different ways in
      which the Romanovs might have been rescued from their Siberian
      detention.

153–4 the American journalist John Reed . . . refusing tips: John Reed, *Ten
      Days That Shook the World* (New York: Vintage, 1960)

154   'I know nothing greater than the *Appassionata* . . . can create such a
      beauty': Maxim Gorky, *Lenin: A Biographical Essay*, trans. Zbyněk Zeman
      (Edinburgh: Morrison & Gibb, 1967)

154   huddled up around their few remaining possessions: See Ivan
      Vladimirov's painting, 1919, *Miserable Life of Russian Nobles and Persons of
      High Rank During the Revolution*, Hoover Institution Library and
      Archives, in which the grand piano is being used as a table. Vladimirov
      lived a double life during the early Soviet era. While publicly praised for
      his works emphasizing the heroism of the new regime, he was covertly
      producing images showing the true horror of the Revolution.

155   Grand pianos were being driven around the city on the back of trucks:
      See Brian Moynahan, *Leningrad: Siege and Symphony* (London: Quercus,
      2013)

155   'Drag pianos out onto the streets . . . they fall to pieces': Vladimir
      Mayakovsky, 'Battle-order to the Army of Art', in *'Vladimir Mayakovsky'
      and Other Poems*, trans. James Womack (Manchester: Carcanet Press,
      2016)

155   Becker ceased output . . . reduced to ten men: Anne Swartz, *Piano Makers in
      Russia in the Nineteenth Century* (Bethlehem: Lehigh University Press, 2014)

155   a situation compounded by trade embargos imposed by European
      countries: See Marina Frolova-Walker and Jonathan Walker, *Music and
      Soviet Power 1917–1932* (Woodbridge: The Boydell Press, 2012)

155 **'We are all either consumed by ceaseless activity . . . the confusion about us':** Letter from Belyayev to Mayakovsky in January 1919, cited in ibid.

156 **Kubatsky was given his own train . . . dressed in his ceremonial military uniform:** This anecdote about the count in Crimea is taken from a study of the changes that swept through Russia's musical intelligentsia during the rise of the Soviet state: Frolova-Walker and Walker, *Music and Soviet Power*.

156 **the number of civilian casualties ran to nearly four times more:** This comparison is made in Anna Reid, *Leningrad: Tragedy of a City Under Siege, 1941–44* (London: Bloomsbury, 2011)

157 **even see a bird flying:** Robert Wilton, *The Last Days of the Romanovs* (London: Thornton Butterworth Limited, 1920)

157 **black bread for breakfast, while all the Empress ate was macaroni:** J. C. Trewin, *Tutor to the Tsarevich: An Intimate Portrait of the Last Days of the Russian Imperial Family, compiled from the papers of Charles Sydney Gibbes* (London: Macmillan, 1975)

158 **a report by Nikolai Sokolov:** Though profoundly wrong in many of its conclusions, the Sokolov Report (first published in France in 1924) continues to provide researchers with a trove of original information relating to the last days of the Romanovs and their murders. Part of Nikolai Sokolov's investigations involved taking detailed inventories of items found at the mineshaft at Ganina Yama and the Ipatiev House, even measuring the depth of the individual bullet holes found in the cellar walls. I used two versions of the Sokolov Report in my research, one abridged and translated from the original Russian edition: *The Sokolov Investigation*, trans. John F. O'Conor (London: Souvenir Press, 1972), and the other the full report in Russian: Nikolai Sokolov, *Ubiïstvo tsarskoï sem'i. Polnaia versiia* (Moscow: LitRes, 2017).

158 **The Bolsheviks shot the Tsar first . . . :** For this widely told story, I have used a number of different sources. One of the most dramatic – and extremely graphic – retellings of the Romanov murders is given in Simon Sebag Montefiore, *The Romanovs: 1613–1918* (London: Weidenfeld & Nicolson, 2016).

159 **fragments of jewellery . . . the same disused mine:** These details are largely taken from Robert Wilton's account of the Romanovs' final days. Wilton, the London *Times*' correspondent in St Petersburg, was among the first Western observers on the scene. He even conducted his reporting in tandem with Sokolov, the official investigator. His conclusions, however, were flawed by his virulent belief that the Russian Revolution, and the murder of the Romanovs, were the result of a global Jewish conspiracy: Wilton, *The Last Days of the Romanovs*.

159   **head had been smashed with a rifle:** Ibid. The account of both imperial
         dogs is told by Wilton.

159   **the Bolsheviks tried to destroy the evidence . . . :** *The Sokolov Investigation*,
         trans. John F. O'Conor. See also Greg King and Penny Wilson, *The Fate of
         the Romanovs* (Hoboken: John Wiley & Sons, 2003)

163   **He was the only person aside from officials inside the cordon:** See Vitaly
         Shitov, *Dom Ipat'eva: letopisnaia khronika v dokumentakh i fotografiiakh,
         1877–1977* (Chelyabinsk: Avto Graf, 2013)   a primary source I owe a
         significant debt to for his unique research into the history of the Ipatiev
         House.

163–4 **recalled sacred songs and women singing . . . 'Let Us Forget the Old
         World':** See Wilton, *The Last Days of the Romanovs*. Also, King and
         Wilson, *The Fate of the Romanovs*

164   **the piano was moved from the hall:** Kent de Price, 'Diary of Nicholas II,
         1917–1918, an annotated translation', *Graduate Student Theses,
         Dissertations, and Professional Papers* (University of Montana: 1966)

164   **told a more sinister version of events:** King and Wilson, *The Fate of the
         Romanovs*

165   **the piano Nicholas II mentions in a diary entry:** de Price, 'Diary of
         Nicholas II, 1917–1918, an annotated translation'

167   **Aleksandr said he had visited the Ipatiev House . . . :** Russian readers can
         find a more detailed description of the events that led Avdonin to the
         Pig's Meadow site, as well as a comprehensive list of everything he found,
         in the 2013 account he wrote of his search: Aleksandr Avdonin, *Ganina
         Iama: istoriia poiskov ostankov tsarskoĭ sem'i*, Second Edition (updated),
         (Ekaterinburg: Real Media Kompaniia, 2013).

168   **Then there was a poem by Mayakovsky:** See Vladimir Mayakovsky,
         'Imperator', in V. V. Mayakovsky, *Polnoe sobranie sochinenii: T. 9.* (Moscow:
         Gos. izd-vo khudozh. lit., 1958)

168–9 **the old Koptyaki Road:** This is the place name Avdonin uses in his book,
         rather than Pig's Meadow. Aleksandr Avdonin, *Ganina Iama: istoriia
         poiskov ostankov tsarskoĭ sem'i*, Second Edition (updated), (Ekaterinburg:
         Real Media Kompaniia, 2013).

174   **'amateur Sherlocks or Pushfuls':** Wilton, *The Last Days of the Romanovs*

9. THE END OF EVERYTHING: THE ALTAI MOUNTAINS

176   **'the End of Everything':** This local phrase is a translation of 'Ukok'.

177   **the town of Barnaul was alive with pianos:** Thomas Atkinson, *Oriental
         and Western Siberia* (London: Hurst and Blackett, 1858)

177   **the eminent German biologist Carl Friedrich von Ledebour:** Audrey le
         Lièvre, 'Nineteenth-century Dorpat and Its Botanical Influence', *Curtis's
         Botanical Magazine*, 14:1 (February 1997)

177 **He gathered close to a thousand butterflies:** Henry J. Elwes, 'On the Lepidoptera of the Altai Mountains', *Transactions of the Royal Entomological Society*, 47:3 (September 1899)

177 **Russia's Prince Elim Pavlovich Demidoff:** 'A Russian is the Richest Man in the World', *New York Daily Tribune* (October 1884)

177 **he bagged thirty-two of the largest wild sheep on the planet:** Elim Demidoff, *After Wild Sheep in the Altai and Mongolia* (London: Rowland Ward, 1900)

177 **a long history of attracting hardy migrants:** 'These peasants, like most pioneers, are not much interested in politics; they ask only to be let alone to carve out their own destinies' – observations made by American travellers Helen Wilson and Elsie Mitchell, who went to the Altai in 1925: *Vagabonding at Fifty* (London: Coward McCann, 1929).

178 **which ravaged the country . . . until 1922:** There is some debate among historians about the year the Russian Civil War came to an end. See Jonathan D. Smele, *The 'Russian' Civil Wars, 1916–1926: Ten Years That Shook the World* (Oxford: Oxford University Press, 2015).

179 **still fresh from the country's civil-war upheavals:** See Nicholas Roerich, *Altai-Himalaya: A Travel Diary* (London: Jarrolds, 1930). He describes the evidence of the horrors from an Old Believer, 'hacked with sabers', to the River Katun where they drowned the Whites.

179 **accompanied by Wagner's music and a portable gramophone:** Andrei Znamenski, *Red Shambhala: Magic, Prophecy, and Geopolitics in the Heart of Asia* (Illinois: Quest Books, 2011)

180 **with the assistance of high culture . . . will humanity thrive:** For Roerich's full credo, see Nicholas Roerich, *Corona Mundi* (New York: International Art Exchange, 1922). See also Ruth A. Drayer, *Nicholas and Helena Roerich: The Spiritual Journey of Two Great Artists and Peacemakers* (Illinois: Quest Books, 2005).

182 **Altaian space junk, shot by Norwegian photographer Jonas Bendiksen in 2000:** The image series also documented the effects of the jettisoned rocket fuel in Russia and Kazakhstan, and the livestock locals claimed were being killed by poisoned soil. See pro. magnumphotos.com/Catalogue/Jonas-Bendiksen/2000/Spaceship-Junkyard-NN144467.html

182 **'the pitch of an unheard-of blending':** Boris Pasternak, *Safe Conduct*, trans. Beatrice Scott (New York: New Directions, 1958). Pasternak's autobiography has a fascinating section on his ambition to be a composer, and the family's relationship with the Russian composer Aleksandr Scriabin. Pasternak's mother was a well-known concert pianist.

183 **'melting pot of nations':** Nicholas Roerich, *Heart of Asia* (New York: Roerich Museum Press, 1929)

184 **four tiny specimens of 'Denisovan Man' have ever been found:** See
       Viviane Slon, Bence Viola, Gabriel Renaud, Marie-Theres
       Gansauge, Stefano Benazzi, Susanna Sawyer, Jean-Jacques
       Hublin, Michael V. Shunkov, Anatoly P. Derevianko, Janet Kelso, Kay
       Prüfer, Matthias Meyer, Svante Pääbo, 'A Fourth Denisovan Individual',
       Science Advances (July 2017)
184 **The Ukok Princess . . . and flakes of gold:** See Natalya Polosmak, 'A
       Mummy Unearthed from the Pastures of Heaven', *National Geographic*
       (October 1994). Polosmak writes eloquently about her discovery, as
       well as the mixed emotions she feels as an archaeologist disturbing a
       grave. She describes carrying the girl's body from her place of
       interment, the corpse supported on a stretcher with white gauze
       pinned down 'like the wings of a specimen butterfly'. When they were
       due to extract the mummy to Novosibirsk, a snowstorm blew in from
       nowhere. Then an engine failed in the helicopter carrying the Ukok
       Princess. 'I believe that thoughts and ideas do not vanish, that they
       still exist in the layers of atmosphere that blanket the earth,' Polosmak
       wrote in her report for *National Geographic.*
185 **'gleams of a remoter world':** Percy Bysshe Shelley, 'Mont Blanc', in *The
       Selected Poetry and Prose of Shelley* (Hertfordshire: Wordsworth Editions,
       2002)

10. THE MOSCOW OF THE EAST: HARBIN

191 **'A passport . . . particularly in Russia':** Thomas Preston, *Before the Curtain*
       (London: John Murray, 1950)
191 **Sokolov was travelling with three suitcases . . . a finger:** Greg King and
       Penny Wilson, *The Fate of the Romanovs* (Hoboken: John Wiley & Sons,
       2003)
191 **likely cut from the hand of the Empress in order to retrieve a ring:**
       Edmund Walsh, 'The Last Days of the Romanovs', *The Atlantic* (March
       1928)
191 **As early as 1907, plays censored by Tsarist Russia premiered in Harbin:**
       Simon Karlinsky, 'Memoirs of Harbin', *Slavic Review*, 48:2 (Summer 1989)
193 **Russian *drosky* drivers in brightly coloured silk shirts:** Walter
       M. Holmes, *An Eye-witness in Manchuria* (New York: International
       Publishers, 1933)
193 **'It was like a dream of old Russia . . . raw and unbeautiful':** Adelaide
       Nichols, 'The Seven Blue Domes of Harbin', *New York Times* (March 1923)
193 **'red on the outside, white on the inside':** Laurie Manchester, 'Repatriation
       to a Totalitarian Homeland: The Ambiguous Alterity of Russian
       Repatriates from China to the USSR', *Diaspora*, 16:3 (December, 2007)

193 **They became prey to Harbin's white-slave traders and 'underworld gentry' . . . swung from telegraph poles:** Amleto Vespa, *Secret Agent of Japan* (London: Victor Gollancz, 1938)

193 **a wide-eyed, twenty-year-old White Guard:** Few records exist of Dmitri Alioshin, a White Russian officer who fled to Harbin after the Revolution and fought briefly in Baron von Ungern-Sternberg's Mongolian army. Alioshin disappeared soon after the publication of *Asian Odyssey*, and a lack of records has raised doubts about his real identity. Regardless, the book gives a rare account of the civil war and Russian Harbin. Dmitri Alioshin, *Asian Odyssey* (New York: Henry Holt & Co., 1940).

193 **There were two operas, six theatres, and music halls in full blast:** F. A. McKenzie, *The Unveiled East* (New York: E. P. Dutton and Company, 1907)

194 **Four years later, jazz was seeping into Siberia . . . travelling along the seams of the Trans-Siberian Railway:** Edwin Ware Hullinger, *The Reforging of Russia* (New York: E. P. Dutton and Co., 1925), cited in Benjamin J. Beresford, *Rhapsody in Red: Jazz and a Soviet Public Sphere under Stalin* (Arizona State University, August 2017). Beresford's dissertation is a lively piece of research on early Soviet jazz – and important to my understanding of how this style of music evolved inside the USSR. One of his primary sources suggested that jazz arrived in Novosibirsk before Moscow.

194 **The Harbin Symphony Orchestra included principals . . . :** See Sheila Melvin and Jindong Cai, *Rhapsody in Red: How Western Classical Music became Chinese* (New York: Algora Publishing, 2004)

194 **Some thirty music schools were flourishing in the city:** Amy Qin, 'In China, Rejuvenating a Classical Music Heritage Linked to a Jewish Community', *New York Times* (August 2016)

194 **When Lundstrem stumbled on a recording:** Eugene Marlow, *Jazz in China: From Dance Hall Music to Individual Freedom of Expression* (Jackson: University Press of Mississippi, 2018)

194 **His brother, Igor, played the saxophone:** S. Frederick Starr, *Red and Hot: The Fate of Jazz in the Soviet Union* (New York and Oxford: Oxford University Press, 1983)

195 **'King of Jazz in the Far East':** See Oleg Lundstrem's obituary by John Fordham, 'Oleg Lundstrem', *Guardian* (October 2005)

195 **Moscow's Bolshoi later moving to Paris for careers at the Folies Bergère:** Alexandre Vassiliev, *Beauty in Exile: The Artists, Models, and Nobility Who Fled the Russian Revolution and Influenced the World of Fashion*, trans. Antonina W. Bouis and Anya Kucharev (New York: Harry N. Abrams, 2000)

195   White Russian 'princesses' worked as dancing girls alongside gypsy performers: John B. Powell, *My Twenty-Five Years in China* (New York: The Macmillan Co., 1945)

195   the less attractive Harbin women, observed an American journalist in 1933, tended to work in dentistry: Lilian Grosvenor Colville, 'Here in Manchuria. Many Thousand Lives Were Lost and More Than Half the Crops Destroyed by the Floods of 1932', *National Geographic Magazine* (February 1933)

195   'Here in Harbin, the whole house rocked with "Bravas!"': Adelaide Nichols, 'Any Night at the Opera in Harbin', *New York Times* (March 1923)

195   Josef Kaspe, who had arrived in Harbin around 1903: Professor Dan Ben-Canaan, the foremost academic on Harbin's Jewish history and diaspora, helped me find my bearings when my hunt strayed briefly into China. Ben-Canaan's book, *The Kaspe File* (Heilongjiang: Heilongjiang People's Publishing House, 2009), gives the most detailed published analysis of the Kaspe history and murder case currently available. My telling of it owes a debt to his work.

196   'Finish it quickly . . . human beings have limited strength': Cited in Ben-Canaan, *The Kaspe File*

197   'a cottage industry': Jamie Bisher, *White Terror: Cossack Warlords of the Trans-Siberian* (London: RoutledgeCurzon, 2005)

197   more than twenty thousand Russian residents in Harbin: Manchester, 'Repatriation to a Totalitarian Homeland'

197   A large proportion of *kharbintsky* . . . piano left to spoil in the Siberian rain: Ibid.

198   From 1936 to 1945, the Japanese turned a Harbin suburb . . . grisly human experiments: The story of Unit 731 – including the shattering testimony of labourers and victims' families – is told in Yang Yan-Jun and Tam Yue-Him, *Unit 731: Laboratory of the Devil, Auschwitz of the East* (Stroud: Fonthill Media, 2018).

198   The city blinks with multi-lane highways: Sophy Roberts, 'Harbin: Opera and Ice Sculpture in China's Frozen Megacity', *Financial Times* (February 2018)

199   Harbin's fifty churches and synagogues . . . during Mao's Cultural Revolution: Kiki Zhao, 'Chinese City With a Russian Past Struggles to Preserve Its Legacy', the *New York Times* (June 2017)

199   'During China's Cultural Revolution . . . like the bones of the bourgeoisie': Richard Curt Kraus, *Pianos and Politics in China: Middle-Class Ambitions and the Struggle over Western Music* (New York and Oxford: Oxford University Press, 1989)

199   In 1966, Mao's Red Guards smashed instruments . . . drove soloists to suicide: Ibid.

11. Beethoven in a Red *Chum*: The Yamal Peninsula

202 **'Muddle instead of Music':** 'Sumbur Vmesto Muzyki: ob opera "Ledi Makbet Mtsenkovo uezda"', *Pravda* (January 1936)

203 **Russia's 'second serfdom':** David R. Shearer, 'Stalinism, 1928–1940', in Ronald Suny (ed.), *The Cambridge History of Russia*, Volume III (Cambridge: Cambridge University Press, 2006)

203 **In Ukraine, an estimated 3.9 million people died from starvation:** See Anne Applebaum, *Red Famine* (London: Penguin, 2017). Other estimates, like those given by Robert Conquest in *Harvest of Sorrow: Soviet Collectivization and the Terror-Famine* (New York: Oxford University Press, 1986) put the figure far higher.

203 **'The Great Retreat':** Nicholas Timasheff, *The Great Retreat: The Growth and Decline of Communism in Russia* (New York: E. P. Dutton & Company, 1946)

203 **Music splintered into a spectrum . . . lead to the labour camps:** I am very grateful for the expert advice of Russian musicologist Vladimir Orlov in navigating this period. Both his work and that of Marina Frovlova-Walker constitute important reading on the nuanced history of Soviet music, its innovations and contradictions.

204 **In this single decade, the number of prisoners in the Gulag doubled then tripled:** Anne Applebaum, *Gulag: A History* (London: Penguin, 2004)

204 **its population swelling by three hundred per cent in the thirties alone:** Shearer, 'Stalinism, 1928–1940'

206 **portable schools, while few in number:** See Andrei V. Golovnev and Gail Osherenko, *Siberian Survival* (Ithaca: Cornell University Press, 1999). The authors say the Red *chums* were less common, and therefore less influential, than the state boarding schools, which they describe in some detail.

206 **Unwilling to adjust to collective rules . . . 1937 to 1938, regarded by some groups of Nenets as a war:** Andrei V. Golovnev and Gail Osherenko, *Siberian Survival* (Ithaca: Cornell University Press, 1999)

206 **'galloping Sovietization':** Ibid.

207 **'a deep blue, like a water-sky':** See Fridtjof Nansen, *Through Siberia, The Land of the Future*, trans. Arthur G. Chater (London: William Heinemann, 1914)

207 **Operation Wunderland:** See Pier Horensma, *The Soviet Arctic* (Abingdon: Routledge, 2003)

208 **'the land of the future':** Nansen, *Through Siberia, The Land of the Future*

209 **In 1893, a Victorian spinster called Helen Peel played the piano:** See Helen Peel, *Polar Gleams* (London: Edward Arnold, 1894)

209 **Nansen wrote how this tough little vessel . . . before disappearing without trace in 1912:** See Nansen, *Through Siberia, The Land of the Future*, and Phil Carradice, *The Ships of Pembroke Dockyard* (Stroud: Amberley Publishing Limited, 2013)

209   **fourteen crew had in fact abandoned ship . . . using a map:** See William
      James Mills, *Exploring Polar Frontiers: A Historical Encyclopedia* (Santa
      Barbara: ABC-CLIO, 2003). By this time, the ship had been re-named
      St. Anna. For a full account of the ship's history, see Carradice, *The Ships
      of Pembroke Dockyard*.

210   **Anna had led protests against the industrial invasion of the Nenets'**
      territory: See Golovnev and Osherenko, *Siberian Survival*

210   **She encourages the community to make money with a modest tourist**
      operation: Sophy Roberts, 'A warm welcome: the Siberian reindeer
      herders opening their tents to tourists', *Financial Times* (July 2017)

211   **their oral traditions were closely bound to elemental sound . . . music**
      played a part in survival: A number of these details are derived from
      the original fieldwork of musicologist Alla Abramovich-Gomon, *The
      Nenets' Song* (Aldershot: Ashgate, 1999) – the first book-length study of
      the Nenets' song tradition, with much of the research undertaken in the
      seventies.

211   **'not a single trace of Western influence':** Ibid.

216   **Railway 501 was one of the most notorious white elephants:** The
      descriptions I give of Railway 501 owe a significant debt to the in-depth
      research undertaken by Lyudmila Lipatova and published in 2016. No
      one can match the first-hand testimonies Lipatova has gathered; not just
      the Gulag stories, but also the evidence of everyday lives in Salekhard at
      the time: L. F. Lipatova, *Dorogi i Sud'by* (Salekhard: GU Severnoe
      izdatel'stvo, 2016).

12. MUSIC IN THE GULAG ARCHIPELAGO: KOLYMA

223   **where Stalin's Gulag ships had offloaded their human cargo . . . :** Hot on
      the heels of the English-language translation of Solzhenitsyn's *The Gulag
      Archipelago*, British historian Robert Conquest published an entire
      volume dedicated to the Kolyma camps. Conquest's *Kolyma* (London:
      Macmillan, 1978) used evidence from almost forty sources – many of
      them first-person testimonies – to tell the story of the Kolyma Gulag
      under Stalin. After perestroika much of Conquest's controversial work
      was published in Russia.

223   **'half-human, half-bird creatures':** Michael Solomon was a journalist
      arrested in communist Romania after the Second World War and sent to
      the Kolyma Gulag. After his release he emigrated to Canada and wrote
      an account of his imprisonment: *Magadan* (Princeton: Vertex, 1971).

224   **'Here we are on the edge of the world . . . playing Vivaldi for fifty**
      gorillas': Georgi Feldgun cited in Anne Applebaum, *Gulag: A History*
      (London: Penguin, 2004), and Brian Moynahan, *Leningrad: Siege and
      Symphony* (London: Quercus, 2013)

224 **For others, such as the Lithuanians singing their hymns:** Miron Ètlis, *Sovremenniki Gulaga: Kniga vospominaniĭ i razmyshleniĭ* (Magadan: Kn. Izd-vo, 1991)

224 **Guards used hoses of freezing water to push their wards back into the holds:** Janusz Bardach and Kathleen Gleeson, *Man is Wolf to Man* (London: Simon & Schuster, 1998)

224 **four-tiered bunks:** Aino Kuusinen, *Before and After Stalin: A Personal Account of Soviet Russia from the 1920s to the 1960s,* trans. Paul Stevenson (London: Michael Joseph, 1974)

224 **cooped up in cages:** Solomon, *Magadan*

224 **Witnesses described the grinding of the ships' engines:** Bardach and Gleeson, *Man is Wolf to Man*

224 **They also remembered the sound of 'wild laughter' . . . caterwauling:** Eugenia Ginzburg, *Into the Whirlwind,* trans. Paul Stevenson and Manya Harari (London: Persephone Books, 2014)

224 **A Polish survivor, Janusz Bardach, described the hard-core criminals . . . some kind of holiday cruise:** Bardach and Gleeson, *Man is Wolf to Man*

225 **'The boat moved off to the sound of the mournful singing . . . reached out towards me from all sides':** Zoe Zajdlerowa was an Irish woman, married to a Pole, who was sent to the Kolyma Gulag after the Soviet Union's occupation of Poland. Her account was initially published anonymously, but Zajdlerowa identified herself in later editions of her book: *The Dark Side of the Moon* (London: Faber & Faber, 1946).

225 **'a melody which was grey like the sea, like our ship, like the fog':** Ibid.

225 **When one of these ships ran aground . . . wait for the rising water:** Martin Bollinger, *Stalin's Slave Ships* (Toronto: Praeger, 2003)

225 **the horrid stench still rising from the holds:** Ibid.

225 **In 1939, the *New York Times* reported . . . :** '700 Believed Dead on Russian Vessel', *New York Times* (December 1939)

225 **At the time, the West was the principal buyer of Soviet gold:** Applebaum, *Gulag: A History*

225 **The watchtowers that lined the road into Magadan were taken down:** Robert Conquest, *Kolyma*

225 **Wallace bought a bottle of perfume:** Vadim J. Birstein, 'Three Days in "Auschwitz without Gas Chambers": Henry A. Wallace's Visit to Magadan in 1944', *The Wilson Center* (April 2012)

225 **he watched a play performed by prisoners:** Conquest, *Kolyma*

226 **Instead of meeting actual Gulag labourers . . . dressed up as miners:** Thomas Sgovio, *Dear America!* (New York: Partners' Press, 1979). In Henry Wallace's own record of events, he wrote: 'The Kolyma gold miners are big, husky young men, who came out to the Far East from

European Russia.' See Henry A. Wallace, *Soviet Asia Mission* (New York: Reynal & Hitchcock, 1946).

226 **'a whole separate continent of the Archipelago':** Aleksandr Solzhenitsyn, *The Gulag Archipelago*, Volume II, trans. Thomas Whitney (London: Harper Perennial, 2007)

226 **over three million prisoners were exiled to Kolyma . . . five hundred thousand made it through:** Kazimierz Zamorski, *Gold Mining and Forced Labour in the USSR* (Washington: Foundation for Foreign Affairs, 1949)

226–7 **Among them was the composer Vsevolod Zaderatsky . . . composed a cycle of twenty-four preludes and fugues:** See the account by the composer's son, Vsevolod Zaderatsky Jr., 'Vsevolod Petrovich Zaderatsky (1891–1953): A Lost Soviet Composer', trans. Anthony Phillips, *International Centre for Suppressed Music, Online Journal* (May 2006).

227 **'My comfort is the music into which I immerse myself, so that I forget the world':** Inna Klause has produced a number of academic articles which relate little-known stories of musicians in the Gulag. Both Zaderatsky's and Varpakhovsky's experiences are documented in her paper: 'Musical Activity of Gulag Prisoners from the 1920s to 1950s', in Amaury du Closel (ed.), *Symposium: Music and Concentration Camps* (Strasbourg: European Council, 2013). The author also talks about the different feelings prisoners had towards being part of the musical ensembles.

227 **'travesty of freedom' and 'people half-alive':** Yelena Vladimirova, 'Kolyma', trans. Catriona Kelly. Cited in Simeon Vilensky (ed.) *Till My Tale is Told: Women's Memoirs of the Gulag* (London: Virago Press, 1999)

228 **Dalstroi, the pseudo-corporation founded in 1931:** A legitimate-seeming corporate front was required to attract the engineers and free workers needed to get this vast mining project off the ground. See Anne Applebaum, *Gulag: A History.*

228 **Solzhenitsyn writes about the famous Soviet tenor Vadim Kozin:** Solzhenitsyn, *The Gulag Archipelago*, Volume II

228 **How Kozin ended up here was quite another story:** Kozin recorded his life and inner thoughts in private diaries which were found after his death. The content of these diaries, and Kozin's biography and arrests, is movingly told in my main source about the singer: Dan Healey's *Russian Homophobia from Stalin to Sochi* (London: Bloomsbury Academic, 2018).

229 **mounted police were needed to keep the concert fans at bay:** Monica Whitlock, 'Searching for Vadim Kozin, the Soviet tango king', *BBC News* (December 2015)

229 **Kozin's surviving diaries, however, reveal a man tortured by the hypocrisy of Soviet society:** Healey, *Russian Homophobia from Stalin to Sochi*

230 **'"All right, Kozin, stop the bowing and get out!"':** Solzhenitsyn, *The Gulag Archipelago*, Volume II

230 **he stood up and called him a pederast:** Healey, *Russian Homophobia from Stalin to Sochi*

230 **Stalin is consistently voted by Russians . . . :** See David Filipov, 'For Russians, Stalin is the "Most Outstanding" Figure in World History, Followed by Putin', *Washington Post* (June 2017)

231 **According to Solzhenitsyn, Kozin tried to hang himself:** Solzhenitsyn, *The Gulag Archipelago*, Volume II

233 **Varlam Shalamov wrote about the region's summer greenery – how it grew with a kind of wild rush:** See Varlam Shalamov, *Kolyma Stories*, trans. Donald Rayfield (New York: NYRB Classics, 2018)

234 **literacy rates in the USSR nearly doubled by the end of the decade:** See David R. Shearer, 'Stalinism, 1928–1940', in Ronald Suny (ed.), *The Cambridge History of Russia*, Volume III (Cambridge: Cambridge University Press, 2006)

234 **new departments at the Moscow and Leningrad conservatories:** See Simo Mikkonen, *State Composers and the Red Courtiers* (Jyväskylä: Jyväskylä University Press, 2007)

234 **a good thing there was no scent to the convicts' tears:** Shalamov, *Kolyma Stories*

13. The Siberian Colosseum: Novosibirsk

235 **Soviet authorities mounted hundreds of loudspeakers:** Albert Pleysier, *Frozen Tears: The Blockade and Battle of Leningrad* (Maryland: University Press of America, 2008)

235 **The authorities also broadcast the tick-tock of a metronome:** See Alexis Peri, *The War Within* (Cambridge and London: Harvard University Press, 2017)

236 **the rhythm of the metronome took on the feeling of a heartbeat:** See Pleysier, *Frozen Tears*

236 **The Soviet poet Vera Inber said Leningraders . . . in a Tchaikovsky concert:** Ibid.

236 **'Music makes me fearless . . . but I go into the melody':** Susanna Ivanova, cited in Boris Skomorovsky and E. G. Morris, *The Siege of Leningrad* (St Petersburg: Books Inc., 1944)

236 **'Your song tells us of a great singing people . . . the meanings of human freedom':** Carl Sandburg, 'Take a Letter to Dmitri Shostakovich', *Washington Post* (July 1942), cited in Brian Moynahan, *Leningrad: Siege and Symphony* (London: Quercus, 2013)

236 **a calling card for the USSR about the urgency of their fight against the fascist advance:** The fascinating ambiguity in Shostakovich's musical

message is revealed in the composer's controversial memoirs published after his death: 'Hitler is a criminal, that's clear, but so is Stalin. I feel eternal pain for those who were killed by Hitler, but I feel no less pain for those killed on Stalin's orders. I suffer for everyone who was tortured, shot, or starved to death. There were millions of them in our country before the war with Hitler began. The war brought much new sorrow and much new destruction, but I haven't forgotten the terrible prewar years. This is what all my symphonies, beginning with the Fourth, are about, including the Seventh and Eighth.' See *Testimony: The Memoirs of Dmitri Shostakovich, as related to and edited by Solomon Volkov*, trans. Antonina W. Bouis (London: Hamish Hamilton, 1979).

237 **'My weapon was music . . . go to any lengths for the sake of victory':** *Literaturnaya Gazeta* (December 1965), cited in Brian Moynahan, *Leningrad: Siege and Symphony*

237 **the composer's rapturous reception earning him the cover of *Time* magazine:** 'Music: Shostakovich & the Guns', *Time* (July 1942)

237 **there were numerous names crossed out (known to be dead), and others marked up in red:** Pauline Fairclough, *Classics for the Masses: Shaping Soviet Musical Identity Under Lenin and Stalin* (New Haven: Yale University Press, 2016)

237 **At the first rehearsal fewer than twenty musicians turned up . . . :** One of the most riveting tellings of the blockade story is by Moynahan, *Leningrad: Siege and Symphony* – a book I have relied on for some of the very human details.

238 **'dressed like cabbages':** Ed Vulliamy, 'Orchestral Manoeuvres', *Observer* (November 2001)

238 **The drummer perished on his way to work:** 'The first violin is dying, the drum died on his way to work, the French horn is at death's door'. Yasha Babushkin, the Radiokom art director, cited in Moynahan, *Leningrad: Siege and Symphony*.

238 **'[W]e were stunned by the number of people . . . Most were thin and dystrophic':** Mikhail Parfionov, cited in Vulliamy, 'Orchestral Manoeuvres'

238 **'Chicago of the Soviet Union':** Richard Nixon, 'Russia as I Saw It', *National Geographic* (December 1959)

238 **Siberian Colosseum:** This is a phrase commonly used. See Peter Conradi, *Who Lost Russia? How the World Entered a New Cold War* (London: Oneworld, 2017)

239 **it could accommodate a column of tanks . . . tractors could be driven from the street to the stage:** For a detailed account of the builders' ambitions, failures and successes, see Ivan Nevzgodin, 'A Great Achievement of the Soviet Construction Technology in Siberia: The

Reinforced Concrete Cupola of the Novosibirsk Theatre', in Ine Wouters, Stephanie Van de Voorde, Inge Bertels, Bernard Espion, Krista de Jonge and Denis Zastavni (eds), *Building Knowledge, Constructing Histories*, Volume I (Leiden: CRC Press/Balema, 2018). One of the challenges to understanding the building's history, remark the authors, is that the chief engineer was executed in 1937 during Stalin's purges.

239   **The original decor was equally extravagant:** Descriptions of the Novosibirsk Opera and Ballet Theatre in its early Soviet days can be found in Eric Johnstone, 'Russian Visit', *Life Magazine* (September 1944) and Richard Lauterbach, *These are the Russians* (New York: Harper & Brothers, 1945).

239   **aviation engineers who assembled the mechanics for a ninety-tonne stage curtain:** Lauterbach, *These are the Russians*

240   **more than twenty-four million Russians, both soldiers and civilians, perished in the Great Patriotic War:** Mark Harrison and John Barber, 'Patriotic War, 1941–1945', in Ronald Suny (ed.), *The Cambridge History of Russia*, Volume III (Cambridge: Cambridge University Press, 2006). These numbers do, inevitably, vary from source to source.

240   **Packing was done in a hurry . . . :** The wartime evacuation of art from Moscow's Tretyakov Gallery is extensively recorded in Z. I. Tregilova's history, which tracks the journeys of some of Russia's most iconic artworks: Z. I. Tregilova (ed.), *Istoriia Tret'iakovskoĭ galerei XX vek, 1941–1945* (Moscow: Tret'iakovskaia galereia, 2015).

240–41 **Museum staff buried what they could . . . A member of Pavlovsk's staff made sketches:** These details are derived from two comprehensive sources: Suzanne Massie, *Pavlovsk: The Life of a Russian Palace* (Leipzig: Liki Rossii, 1990), an extraordinarily rigorous piece of historical research which reads like a thriller as the museum trains make their escape from Leningrad to Siberia; and R. R. Gafifullin, *In Memoriam: Pavlovsk. Sobranie dvortsa-muzeia, Poteri i utraty* (St Petersburg: GMZ 'Perriavlovsk', 2015).

241   **Stalin's heir apparent, nicknamed 'The Pianist':** Simon Sebag Montefiore, *Stalin: The Court of the Red Tsar* (New York: Alfred A. Knopf, 2004)

242   **'Crate 63':** I am indebted to the work of Aleksei Guzanov and Nataliya Kulina at Pavlovsk Palace, who dug into the archives on my behalf to reveal the previously untold Siberian tale of Catherine's Zumpe piano. For more on the railway journeys to Novosibirsk, see Massie, *Pavlovsk: Life of a Russian Palace*.

242   **The Tretyakov employees slept in a dormitory in the make-up rooms:** Tregilova (ed.), *Istoriia Tret'iakovskoĭ galerei XX vek, 1941–1945*

242–3 **The Pavlovsk workers occupied the basement:** Massie, *Pavlovsk: Life of a Russian Palace*

243 **Mravinsky travelled with his mother, wife and several domestic cats:**
See Gregor Tassie, *Yevgeny Mravinsky: The Noble Conductor* (Lanham:
Scarecrow Press, 2005)

243 **Mravinsky's orchestra went on to play . . .:** Ibid.

243–4 **The Philharmonic also travelled to various Siberian towns . . . equal to
the orchestra's Leningrad appearances:** Ibid.

244 **'Treasures Saved from the Germans':** See Tregilova (ed.), *Istoriia
Tret'iakovskoĭ galerei XX vek, 1941–1945*

244 **'Not one of the orchestras that have performed my work . . . a perfect
fulfilment of ideas':** D. D. Shostakovich, *Sovetsky Sibir* (July 1942)

244 **An article in the newspaper *Soviet Siberia* described . . . this animal-like
howling:** I. Sollertinskii, 'Sed'maia simfoniia Shostakovicha', *Sovetsky
Sibir* (July 1942)

244–5 **'Far off in the middle of Siberia . . . the city of Lenin':** D. D.
Shostakovich, 'Zamechatelniye orkester', *Literature i Isskustvo* (August 1942),
cited in Tassie, *Yevgeny Mravinsky*

253 **there were over four hundred thousand primary-age children
enrolled . . . twenty-four college-level conservatories:** See Maria
Pisarenko, 'Cultural Influences upon Soviet-era Programmatic Piano
Music for Children', *UNLV Theses, Dissertations, Professional Papers, and
Capstones* (Las Vegas: University of Nevada, 2017)

256 **a massive panic migration:** In Antony Beevor's *The Second World War*
(New York, Boston and London: Little, Brown & Company, 2012), the
British historian writes that after the Soviet offensive, which included
extraordinary levels of mass rape, only 193,000 Germans of the pre-war
population of 2.2 million were left in East Prussia. In *Berlin: The
Downfall, 1945* (New York: Viking, 2002), Beevor describes the Red Army
leaving eastern Germany with tanks filled to the brim with plunder. Both
books are important reading to understand the depth and horror of what
occurred.

256 **Aleksandr Solzhenitsyn, then an artillery captain stationed in East
Prussia:** See Aleksandr Solzhenitsyn, *Prussian Nights*, trans. Robert
Conquest (London: Fontana Press, 1978)

256 **collections were also burnt or looted by civilians before the Red Army
arrived:** See Max Hastings, *Armageddon: The Battle for Germany, 1944–45*
(London: Macmillan, 2004)

14. Vera's Mühlbach: Akademgorodok

258 **seventy thousand construction workers:** This statistic was published in
Richard Nixon, 'Russia as I Saw It', *National Geographic* (December 1959).

259 **ninety per cent of the country's natural resources:** See Committee on
Improving the Effectiveness of Environmental Nongovernmental

Organizations in Russia et al., *The Role of Environmental NGOs – Russian Challenges, American Lessons* (Washington DC: National Academy Press, 2001)

259 **On paper, Akademgorodok looked spectacular:** For comprehensive descriptions of Akademgorodok's founding, purposes and achievements, I have leaned heavily on Paul R. Josephson's *New Atlantis Revisited: Akademgorodok, the Siberian City of Science* (Princeton: Princeton University Press, 1997).

259 **'the little town with probably the biggest I.Q. anywhere':** See Daniel Ford, 'Rebirth of a Nation', *New Yorke*r (March 1998)

259 **For the country's intelligentsia with a renegade bent:** Josephson, *New Atlantis Revisited*

259 **Within a decade of breaking ground . . . fifteen functioning research institutes:** Ibid.

259 **'a miracle':** Raissa L. Berg's autobiography captures the nuances of daily life in newly built Akademgorodok, detailing the preferential treatment of the city's 'elite' academics: Raissa L. Berg, *Acquired Traits*, trans. David Lowe (London: Penguin, 1988).

260 **Vera Lotar-Shevchenko was born Vera Lautard . . . Mediterranean resort of Nice in France:** I am indebted to a number of detailed accounts of Vera's life, principally: Liubov' Kachan, 'Zhalet' sebia – kakaia erunda!', *Novo Russkoe Slovo* (April 1999); Simon Soloveychik, 'Pianistka', *Komsomol'skaia Pravda* (December 1965); and the Russian-language documentary *My eshchë budem zhit' nastoiashcheï zhizn'iu* (1991) directed by Valeriï Klabukov. With the help of Anastasia Bliznyuk, I also gathered various accounts by the Akademgorodok historian Mikhail Kachan, and Georgiï Ugodnikov, who studied piano under Vera in Nizhny Tagil. There are further accounts by local historians in Nizhny Tagil, and others written by people who knew Vera, on historyntagil.ru. Some of the sources are contradictory, not least the fundamentals: there are variations in Vera's date of birth and death (with arguments that even the year on her gravestone is wrong). Her definitive biography is further complicated by the fact that Vera left no known diaries or memoirs. In my version of her life, I have no reason to doubt the truth of these sources. While I did my best to seek verification from living people who knew her, my telling also conveys a deliberate level of uncertainty here and there, given some of the contradictions.

261 **Another source cited her teacher as the Italian, Ernesto Consolo:** 'Concerts "Vera Lautard"', *Figaro* (November 1920)

261 **'velvet' playing style:** The description given by Kachan, 'Zhalet' sebia – kakaia erunda!'

261 **'rare brilliance':** 'Concerts "Vera Lautard"', *Figaro*

263 '[n]othing that is not there and the nothing that is': Wallace Stevens, 'The Snow Man', in *The Collected Poems of Wallace Stevens* (New York: Alfred A. Knopf, 1954)

264 There is an old recording of Vera playing . . . : ADGO, 'Vera Lotar-Shevchenko plays Beethoven Piano Sonata No. 32, Op. 111', *YouTube* (June 2017)

264 beauty at its very limit: Soloveychik, 'Pianistka'

265 Vera refused an encore, telling the audience how hard it had been to perform: This account of Vera's performance in the Novosibirsk Opera and Ballet Theatre is given in the Russian-language documentary *My eshchë budem zhit' nastoiashcheï zhizn'iu* (1991) directed by Valeriï Klabukov. The Akademgorodok historian Mikhail Kachan, however, believed the Estonia-Steinway event occurred in a different concert hall in another Siberian city.

266–7 large numbers of political prisoners granted amnesty, or 'rehabilitated': 'If 7,000-odd people had been rehabilitated in the three years preceding the secret speech, 617,000 were rehabilitated in the ten months that followed it' – Anne Applebaum, *Gulag: A History* (London: Penguin, 2004).

267 In 1958, the Texan pianist Harvey Van Cliburn . . . with Khrushchev's approval: See Stuart Isacoff, *When the World Stopped to Listen* (New York: Knopf Doubleday, 2017)

267 'dressed as if ready for a football game': James Reston, 'Siberia and Surprises', *New York Times* (July 1959)

267 Mrs Nixon went to a Siberian fashion show: 'Mrs. Nixon Views Siberian Fashions', Ibid.

268 began his eighteen-year tenure as General Secretary: The use of this title, as opposed to First Secretary, was a telling throwback to the language of the Stalin era. See Stephen E. Hanson, 'The Brezhnev era', in Ronald Suny (ed.), *The Cambridge History of Russia*, Volume III (Cambridge: Cambridge University Press, 2006).

268 The event was announced with a banner . . . : See Alexander Galich, *Songs and Poems*, trans. Gerald Stanton Smith (Ann Arbor: Ardis, 1983)

268 Then all two thousand people in the audience rose to their feet: Galich, *Songs and Poems*

268 Galich was fetched from the city hotel for a 2 a.m. encore: Josephson, *New Atlantis Revisited*

270 the top four floors of the projected twelve-storey hotel were quickly lopped off: Ibid.

271 1905, when the factory was producing two hundred and fifty grand pianos a year: Anne Swartz, *Piano Makers in Russia in the Nineteenth Century* (Bethlehem: Lehigh University Press, 2014)

271 **The German maker was among the foreign artisans:** Robert Palmieri
(ed.), *The Piano: An Encyclopedia*, Second Edition (New York and London:
Routledge, 2015)

274 **Klavdiya Shulzhenko, 'Russia's Vera Lynn':** Anna Reid, *Leningrad: Tragedy
of a City Under Siege, 1941–44* (London: Bloomsbury, 2011)

274 **the spire of the Admiralty scaled by mountaineers:** See also Albert
Pleysier, *Frozen Tears: The Blockade and Battle of Leningrad* (Maryland:
University Press of America, 2008)

275 **Lagoda's ice held for six months . . . half a million people:** See Harrison
E. Salisbury, *The 900 Days: The Siege of Leningrad* (London: Macmillan,
2000)

275 **knew the 'Road of Life' by another name: the 'Road of Death':** Ibid.

277 **Rönisch was a manufacturer from Dresden . . . :** The history of Rönisch
pianos in Russia is told in detail by Swartz, *Piano Makers in Russia in the
Nineteenth Century.*

278 **J. Alfred Prufrock measured out his life with coffee spoons:** T. S. Eliot,
'The Love Song of J. Alfred Prufrock', in *The Wasteland and Other Poems*
(London: Faber and Faber, 1999)

278 **thirty million people outside America were listening in:** John S.
Wilson, 'Who is Conover? Only We Ask', *New York Times* (September
1959)

Part Three: Goodness Knows Where

281 **'Often the object of desire . . . becomes more real than reality itself':**
Umberto Eco, *The Book of Legendary Lands*, trans. Alastair McEwan
(London: MacLehose Press, 2015)

281 **''Tis wonderful how soon a piano gets into a log-hut on the
frontier':** Ralph Waldo Emerson, *The Collected Works of Ralph
Waldo Emerson*, Volume VII (Cambridge and London: Belknap
Press, 2007)

281 **'There are many kinds of endings – triumphant and tragic . . .
mysterious, unseal an enigma':** Alfred Brendel, *A Pianist's A–Z: A Piano
Lover's Reader* (London: Faber & Faber, 2013)

15. A Game of Risk: Kamchatka

283 **In 1986, the legendary Soviet pianist Sviatoslav Richter took a piece of
cardboard . . . :** See Valentina Chemberdzhi, *V puteshestvii so
Sviatoslavom Rikhterom* (Moscow: M. RIK 'Kul'tura', 1993) – a
comprehensive portrait of the pianist's Siberian travels, which
Chemberdzhi experienced. Sensitive to Richter's complex character and
melancholy, her account is a fascinating read.

284 **Liszt performing on a rattling Tompkinson upright in an Irish hotel sitting room:** Alan Walker, *Franz Liszt: The Virtuoso Years* (Ithaca: Cornell University Press, 1993)

284 **'it's hard to imagine a grand piano in a yurt or in the taiga!':** Chemberdzhi, *V puteshestvii so Sviatoslavom Rikhterom*

284 **'In deepest Russia . . . I've played on terrible pianos, and played extremely well':** Bruno Monsaingeon, *Sviatoslav Richter: Notebooks and Conversations*, trans. Stewart Spencer (London: Faber & Faber, 2001)

284 **visited Khabarovsk, Chita . . . Ulan-Ude, Irkutsk, Krasnoyarsk and Barnaul:** Richter's full itinerary, and many an anecdote along the way, is given in Chemberdzhi, *V puteshestvii so Sviatoslavom Rikhterom*

284 **In Abakan on the Yenisei River . . . Siberians could hear him perform live:** Ibid.

284 **scribbled on pieces of paper . . . sometimes in less than thirty minutes:** Monsaingeon, *Sviatoslav Richter*

284 **'[T]hrough word of mouth the hall would be full. That's not done in the West':** Ibid.

284 **'All that matters is that people come not out of snobbery but to listen to the music':** Ibid.

285 **'In tsarist Russia's last years . . . And we call that socialism!?':** Gorbachev's visit to Nizhnevartovsk and this quote is given in William Taubman, *Gorbachev: His Life and Times* (London: Simon & Schuster, 2017).

285 **extraordinary queues on the day McDonald's opened:** Francis X. Clines, 'Upheaval in the East; Moscow McDonald's Opens: Milkshakes and Human Kindness', *New York Times* (February 1990)

285 **In Leningrad, rock surged out of illegal clubs:** Mark Yoffe and Dave Laing, 'History of Soviet and Russian Rock Music', in John Shepherd, David Horn, Dave Laing, Paul Oliver and Peter Wicke (eds), *Continuum Encyclopedia of Popular Music of the World: Locations*, Volume VII (London and New York: Continuum, 2005)

286 **By 1992, queues outside food stores had returned to city streets:** Serge Schmemann, 'Yeltsin Takes to Now-Restive Streets', *New York Times* (January 1992)

286 **One of the regions that emptied out most dramatically:** See Stephanie Hitztaler, 'The Relationship between Resources and Human Migration Patterns in Central Kamchatka during the Post-Soviet Period', *Population and Environment*, 25:4 (March 2004)

288 **Getting to Kamchatka . . . :** For a full account of the challenges of reaching Kamchatka, see James R. Gibson, *Feeding the Russian Fur Trade* (Madison: University of Wisconsin Press, 2011).

288 **'[H]ere there were not what we call roads . . . choosing paths in various directions':** Lyudmila Rikord, cited in ibid.

289 'I consider myself particularly fortunate . . . bringing to Kamchatka a pianoforte': V. I. Golovnin, *Around the World on the Kamchatka*, trans. Ella Wiswell (Honolulu: Hawaii University Press, 1979) about an epic voyage little known outside Russia.

289 '[T]he pleasure of playing the piano in such an isolated spot, for someone who loves music, is immense!': Ibid.

289 Golovnin's seaborne piano delivery had taken eight months and eight days: Ibid.

290 Kamchatka was the place at the back of the classroom: Boris Pasternak, *Safe Conduct*, trans. Beatrice Scott (New York: New Directions, 1958)

290 One in ten of Kamchatka's population left: Hitztaler, 'The Relationship between Resources and Human Migration Patterns in Central Kamchatka during the Post-Soviet Period'

295 'America's best friend': T. De Witt Talmage, 'Truth about Russia', *Herald and News. Vermont* (November 1892)

295 The country's two leaders were being favourably compared: Ibid.

295 'waste space on the map of the globe': Perry Collins, *Overland Explorations in Siberia, Northern Asia and the Great Amoor River Country* (New York: D. Appleton and Co., 1864)

295 his bestselling indictment of the Tsarist exile system: See George Kennan, *Siberia and the Exile System*, Volumes I & II (New York: The Century Co., 1891)

295 He writes about the captain of the port . . . refined musical tastes: George Kennan, *Tent Life in Siberia* (New York: G. P. Putnam's Sons, 1893)

296 'an occasional but rare piano': Thomas Wallace Knox, *Overland through Asia* (Hartford: American Publishing Co., 1870)

296 'Evidently, many of those rough but kindly people . . . the evening's entertainment': Washington Vanderlip and Homer Hulbert, *In Search of a Siberian Klondike* (New York: Century Co., 1903)

296 'classical concerts were replaced by the howling of sledge-dogs': Elim Demidoff, *A Shooting Trip to Kamchatka* (London: Rowland Ward, 1904)

296 At volcanic mud baths . . . an old stained piano: Ibid.

299 Nazi SS execution squads were shooting, hanging and burning communist partisans: 'Einsatzgruppen', in Israel Gutman (ed.), *Encyclopedia of the Holocaust*, Volume II (New York: Macmillan, 1990)

300 'The Boy and the Bird': See Vasiliĭ Peskov, *Polnoe sobranie sochineniĭ, Tom 5: Moshchenye reki* (Moscow: LitRes, 2017)

16. SIBERIA'S LAST PIANO: THE COMMANDERS TO THE KURILS

305 'too much certainty is a miserable thing': Horatio Clare, *Orison for a Curlew* (Toller Fratrum: Little Toller Books, 2015)

305   measured using a mechanism fashioned from piano wire: Albert
         E. Theberge, 'George Belknap and the Thomson Sounding Machine',
         Hydro (April 2014)

305   piano wire was also used by the Soviets to hang traitors during the
         Second World War: Peter Julicher, *'Enemies of the People' under the Soviets*
         (Jefferson: McFarland and Company, 2015)

306   Current research suggests there are no more than two hundred and
         fifty nesting pairs left in the world: This figure was accurate in July
         2019, according to the most up-to-date information provided by the
         RSPB (The Royal Society for the Protection of Birds). The same source
         rated the bird as 'critically endangered'.

307   annotated book on birds of the Russian Far East: Mark Brazil, *Field
         Guide to the Birds of East Asia* (London: Christopher Helm, 2009)

309–310 'By another spring I may be a mail-carrier in Peru . . . Let us migrate
         interiorly without intermission': Henry David Thoreau, *The Writings of
         Henry David Thoreau* (Boston: Houghton Mifflin, 1906)

310   Among them is one book I adore . . . : Kate Marsden, *On Sledge and
         Horseback to Outcast Siberian Lepers* (London: Record Press, 1892).
         Marsden's map, published in her book, is a treasure in the annals of
         Siberian adventures.

310   'of course, it was quite natural for the gentlemen . . . get at the end of
         the journey before setting off': Ibid.

310–11 'Even my own attention, I must confess . . . in thinking what to wear': Ibid.

313   the land-and-sea journey made in the eighteenth century by the
         explorer Vitus Bering: Peter Ulf Møller and Natasha Okhotina Lind,
         Until Death Do Us Part (Fairbanks: University of Alaska Press, 2008)

313   In July 1741, Bering made landfall on Kayak Island . . . : For Bering's
         story, see Glynn Barratt, *Russia in Pacific Waters, 1715–1825: A Survey of
         the Origins of Russia's Naval Presence in the North and South Pacific*
         (Vancouver: University of British Columbia Press, 1981).

313   Steller described these creatures as over seven metres in length . . . able
         to feed forty hungry sailors for two weeks: See George W. Steller, *'De
         bestiis marinis, or, The Beasts of the Sea (1751)'*, trans. W. Miller and J. E.
         Miller, *Faculty Publications*, UNL Libraries, 17

315   indigenous Aleuts originally imported from the Aleutian Islands to
         harvest the pelts: James S. Olson (ed.), *An Ethnohistorical Dictionary of the
         Russian and Soviet Empires* (Westport: Greenwood Press, 1994)

319   This has always been sensitive border territory: John J. Stephan, *The
         Kuril Islands: Russo-Japanese Frontier in the Pacific* (Oxford: Clarendon
         Press, 1974). This detailed, elegantly told history of the Kurils is one I
         have relied on closely – and one of the main reasons why I wanted to
         travel this far east and see the islands for myself.

319 **on Russian maps first drawn by the Tobolsk map maker Semion Remezov in 1700:** Ibid.

319 **The Japanese strike force set sail from the island of Iturup:** Ibid.

320 **'the end of the world':** Ibid.

320 **Then came a series of muffled booms:** Henry James Snow, *In Forbidden Seas* (London: Edward Arnold, 1910)

321 **the Kuril Islands' only purpose was to provide a refuge for the shipwrecked:** Jean-François de La Pérouse, *A Voyage Round the World in the Years 1785, 1786, 1787 and 1788*, Volume II (London: J. Johnson, 1799)

321 **Franklin D. Roosevelt valued them as so utterly irrelevant . . . for less than the time:** Stephan, *The Kuril Islands*

321 **reducing the Kurils' sea-otter population to near extinction:** See Ann B. Irish, *Hokkaido: A History of Ethnic Transition and Development on Japan's Northern Island* (Jefferson and London: McFarland & Company, 2009)

321 **'Fog Archipelago':** John D. Grainger, *The First Pacific War: Britain and Russia, 1854–1856* (Suffolk: Boydell Press, 2008)

17. PROVENANCE REGAINED: KHABAROVSK

324 **hall Richter played:** He complained it was over-heated, badly ventilated and with poor acoustics. See Valentina Chemberdzhi, *V puteshestvii so Sviatoslavom Rikhterom* (Moscow: M. RIK 'Kul'tura', 1993)

325 **Léopold Stürzwage, who opened a Moscow workshop:** Martha Novak Clinkscale, *Makers of the Piano: 1820–1860*, Volume II (Oxford: Oxford University Press, 1999)

325 **Stürzwage's heir, also called Léopold:** See Maksim Sergeev, 'Professiia fortepiannovo mastera v Rossii. Tsekhovoĭ remeslennik kak klassicheskiĭ tip nastroĭshchika fortepiano', *Opera Musicologica*, 2:28 (2016)

325–6 **'You regard the world with one eye, and with the other you look inside yourself':** Cited in Mason Klein, *Modigliani Unmasked* (New Haven and London: Yale University Press, 2017)

326 **'Exile is strangely compelling . . . the loss of something left behind forever':** Edward W. Said, *Reflections on Exile* (Cambridge: Harvard University Press, 2000)

EPILOGUE

337 **'You cannot fathom Russia with the mind . . . believe in it':** See Robert Chandler, Boris Dralyuk and Irina Nachinski (eds), *The Penguin Book of Russian Poetry* (London: Penguin, 2015). The anthology includes two different translations of Tyutchev's iconic quatrain of 1866.

337 'I never choose a piano and don't try them out before a concert . . . walk
     on water': Cited in Bruno Monsaingeon, *Sviatoslav Richter: Notebooks and
     Conversations*, trans. Stewart Spencer (London: Faber & Faber, 2001)

337 'Siberia is an extensive and chilly land . . . Ask the Public Prosecutor to
     exile you here': Anton Chekhov, 'Letter to his brother, June 1890' in
     Anton Chekhov, *Sakhalin Island*, trans. Brian Reeve (Surrey: OneWorld
     Classics, 2007)

339 'Febris Sachalinensis': Chekhov, *Sakhalin Island*

339 'Kurllltls': See John J. Stephan, *The Kuril Islands: Russo-Japanese frontier in
     the Pacific* (Oxford: Clarendon Press, 1974)

339 Siberia has the virtue of not startling . . . left part of himself in
     Siberia for ever: Valentin Rasputin, *Siberia, Siberia*, trans. Margaret
     Winchell and Gerald Mikkelson (Evanston: Northwestern University
     Press, 1996)

340 Holman's presence in Irkutsk had put him under suspicion: James
     Holman, *Travels through Russia, Siberia, Poland, Austria, Saxony, Prussia,
     Hanover, &c. &c. Undertaken during the Years 1822, 1823 and 1824, While
     Suffering from Total Blindness, and Comprising an Account of the Author
     Being Conducted a State Prisoner from the Eastern Parts of Siberia* (London:
     Geo. B. Whittaker, 1825)

341 'My main aim in conducting the census . . . the impressions received
     during the making of it': Chekhov, *Sakhalin Island*

341 'I'm interested to be where I was not': Cited in Valentina
     Chemberdzhi, *V puteshestvii so Sviatoslavom Rikhterom* (Moscow:
     M. RIK 'Kul'tura', 1993)

341 'proclivity for adventure': Catherine the Great, 1869, cited in Alexander
     Etkind, *Internal Colonization: Russia's Imperial Experience* (Cambridge:
     Polity, 2011)

341 Was it all just a grand romance?: These ideas are explored in Barbara
     Fuchs, *Romance* (New York and London: Routledge, 2004).

350–1 '[John] Field did not so much play his own nocturnes, but dreamed
     them at the piano': Cited in David Dubal, *The Art of the Piano*
     (Cambridge: Amadeus Press, 2004)

353 George Kennan had encountered one of the finest drawing rooms in
     Russia . . . a grand piano: George Kennan, *Siberia and the Exile System*,
     Volume I (New York: The Century Co., 1891)

353 What this country endured is hard to fathom: 'The terrible impact of all
     of Russia's combined calamities, the Revolution, civil war, Stalin's Terror,
     plus World War Two, can be glimpsed in one dramatic demographic
     fact,' writes the American author Suzanne Massie. 'In 1950, eighty-five
     million Russians who should normally have been alive were not. Of
     these, forty-five million men – one in two – were, in the parlance of

demographers, simply "not there".' *Pavlovsk: The Life of a Russian Palace* (Leipzig: Liki Rossii, 1990).

A BRIEF HISTORICAL CHRONOLOGY

358 'the pianoforte is the most important of all musical instruments . . . the invention of printing was to poetry': George Bernard Shaw, *The Fortnightly Review* (February 1894) in Louis Crompton (ed.), *The Great Composers* (Berkeley: University of California Press, 1978)

Index

Index

Index

About the Author

Sophy Roberts is a British writer whose work focuses on the wild places from Papua New Guinea to the Congo. She began her career assisting the writer Jessica Mitford, and trained in journalism at Columbia University in New York. She regularly contributes to the *Financial Times* and *Condé Nast Traveler*, among others. *The Lost Pianos of Siberia* is her first book.